AF756021

ŚRĪ-CAKRAŚAṀVARA-TANTRA

TANTRIK TEXTS

UNDER GENERAL EDITORSHIP
OF
ARTHUR AVALON

VOL. VII

SHRĪCHAKRASAMBHĀRA TANTRA
A BUDDHIST TANTRA

EDITED BY

KAZI DAWA-SAMDUP

ADITYA PRAKASHAN
24 Ansari Road
New Delhi 110002

First published: Thacker, Spink & Co., Calcutta, 1919
Reprinted: New Delhi, 1987

₹1[illegible]00.00

Published by: Rakesh Goel
for: Aditya Prakashan, New Delhi in arrangement with Ganesh & Company, Madras.

Printed in India at, D.K. Fine Art Press, Delhi-110052.

CONTENTS

(the titles have been supplied by Lokesh Chandra)

PREFACE
by
Lokesh Chandra

The fundamental tantra of Cakrasaṁvara, the Laghusaṁvara (Toh. 368), belongs to the division of anuttara-yoga-tantras. This division also contains the mystic songs of the mahāsiddhas in the Tanjur. The classifications set by Bu-ston and Tsoṅ-kha-pa differ in details from the three subdivisions of the anuttara-yoga, propounded by Jayapaṇḍita Blo-bzaṅ-ḥphrin-las (A.D. 1642–):

1. Neither Father nor Mother tantras (Tsoṅ-kha-pa does not admit this subdivision)
2. Mother tantras
3. Father tantras

The three subdivisions are classified further as follows:

1. Neither Father nor Mother tantras
   - Nāma-saṅgīti (Toh. 360)
   - Kālacakra (Toh. 361–365)
2. Mother tantras (seven groupings: a–g)
   - a. Ston-pa (Śāstā, i.e. Śākyamuni)
     Sarva-buddha-samāyoga (Toh. 366)
   - b. Heruka (i.e. Akṣobhya)
     - (i) Saṁvara (Toh. 368–415)
     - (ii) Hevajra (Toh. 417–423)
     - (iii) Buddhakapāla (Toh. 424)
     - (iv) Mahāmāya (Toh. 425)
     - (v) Ārali (Toh. 426–427)
   - c. Vairocana
     Catuḥpīṭha (Toh. 428–430)
     Caṇḍamahāroṣaṇa ... (Toh. 431–434)
   - d. Vajraprabha (i.e. Ratnasambhava)
     Vajrāmṛta (Toh. 435)

e. Padmanarteśvara (i.e. Amitabha)
Lokanātha (Toh. 436)
Tārā-Kurukullā (Toh. 437)
f. Paramāśva (i.e. Amoghasiddhi)
Namas tāre ekaviṁśati (Toh. 438)
Vajrakīlaya (Toh. 439)
Mahākāla (Toh. 440)
g. Vajradhara
Yathālabdha-khasama (Toh. 441)

3. Father tantras (six groupings: a–f)
a. Akṣobhya
Guhyasamāja (Toh. 442–451)
Vajrapāṇi (Toh. 454–464)
b. Vairocana
Yamāri (Toh. 467–475, 478)
c. Ratna-kula (lacking)
d. Padma-kula
Bhagavad-ekajaṭa (Toh. 476)
e. Karma-kula (lacking)
f. Vajradhara
Candra-guhya-tilaka (Toh. 477)

From the above it becomes clear that the four items of Dawasamdup's translation pertain to different groupings of anuttara-yoga: Cakrasaṁvara 2b(i), Mahāmāyā to 2b(iv) and Tārā to 2f. The present English translation does not pertain to the fundamental text (mūla-tantra), namely, the Laghu-saṁvara.

*

According to the Second Dalai Lama Dge-ḥdun-rgya-mtsho (Dpal Ḥkhor-lo-sdom-paḥi rim-pa daṅ-poḥi lam-la slob-paḥi tshul go bde-bar rjod-pa ḥdod-pa-ḥjo-baḥi sñiṅ-po, in vol. PHA), the literature of Cakrasaṁvara is divided in two basic groups: tantra proper and commentarial works. The tantras, in their turn, are subdivided in three groups: (a) the original Tantras (rtsa rgyud) in three versions, the large one in three hundred thousand verses, the middle one as the Khasama-tantra, and the short one (Laghusaṁvara), (b) the explanatory tantras namely Vajraḍāka, Śaṁvarodaya, Yoginīsañcāra, Abhidhānottara, Sampuṭa; (c) the parallel tantras (phyogs mthun) as Herukābhyudaya, Ḍākārṇava (Tucci 1936: III/2.29)

*

As the main emphasis of the present work is on the maṇḍala we shall detail its description and significance. There are two main liturgies of the maṇḍala of Śaṁvara:

(i) According to the liturgy of Luipa (Tucci 1936: III/2.17ff., Tucci 1949:2.232, pl. G). This method of mystical realisation was glossed by Tsoṅ-kha-pa, and it describes the deities constituting the maṇḍala of Śaṁvara, which have to be evoked in the various moments of the complex ceremonial. The lists are of the greatest iconographic interest because they contain accurate and complete descriptions of deities.

(ii) The one centring on Kānhapa's ritual (Tucci 1949:2.603, pl.220).

As far as various interpretations go, Ṅag-dbaṅ-rigs-ḥdzin-rnam-rgyal-rdo-rje, in his *Bcom-ldan-ḥdas dpal Ḥkhor-lo-sdom-paḥi spyi bśad theg-mchog bdud-rtsiḥi dgaḥ-ston ye-śes-chen-poḥi sman mchog,* lists nine different methods, each of which goes back to a famous master of the tantric schools. The Tibetan tradition has especially taken its inspiration from three methods of exegesis and liturgy: either from that of Luipa, or from that of Ghaṇṭāpa, or of Kānhapa. Without entering in details, it is right to say that Rin-chen-bzaṅ-po and in general the Kadampa have followed the first system, namely the one of Luipa. The other six methods, i.e. those of Prabhūtacandra, Kambala, Nāgārjuna, Indrabhūti, Maitripa, Trinetra, did not have a diffusion equal to that enjoyed by the first three of them.

In his fundamental work the Indo-Tibetica (1936: III/2. 17ff.), Tucci has dealt the Śaṁvara-maṇḍala at length. His findings are summarised herein, from Italian into English. This maṇḍala is one of the richest and most complex. In the numerous groups of the acolytes of Śaṁvara we find well-known deities of the Hindu pantheon, almost as to testify the tendency, appearing earlier in Buddhism, of uniting itself with the popular religious traditions and of accepting them, and then transform them completely in its symbolism.

MAṆḌALA OF CAKRASAṀVARA

1. The maṇḍala of Śaṁvara is given by Abhayākaragupta (11th century) in his Niṣpannayogāvalī as follows: 5+16+16+16+8 (= 61 deities) or 37 deities if the couples in the kāya, vāk and citta cakras are counted as one (5+8+8+8+8).

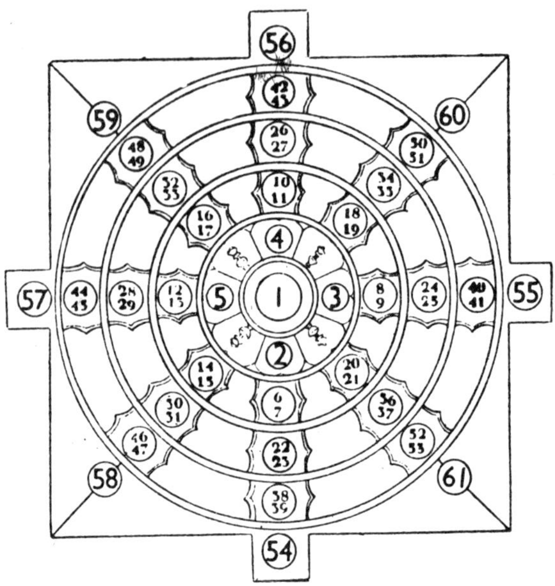

The central deity is the Four-faced *(caturmukha)* Twelve-armed *(dvādaśabhuja)* Sambara (Bde mchog 1), embraced by his Prajñā Vajravārāhī. In the four directions they are surrounded by Ḍākinī (Mkhaḥ ḥgro ma 2), Lāmā (Lā ma 3), Khaṇḍarohā (Dum skyes ma 4), and Rūpiṇī (Gzugs can ma 5). In the intermediate corners are the four holy vessels *(abja-bhājana).*

Hereafter are three circles *(cakra)* of the three planes of citta, vāk and kāya. Each circle has eight yab-yum i.e. sixteen deities in the eight cardinal and intermediate directions. The Prajñā of every deity has her own specific name.

The deities in the citta circle *(citta-cakra)* are: Khaṇḍa-kapāla (Thod paḥi dum bu 6) + Pracaṇḍā (Rab tu gtum mo 7), Mahākaṅkāla (Keṅ rus chen po 8) + Pracaṇḍākṣī (Gtum paḥi mig can ma 9), Kaṅkāla (Keṅ rus 10) + Prabhāvatī (Ḥod ldan mo 11), Vikaṭadaṁṣṭrī (Mche ba rnam par gtsigs pa 12) + Mahānāsā (Sna chen ma13), Surāvairī (Chaṅ dgra 14) + Vīramatī (Dpaḥ boḥi blo gros ma 15), Amitābha (Ḥod dpag med 16) + Kharvarī (Miḥu thuṅ ma 17), Vajraprabha (Rdo rje ḥod 18) + Laṅkeśvarī (Laṅ kaḥi dbaṅ phyug ma 19), and Vajradeha (Rdo rjeḥi lus 20) + Drumacchāyā (Śiṅ grib ma 21).

The vāk circle *(vāk-cakra)* has the ensuing deities: Aṅkuraka (Myu gu can 22) + Irāvatī (Sa bsruṅs ma 23), Vajrajaṭila (Rdo rje ral pa can 24) + Mahābhairavā (Ḥjigs byed chen mo 25), Mahāvīra (Dpaḥ bo chen po 26) + Vāyuvegā (Rluṅ gi śugs can ma 27), Vajrahūṁkāra (Rdo rje hūṁ mdzad 28) + Surābhakṣī (Chaṅ ḥthuṅ ma 29), Subhadra (Rdo rje bzaṅ po 30) + Śyāmā-devī (Lha mo sṅo bsaṅs ma 31), Vajraprabha (Rdo rje ḥod 32) + Subhadrā (Śin tu bzaṅ mo 33), Mahābhairava (Ḥjigs byed chen po 34) + Hayakarṇī (Rta rna ma 35), and Virūpākṣa (Mig mi bzaṅ 36) + Khagānanā (Bya gdoṅ ma 37).

In the kāya circle *(kāya-cakra)* we find: Mahābala (Stobs po che 38) + Cakravegā (Ḥkhor loḥi śugs can ma39), Ratnavajra (Rin chen rdo rje 40) + Khaṇḍarohā (Dum skyes ma 41), Hayagrīva (Rta mgrin 42) + Śauṇḍinī (Chaṅ ḥtshoṅ ma 43), Ākāśagarbha (Nam mkhaḥi sñiṅ po 44) + Cakravarmiṇī (Ḥkhor loḥi go cha ḥdzin ma 45), Śrī Heruka (Dpal he ru ka 46) + Suvīrā (Śin tu bzaṅ mo 47), Padmanartteśvara (Padma gar gyi dbaṅ phyug 48) + Mahābalā (Stobs chen ma 49), Vairocana (Rnam par [snaṅ] mdzad 50) + Cakravartinī (Ḥkhor los sgyur ma 51), and Vajra-sattva (Rdo rje sems dpaḥ 52) + Mahāvīryā (Brtson ḥgrus chen mo 53).

The gates of the four cardinal directions are occupied by Kākāsyā (Khva gdoṅ ma 54), Ulūkāsyā (Ḥug gdoṅ ma 55), Śvānā-syā (Khyi gdoṅ ma 56) and Śūkarāsyā (Phag gdoṅ ma 57). In the intermediate corners *(koṇa)* are Yamadāhī (Gśin rje brtan ma 58*), Yamadūtī (Gśin rje pho ña 59), Yamadaṁṣṭrī (Gśin rje mche ba ma 60), and Yamamathanī (Gśin rje ḥjoms ma 61).

Variations: The Niṣpannayogāvalī notes two further variations when the central deity *(cakreśa)* is Sambara. If his Prajñā Vajravārāhī comes into the centre *(cakresa)* then she too has three variations. This gives us six types of maṇḍalas of Sambara and his Prajñā. 500 Gods R 7a, b, c, 8a, b, c illustrate these six types under the captions Śaṁvara (7a), Dvibhuja Śaṁvara (7b), Pīta Cakraśaṁvara (7c), Rakta Vārāhī (8a), Nīla Vārāhī (8b), and Pīta Vārāhī (8c).

References: Niṣpannayogāvalī introd. p.44, Skt. p.26, Tib. 135a3, Vajrāvalī 36b5, Lokesh Chandra 1986: nos. 977–982, Samuccaya 182b3, Kanjur (Toh. no.) 368–415, Tanjur (Toh. no.) 1401–1606, Tucci 1949:332, 603 (illustrated on plate 220), Tucci 1961: plate II (p.140), Tucci 1936: III/2 16ff., Gordon 1952: 25, Odette Monod-Bruhl, Peintures Tibétaines, illustrates a different type of maṇḍala, Bhattacharyya 1958: 161 (twelve-armed).

2. The Rgyud-sde-kun-btus, which embodies the Sa-skya-pa tradition of Kun-dgaḥ-bzaṅ-po (15th century) illustrates the 62deity maṇḍala of Śaṁvara according to Luipa (Bde-mchog lu-i-pa lha-drug-cu-re-gñis). The deities are represented by their emblems (see illustration opposite).

3. The maṇḍala of Luipa/Tsoṅ-kha-pa as given by Tucci (1936:III/2.31–41) has 102 deities (18+10 krodhinī + 5 pūjā devī + 16 vidyā + 8 dikpāla + 8 kṣetrapāla + 8 nāga + 24 protectors):

1. Heruka, blue, r.h. vajra, l.h. bell, ālīḍha, embracing his consort Vajravārāhī, red, hands hold vajra and kapāla. If Heruka has one head it is of normal body colour, when the faces are more than one the sequence is central, right and left, and only the central head is of body colour.

---

*The Sanskrit ms. B in Bhattacharyya's edition reads *-ṭī* or *-ḍī.* This reading points to Yamadāḍhī, a Mid-Indic form of Yamadṛḍhā. Tibetan *-brtan ma* is equivalent to *-dṛḍhā.*

2. Vairocana, white, r.h. discus upraised, l.h. bell on hip, ālīḍha.

3. Vajrasūrya, yellow, r.h. jewel. l.h. bell on height of breast, ālīḍha.

4. Padmanarteśvara, red, r.h. red lotus, l.h. bell on height of breast, ālīḍha.

5. Vajrarāja, green, r.h. viśvavajra, l.h. bell on height of breast, ālīḍha.

6. Vajrasattva, white, r.h. vajra on breast, l.h. bell on hip, ālīḍha.

7. Heruka, black, r.h. vajra, l.h. bell on hip, ālīḍha.

8. Mohavajra, white, r.h. discus, l.h. bell on hip, ālīḍha.

9. Dveṣavajra, black, r.h. vajra on breast, l.h. bell on hip, ālīḍha.

10. Mātsaryavajra, yellow, r.h. jewel, l.h. bell on breast, ālīḍha.

11. Rāgavajra, red, r.h. red lotus, l.h. bell near breast, ālīḍha.

12. Īrṣyāvajra, green, r.h. viśvavajra, l.h. bell on breast, ālīḍha.

13. Īśvaravajra, white, r.h. vajra on breast, l.h. bell on hip, ālīḍha.

14. Ltuṅ-byed-ma, yellow, 4 arms: r.h. knife, discus, l.h. kapāla, khaṭvāṅga, ālīḍha.

15. Gsod-byed-ma, black, 4 arms: r.h. knife, vajra, l.h. kapāla, khaṭvāṅga, ālīḍha.

16. Ḥgugs-byed-ma, red, 4 arms: r.h. knife, padma, l.h. kapāla, khaṭvāṅga, ālīḍha.

17. Narteśvarī, green, 4 arms: r.h. knife, sword, l.h. kapāla, khaṭvāṅga, ālīḍha.

18. Padmajāla, pearly 3 heads: pearly, white, red, r.h. knife, head of Brahmā, hook, l.h.: kapāla, khaṭvāṅga, noose.

TEN KRODHINĪ

19,20. Two Kākāsyā, black, r.h. vajradaṇḍa, l.h. phur-bu (kīlaka)

21. Ulūkāsyā, green, hands as in 19.

22, 23. Śvānāsyā, red, hands as in 19

24. Sūkarāsyā, yellow, hands as in 19.

25. Yamadṛḍhā, blue on right and yellow on left, hands as in 19.

26. Yamadūtī, yellow on right and red on left, hands as in 19.

27. Yamadaṁṣṭrī, red on right and green on left, hands as in 19.

28. Yamamathanī, green on right and blue on left, hands as in 19.

FIVE PŪJĀDEVĪ

29. Puṣpā, white, 4 hands: r.h. vajra, vessel with flowers, l.h. bell, vessel with flowers.

30. Dhūpā, grey, 4 hands: r.h. vajra, vessel with incense, l.h. bell, vessel with incense.

31. Dīpā, red-yellow, 4 hands: r.h. vajra, vessel with lamp, l.h. bell, vessel with lamp.

32. Gandhā, green, 4 hands: r.h. vajra, vessel with perfume, l.h. bell, vessel with perfume.

33. Naivedyā, multicolour, 4 hands: vajra, vessel with offering, l.h. bell, vessel with offering.

SIXTEEN VIDYĀ

34. Vīṇā, blue, 4 hands: r.h. vīṇā, vajra, l.h. bell.

35. Vaṁśā, yellow, 4 hands: r.h. vaṁśā, vajra, l.h. bell.

36. Mṛdaṅgā, red, 4 hands: r.h. mṛdaṅga, vajra, l.h. bell.

37. Murajā, green, 4 hands: r.h. muraja, vajra, l.h. bell.

38. Hāsyā, red, 4 hands: two hands in the attitude of laughing, r.h. kapāla, l.h. khaṭvāṅga.

39. Lāsyā, blue, 4 hands: r.h. vajra, kapāla, l.h. bell on hip, khaṭvāṅga.

40. Gītā, yellow, 4 hands: cymbals in two hands, r.h. kapāla, l.h. khaṭvāṅga.

41. Nṛtyā, green, 4 hands: two hands beating rhythm, r.h. kapāla, l.h. khaṭvāṅga.

42. Puṣpā, white, 4 hands: r.h. vase of flowers, ḍamaru, l.h. kapāla, khaṭvāṅga.

43. Dhūpā, pearly, 4 hands: r.h. vase of incense, ḍamaru, l.h. as in 42.

44. Dīpā, yellow, 4 hands: r.h. lamp, ḍamaru, l.h. as in 42.

45. Gandhā, red, 4 hands: r.h. vase of perfume, ḍamaru, l.h. as in 42.

46. Rūpā, white, 4 hands: r.h. mirror, ḍamaru, l.h. as in 42.

47. Rasā, red, 4 hands: r.h. vase of honey, ḍamaru, l.h. as in 42.

48. Sparśā, green-yellow, 4 hands: r.h. multicolour dress, ḍamaru, l.h. as in 42.

49. Dharmavajrī, red, 4 hands: r.h. triangle, ḍamaru, l.h. as in 42

SECOND CYCLE

EIGHT DIKPĀLA

50. Indra, yellow, 4 hands: two hands joint in adoration, r.h. vajra, l.h. kapāla, on white Airāvata elephant.
51. Kubera, yellow, 4 hands: two hands joint in adoration, r.h. ichneumon, l.h. kapāla, mount: man.
52. Varuṇa, white, 4 hands: two hands joint in adoration, r.h. nāgapāśa, l.h. kapāla, mount: makara with seven crests.
53. Yama, blue, 4 hands: two hands joint in adoration, r.h. daṇḍa, l.h. kapāla, mount: buffalo.
54. Maheśvara, white, 4 hands: two hands joint in adoration, r.h. trident, l.h. kapāla, mount: bull.
55. Agni, red, 4 hands: two hands joint in adoration, r.h. rosary and kamaṇḍalu, l.h. kapāla, mount: ram.
56. Yakṣa, blue, 4 hands: two hands joint in adoration, r.h. sword, l.h. kapāla, mount: ghost.
57. Vāyu, pearly, 4 hands: two hands joint in adoration, r.h. standard, l.h. kapāla, mount: śabala antelope.

EIGHT KṢETRAPĀLA

58. with the head of an elephant, white, r.h. bali, l.h. kapāla.
59. with the head of a man, yellow, r.h. bali, l.h. kapāla.
60. with the head of a makara, white, r.h. bali, l.h. kapāla.
61. with the head of a buffalo, black, r.h. bali, l.h. kapāla.
62. with the head of a bull, white, r.h. bali, l.h. kapāla.
63. with the head of a goat, red, r.h. bali, l.h. kapāla.
64. with the head of a ghost, black, r.h. bali, l.h. kapāla.
65. with the head of a gazelle, green, r.h. bali, l.h. kapāla.

EIGHT NĀGA (two hands of all the eight nāgas are in adoration, upper part is human and the lower serpentine)

66. Vāsuki, white
67. Takṣaka, red
68. Karkoṭa, blue
69. Padma, white

70. Mahāpadma, white
71. Ananta, multicolour
72. Kulika, white
73. Śaṅkhapāla, yellow
74. Heruka, blue, 4 heads (blue, green, red, yellow), 12 hands: two hands embrace prajñā holding vajra and bell, r.h. ḍamaru, hatchet, knife, trident, l.h. khaṭvāṅga, kapāla, noose, head of Brahmā. Āsana: the right leg in ālīḍha, left in pratyālīḍha, crushing Kālabhairava and Kālī. Prajñā: Vajravārāhī with two faces, two hands (r.h. tarjanī, l.h. kapāla).
75. Ḍākinī, black, 4 hands: r.h. knife, ḍamaru, l.h. kapāla, khaṭvāṅga.
76. Lāmā (corr. Rama), green, hands as in 75.
77. Khaṇḍarohı, red, hands aṣ in 75.
78. Rūpiṇī, yellow, hands as in 75.

24 PROTECTORS OF 24 PLACES OR REGIONS OF VAJRAKĀYA, ACCOMPANIED BY THEIR CONSORTS CITTA-CAKRA, SPHERE OF ĀKĀŚA

79. Khaṇḍakapāla at Pullīra Malaya, blue, 4 hands: two hands embrace the prajñā who is holding a vajra and bell, r.h. ḍamaru, l.h. khaṭvāṅga. Pracaṇḍā, two arms embrace the deity, r.h. tarjanī, knife, l.h. kapāla, open hair.
80. Mahākaṅkāla at Jalandhara (upper portion of head), Pracaṇḍākṣī, blue, 4 hands as in 79.
81. Kaṅkāla at Oṭṭiyāna (right ear), blue, 4 hands as in 79. Prabhāvatī.
82. Vikaṭadaṁṣṭrī at Arbuda (nape), blue, 4 hands as in 79, Mahānāsā.
83. Surāvairī at Godavari (left ear), blue, 4 hands as in 79, Vīramatī.
84. Amitābha at Rameśvara (space between the brows), blue, 4 hands as in 79, Kharvarī.
85. Vajraprabha at Devīkoṭa (two eyes), blue, 4 hands as in 79, Laṅkeśvarī.

86. Vajradeha at Mālavar (two shoulders), blue, 4 hands as in 79, Drumacchāyā.

VĀK-CAKRA, SPHERE OF PṚTHIVĪ

(nos. 87–102: r.h. ḍamaru, l.h. khaṭvāṅga)

87. Aṅkuraka at Kāmarūpa (two armpits), red, Airāvatī.
88. Vajrajaṭila at Oṭe[viśa] (breasts), red, Mahābhairavī.
89. Mahāvīra at Tiśakune (navel), red, Vāyuvegā.
90. Vajrahūṁkāra at Kośala (tip of nose), red, Surābhakṣī.
91. Subhadra at Kaliṅga (mouth), red, Śyāmādevī.
92. Vajraprabha at Lampaka (neck), red, Subhadra.
93. Mahābhairava at Kāñcī/Campā (heart), red, Hayakarṇī.
94. Virūpākṣa on Himalaya (pupil), red, Khagānanā.

KĀYA-CAKRA, SPHERE OF PĀTĀLA

95. Mahābala at Pretapurī (sexual organ), white, Cakravegā.
96. Ratnavajra at Gṛhadevatā (anus), white, Khaṇḍarohā.
97. Hayagrīva in Saurāṣṭra (thigh), white, Śauṇḍinī.
98. Ākāśagarbha in Suvarṇadvīpa (calf), white, Cakravarmiṇı.
99. ŚrīHeruka at Nāgara (fingers), white, Suvīrā.
100. Padmanarteśvara in Sindhu (upper part of foot), white, Mahābalā.
101. Vairocana at Maru (four thumbs), white, Cakravartinī.
102. Vajrasattva at Kulūṭa (knees), white, Mahāvīryā.

The ideas connected with the two components of the word Cakra-śaṁvara have been tabulated by Lessing (1942:118) as follows on the basis of Tucci (1936:III/2.18–19):

Cakra	Śaṁvara
1. All the dharmas or essences, as pluralities.	1. The one Essence which is at the basis of all of them.
2. The first four aspects of gnosis (knowledge, *jñāna*)	2. The fifth aspect: gnosis of the absolute, also symbolized as a mirror.
3. The four Ḍākinīs	3. Heruka.
4. Four lower forms of	4. Highest, innate *(sahaja)*

mystic bliss.	bliss *(mahāsukha),* feeling of co-substantiality with the absolute.
5. The four Tathāgatas (Akṣobhya, Amitābha, Ratnasambhava, Amogha-siddhi).	5. Vairocana.

The iconographical characteristics of Cakra-śaṁvara and his consort Vajra-vārāhī, can be seen in the following table:

	Cakraśaṁvara	Vajravārāhī
colour	dark blue	cherry-red
posture	standing	encircling yab
faces	4	1 face with 3 eyes
arms	12	2
dress	nude, elephant's skin, apron of tiger's skin	nude
ornaments	partly those of the Terrible Ḍharmapālas, partly of Bodhisattvas	skull crown: ornaments of Bodhisattva

The following table shows the attributes and symbolism of Cakraśaṁvara according to Dawasamdup (1919:22 as summarised by Lessing 1942:119, 120):

Attribute	Symbolizes:
1. Colour: blue.	dharmadhātu-jñāna.
2. three eyes.	all the three world-systems (trailokya) are under his vision; he knows the three times (past, present, future)
3. twelve hands.	he knows the twelve nidānas and the twelve bhava-saṁ-

	krānti (T. *srid-pa-ḥpho-ba,* projections of consciousness, etc., into another form).
4. vajra and bell in both "original" hands.	his bodhicitta is both insubstantiality *(śūnyatā)* and compassion *(karuṇā).*
5. these same two hands embrace his spouse.	*upāya* (action) and *prajñā* (transcendental wisdom, contemplation), cf. yum no. 11.
6. second two hands hold elephant's hide (T. *glaṅ-lpags*).	emblem of ignorance *(avidyā,* the metaphysical root of existence).
7. third right hand holds skull drum *(damaru).*	he proclaims joyous tidings.
8. fourth right hand, battle-axe *(paraśu).*	cuts off birth and death, root and trunk.
9. fifth right hand wields chopper *(kartarī,* T. *gri-gug).*	severs pride, destroys the sins of the world-systems.
10.sixth right hand wields trident *(triśūla).*	"
11.third left hand: magic wand *(khaṭvāṅga).*	he is endowed with supreme bliss.
12.fourth left hand: skull bowl filled with blood *(kapāla).*	he does away with all ideas of substance and non-substance.
13.fifth left hand: vajra-noose (pāśa).	his knowledge holds the nature of sentient beings.

VAJRAVĀRĀHĪ. Her attributes and their symbolism is given below:

1. One red face: all dharmas (essences, elements) are "of one taste" (ekarasa), i.e. dissolving all polarities, contrasts in reality (tattva).
2. Two hands: saṁvṛtisatya (phenomenal or empirical truth) and paramārthasatya (noumenal or gnosic truth).
3. l.h. embraces the yab, holds a skull bowl filled with blood: she confers supreme bliss.
4. r.h. holds a chopper (kartarī) with vajra-mark and makes the menacing gesture (tarjanī-mudrā): her wisdom cuts all reasoning, destroys all fiends (Māras) and defilements (kleśa).
5. Loose hair: she unties the knot which keeps all dharmas together so that they do not appear as what they are.
6. Nudity: freedom from the obscuration of the defilements of the mind (kleśa).
7. Three eyes: cf. Cakraśaṁvara, no.2.
8. Crown of five human skulls: cf. Cakraśaṁvara, no.22.
9. Garland of fifty skulls: cf. Cakraśaṁvara, no.23.
10. Five bone ornaments (pañcamudrā, the ashes missing): cf. Cakraśaṁvara no.25.
11. The two calves of the legs embracing her consort: she is inseparable from upaya, cf. Cakraśaṁvara no.5.
12. Conjugal embrace: unio mystica of phenomenal world, or method, action (upāya), compassion (male) with insubstantiality (śūnyatā), transcendental wisdom (prajñā), contemplation, tranquility, great bliss (mahāsukha).
13. Fire-halo: supreme wisdom consumes all exterior and interior obstacles.
14. Sixth left hand: the head of four-faced Brahmā: he has shaken off all samsaric delusions (moha, Tib. gti-mug).
15. r. leg outstretched treads on the prostrate body of blue Kālī (T. Dus-mtshan-ma), goddess of Time (see no.17): out of compassion be continues to live in the world of sentient beings.

16. Chopper and skull in the hand of this goddess (attributes vary): the extreme view about Nirvāṇa, i.e. the belief (to be avoided) that Nirvāṇa is eternal passiveness, the sole eternal reality (cf. no.18).
17. l. leg bent, treads on red Bhairava (T. Ḥjigs-byed) the Destroyer. No.15 combined with 17 is the ālīḍha posture: in his consciousness there is neither subject nor object (neither pudgala nor dharma, cf. no.26).
18. Skull drum and chopper in the two right hands and magic wand and skull in the two left hands of Bhairava (see no.17): the extreme view about saṁsāra, i.e., the belief in an external action, cf. no.16.
19. Hair tied in a knot adorned with cintāmaṇi (also explained as sun, at his right side): all merits have been accumulated by him.
20. l. side of hair-knot adorned with a crescent: his bodhicitta is constantly reaching higher stages.
21. Crossed vajra on crown of head: his acts benefit all sentient beings.
22. Crown of five skulls on each of the heads: he possesses five kinds of wisdom.
23. Garland of fifty heads: the fifty letters of the alphabet from which he has sprung have been purified.
24. Frowning face, bare fangs: Mara and all heresies are subdued.
25. Ṣaṇ-mudrā: the six bone ornaments symbolize the six perfections, pāramitās. (1) ear-rings: patience (kṣamā), (2) neck-ornament: charity (dāna), (3) bracelets: discipline (śīla), (4) gridle: energy (vīrya), (5) wheel of bone on crown of his head: meditation (dhyāna), (6) ashes from crematories and the sacrificial thread (yajñopavīta): transcendental knowledge (prajñā)
26. Wearing tiger-skin loosely around his loins: he has subdued Māra and overcome the contrast of grāhya-grāhaka, i.e. subject and object, mind and matter (pudgala and dharma, cf. no.17).

Tucci (1961:68–72) gives another symbolical interpretation of Cakrasaṁvara and Vajravārāhī: "Śrī Cakra-Saṁvara (Heruka) is thus described: In the middle of the lotus, on the solar seat, is the God of the deep blue body. He has four faces. The first (in the middle) is of deep blue, that to the left green, that at the back of his head red, and that to the right yellow. Each face has three eyes. On his forehead he wears a diadem of five-pointed vajras.

"With his outstretched right leg he crushes the head of Kāla-bhairava who has four arms; two are joined together in the attitude of adoration, in the second on the right he has the magic drum (ḍamaru) and in the second on the left he has the sword. The left leg is drawn back and tramples on the chest of Red Kālī who also has four arms; two are joined together in the attitude of adoration and of the other two that on the right holds a skull (kapāla) and that on the left a khaṭvāṅga.

He has twelve hands. "(Heruka) with his two principal arms embraces Vajravārāhī, while, at the same time, holding in his right hand a five-pointed vajra and in his left the small bell (to symbolize that he is the union of illumination and compassion). The hands of the two arms underneath are in the attitude of menace (tarjanīmudrā); with them he holds and stretches out at the level of his eyes a vestment made of the white and blood-stained skin of an elephant and with the left hand the left foot of this skin. In his other right hands he holds aloft, respectively, the magic drum, the hatchet, the knife and the trident. In his left hands the khaṭvāṅga (marked with the vajra symbol of illumination), a cranium full of blood (symbol of supreme beatitude), the admantine noose and the head of Brahmā with four faces.

"He bears the ascetic forelock marked with double vajra arranged as a cross (viśvavajra). On each head is a diadem of black vajras on which are fixed five skulls above and five below. On the left side of his face he has a slightly sloping crescent. The faces are deformed and made terrifying by the four jutting teeth and the sneering grimace.

"He has nine modes: three of the body, robust, heroic and ugly; three of words, savage, terrible and awe-inspiring; three of the spirit, compassionate, dignified and serene. At his belt he wears an apron of tiger-skins. Suspended from his neck is a garland of fifty freshly severed human heads strung on a thread of human guts. He is marked with six seals (mudrā) and his body is smeared with the ashes of burnt corpses.

"The coupling of the "mother" and "father" signifies the fusion of the two coefficients of salvation, that is, on the one hand, the "means", namely compassion or the active element (since this "means" when it has attained particular efficacy permeates the most vital parts of the body), and, on the other hand, "wisdom". During the union with the "mother", the "moon", that is the thought of illumination seated in the head, melts and permeates the whole body. From it proceeds the "great bliss of the mean" which symbolizes meditation on the four fundamentals of liberation which have as their object the insubstantiality of the All, identified with mystical wisdom: this bliss is symbolized by the khaṭvāṅga, the skull symbolizing that he is beyond all notions of substance and no substance.

"Each has a crown of five skulls, to signify the possession of the five gnoses. All this suggests purification from thirst for action etc., liberation from mental obscuration, evocation of all the Buddhas, the excision of false concepts concerning the extreme theses and the errors of the three "doors" (that is body, word and spirit), the piercing of all moral infections and the union with pure consciousness, the submission of the two extreme theses, namely that of eternity or of the continual existence of saṁsāra, and that of annihilation, namely the non-existence (of the individual) in nirvāṇa. In a word, the submission of the whole phenomenal world by means of the concept of insubstantiality.

"The elephant skin is the symbol of ignorance, the drum that of the good news of the Law, the axe because it cuts out saṁsāra and its roots. He clutches a knife because he slashes pride and sins. He holds a trident because he puts an end to greed, wrath and mental perturbation. The skull is filled with blood because he is beyond material and non-material things. He holds the adamantine noose because gnosis reveals the essence of creatures. He holds, by the hair, the head of Brahmā to indicate that he is free of all illusions.

"The skulls that form the necklace of the God signify the incorporation of light that proceeds from the peace attained by the suppression of all extremes. The twelve hands indicate purification from all spot or stain as regards the interpretation of the twelve-fold causal concatenation. The deformed faces signify the denial of all theories, the sneer of the projecting teeth indicates the overcoming of the four Māra. The upstanding ascetic's tuft symbolizes the conception of ascending merit, the garland of vajras, quiescence in the quintuple gnosis which is attained when merit reaches its greatest development. The God has three eyes because with his wisdom he discovers everything in all three times and in the triple space. He bears on the top of his head a double vajra in the form of a cross because, with four-fold action, he accomplishes the good of all creatures. The six seals signify the perfection of the methods (literally "paths") which lead to the six mystical perfections. He is adorned with all the magnificence of that spiritual serenity which is the conglomeration of the five Buddhas and of the four mothers.

"In front of the Blessed One is the head of Vajravārāhī, whose body is red because dedicated to the good of creatures. She has only one face to indicate the essential sameness of all things, two hands, because truth is twofold, absolute and relative, and three eyes. She is naked with dishevelled hair because she has been set free from the illusions that hide the essence of things. She wears a girdle adorned with portions of skulls because she bestows supreme bliss and with her right hand, in the gesture of menace (tarjanīmudrā), she clutches the vajra and terrifies the demons of the ten points of space.

"Since she is the symbol of intuition of the universe's insubstantiality, she is like the fire which at the end of the ages destroys the worlds. She is resplendent with solar brilliance as she expresses the possession of the purest wisdom. She rejoices in blood, she drips blood, she presses with her legs the thighs of the "father", consubstantial with the Great Compassion, since she accomplishes the good of creatures while remaining in the highest beatitude which consists in the Supreme Vision. She is decked with five seals, but is not smeared with ashes, she wears a garland of fifty skulls and has upon her forehead a diadem of five skulls".

*Meaning of the maṇḍala**. The maṇḍala expresses inner and intimate experiences, symbolically conveyed by deities. Hereby one ascends gradually to the enjoyment of and participation in profound ecstasy in which, passing from vision to vision, the initiated believes himself to be transformed to those planes of supreme spiritual experiences, of which the tantras knew the schematic doctrine and the maṇḍalas the enigmatic representation. The masters who elaborated these methods of mystical realizations were undoubtedly profound knowers of the human psyche. Starting from interior experiences, they were able to discover the slender bonds uniting the physical world with the psychical one, the extreme of the body with the threshold of the soul. They imagined systems of concentration and meditation capable of producing phenomena of self-hypnosis; and found the way to visualize their experiences and especially to master the mobile world of our psyche, by concentrating on it and identifying it in a unity of experience.

The sādhana is an organic unit which moves the entire psychic substratum of the individual; it promotes, guides and addresses the visions. It is able to regulate the fluctuating images, which faith fills with spirit, by evoking the phantoms in vivid and luminous forms, exteriorizing them before the eye of the initiated, who is dominated by the presence of the god in himself. Thus the rite of the utpatti-krama or evocation is concluded, and this

*I am grateful to Dr. Uma M. Vesci for kindly translating Indo-Tibetica III/2. The meaning of the maṇḍala, the twentyfour vīras, and eight cemeteries are adapted from Uma Vesci's English rendering of Tucci's Italian text.

rite takes out from the spiritual background of the mystic the forms of the gods, and they are absorbed in him again, giving him the certitude that the gods too are not realities existing in themselves, but projections of our religious consciousness, sudden colorations of that unattained lucidity that is in the whole; in a word: they are symbols and not beings. In the rite, the painted and visible maṇḍala has, in a second and higher time, to be transported in the body of the meditating person. In his body, ideally identified with the cosmos, the mystic, sees reflected the incessant process of emanation and reabsorption of the worlds and therefore the vanity and vacuity of the flowing of ephemeral manifestations (emerging) from that ground which always is, and remains, the cause of every becoming. This will appear clear to one who examines, for instance, the sādhana of Śaṁvara according to the system of Lui-pa, interpreted and commented upon by Tsoṅ-kha-pa.

The twentyfour vīras and the cosmic man. These twentyfour deities preside over twentyfour places of India and therefore in the esoteric ritual, they are localized in as many centres of our body. Some Tibetan sources relate that in ancient times Rudra (Drag-po) and Kālī (Dus-mtshan-ma) came to the country of Magadha and became masters of entire Jambudvīpa. Then they enthroned in twentyfour places twentyfour deities that in a certain way were their viceroys. They are: four gods of heavenly space, four gandharvas, four yakṣas, four rākṣasas, four nāgas, and four asuras. However, in spite of invitations, these gods did not come to take possession of the country given to them. This is why in their places have been installed the corresponding images of stone, still venerated in these sacred places. The legend was narrated for the first time in Tibet by Bu-ston and is repeated by Kloṅ-rdol in his ***Bstan-sruṅ dam-can rgya-mtshoḥi miṅ-gi graṅs*** (PA, fol.9, of his complete works).

These twentyfour vīras are not only enthroned, during the ritual, in the various parts of the body of the mystic, but they divide among themselves the dominion of the earth. In fact, in the tantric traditions they circumscribe the geographical vajrakāya, that is to say the adamantine body which is the concrete projection of the supreme being in the world of matter. But, while in the school properly Indian, this 'adamantine body' is identified with the twentyfour places mentioned above, corresponding, except for a few exceptions, to countries easily identifiable on Indian territory in a broad sense, in later times, possibly when the fortune of Buddhism started declining, the zone of the geographical Vajrakāya has been limited to the Himalayan region. This transposition which had often violated the geographical traditions of India, is already an accomplished fact in the tantric schools of Tibet. For instance, Urgyan-pa and Stag-tshaṅ-ras-pa, perform their pilgrimages from Tibet to the valley of the Swat taking care to visit the twentyfour places of the Vajrakāya presided over by the twentyfour vīras, according to the theories of the Śaṁvaratantra. Now, these places are through Zanskar, Kashmir, Kulu, Hazara district and Swat.

This adamantine body is reconstructed, so to say, during the liturgical process, in the body of the person who meditates. He, in the microcosmos of his person, sees reproduced the double moment of the evolution and involution through which the primordial consciousness is actualized in the multiplicity of contingency and then goes back to itself.

In other words, we find the twentyfour vīras in the physical world, in the maṇḍala symbolising that very world schematically in a conventional representation containing the symbols and representing their history and their mechanism, and finally in the very body of the mystic. This latter aspect of the liturgy will not wonder us when we remember that in it the I is equated to the universe and on this presupposition are based both the theory and the praxis of Haṭhayoga. In tantric ritualism has remained, even more than in the other religious systems of India, the old and primal intuition of the cosmic Puruṣa, of the entire world derived from primeval Man or imagined in the shape of a Man. The world is born from the dismembration of the cosmic man and is recomposed during the sacrificial process. Thus it was already in the Vedic ritual of agnicayana. The twentyfour gods enthroned in the twentyfour places of the earth, as also in twentyfour parts of the human body, delimit the surface of the cosmic Puruṣa or of his reflection, but the one and the other always mystical maṇḍala in which, for him who knows it, is reproduced the alternate process of the becoming in its three moments of creation, duration and return. In order to make more perfect the equation between macrocosmos and microcosmos it asserted that as every individual is constituted of three planes, i.e. the physical *(kāya),* the verbal *(vāc)* and the spiritual *(citta),* so also the twentyfour gods presiding over as many points of the cosmos—namely of the cosmic man—are divided in three corresponding planes: namely, we have three circles, each of which is equivalent to a plane with eight series of deities, four for each fundamental cardinal direction, and four for the secondary cardinal directions.

This theory of the twentyfour vīras is not isolated. It is perhaps to be placed besides the twentyfour forms of Kṛṣṇa (his emanations are termed vaibhava-vilāsa) listed and described in the Kṛṣṇaite schools (see for instance Caitanya-caritāmṛta, madhya-līlā, ch.20). They too, except Nārāyaṇa who dwells in the heavenly Vaikuṇṭha, have their separate heavens in the eight cardinal directions around the supreme heaven *(Parama-vyoma)* but they come down in the world to preside over certain special places. They are also seated in the various parts of the body.

The eight cemeteries. The outermost rim of the maṇḍala represents the eight cemeteries well known to the ascetic schools of India, fearful places where the Siddhas retire to gain their wonderful powers, to dedicate themselves to meditation and to train themselves in the complex methods of Haṭhayoga.

These cemeteries have always had an essential part in the training of ascetics, as those places where there appeared, in its sickening crudity, the corruptibility of our physical being and there was experienced the fatal dissolution of the flesh and the inanity of the passions. The very Buddha himself, according to hagiographic traditions, passed whole years there before acquiring supreme illumination. The Majjhima-nikāya has pages of highest poetry when it describes these places of death and silence, in whose fearful solitudes Śākyamuni strengthened slowly the sense of detachment from earthly things, the will of separating himself from all that is frail and perishable, the longing for seeking the incorruptible and the eternal. But in the tantric schools the cemetery is no longer the place where one goes to meditate on the sad destiny of our flesh, and it is not even only the gruesome symbol of the death of passions.

Those incomparable analysts of the human psyche coming out from the tantric milieux looked for violent impressions, gave free vent to their imagination, to evoke in the silence of these fearful recesses visions and hallucinations of demons and phantoms, to destroy them later on with the fire of ascesis and of meditation; in this way they could acquire the indestructible awareness that demons and gods are not objective and transcendent realities, but ephemeral projection of our mind not yet mastered, and therefore they could realize the ineffable truth of the insubstantiality of whatever appears. It is the analysis and disintegration of the psychical complex in order to descend into that irreducible element of our ego, by discovering which they thought to find the ground of being itself.

Among all the gruesome places of meditation eight have become especially famous; legend populated them with divine beings or narrated about famous Siddhas who would have acquired in those places their thaumaturgical powers.

Why they are just eight it is easy to imagine. It is true that the esoteric schools considered them as symbols of the conscient elements of the human personality. They put us in contact with the external world and give us its sensation and raise in us the desire of it. And they are in fact eight: five for the five senses with the addition of the *mano-vijñāna* or mental sensation, the *mano-kliṣṭa-vijñāna* or mental sensation obscured by karmic dispositions, and the *ālaya,* i.e. the constant centre of the individual, in which is summed up the experience of his past lives and from which his future existence evolves. Nevertheless, it is clear that this symbolism represents a secondary element, which has been developed on the already formed scheme of the eight cemeteries. They had to be eight in relation to the eight cardinal directions, the four principal and the four intermediary ones.

According to the liturgy connected with Śaṁvara, these cemeteries are considered as indispensable concomitants of the maṇḍala. They have to be represented covered with corpses without head, stiff and hung on trees, lying with the back on earth, impaled, transfixed by a spear, cut in the middle; covered with skulls, thigh-bones, grinning heads and spread over with other bones or with full skeletons (Tsoṅ-kha-pa).

And Lui-pa adds that these cemeteries must be imagined full of howls of dogs and jackals, of lions, tigers, boars, cats, sheep, wolves and of inauspicious birds as crows, owls etc., of corpses ripped up by poles, full of skeletons, skulls cut in the middle, bones, burnt pyres or half-burnt pyres, pisacas eaters of corpses, divine ascetics in the act of giving offerings, Yoginīs in great numbers, knives, skulls and khaṭvāṅgas, dry twigs and vases full of food, and white caitya.

Even the trees filling the background of the cemeteries have their meaning. They represent the eight species of trees, each characteristic of the corresponding cemetery: *śirīṣa* (Acacia siris-sa), *cūta/āmra* (Mangiphera indica), *aśvattha* (Ficus religiosa), *harikela/vaṭa* (Ficus bengalensis), *karañja* (Pongamia glabra), *latāparkaṭī/pārthiva/arjuna* (Terminalia arjuna).

Alternating with the described scenes we can see some mountains near which stupas are depicted. But one has not to believe that these figures have a decorative function, a kind of background to the terrific landscape of the front. Mountains and stūpas are also a symbolic element necessary to the representation of the sacred maṇḍala of Śaṁvara. The mountains too have to be eight for reasons of cosmographic symmetry, and near each of them a stūpa has to be drawn. These eight mountains starting from east and turning to the left, not to the right, are: the mountain made of gems the Sumeru, the Mandara (green), Kailāsa (white), Malaya (yellow), to the north-east turning to the right, Mahendra (black), Gandhamādana (yellow), Himālaya (white), Śrīparvata (blue).

The figures in adoring attitude represent the eight nāgas of which the liturgical manual of Tsoṅ-kha-pa has given us summary description. Above the figure of every nāga is depicted a cloud, symbol of that connection between the nāga and the waters, having very old origins, from India to China. In this case too the clouds are not anonymous, almost a simple expression of this original meaning of the nāgas; they are eight and each of them has a name. In the same way the coupled figures of the eight kṣetrapālas are indissolubly connected with the eight cemeteries.

The representation of these cemeteries and of their details is neither left to the will or discrimination of the artist, nor are they mere ornament. It answers, in fact, to symbolic schemes well determined, whose origin has to be looked for in the tantric traditions of India. The eight cemeteries are thus described by Suratavajra in his Vajra-pradīpa-ṭippaṇī:

अथ श्मशानानि कथ्यन्ते यथानुक्रमयोगतः। पूर्वे चण्डोग्रं नाम महाश्मशानं। शिरीषवृक्षे गजमुखो महर्द्धिकः सितः। इन्द्रो दिक्पतिः गौरः सहस्राक्षः शुक्लैरावतासनासीनः। वासुकिर्नागराजः पीतः गर्जितो मेघो विश्ववर्णः। सुमेरुः पर्वतश्च भूरत्नमयः। सितवज्रो नाम चैत्यः श्वेतः॥

दक्षिणे करङ्कभीषणं नाम महाश्मशानं। आम्रवृक्षे महिषमुखो महर्द्धिकः कृष्णः। यमो दिक्पालो महिषारूढः कृष्णः। पद्मो नागः सितः। आवर्त्तको मेघो विश्ववर्णः। मलयः पर्वतो गौरः। पिशुनवज्रो नाम चैत्यः कृष्णः॥

पश्चिमे ज्वालाकुलं नाम महाश्मशानं। अशोकवृक्षे मकराननो महार्द्धिकः श्वेतः। वरुणो दिक्पतिः सितः। कर्कोटको नागो रक्तः। घोरो मेघो विश्ववर्णः। कैलासः पर्वतः सितः। संज्ञावज्रो नाम चैत्यः सितः॥

उत्तरे गह्वरं नाम महाश्मशानं। अश्वत्थवृक्षे मनुष्यमुखो मह-

र्द्धिको गौरः। कुबेरो दिक्पतिः गौरो नरवाहनः। तक्षको नागः कृष्णः। घूर्णितो मेघः विश्ववर्णाः। मन्दरः पर्वतः श्यामः। चित्तवज्रो नाम चैत्यो गौरः॥

ऐशान्यां लक्ष्मीवनं नाम महाश्मशानं। वटवृक्षे गोमुखो महर्द्धिकः सितः। महेश्वरो दिक्पतिः सितो गोवाहनः। शङ्खपालो नागः पीतः। चण्डो मेघो विश्ववर्णाः। महेन्द्रः पर्वतः कृष्णः। वाग्वज्रो नाम चैत्यः श्वेतः॥

आग्नेय्यामट्टहासो नाम महाश्मशानं। करञ्जवृक्षे छागाननो महर्द्धिको रक्तः। हुताशनो दिक्पतीरक्तः छागासनः। महापद्मो नागो श्यामः। घनो मेघः विश्ववर्णाः। गन्धमादनः पर्वतः पीतः। कायवज्रो नाम चैत्यो रक्तः।

नैरृत्यां घोरान्धकारो नाम महाश्मशानं। लतापर्कटीवृक्षे शवमुखो महर्द्धिकः कृष्णः। राक्षसो दिक्पतिः शवासनः कृष्णः। अनन्तो नागः पांडुरः। पुराणो मेघो विश्ववर्णाः। हेमः पर्वतः श्वेतः। रत्नवज्रो नाम चैत्यः कृष्णः।

वायव्यां किलिकिलारवं नाम महाश्मशानं। पार्थिववृक्षे मृगाननो नाम महर्द्धिकः श्यामः। मारुतो दिक्पति श्यामो मृगारूढः। कुलिको नागः कर्बुरः। वर्षणो मेघो विश्ववर्णाः। श्रीपर्वतो नीलः। धर्मवज्रो नाम चैत्यः श्यामः॥

The maṇḍala of Śaṁvara at Tsaparang. It is represented in the middle of the temple which is but a poor ruin. The few fragments remaining, made clear by the liturgical texts, allow us to reconstruct it ideally in its entirety. The few statues snatched from destruction, although mutilated and without symbols, nevertheless can be identified, especially with the help of their colours, which, as every smallest detail in this mahayanic art, have a precise meaning.

The small temple of Tsaparang presents something if not unusual, at least not very frequent, namely, the maṇḍala is not painted but is built with wood and stucco. When it was intact, it would have constituted a splendid example of an architectonic maṇḍala. In fact, normally the maṇḍalas, if they were not frescoed, were drawn every time by means of coloured powders on the floor, or over a surface appositely prepared. Now the details of the maṇḍala at Tsaparang have fallen down and are destroyed. The arches that adorned the pavilions *(vimāna)* or were over the 'doors' are lying here and there broken in confused heaps. Tucci reached just in time to find, among the ruins, the statues or fragments of statues of the deities originally disposed around the maṇḍala in the place assigned to each of them. They are described at length and copiously illustrated by Tucci in his *Indo-Tibetica* III/2.

Saṁvara to Śambhala. The word saṁvara has several orthographic variations: saṁvara, sambara, sambhāra, śaṁvara, śambara, śambhara. The original word saṁvara means 'obligation, vow', whence Tibetan *sdom-pa* 'restraint, obligation, vow'. In Tamil, sambara refers to the Buddhist community. This is reflected in place names like Sambalhora (in Muzaffarnagar), Sambalpur (in Orissa and Madhya Pradesh), Sambhal (in Moradabad). In course of time, Śaṁvara of the Cakra-śaṁvara became Śambhala of the Kālacakra.

LITERATURE CITED

Bhattacharyya 1958

Benoytosh Bhattacharyya, *Indian Buddhist Iconography,* Calcutta (Firma K.L. Mukhopadhyay).

Gordon 1952

Antoinette K. Gordon, *Tibetan Religious Art,* New York.

Lessing 1942

Ferdinand Diederich Lessing, *Yung-ho-kung,* an iconography of the Lamaist cathedral in Peking, Stockholm.

Lokesh Chandra 1986

Lokesh Chandra, *Buddhist Iconography of Tibet,* Kyoto (Rinsen Book Co.).

Toh.

Hakuju Ui et al., *A Complete Catalogue of the Tibetan Buddhist Canons* (Bkaḥ-ḥgyur and Bstan-ḥgyur), Sendai (Tohoku Imperial University), 1934.

Tucci 1936

Giuseppe Tucci, *Indo-Tibetica,* III/2. I Templi del Tibet Occidentale e il loro Simbolismo Artistico, Tsaparang, Rome (Reale Accademia d'Italia).

Tucci 1949

Giuseppe Tucci, *Tibetan Painted Scrolls,* Rome (La Libreria dello Stato).

Tucci 1961

Giuseppe Tucci, *The Theory and Practice of the Mandala,* London (Rider & Co.).

FOREWORD.

It was my intention in starting this Series of Tantrik Texts to include therein specimens from all the various schools of Āgama, Vaishnava, Shaiva, Shākta and Bauddha. For, whatever may be the difference as regards doctrinal and ritual details, there are marked similarities in spirit, general outlook, and method between all the Āgamas; and though, as I have often said, the use of the phrase "the Tantra" is vague and incorrect, an examination of the Tantras of the Āgamas of differing schools do enable us to extract therefrom certain common features which, when found in any work, enables us to describe it as being of a "Tantrik" character. The inclusion therefore of Tantras of varying schools in this Series will establish this point. So a coming volume will contain a Tantrik Prakarana of the Kashmir School called Kāmakalāvilāsa. The Buddhist Demchog Tantra here printed is the first Buddhist Tantra to be published, and the first to be translated into any European tongue.

As in the case of the Indian Tantra, the Buddhist Tantra has suffered neglect. In both cases one of the reasons has been the great difficulties of the work. Nevertheless, as in the case of the Indian Tantra, a very imperfect knowledge and understanding of the subject has not stood in the way of adverse and absurd judgments. Thus, when speaking of the doctrinal theories of the great saint and poet Milarepa, it has been said, the italics being mine ("Tibet and the Tibetans" by the Rev. Graham Sandberg, 260): "As is *invariably* the case in Buddhist philosophical statements, were we to quote here (as we do later) these enunciations, they would be found to contain *no* real recondite wisdom, *nor even any scheme of metaphysics and morality* which could be dignified with the title of an ethical system. They are, mostly, *mere pretentious phrases* which have little consistency, and the profundity is only apparent and will not bear analysis. There is *nothing* ennobling to the individual, or calculated to make the world better; or even, in the Buddhist sense, less steeped in misery, in the doctrines of sublime vacuity and indifference to all earthly claims with which Buddhism, whether Indian or Tibetan, occupies itself. It is essentially the religion of *phraseological terms* and *onomato-poetical* positions. Even the universal philanthropy preached becomes *degenerate* when it would condescend to practical individual exercise." Though perhaps this is an extreme statement, many other Western authors expatiate on the "meaningless" "charlatanism" and "degeneracy" of Northern Buddhism. When will they learn, in this as in other cases, not to discredit common humanity by supposing that any large body of men have devoted themselves throughout the ages to "meaningless" doctrines and practices! If they are meaningless to them, it is because they do not know the meaning. And what is yet known of the Buddhist Tantra? Very little indeed. Religious prepossessions will naturally assign to the critic's own religion (if he have one) a superior worth; for if he did not believe it superior to all others, he would not presumably follow it. Racial prejudice often grudges to the Asiatic the possession of any real merit, much less superiority over Western theories of life. Nevertheless the true spirit of scholarship will endeavour to be just, and if any doctrine or practice is not understood, it is better and safer to admit this ignorance than to allege meaningless and absurdity—a charge which often implies nothing more than irritation in the face of what is not understood. We are, many of us, too disposed to hold that what *we* cannot understand has no meaning at all. That is because we overflatter both our abilities and knowledge. It is surely the acme of absurdity to deny that Northern Buddhism has any scheme of metaphysic, when it has developed some of the most subtle and logically welded themes which the world has ever known ; or to deny that it has an ethical system, seeing that Buddhism as also Brahmanism have produced the most radical analysis of the basis of all morality and have advocated every form of it which any other religion has affirmed to be of worth. It is a commonplace however, which is nevertheless to be remembered, that in all religions there is a mass-religion suitable to the less developed minds of the majority of the community and the religion of the highly educated, the spiritually developed, and the sages. Even present-day Christianity, which prides itself on having no esoteric teaching, shows those differences which we might naturally expect when minds differ in both capacity and knowledge. There is thus a high philosophic Tantricism and that of the crowd with its cruder beliefs. Whilst the adherents of the former are blamed for "their sublime vacuity and indifference to earthly claims," the majority are called to book for making religion a means to secure material gain—as if man all the world over did not seek and pray for earthly benefits. So whilst the mass believe in the objectivity of the multitudinous Devatās, the initiate is aware that they exist only in the mind, and by means of the mind, which gives them the life which they possess. But though their existence is that of the mind, that is not to say that they are nothing. And so the Brihadāranyaka Upanishad says that those who adore the Devas, thinking that they are different from themselves, such men the Devas make their beast of burden. In the philosophic presentment and its accompanying ritual, the idea of the Void (Shūnyatā) dominates. After the Chela has gained a clear vision of the Devatās, occupying the different parts of the Mandala of worship, he arrives at a point in which the Devatās gradually melt the one into the other, and are all absorbed in the principal Devatā which occupies the centre of the Mandala, and this in its turn gradually effaces itself and is absorbed in the Bindu (Thigle) between the eyebrows (Ājnā-chakra) where is the Point of Light which itself disappears in the Void. Similar principles govern the worship of the Indian Shrī-chakra. Both are instances of the Tantrik method by which the Sādhaka is made to *practically* realise that he is one with all that is, and that all is at base Shūnyatā or Paramātmā, as the case may be. It is not enough to theoretically affirm that identity, Proof must be given of it; and the only real proof anywhere is direct (Pratyaksha) experience. So to take another instance: the mass of Buddhistic believers may think that union with the Dākinīs consists in gaining the favour of female-spirits. Esoterically however the adept projects his creative will into the Matrix of the Mother-Energies which are the Mātrīs and Dākinīs and there engenders active forms and powers which are indeed himself as such, since all that is without is within.

And so also the Buddhas project the Bodhisattvas who create in their turn. But beside all this mysticism which, whether rightly founded or not (a matter with which I am not concerned), is, as a system, philosophically profound, there are to be found amongst Buddhist and Indian Tantrikas inferior practitioners given over to an evil magic which is yet by no means always " charlatanism " as most Orientalists aver, and to abuses in connection with what in India is known as the Chakra ritual. The ignorant lay-folk in these and other countries envisage spiritual truths so grossly that they come to be called superstition. All evil and ignorance is so much by its nature on the surface and affords so apt a subject for adverse judgment that it is readily seized upon, and the more so that it is convenient material for religious polemic. Nevertheless I repeat that we must do credit both to our intelligence and sense of justice by endeavouring to understand any religion in its highest and truest aspect. The Tantras, whether Buddhist or Indian, contain both a profound doctrine and a wonderfully conceived praxis. And so it was said of Marpa, the founder of the Kar-gyu-pa sect, that " his Dorje (Vajra) revelled in the profoundest of Tantras."

The translator of this work is a Sikkhimese, Kazi Dawa-samdup (zla-va-bsam-hgrub) who, when I first made his acquaintance, was chief interpreter attached to the staff of H. E. Lonchen Shatra, the Tibetan Plenipotentiary to the Government of India. Before that, he was Translator and Interpreter to the Government of India in Buxa-Duar and Rajshahi, and (as he is now) the head of the State school at Gangtok in Independent Sikkim. He was also attached to the political officer's staff on the visit of His Holiness the Dalai Lama to India. Kazi Dawa-samdup is a

Tibetan scholar, whose version of some portion of Milarepa's Hymns have been adopted by the Government of India as a text-book for the high proficiency examination in Tibetan. He has also got a good knowledge of English and some knowledge of Sanskrit which has been very useful in the discussions we have had as to the rendering to be given to particular passages or words. For it is to be remembered that the Tantrik doctrines were introduced into Tibet from India, and many Tantras which are in Tibetan were formerly in Sanskrit. The Mantras in the text translated are in Sanskrit, though Tibetan script is employed. These Mantras are generally incorrectly written, and it is often difficult to state them correctly. I have not in general attempted to do so. I have kept to the spelling and accents of the texts. As regards some of the longer and more important Mantras, I have suggested a correct reading. As regards this, I acknowledge with thanks the assistance of Mahāmahopādhyāya Satish Chandra Vidyābhūshana, Principal of the Sanskrit College, Calcutta, and himself a Tibetan scholar.

I have not had more than one part of this Text translated for two main reasons. The first Part will give the ordinary English reader an idea of the general character of the ritual work, which is sufficient for my present purposes. In the next place, the translator and myself lost through their death the advantage of the very learned assistance of the Guru of the former and of the Enche Geshe.

The translator not being an initiate in this particular Tantra was unwilling, for the present, to continue the translation of the other Parts without the assistance of its learned votaries. Summaries have therefore been given of the Parts subsequent to the first which has been fully translated. This will probably serve the purpose of the ordinary English reader. Tibetan scholars have here the text to translate if they can. The translator has given full explanatory notes to the text, and has written a useful Introduction on the Vajrayāna and Mantrayāna, to which this Demchog Tantra belongs, the valuable manuscripts of which, with others, I acquired some five years ago, shortly after which the preparation of this volume was begun.

The term Vajra (rDo-rje) has as one of its meanings "diamond," and so we get the quaint translation by those who do not understand the subject "Diamond Sow" for the Goddess Vajra-vārāhī (rDo-rje-Phagmo); and so also we find Vajrachitta translated as (though in this case more congruously) "Pensée de Diamant," "diamond thought." Vajra also means thunderbolt. Want of knowledge and a predilection for facile and gross meanings leads to absurd results, of which the Orientalist (whose lack of information is alone responsible for them) complains. I have already pointed out in the summary I have elsewhere given ("Origin of the Vajrayāna Devatās") of the fifth Chapter of the Golden Rosary of the history of the Lotus-born (Padma thangyig-serteng), that just as the diamond is hard and practically indestructible and the thunderbolt is powerful and irresistible, so Vajra is used for That which is steady, lasting, indestructible, powerful and irresistible, and is used in connection with its expressions in the phenomenal world. Thus in the Tantrik ritual we find Vajra-bhūmi (Vajra-earth), Vajra-pushpa (Vajra-flower) and so forth. These are not "diamond" earth or flowers, but limited phenomenal expressions of the ultimate Vajra offered in worship to that Vajra. Again, the chief priest in the Tantrik rites is called Dorje-Lopon. We read of Vajra-jnāna and Vajra-chitta as in the phrase from the Subhāsita Sangraha (II. 59) " Smaranam citta vajrasya sārāt sāratar am param." Here Vajra indicates firm, steady mind, free from Kalpanā. The spot at Bodhgaya where Buddha attained enlightenment is called Vajrāsana.

Vajradhara (rDo-rje-hChang) embodies in Himself all the five Dhyāni Buddhas and is called the sixth Buddha or Drug-pa-dorji-chang (Drug-pa-rDo-rje hChhang) who is the Dhyāni Buddha of the thirteenth highest Vajra state or Bhūmi in Sambhoga-kāya (bcū-sūm-rDorje-hDzin-pahi-sa). The five Dhyāni Buddhas are Vajra-sattva (East), Ratnasambhava (South), Amitābha (West), Amog-hasiddhi (North), Vairochana (Centre). Over all there is Vajradhara. He is of a blue colour and has two hands, which are crossed on his breast. The right hand holds a rDo-rje (Vajra) and the left a bell. Vajra-sattva (rDo-rje-Sems-dpah) is the Eastern Dhyāni Buddha, of whom Milarepa is believed to have been an incarnation. He is white. The right hand is on the heart and holds a Dorje (Vajra) pointing upwards, and the left on the lower body and holds a bell ; the right and left hands holding a Vajra and Bell. He is invoked for the absolution of sins. Vajrapāni (Phyagna-rDorje) is one of the three Bodhisattvas, or beings near Buddhahood, who are at certain Bhūmis on the way thereto, who represent the three principles of a Buddha ; *viz.*, Jampal-yang, or Manjusri (hJam-dPal-dVyangs), of an orange colour, representing Wisdom, holding in the right hand a sword emblematic of Prajnā (Shes-rabs), and in the left a lotus with a book on it, signi-fying learning and pure rebirth ; Avalokiteshvara

(Chen-rezi) of a white colour, with four hands (two joined in prayer, the others holding a crystal rosary and eight-petalled lotus), representing the Mercy of a Buddha; and Vajrapāni, of a blue colour and fierce type (Krodha Bhairava), representing the Might or Power of a Buddha, holding a Vajra in his right hand. His left hand makes a menacing Mudrā. He stands with legs wide apart and is surrounded by flames instead of a rainbow halo.

Vajrayāna, (Dorge-thegpa) or Vajra-vehicle, is so called because of its powerful disciplines and ritual methods for the attainment of that thirteenth state (Bhūmi), which is Vajradhara (rDorje-hChang). Buddha Vajra-sattva (rDo-rje Sems-ḍpah) is the eastern Dhyāni Buddha. Vajra is thus the primordial pure Vajra Consciousness. Vajra too is all Tathāgatas, that is those who have aforetime become illuminate. The image of Vajra-sattva is represented sitting with the legs crossed, holding the Vajra (rDo-rje) in his right hand and in his left a Bell. The Bell is Shes-rab (Prajnā) or Wisdom, which is Shūnyatā the Void, and the Vajra is Thabs (Upāya) or Method, which is Karunā or Compassion. This indicates that by means of the high and indestructible (Vajra) method, which is Compassion for all sentient beings, one attains the final end (Dharmakāya or Chös-Sku), which is the imperishable unchanging state of the " Two in one " wisdom (Zung-hjug-yeshes), which is the Bhūmi or state called Vajradhara (rDo-rje-hChang).

What then is Shūnyatā (sTongpa-nyid)? The word sTong-pa means empty, and sTongpa-nyid is Emptiness or the Void. This means " nothing "; but not " nothing " in the sense of what is commonly called Nihilism. It is absurd to suppose that the Buddhist seeks, and is on the way to, this. It is " nothing " in the relative sense—that is nothing *to us*, because it has none of the qualities of things which we know, such as form, colour, taste, smell, weight, and temperature. These are of the material plane. The state here described is beyond the phenomenal world and cannot be described in the imagery of that world. Of it, as of the Indian Paramātmā, it can be only said "it is not this," "it is not this" (neti, neti). In fact, the Indian Tantra also employs the term Shūnya to denote the Brahman. (*See*, for instance, Tantrik Texts, Vol. II, and "The Serpent Power," which I hope to have ready shortly after the appearance of this.) The empty space in the Bindu is designated the quiescent Parabrahman, just as the form of the Bindu itself is the creatively active Īshvara.

This leads me to say a few words on the Buddhist doctrine of Anātmā. Without claiming to have studied the Buddhist doctrines in the same degree that I have done some of those of Brahmanism, what I know of them leads me to the conclusion that the alleged difference between the Advaita Hindus and Buddhists (at any rate of the school here represented) on the subject of Ātmā is, to a considerable extent (though there are also differences), a question of words. It has been said by a Western Buddhist scholar that the Hindu belief in Ātmā is belief in an immortal, unchanging Ego, a subtle form in the body and not of it, being a separate entity; whilst a personality or Pudgala according to the Buddhists is an aggregate of Khandhas, material and immaterial, in the way of body, mind and tendencies, in which there is no abiding Ātmā. The states of mind lead to rebirth or liberation. Man is in no sense an abiding entity. At death the general result of the mental workings cause a new consciousness to arise in accordance with the Vāsanā or general tendency, which fresh name and form (Nāmarūpa) is " the same and yet not the same " ; a being which is the resultant of the previous one. It is, however, a mistake to suppose that Indian Monism (Advaitavāda) posits an unchanging immortal Ego. It speaks of three bodies—supreme, subtle, and gross. The latter is the physical, the second the psychical body of mind, *viz.*, Buddhi (including Ahangkāra), Manas, the senses (Indriya), the five Prānas, or, according to Sāngkhya, the five Tanmatrās known as the " 17." The third or spiritual body is that of Bliss (Ānanda) which is the eternal, changeless Ātmā. The subtle body is the soul which may be said to be an entity in the gross body. Ahangkāra, which is one of its elements, is the Ego-making function of the mind. This subtle body survives at death and transmigrates. But it is not changeless, nor immortal. On the contrary, it being a product of Prakriti, is changing. Nor is it as such immortal, for it ceases to be on liberation when the individual Ego also ceases to be. What is changeless and eternal is the Ātmā. This Ātmā is not a thing, an object, an Ego, or person, but relatively to worldly experience a state of consciousness. Relatively to this experience it is called " Being-Consciousness-Bliss," but in truth nothing can be said as to what It is in Itself. This is only known by being It. For, to truly know a thing is to be that thing. By knowing, that is realizing in oneself Brahman, one becomes Brahman. It is this ultimate State which in the Indian Shākta Tantra is called Shūnya, and by the Vajrayāna Buddhists, Shūnyatā (sTong-pa-nyid). The former call it the Absolute Real, though the Buddhists appear to be satisfied to say no more than it is Shūnyatā. It may be contrasted with appearance (sNang-va-dang) or name and form (Nāmarūpa).

Shūnyatā (Shes-rabs) is associated with Karunā (Thabs) The latter is the Power, Means (Upāya) or Method by which anything is done as compared with Shes-rabs, the wisdom (Prajnā), which guides and utilises it. Shes-rabs (Prajnā) utilises Thabs (Upāya) in order that Nirvāna may be attained. The Mahayāna Buddhist does not seek liberation (or salvation, as the Christian would call it, though the latter term belongs to a different order of ideas) for himself alone. His object is that all beings may share that lot : a truly noble doctrine. In and for purposes of worship, Wisdom is regarded as female and Power or Method as male. They are pictured as being in sexual union, the Male standing and the Female clinging to him with either one or both lower limbs circling his back. This denotes that Wisdom and Method are ever in union.

This also teaches the Sādhaka to avoid the extremes of passive Nirvāna and eternal active Sangsāra or phenomenal universe. The two are one. This doctrine is "Not two knowledge" (gNyismed-yeshes), that is, Monism or Advaitavāda. The Perfect Mind (Byang-chub-sems) is the purified mind of the Buddha. The five aspects of the Buddha Consciousness are exoterically the five Dhyāni Buddhas and esoterically the five Wisdoms (Yeshes or Jnāna) which are described in the notes to pp. 4-5 of the translation. The causal chain leading to the appearance in mind of the phenomenal universe are the Nidānas, according to which, as in Brahmanism, the world springs from the desire generated by the Vāsanā which is the seed of it and of the will to worldly life. Destruction of this desire leads back to Nirvāna which is not annihilation in the sense of nothingness, but a supremely blissful state of Changeless Being. Hence the Devatā here worshipped is called Demchog (bDe-mChog), which means Great or Highest Bliss (Mahāsukha or Paramānanda). The Buddhist, like all Mankind, seeks as his end unchanging and indestructible happiness. " Annihilation " means annihilation of the world-experience of forms, which, as forms, are bound up with suffering. Liberation is sought from suffering, that is form.

Māyā is in Tibetan Gyūma (sGyūma), which means a magical and illusory show, such as that of a magician or conjurer. So Shangkarāchāryya calls the Lord a Māyāvin or Magician, the world being a show of His Magic Power. Knowledge is also real (Pāramārthika) and empirical (Vyāvahārika).

The similarities between this doctrine and Māyāvāda Vedānta are obvious. This was long ago perceived when the Padma Purāna spoke of Shangkarāchāryya's system called Māyāvāda as "a bad doctrine and a covert form of Buddhism" (Māyāvādam asachchhāstram prachchhanam bauddham). It is however equally obvious that there are also differences between the two doctrines. It was Shangkara's object to refute the Buddhists and Atheists (Nāstika), in the sense in which that term is used in Sanskrit, namely, persons who did not accept the Scriptural authority of Veda. Probably it would be correct to say that Shangkara adjusted his exposition of Vedānta to meet the original Māyāvāda of the Buddhists and so promulgated a new presentment of Māyā without abandoning what he believed to be essential principles of Brahmanism. In fact he was a worshipper of the Supreme Mother or Shakti whose Shrī Yantra may be seen in his Maths. The Shākta Tantra is also a form of Advaitavāda presented in a way suitable for its purpose, namely, the practical end of worship. Therein Māyā is a Power (Shakti) of the Supreme Consciousness. In

Northern Buddhism as in Brahmanism, the Bodhisattvas and Devatās are accompanied by their energies (nü-ma) in female form, the Deva being called Yab and his Shakti Yum.

On the ritual side also there are many similarities between this form of Buddhist Tantra and the Indian Shākta Tantra, such as the use of images, Mandalas, Bīja, Mantra, Mudrā, Upachāra, Abhisheka, Dhyāna, Symbolism, the worship of Āvaranadevatās and so forth. The reader will find some very interesting methods of meditation both in the text of Part I and in the Synopsis of Part VII which describes the concentration on Points of Light by which the sense organs are controlled in the face of distractions and the temptation to lust and other passions caused by objects of enjoyment. The movement of some forms of the Mantra-Shakti is described at pp. 52-53 of Part I. Where ritual details vary, the spirit, purpose and psychological method are similar. To my mind, one of the most distinctive marks of the Tantrik system is its profound application of psychology to worship, and the manner in which it not only formally teaches through symbols, but actually *creates*, through its ritual methods, the *states of mind* which are set forth as the end of its teachings. As the translator and editor of this text acutely observes, the Buddhist Tantra does not so much say, " Here is the answer or theory. Train your mind to believe so " ; but " Here are the problem and the means. Work out the answer for yourself." Any ritual which accomplishes this (whatever be its form) has true value. It can, however, only achieve this by profound observation of the workings of the human mind and by the framing of ritual forms which are in conformity therewith. The subject is both deep and extensive, and I cannot deal with it here. The reader may find some explanations, which may be of use to him on this point in my "Shakti and Shākta." Here, however, I may give an example of my meaning. The Tantra is called Shrī-chakra-sambhāra, and deals with the worship of the Deity (bDe-mchog). It is thus a Demchog Tantra. Shrī is an auspicious prefix. Chakra means here Mandala (hKhorlo), that is a material or mental image of the Deity in His abode with its guardians, and surrounding Devātas, and so forth. The Tantra has been given the Sanskrit name Shrī Chakra Sambhāra. The last word, however, is spelt differently in the Text. Sometimes it is spelt Sambhara, sometimes Sambara, and again Sambāra. Sambhāra, Sambhara and Sambara and Sambhri (root) have in Sanskrit the sense of "collection," that is of the materials, means and requisites for any purpose: and here mean, in this sense, all that is collected together in the Mandala of Worship, the Īshtadevatā, His abode, surrounding or Āvarana Devatās, guardian Spirits, and so forth. The equivalent Tibetan word is sDompa, which means a collection, and added figure or sum, and also a vow in restraint of certain acts. In this latter sense, it is outer, inner, and hidden. The obscuring or defiling passions (Klesha) of Lust, Anger, and Delusion (Moha) are in the outer vow restrained, together with Egoism (Ahangkāra) by Jnāna (Yeshes). By the inner vow, belief in a self and outer material objects are restrained in the Chakra of the Devatās. By the hidden vow the Nādis, Vāyus, and the Sūkshma Bīja of the body are restrained in the Chakra of the heart. And, lastly, all consciousness and ideas are restrained in the pure state (gNyüg-ma), which is the Void (sTongpa-nyid). The Tibetan word (bDe-mchog) means Highest Bliss (Mahāsukha), which is the state of the Devatā here worshipped, and who is also thus called Demchog. Vajra-yoginī (rDo-rje rNal-hbyorma) or Vajra-vārāhī (rDo-rje Phagmo), the so-called " Diamond Sow," is His consort. He is Method (Thabs) or Compassion, and She is the Wisdom (Shes-rabs) which is the Void or Shūnyatā. The same Devatā is addressed by both names. She is called Vajra-yoginī, as consort of Vajradhara, and Vajra-vārāhī when She is the chief Devatā of the Vārāhī Maṇḍala.

On the subject of the Three Bodies of Buddha to which reference is here and in all Tantras made, I would refer to the Opuscule "Les trois corps du Bouddha" which its author M. Masson-Oursel was good enough to send me on its publication the year prior to the war (Extrait du Journal Asiatique, Mai-Juin 1913). The word which we translate as " body, " but which must not be here understood in the gross sense of that term, is in Sanskrit Kāyā, in Tibetan Sku, and in Chinese Chen. The first or Dharma-kāya (translated by M. S. Levi as " essential body ") is beyond form (Arūpa), mind and speech, the eternal omnipresent law of all Becoming, holding within itself in undifferentiated mass all particular Dharmas and in creation manifesting as them. This is what is referred to as the Dharmadhātu or Dharma-substance from which Matrix all the Blessed Ones, the Tathāgatas, issue. This is the body of the Buddha in Nirvāna and the base of the two others which are its (relatively) passing aspects to the dual consciousness of form. The Sambhoga-kāya is the body of bliss or enjoyment with form (rūpa-vān) and therefore visible to the Bodhisattvas in Heaven consisting of the five Skandhas—Rūpa, Vedanā, Samjnā, Samskāra, Vijnāna—and is an intermediate manifestation of the Dharmadhātu. The third or more " material " body of the Buddhas is Nirmāna-kāya or that which is "made" and incarnate on earth as a human personage. The Dharma-kāya is an indivisible unity beyond all duality. The Sambhoga-kāya without dividing and particularising itself is the Body of Glory manifest only to the Bodhisattvas who more nearly approach the state of a perfect Buddha. In Nirmāna-kāya the essence of Buddha is exteriorised into multiple individual appearances visible to men, such as the forms in which the Buddhas have appeared on earth. We have thus to do here with what in Western language may be described as a doctrine of emanation or transformation or Tul-pa (sPrülpa). Similarly in the Indian Tantrik doctrine of Ābhāsa, the Supreme whilst resting one and the same in Its own true nature (Svarūpa) produces in Its creative aspect a principle (Tattva) from itself which again evolves another and so on, each cause remaining what it was whilst producing an effect.

I append here a short summary of the general principles of Buddhist doctrine as given in the "Path of Good Wishes" of the Buddha Samanta Bhadra called Thogmahi Sans-rGyas Küntu-bZangpo or sMon Lam-stops-po-che translated by Kazi Dawa-samdup. The "Good Wishes" are in italics. The brackets enclose explanations in roman character.

THE GOOD-WISHES.

"Then the all-good Buddha, Küntu-bZangpo, uttered these good wishes whereby the sentient beings of the Sangsāra cannot but be saved.

1.

Ho [Listen]! *All which is visible and invisible* (sNang-srid), *whether Sangsāra or Nirvāṇa, is at base* (gZhi) *one* (that is Shūnyatā) *with two paths* (Avidyā and Vidyā) *and two ends* [Sangsāra and Nirvāna. This ultimate base is in Advaita Brāhmanism the Parabrahman also called Shūnya. By its Shaktis Vidyā and Avidyā liberation (Moksha) and bondage (World) is attained]. *These* (paths and ends) *are the wondrous play of Ignorance* (Avidyā) *and Knowledge* (Vidyā). *By the power of these good wishes of Küntu-bZangpo, may all attain Buddhahood in the Dharma-dhātu* [Chös-dVyings; that is the ultimate Dharma-kāya in Nirvāna which is Shūnyatā or Void. All have an inherent right and capacity to Enlightenment. But all beings do not attain it simultaneously. Therefore Sangsāra is Eternal].

2.

The Foundation of all [Kün-gZhi. Kün = all; gZhi = basis or underlying principle, which according to Atiyoga (rDzogs-chhen) is simple or uncompounded. All visible objects are compounds] *is uncreated* (Rang-byung or "come out of self") *and independent, uncompounded* (hDus ma-byas) *and beyond Mind and Speech. Of It neither the word Nirvāna nor Sangsāra may be said* [these are terms of the dualistic world, Nirvāna (Myang-hdas) being contrasted with, and having meaning only in reference to, Sangsāra (hKhorva). They are both ideas formed by the mind of certain states. But Shūnyatā, the Void, is beyond the finite mind with all its imaginings. The state of Shūnyatā is free of all defined notions which have no meaning in this absolute state. Similarly whilst in Advaita Brahmanism the Parabrahman is, relative to the Sangsāra, Being-Consciousness-Bliss or Sachchidānanda, what It is in Itself is unknowable except by and to Itself]. *To realise It is to be a Buddha, and not to realise it is to stray into Sangsāric being. May all sentient beings in the three Regions* (Lokas) *realise this indescribable Basis of all.*

3.

I Küntu-Zangpo knowing the Basis which is without cause to be self-produced, did not sully it by the thought that It was without or within. It is not obscured by the darkness of unconsciousness. No faulty notion of self darkens it [Rang-snang. The first word means self and "Snang" is notion or appearance. That is the notion of self. The apparent self is the cause of all error].

For those who are in the state of true knowledge [Rang-rig. Rang = self and "Rig" is knowledge, that is knowledge that the sense of self is unreal and phenomenal only, and that the ultimate is Shūnyatā] *there is no fear, were even all the three regions to be destroyed. They are not attached to the objects of sense enjoyment. To the self-subsisting experience beyond ideas* [rTog-med. rTogpa is in

Sanskrit Kalpanā, and rTog-med means without that or Nirvishesha Jnāna, beyond all limited knowing, for ideas are limitations] *there is no material form* [dNgös-pohi-gZugs ; that which can do something or fulfil some purpose or Dön-byed-nus-pa-dNgospo. That is, things with form (rūpa). Form is the work of the finitizing principle of Māyā] *or the five poisons* [that is Lust, Anger, Infatuation, Pride, Jealousy, which are sinful attachments to form]. *Then from clear unobstructed mind* [Rigpa or pure Buddhi. Sems, Blo, and Rigpa all mean mind, but the last is, though Sangsāric, purified mind (Sems) and therefore something lower than Prajnā (Shes-rabs) or Yeshes (Jnāna), into which by training it may be and is here exalted. The arts and sciences are also called Rigpa, because they are the proper field of high intellect. By the action of Avidyā and Moha, mind is obstructed. Here Rigpa is that pure state of mind which may be trained into the Yeshes, the embodiments of which are the Dhyāni Buddhas] *come five Wisdoms* (Yeshes, see notes pp. 4-5, *post*) *though they are in essence one, from which are produced the five Buddhas* (Vairochana and the rest which either Küntu-Zangpo or rDorje-hChhang of the Kargyudpas embodies). *From the going forth of the Wisdom of the five Buddhas the forty peaceful Buddhas are produced.* [The term " Buddha " is here used to describe the whole class. These are the five Dhyāni Buddhas and their Spouses, the eight Bodhisattvas called Nyevahi-Sras-chen-brGyad, namely, Manjusri, Avalokiteshvara, Vajrapāni, Ākāshagarbha, Kshitigarbha, Maitreya, Samanta Bhadra, and Dib-pa-nam sel, which, with their Consorts, make 16, and the six Buddhas who work on behalf of the beings of the Lokas. These 32 occupy the Heart-chakra. There are ten other Devatās of the Throat-chakra. These

42 peaceful (zhi) and 58 wrathful (khro) make in all an 100 Devatās. Forty are here mentioned and sixty in the next verse in round numbers instead of 42 and 58. Such round numbers are also used to guard the mysteries.]

5.

From the shining forth of the Power (rTsal) *of the five Buddhas come the* 60 *blood-drinking* (that is wrathful) *Devatās.* [60 should be 58, made up as follows, *viz.*, the ten Herukas, aspects of the Buddhas and their Shaktis, Buddha-Heruka, Vajra-Heruka, Ratna-Heruka, Padma-Heruka, Karma-Heruka; four door-keepers; eight Devatās in the eight directions—Keurima (E.), Cheurima (S.), Pramoha (W.), Petali (N.), Puskasi (S. E.), Kasmari (S. W.), Chandika (N. W.), Smeshali (N. E.); the eight animal-headed Devatās called Phramenmas (*see* Arthur Avalon's "Essay on the Vajrayāna Devatās"); four other door-keepers with heads of Tigress, Sow, Lioness, and Snake; and 24 Yoginīs in four sets of six, each performing peaceful, grand or nourishing, fascinating, and stern or destructive powers. The Blood-drinking Devatās are situate in the Brain Mandala.] *In Me there has been no error in straying away from knowledge of the Foundation. As I am the Buddha, may all sentient beings in the three Regions by the power of this My good wish gain the great wisdom* (Yeshes chenpo) *through the self-produced Mind* (Rang-byung-Rigpa).

6.

There will be no end of my Avatāras (sPrülpa), *who will appear in inconceivable millions of numbers and shapes, and who will adopt various methods suitable for the control of every kind of being. By the power of My grace and good wishes, may all sentient beings of the three Regions* (Lokas) *escape from the six Sangsāric worlds* (that is, of Deva, Asura, Men, Preta, Tiryak, and Naraka).

7.

Beings who aforetime erred, did so because they knew not the Foundation. They were overpowered by the unconscious dark state. This was the cause of ignorance and error. Immersed in ignorance and obscured by delusion [which produces the Māyā of selfness. From the notion of "I" comes that of "other"; then "mine" and "thine" and all errors and sins], *the knower* (Mind) *was afeared and confused. Then came the idea "I" and "Other" and hatred. As these gained force a continuous chain of Sangsāric evolution was produced. Through that the five poisons of the obscuring passions of lust, anger, covetousness, delusion, jealousy increased, and an endless stream of evil Karma issued forth. Therefore, as the root source of error in sentient beings is unconscious* (Dran-med) *ignorance, may all by the power of the good wishes of Me, the Buddha, attain the clear pure mind* [Rigpa; the undisturbed true level of mind which is that of Dhyāna. When this is had, enlightenment comes] *inherent in every being.* [Pure mind is inherent in all and may be attained by all. It is said that the essence of the Sugatas or Buddhas pervades all beings, as butter in milk. As milk when churned, yields up butter, so each mind being developed, Nirvāna arises.]

8.

The root-ignorance [Lhan-skyes-Marig or Sahajā Avidyā, the general ignorance of the true state, which is called Kün-brTags-Marig when so intensified as to produce the notion of "other," "mine" and so forth (Parikalpitā Avidyā)] *is the abyssal ground of the knower's unconsciousness* (Dran-med Marig). *The other ignorance* (Kün-brTags-Marig) *is that which regards self and others to be different and separate. These two forms of ignorance are the root cause of error in all sentient beings. By the power of these good wishes of Me, the Buddha, may the gloom of unconsciousness* (ignorance of the true) *which obscures all beings in the Sangsāra, be dispelled. May they be cleared of their error which regards beings as separate from one another, and may their inherent pure mind* (Rigpa-rang-ngo-shes-par-shog) *be realised.* [That is, may Vidyā arise. May it come to know itself. The phenomenal or Vyāvahārika self is admitted, but it is the product of Māyā. This is the doctrine of Anātmā, for it has no independent permanent being (rTag-gcig-rang-dvang-can) for the attainment of the true or essential state shows this.]

9.

The thought which regards beings as separate (gNyis-hDzin bLo-ni, literally "as two") *begets a hesitating doubting state* (the-Tshom-za). *A subtle feeling of attachment arises which on being allowed to gain force gradually resolves itself into strong attachment and a craving for food, clothing, dwellings, wealth, and friends—the five objects of enjoyment—lovers, wives, and husbands. These are the chief errors of worldly people. There is no end to the action flowing from the ideas of dualism* [which regards things as external reality, and the Mind which perceives them as inner reality. If Sangsāra be left to itself, it goes on producing Sangsāra for ever. To attain release therefrom, effort guided by wisdom is necessary. This release is the Buddhist Shūnyatā and the Brahmanic Moksha]. *The fruit of these cravings is birth as a Preta* (what English Orientalists call "tantalized ghosts"), *who is tormented by pangs of hunger and thirst* [that is, the ordinary normal being gives way to desires and covetousness, the punishment whereof is in Pretal Loka. If the Karmic act be influenced by anger, then Hell (Naraka) is man's portion. Acts done under the influence of stupidity, such as killing for sport, or "for the fun of it," in ignorance of the Karmic results, procures for the actor birth in the brute world]. *By these, My good wishes, may all those beings, who suffer from their desires, strive not to studiously avoid them, nor* (weakly) *to give way to them, but to let the knower* [Shespa = Mind that is Sems, bLo, Rigpa : terms which essentially denote the same thing. Shespa conveys the idea of mind engrossed in perception of external objects subject to feeling and so forth] *take its own course and attain its own* (exalted) *position.* [Shespa-rang-so-blod-pa-yis, literally "detaching the teeth-hold of the knower," that is, detaching the knowing mind from its objects, thus letting it attain its own level free of them. This is a profound counsel. Merely to run away will effect no cure. The same temptation will recur. To surrender is to lose the fight for the supreme end. Let the mind take up a position of detachment from the objects which attract, and let it detachedly examine them, and the cause of their power over it, and so attain dominance.] *May it realise the discriminating wisdom* [Kün-rTog-yeshes, that is, is So-sor-rTog-pahi-Yeshes of the Demchog Tantra described in notes pp. 4, 5 of the Text *post.* This is Jnāna (Yeshes)—(whereas Kün-brTags-Marig-pa is Avidyā)—which knows that all ideas (of separate objects) are illusory].

10.

From the idea of something external, there arises a subtle feeling of dread [As Brahmanism says, fear arises from duality. He who becomes Brahman by realising unity is fearless] *moves the knower at first faintly. As this feeling gains strength, it resolves itself into a vague sense of enmity, and the thought "it will kill me" arises. When this hatred produces its evil Karma, burning in Hell becomes intense. By the power of the wishes of Me, the Buddha, may all the sentient beings of the six Lokas, when they feel great anger arising in their mind, learn neither to avoid it studiously, nor to give way to it* (weakly), *but to leave it to itself and let the mind attain its own* (exalted) *position.* [It is not possible at once to totally eradicate an evil passion, or to avoid all acts which might conduce to it.] *May it attain the clear wisdom* [gSalvahi-Yeshes. That is the mirror-like wisdom Melong-lTabuhi-Yeshes, described in notes to p. 5 of the Text *post*].

11.

From pride which puffs up the Mind is produced a feeling of contempt for others, together with overweening self-conceit. This leads to disputes and quarrels. When these have Karmic fruit, there is birth in the Deva world. [The state of a Deva though higher than that of a man is not of the highest. The cause of birth in Devaloka is pride combined with good action, which, without pride, would have produced better result, yet with pride confers only the lesser boon of Deva-life. A Deva has a long life of pleasure, but, like human beings, is liable to death and fall when his stock of merit is exhausted. Towards the term of a Deva's life his beauty fades, his gardens wither, his fountains run dry. Upon his wish-granting Kalpataru a blight falls. His companions and the Devīs cannot approach him because of the stench his body commences to emit. Being endowed with Deva eyesight, he sees where he will be reborn in a lower world. He is conscious that his stock of merits is spent, and no fresh stock acquired. He is conscious of the evil result of the life of thoughtless pleasure heaped over against him, leading him to rebirth on a less happy plane. He is weighed down with remorse. He foretastes the miseries of his fate in the comparison he makes of the pleasures of the Deva-life he is leaving behind and the miseries of the life to come. This is the fate and misery (hPho-lTung) which prevails in Devaloka. Pride has taken them there, because the Devas think themselves the highest and best. Pride is their obscuring passion (Klesha). As like seeks like, pride seeks the plane where pride prevails, that is Devaloka.] *From there they fall, suffering Hell after death. By the power of these My good wishes, may all such as are given to pride know how to detach therefrom the knower* [Shes-pa = Sems, bLo, Rigpa, different names of mind ; the latter being in its highest state clear and freed of all obscurity. The highest state naked of imaginings and void is called the Great Perfection (rDzogs-pa-chenpo). Here Rigpa is not part of the Skandha, but may be said to be the innermost essence of Vijnāna (rNam-shes)] : *thus letting the feeling alone and the Mind* (Rigpa) *attain its own* (exalted) *position. May it realise the truth that all is one, that each is* (in essence) *alike.* [For all being is pervaded by the Sugata Dhātu or Essence of the Buddhas (bDe-gShegs-sNyingpo) ; just as in Brahmanism Brahman is the All-pervader. Here the realisation is that of one of the five wisdoms called Nyam-nyid-Yeshes described in notes to p. 5 of the Text *post.*]

12.

From the propensity [Bag-chags, that is, predisposition arising from habit. Thus the Bag-chags of dreams at night is what has been done in the day] *to regard oneself and others as different arises the desire to praise oneself and depreciate others : an act which leads to suffering. When the wish to vie and fight with others is strengthened, there is birth in the Asuraloka, wherein beings are ever engaged in wounding and killing each other. This hurls them into Hell. By the power of these good wishes of Me, the Buddha, may all such beings cease to look upon each other as enemies. Let the feeling of enmity alone by itself and let the knower attain its own* (exalted) *position. May it realise the unobstructed power of Divine Service* [hPhrin-las pronounced Tinlas. When a Samsāric being (Pudgala) becomes, by virtue of his merits, a Saint, then he devotes himself to the service of sentient beings. Bodhisattvas and Buddhas are ever thus engaged. The acts they perform for the benefit of others are of four kinds, the peaceful (Shānti), the grand or nourishing (Pushti), the fascinating or overpowering (Vashīkaranam), and the stern or destructive (Māranam and the like). These are Tinlas—their Mission]. *Lack of intelligence and memory* (Dran-med, a state of unconsciousness), *indifference, distraction, being overpowered by sleep and forgetfulness, swoon, and sloth, are all forms of stupidity leading to birth in the brute world* (Tiryakloka). *By the power of these good wishes of Me, the Buddha, may the overpowering gloom of stupidity be dispelled and lit up by the rays of clear consciousness. May such attain the pure wisdom* [rTog-med-Yeshes, unrestricted by the finite forms of thought]. *All sentient beings of the three worlds* (Loka) *are in their essence alike to Me, the Buddha. Unconsciousness* (want of true knowledge or Avidyā) *is the Cause of these errors. At present they are engaged in useless actions* (Dön-med-las, that is, such actions as do not tend to self-development and emancipation). *The six acts aforesaid* (acts done in the six Lokas which lead to rebirth in them) *are but dreams and delusions. I am the most ancient Buddha* [that is, of the most remote past known to man; not the first in status or time. Both Nirvāna and Sangsāra being eternal there is no first Buddha in point of time] *that My incarnations may control the beings of the six Regions. By the power of the good wishes of Me, Samanta Bhadra* (Küntu-bZangpo), *may all sentient beings, without exception, attain Buddhahood in the Dharma-kāya* [Chos-dVyings which is the Void (Shūnyatā) and Compassion (Karunā)].

This great subject being for want of exploration one of difficulty, its treatment is not likely to escape all error. But those who are free of wrong notions as to the meaning of Shūnya, of Anātmā (in Buddhism), and of Ātmā (in Advaita Brahmanism), and have some knowledge of the Tantric ritual in both systems, will I think discern essential similarities between the two. To quote the words of a review of a recent work on Buddhism: " With each fresh acquirement of knowledge as to Buddhism, it seems more difficult to separate it from the Hinduism out of which it emerged, and into which it relapsed."

ARTHUR AVALON.

Ranchi:
27th September, 1918.

INTRODUCTION.

THE term Thegpas or Yāna, to give it the Sanskrit equivalent, means Vehicle, and presents the same idea as sect, school, and method. There are broadly two chief Yānas commonly spoken of, namely, Hīnayāna, and Mahāyāna. The Southern Buddhists of Ceylon and Burma belong to the former, and those of Tibet, China, and Japan to the latter. The term Hīnayāna, which is not of a complimentary character, is not given to themselves by the Southern Buddhists but by the Mahāyānists, followers of the Greater Vehicle. The Southern school is called Lesser Vehicle because its followers seek Nirvāna and Arhatship each for himself, whilst the Mahāyānists strive for the enlightenment of the whole universe. What is it to be saved oneself if others are still lost and suffering? Vajrayāna, or Mantrayāna as it is also called, is a development and particular branch of the Mahāyāna. Vajrayāna is a form of Tantrik Northern Buddhism. The Mantrayānic Buddhist doctrine speaks of nine Yānas, each Yāna being divided into four parts, namely, the view (lTa-va; in Skt. Drishti), the meditation (sGompa; in Skt. Dhyāna), the practice (sPyodpa; in Skt. Chārya), and the fruit (LBras-bu; in Skt. Phala).

The first three Vehicles constitute the original divisions as they existed in the time of the first three convocations which were held after the Pari-nirvāna of Our Lord the Buddha in India. These three Vehicles are (1) Shravaka-yāna (Nyan-thös-kyi-thegpa); (2) Pratyeka-Buddha-yāna (Rang-rgyal-gyi-thegpa); (3) Bodhisattva-yāna (Byang-chub sems-dpahi thegpa). Subsequently these three

Vehicles were with the advent of Padma-Sambhava developed in Thibet into nine. He was the founder of the Mantrayāna school in Thibet and of the Great Perfection school (rDzogs-chen).

The development or " fruit " of the first three is the Vajrayāna and Mantrayāna which is divided into six parts or stages: (4) Kriyā-tantra-yāna (Byavahi-rGyud-kyi-thegpa); (5) Chārya or Upāya-tantra-yāna (Spyöd-pahi-rGyud-kyi-thegpa); (6) Yoga-tantra-yāna (rNal-hbyor-rGyud-kyi-thegpa). The latter is again sub-divided into three: (7) Mahā-yoga-tantra-yāna (Mahā-yoga or Ma-rgyüd-kyi-thegpa); (8) Anuttara-yoga-tantra-yāna (Anu-yoga or Blamed-rgyüd-kyi-thegpa); and (9) Ati-yoga-tantra-yāna (Ati-yoga hi-thegs-pa).

Ati-yoga is considered the highest of all. This is the pure Advaita-tantra or monistic school in which all is realised as the Eternal Buddha. The Tibetan word here rendered by the Sanskrit term Advaita is gNyis-med = One, that is Shūnyatā. The four accepted schools in Buddhist Philosophy are: (1) Bye-brag-smrava: in Sanskrit Vaibhāshika; (2) mDo-sDe-pa or Sautrāntika; (3) Sems-tSampa—a term which means " only mind "—or Vijnānavāda; (4) dVuma-pa or Mādhyamika. According to the first all things (Dharma), both outer and inner, that is, matter and mind, are real; a position accepted by the second with some modification. In the third school external objects are not real, but the mind alone is so. According to the last school neither external objects nor internal mind are real, in the sense that they appear to be so. But the real, if it can be called such, for reality in a sense is also denied to it, is the Void or Shūnyatā for which there is no word, since it is beyond mind and speech. All schools admit the phenomenal " I " or personality which clings to a being or aggregate so long as he is not truly enlightened; but they all deny that this "I" which they call Ātmā is real. The Tibetan definition of the Ātmā, which they deny, is something which is one (gCig) independent or free (rang-dvang-can), and permanent and eternal (rtag). Shūnyatā is an inexpressible mystery in and behind the incessant flow of the stream of seeming, which can be described by no term borrowed from the world of appearance, for none of these terms has a meaning except in relation to its opposite. Thus "one" is an idea belonging to the world of numbers; freedom and permanence are only understood with reference to the phenomena of dependence and change. The Advaita Buddhist Tantra is thus the doctrine of Shūnyatā. This means that the universe (hKhorva = Sangsāra), and Nirvāna are not two but one or Shūnyatā, just as the mind and body in any individual are aspects of one unity. So the Prajnā-pāramitā-hridaya-garbha says: "gZūgs-sTong-pa-ho, sTong-pa-nyid-gZugs-so": that is Form (Rūpa) or Matter is the Void and the Void is Form. The one is not other than the other. The work here published belongs to Anu-yoga the highest but one division of Anuttara-yoga which is known as the Mother-Tantra (Ma-rgyüd-lung), which, it is said, deals with the three Mandalas (*i.e.*, in ordinary worship the Devatā, His abode His court-followers) known as the Eternal Self-existing Mandala (Ye-ji-bzhinpahi-dkhyil-hkhor), the Eternal Self-created Mandala (Rang-bzhin-lhun-grub-kyi-dKhyil-hKhor) and the Great Bliss Mandala which is that of the Bodhisattva. The Mahā-yoga-tantra is known as the male or Father Tantra (Phargyüd). The highest or Atiyoga Tantra is the "not two" or non-dual Tantra (gNyes-med-rgyüd). My informant a Khamba

Lama Tshewang-Runchen gave me from a Thibetan Manuscript (which he said he had studied thoroughly), a short summary of these Yānas showing the various views entertained at these several stages regarding Anātmā, Momentary Cognition, Appearance and Reality, the Void (Shūnyatā), and the four dogmatical extremes " is, is not ; the appearance is true ; the Void (Shūnyatā) is true." As, however, the definitions given were not approved by the learned Enche Geshe-Chön-mdzad La who has helped me in this work (but who unfortunately died last April), I forbear to give them.

The Sanskrit term Sambhāra is the equivalent of sDompa, that is, " a collection " meaning the Mandala of the Devatā and all therein. It has also the meaning " vow of restraint " as explained in the foreword of the general Editor. The state of the Devatā embracing, as part of Himself, His Mandala is that of the Highest Bliss (bDe-mChog). bDe-mChog means " Bliss highest "; in Sanskrit Paramānanda or Mahāsukha. The present work is a Tantra of both the dKar-rgyud-pa and the Saskya-pa sects. By this is meant that there are several rites of Dem-Chog in which the number of faces, hands of the chief Devatā and surrounding Devatā vary ; as also the text. One sect may therefore follow this Tantra in one form, and another in another. The yellow-hat sects of the state monastery of Tashi-Lhünpo have also got this Tantra, and my late Guru, a highly advanced Lama of the Dukpa-dKargyud sect, wrote to me to say that the Mandala with 62 Devatas (very difficult of practice) exists also in Bhutan. The former has two divisions, the Karma-dKar-gyüd whose chief seat is sTöd-lung-Tshoorphug, about two days' journey to the north of Lhasa. Its Avatāra Hierarch is the highly venerated rGyalva-Karma-pa.

This school has several adherents in Sikkhim and Khams as well as in other parts of Thibet. The second division is the dBrugpa dKargyüd sect, which counts several very rich monasteries in Khams, the Hemis monastery in Ladakh, and is the state religion of the whole of Bhutan. In Thibet itself there are the Ralung, Sangachelling and several other smaller monasteries near the Tsari and the Poba districts. The Saskya Sect still has its centre at Saskya in Thibet over which its Hierarchs ruled shortly before the date of the fifth Dalai Lama.

The line of the bDe-mchog-Tantra Gurus (Saskyan branch), is here given from the Pag-Sam-Jön-zang (History of Buddhism in Thibet) by Sumpa-mKhan-po-Yeshes dPal-hbyor. The Gurupangkti is as follows:—(1) rDo-rje-hChang or Vajra-dhara a celestial guru of the Akanishta Heaven (Hog-min). (2) Phyag-na-rDo-rje or Vajrapāni another celestial guru. (3) mDah-bShum or Suraha an Indian Saint. (4) Klu-sgrub or Nagarjuna. (5) Shrī Shvavari or dPal-lDom. (6) Looyipa, an Indian Sage. (7) SLob-dpon-rDo-rje-dril-bu-pa. He is also said to be another source of the Demchog Tantra having obtained teaching directly from Shrī Chakra Sambhāra (dPal-hKhorlo-sdompa) Himself and thus was invested with a fresh power. (8) Rüg-stsal-zhabs or Kacchapāda. (9) Jalan-dhara. (10) Nagpo-sPyodpa or Krishnāchāryapāda. (11) Guhya. (12) rNam-rgyal-Zhabs or Vijayapāda. (13) Tailopa. (14) Naropa. (15) A Newar Phum-mthing the greater (hJigs-meds-grags). (16) Ngag-dVang-Grags-pa or Ngag-dVang-phyūg. (17) Ngag-gi-dVang-phyug. (18) gLag-Skya-Shes-rab-brtregs. (19) The Saskya Hierarch hGro-mGön-hPhagspa-Kün-dGah-sNing-po shortly called hPhagspa or Su-chen (b.circ 1233 A. D.).

to whom reference is later made. The remaining Gurus can only be obtained from Saskya.

From a note at the end of the MS. it would appear that it was written out at the dictation of a venerable Pandit Lama (Phagspa = Ārya), whose name is not given; but the places and dates are stated where each Chapter or Part was completed. In the "Blue Records" of Thibet (Teb-ther-sNgönpo)—a history of Buddhism and its different schools—one of the Hierarchs of Saskya the abovementioned Guru hGro-mgön-hPhags-pa by name, attained great celebrity as a Saint and learned man. He had several eminent disciples. The "Blue Records" say that he became the Guru of the Sechen (Tartar) Emperor of China. The MS. says that the first part was written at Svayambhunath (Shing-kün) in Nepal at the request of a prince called Ji-big-Demur. This may be the name of either a Newar or more probably Tartar Prince, for Demur may be Temur or Taimur which is part of the name Tamerlane to whose line the Sechen Emperor of China belonged. It is possible that the Hierarch who visited both China and Nepal may have been attended by a Prince of the Imperial Chinese Tartar family on a pilgrimage to the holy Buddhist Temples of Nepal—then under the rule of Newar Buddhist Kings, and caused a Thibetan translation to be made from a previously existing text in Sanskrit. In such case the very valuable MSS. which Mr. Avalon, the general Editor, has acquired should be 660 to 665 years old. For this was the Hierarch to whom the Chinese Sechen Emperor made over the whole of Thibet and the date of his accession to the sovereignty over Thibet is given as being some time about 1253 A. D., in Thibetan almanacs.

The original MSS. is in the old "headless" style (dVu-med) of Thibetan writing. It is noteworthy as denoting the importance of the personage on whose behalf the work was written out, that in this volume of ninety leaves of seven different parts, each bears the name of the copyist and the date and place at which they were written. Two or three writers were thus employed, each of them highly trained.

The whole series consisting of some 240 folios all bear upon the same subject,—namely, Demchog, in its different stages and parts. But the other books are not in the same hand, nor of the same age, though they form a very valuable collection. Unfortunately it is not quite complete, though sufficiently so to enable the Sādhanā prescribed to be carried out successfully.

The collection consists of eleven parts, *viz.* :—

(1) A set of dances according to the bDe-mchog-Tantra called "Dance Book of the Best of Gifts" (Mchog-dbyin-rDo-rjehi gardpe), consisting of four folios.

(2) Another Vajramālā dance (rDo-rje-hphreng-vahi-Kün-bsKyöd-kyi-gar), three folios.

(3) The Sādhanā of Sambhāra or Demchog entitled "Method of attaining the highest simultaneously born bliss" (bDe-mchog-lhen-skyes-kyi-bgrub-thabs) of seven folios.

(3) "The Method of meditation on Demchog" (bDe-mchog-lhan-kye-bGom-thabs) of five folios.

(4) "The feast or worship of Vajra-yoginī" (zDorje-rNal-hByor-mahi-tsogs-hkhor) of six folios. (173rd folio to front page 178th.)

(5) Homa of Shrī Vajrayoginī (dPal-rDo-rje-rNal-hByor-mahi-sByin-sreg-gi-choga). Front page of 178th folio—last two lines—to the back page of 181st folio. (4 folios.)

(6) " Notes on the method of making the waters of initiation enter oneself " (dVang-chog-bdag-hjug-la-lTös-pahi-tho-yig). (Of 82 folios from 372nd folio to the 453rd folio.)

(7) Meditation on the twenty-one Tārās—10 folios = 259th to the 269th folios.

(8) " The King of Shrī-Sambhāra-chakra Tantra" named the Ca-ma-Gala-grita—ornament of sepulchral things " (dPal-hkhor-lo-sdom-pahi - rgyud - kyi - gyalpo - dur - Khröd-Kyi-rgyan dPal Heruka), in twelve folios. " Sepulchral things " has a two-fold signification. Exoterically reference is made to the bone ornaments carried by the Heruka obtained from the skulls and bones in the cemeteries. Esoterically it is denoted that meditation on the Heruka (Demchog) extinguishes existence in the Sangsāra. The end of worldly life is the cemetery or death. But from the cemetery which is Sādhanā is born enlightenment. (This is in a very different hand, and of much older date. It gives the name of the Indian Pandit Gayadhara, and the Thibetan translator—Shag-Yeshes—and contains very finely written footnotes under each line of text.)

(9) " The Rosary of worship of Demchog " (bDe-mchog-chod-Phreng), in twenty-one folios. (This also is in the same hand as the Part 8

—and the name of the compiler or contributor of this part is given as BLo-grös-rGyal-mtshan—and the place is "Khai-phing-hoo," 'the great king's palace,' possibly somewhere in China because this is neither a Thibetan nor Nepalese name. Date: Water-Dog year, 25th of the month of rGyal.

10th Part.—The Homa-ritual (burnt offerings) or sacrificial fire, of dPal-hKhor-lo-sdompa, explained at length (mNgön-rtogs) in nine folios. There are four kinds of Homas—the peaceful (Zhiva), the grand (rgyaspa), dVang-va (the overpowering or fascinating—Vashīkarana) and the fierce, stern or destructive (Mārana). It is said to be done by one Pandita (sLob-dpön-Rinchen-rDorje).

(11) The work here published "Vajra-yoginī," Shrī Mahāmāyā and Tārā (dPal-hKhor-lo-bDe-mchog, rDo-rJe-rNal-bYor dPal-sGyuma-Chen-mo-sGrolma) in nearly 90 folios. This last is divided into seven parts, all of which have been here printed in the printing character with heads (dVuchen).

The first part which closes at the 27th folio I have translated in full so as to give the reader a general idea of the nature of the work and the methods of meditation. Of the other parts a short Synopsis has been given following on the translation of the First Part.

Gangtok, Sikkhim:
1st *May*, 1918.

KAZI DAWASAMDUP.

SHRĪ SAMBHĀRA CHAKRA.

Vajra-yoginī, Shrī Mahāmāyā and Tārā.

(dPal-hKhor-lo-bDe-mChog ; rDo-rJe-rNal-hByor. dPal-sGyuma-Chen-mo sGrolma.)

THIS is a clear exposition of the ritual of the Mandala [1] of Shrī Chakra of Great Bliss.[2]

Obeisance to the Guru and Shrī Heruka.[3] Having bowed with reverence to the Guru, the essence of all the Buddhas and to Shrī Heruka I now expound the Sādhanā [4] of Shrī Chakra Mahāsukha.

He whose mind is firm in Bodhisattva resolve ; [5] who has obtained the highest initiation,[6] who understands the Mantras and is foremost among Yogīs will of a surety obtain the highest boons, both temporal and spiritual, if he follows the course prescribed, namely, the imaginative [7] and meditative [8] ; if he practises to make his mind tranquil ; if he offers rice cakes [9] and other food offerings ; and if in short he assiduously applies himself to all the four branches [10] of a Yogī's duty.

---

(1) dKyil-dKhor. (2) Shrī-Chakra-Mahāsukha ; the Devatā whose state is that of great bliss (Mahāsukha). (3) A Vajrayāna Devatā. (4) Ritual : practice whereby Siddhi (success, here spiritual attainment) may be obtained. (5) That is whose mind is firm in righteousness. (6) Literally "Conferring of power" (dVang). (7) By this is meant the mental process whereby the imagination is exercised to produce certain pictures and ideas. (8) That process whereby the mind ceases to imagine and passes into the tranquil state. In the first the mind projects and in the second withdraws its own projections. (9) gTorma. (10) Namely, pertaining to Samādhi, the Path (or conduct), Offerings (of rice cakes) partaking of food.

The devotee when about to go to sleep should firstly, imagine his body to be that of Buddha Vajra-Sattva and then at length merge into the tranquil state of the Void.[1] Arising from that state he should think that the double drums[2] are resounding from the midst of the heavens proclaiming the Mantras of the twenty-four Heroes.[3] Arising from his sleep in this state of divine

---

(1) Shūnyatā (sTong-pa-nyid or emptiness) or the ultimate formless (Arūpa) Reality as contrasted with appearance (sNang-va) or form (Rūpa). This is not, as has been ignorantly supposed, absolutely nothing, and therefore the term nihilism is out of place. It is relatively nothing ; that is *to us* since it has none of the qualities of the things we know, such as form, colour, taste, smell, weight, temperature. There is nothing to which it can be likened and therefore no words can define it. It is beyond the circle of phenomenal existence and therefore the state is marked by neither Avidyā, Sangskāra, Vijnāna, Nāmarūpa or property of any kind. As the Prajnāpāramitā-hridaya-garbha says of it (like the Paramātmā), it can only be said, "not this," "not this" (neti, neti). Shūnyatā is united with every form of experience as its background. (2) Damaru—small drums of the shape of an hour-glass such as that held by Shiva. (3) dPahvo (Vīra) that is the twenty-four male Devatās of the twenty-four Tīrthas. The ordinary use of the term Hero in Thibet as elsewhere refers to the martial hero. But it has an application to Sādhanā also. Here the reference is to certain Divinities. A Yogī who has attained Siddhi through Sādhanā with meat, wine, and women, may be called a Vīra or Heruka; such as the mad Heruka of Kongbu, Kongsmyön Heruka, otherwise called Lhabtsün-nam-mkhah-hiigs-med, the pioneer rNyingma Lama Saint, who entered Sikkhim some 300 years ago by the Kangs-chen Pass and whose school is now the Chief of the State Monasteries in Sikkhim, *viz.*, Pemiongchi ; and hBrug-sMyon Heruka, otherwise called hBrug-smyön-Kundgah-legs-pa who entered Bhutan at a still earlier date. The Yoginī or Heroine is rNal-hByorma and sometimes dPah-mo. By these terms is generally understood in Thibet the divine Dākinī, Vajra-vārāhī, or some manifestation of Her. In Sikkhim, according to pre-Buddhistic Bon beliefs, still there prevailing, the Seer of the wild men of the highlands is called dPah-vo and Nal-hByorma (pronounced Naljorma), a woman who claims to be a medium for local spirits and those of dead persons plaguing people with their evil influence.

body [1] he should regard all things around him as constituting the Mandala of himself as Vajrasattva.[2]

If beneficial to his devotions, he may perform the ablutions as he had done while receiving initiation. Then seating himself with ease facing the South let him sanctify his body by tasting the drop of Amrita.[3]

Then he should begin by repeating the Refuge formula [4] and the Good Wishes formula.[5] Then let him meditate on himself as Demchog [6] and his Consort. [7] Imagining his own body to be that of the Devatā is the bliss pertaining to the body. Saying "Shrī He-ru-ka Aham," [8] he should meditate on each syllable of the Mantra as follows:—

"Shrī" is non-dual experience; [9] "He" is the cause and the void or Dhātū; [10] "Ru" is uncompounded; [11] "Ka" is not abiding anywhere.[12] Thinking oneself

---

(1) Lhahi-Sku, that is Deva-deha. The body is divine in fact, and known to be such when consciously identified with Divinity. (2) He thinks of himself as Buddha Vajrasattva (rDōrje sems-dpah) and of all objectivity as the Mandala (*v.post*) of the latter. (3) Rilbu, The Amrita, is a drop of wine (the extra-ritual use of which is forbidden) taken on the tips of the ring finger. (4) Buddham sharanam gachchhāmi, Dharmam sharanam gachchhāmi, Sangham sharanam gachchhāmi (I take refuge in Buddha, the Law and the Assembly). (5) May all sentient beings have happiness and be endowed with the cause thereof. May all sentient beings be free of pain and its causes. May all sentient beings ever enjoy happiness unalloyed with pain. May they feel supremely equable (*i.e.*, free both of Rāga and Dvesha). (6) Mahāsukha, the state of the Devatā of this Tantra. (7) Vajra-Vārāhī or Yoginī. (8) "I am the revered and glorious Heruka." (9) gNyismed-yeshes; which literally means "not two-knowledge;" monistic or advaita experience; yeshes being Jnāna. (10) Hetu and Shūnyatā, *i.e.*, rgyu-sogs-sTong-pa-nyid. (11) tshogs-dang-bralva, separation from combinations. It is not a compound. It is homogeneous as is pure Kevala, or Shuddha Jnāna. (12) Gang-duhang-mi-gnaspa. It cannot be said to be in any place for it is all-pervading (Sarva-vyāpin) and dependent on nothing (nirālamba).

to be the Self [1] which embodies all these, whatsoever a man says is Mantra.[2]

Let him imagine in the centre of his own heart the letter "A" evolved from the experience which knows that forms are unreal.[3] On it let him think of the clear Lunar disc which symbolises world-experience,[4] and upon that the Mantra "Hūm," which symbolises mind [5] devoid of objective content. [6] Of this "Hūm" the letter "U" stands for the knowledge which accomplishes all works; [7] the body of the letter "H" for that knowledge which distinguishes; [8] the top of the letter "H" for the

---

(1) bDag-nyid. The first word is " I : " the second points at something—the very I or self. He thinks " I am the non-dual experience, single (homogeneous), all-pervading, the Dhātu. (2) That is, his speech is pure and holy as is his whole body. (3) Mi-rtog-pahi-yeshes: literally " thinking-not " knowledge: that is Jnāna which is that Wisdom which knows that all forms have no real existence as such in themselves, that is which knows that the true nature of forms is Shūnyatā. The definition is Mi-rtog-yeshes, bDen-pas-ma-grub-pahi-khyad-par-du-byas-pahi-gzugs-rTogs-pahi or shortly Dehi-ngo-vo-ham-ye-nas-gNas-lugs-shes-pa-la-zer. The mind which regards forms as real things (which they are not) is called hJig-rTen-pahi-yeshes or "Worldly Wisdom." (4) hJig-rtenpahi yeshes; world-knowledge of objects; Vishaya Jnāna. (5) Sems: chitta. (6) Mind (sems) as distinguished from objective contents or thoughts. (7) There are five "wisdoms," "knowledge," or aspects of consciousness (Yeshes=jnāna) which are here defined from the seventeenth century Tibetan work by Bustön Rinpoche, called Bustön-Chös-hbyung. The first here described is Amogha-Siddhi or Bya-ba-grubpahi Yeshes, (pronounced Ja-wa-dub-pai-yeshes,) literally " having done act successfully." Amogha-Siddhi is irresistible power of doing everything; omnipotence. The first is defined by Bustön Rinpoche as " The wisdom which accomplishes all works (Bya-va-grub-pahi-yeshes), is that which fulfils all the needs and interests of sentient beings by manifesting itself in various forms and under varying conditions (*sNa*-tshogs-su-sprul-nas-sems-can-gyi-dön-bsgrub-pas-bya-grub-yeshes-so). (8) Sosor-rtog-pahi yeshes, (pronounced sosor-togpai-yeshes) literally " different knowing ;" that knowledge which is defined by

[5]

equalising knowledge ;[1] the crescent (Chandra) for the mirror-like knowledge ;[2] and the Bindu (Thiglé) above that for the changeless knowledge.[3] Meditation on these different parts of the Mantra symbolising the mind is the

---

Bustön Rinpoche as the "Distinguishing Wisdom" (Sosor-rtog-yeshes) is the knowledge of all objects with their differences : (that is the knowledge which knows all which is abstract or concrete with their different names and so forth). (So-sor-rtog-pahi-yeshes, shes-bya-thams-cad-thogs-med-du so-so kün-rtogs yeshes-so.) (1) mNyam-pa-nyid-kyi-yeshes : (pronounced Nyampa-nyid-kyi yeshes,) literally "equal-intensifying of knowledge." Whereas in the last form of experience there is the recognition of difference ; here is seen the sameness (Sāmya) of all—Samatā Jnāna. This is defined by Bustön Rinpoche as "The equalising wisdom" (mNyampa-nyid-kyi-yeshes) and is the result of meditation on the sameness of the nature of all beings, oneself and others, producing attainment of the highest Nirvāna. (Rgyu-bdag-gzhan-mNyam-par-sGom-pahi-hbras bu, mi-gnas-pahi-Myang-hDas-la-bzhugs pas-na, mNyam-nyid-yeshes-so.) (2) Melong-lta-buhi-yeshes : (pronounced Melong-tabui-yeshes,) literally "mirror-like knowledge," defined by Bustön Rinpoche as "The Dharmadhātu" being perfectly pure and uncognising, like the mirror, is called mirror-like (Chös-kyi-dvyings-rnampar-dag-pa-dang melong-ltar-gsal-la-mi rtog-pas—na-melong-lta-buhi-yeshes-so). The mirror is itself pure ; reflects but is not itself affected. (3) Dharma-dhātu-Jnāna : or Chhös-kyi-dvyings-kyi-yeshes, pronounced Chö-kyi-ing-kyi yeshes. The explanation of this term (obtained from Geshe-La, the most learned Lama now living in Sikkhim named Kusho Chö-mzad La, of Enche (dVen-bchas Monastery) is, "That which is not liable to change or transition is Dharmadhātu." Dharmadhātu-Jnāna is said to be "The wisdom which knows that the things which are coloured differently and the like are really not so, but they are all of one nature and taste." The Tibetan word, Thiglé or Bindu in Sanskrit. (See Arthur Avalon's "Shakti and Shākta" and "Studies in the Mantra Shāstra") means a spot or point or drop such as a spot on a leopard's skin, a drop of semen, a cypher and the metaphysical "point" which is the Mantra expression of the Indian Īshvara and the Highest Truth in the Tibetan rNyingma doctrine called the "Great Perfection" (rDzogs-pa-chenpo). So Dharmakāya or Chos-sku is defined as that which is devoid of all natural and accidental impurities. Hūm is in Sanskrit characters ཧཱུྃ ; ུ is the first knowledge ; ཧ is the second ; —is the third ; ◡ is the fourth ; and

method by which the latter is qualified for pure experience and enjoys the bliss which arises from contemplation on the bliss [1] of the divine mind.[2]

From the Mantra " Hūm " rays of blue, green, red, and yellow light shoot forth through the four heads of the Devatā [3] and gradually fill the whole universe. Then think in the following order:—

" May all sentient beings enjoy happiness and be endowed with the cause thereof "—" May they be freed of all pain and of the causes thereof "—" May they never be separated from the highest happiness "—" May they be free both of attachment as well as hatred, and may they have all their eight worldly wishes [4] pruned and levelled." [5] Think fully on these wishes in their order the one after the other.

Then snapping the thumb and middle finger of the left hands and pointing the latter in the ten directions [6] let him think it to be such directions and repeat the Mantra " Sukhe bhavantu " (Be happy). By this means he dedicates all the merits that he acquires to the benefit of others. This is the meditation on the four abodes.[7]

Again think that rays of various coloured light beam forth from the Mantra " Hūm " filling the whole body and shining thereout in all space, cleansing the sins and ignorance and the propensities born of habit of all sentient beings, changing them all into myriad forms of

---

O is the fifth. (1) Gawa-(dgahva). (2) Thugs. (3) That is bDe-mchog. (4) Name, fame, wealth, etc. (5) That is they are not to be extirpated but cut down and levelled, moderated and if possible brought down to their minimum force. (6) The eight points of the compass, Zenith and Nadir. (7) That is the four states of Dhyāna comprising thirteen lokas : four in the first stage and three in each of the others, from Brahmakāyika to Brihatphala.

Khorlo-De-mChog.[1] Then having withdrawn[2] inwards all the rays of light and absorbed them into one's own self, meditate again as follows :—

Let the worshipper think the Rūpa-skandha[3] to be Vairochana;[4] his Vedanā-skandha[5] to be Vajra-sūryya;[6] his Samjnā-skandha[7] to be Padma-nateshvara;[8] his Sangskāra-skandha[9] to be Râja-Vajra and his Vijnāna-skandha[10] to be Buddha Vajra-sattva.[11] Meditate thus upon all the principles constituting the self as having become each a Tathāgata: the whole constituting the revered and glorious Heruka. (Then meditate on the five senses as five male Devatās.)

Heruka's eyes are Vajra-delusion (Moha); ears Vajra-anger; mouth Vajra-greed; nose Vajra-miserliness; body Vajra-jealousy;[12] and all the senses (Āyatana) Vajra-Īshvara.[13] (The five constituent elements of the body should then be meditated upon as five female Devatās.) The Earth element[14] is Tung-bar-byed-ma;[15] the water element[16] is Sod-par-jed-ma;[17] the fire element[18] Gug-par-jed-ma;[19] the air element[20]

---

(1) hKhorlo-bDemchog. Shrī-chakra-mahāsukha. (2) This is an instance of the imaginative and meditative method above described. (3) Bodily aggregate. (4) rNampar-sNang-mdzad (5) Aggregate of sensation. (6) rDo-rje-Nyima. (7) Aggregate of feeling. (8) Padma-gargyi-dVang-phyug "Padma Lord of Dances." (9) Aggregate of tendencies. (10) Aggregate of cognition. (11) rDo-rJe-sems-dpah. Just as the five Yeshes are personified as the five Dhyāni Buddhas in the case of Ādi Buddhas, so in this mandala (the whole body being such) there are five Devatās. (12) That is the eyes and so forth are considered to be Vajra delusion, gTimug-dorje; wrath, zhe-sdang-rdorje; miserliness (Serna-dorji), covetousness (Dots-chags-dorji), jealousy (Phrag-dag-dorji). (13) Dorji-Wang-chug. (14) Prithivī. (15) "She who causes fall." (16) Apas. (17) gSod-par-byed-ma "She who kills." (18) Agni. (19) hGug-par-byed-ma "She who summons." (20) Vāyu.

Padma gargyi-wang-chug [1] and the ether element [2] is Padmai-dra-wa-Chan. [3] As one desires a precious object by means of which only one can acquire merits the purification and mental transmutation of all the aggregates the elements, and the functions of the various organs of the senses into Devatā furnish such an object.

Again with the beams of light shooting forth from the " Hūm " in the heart, let the worshipper invoke his Vajra-guru [4] surrounded by the line of Gurus in the upper Heavens before him. Below them is the principal Devatā (Khorlo-Demchog) surrounded by the sixty-two Devatās of the Khorlo-Demchog Mandala (Chakra-sambhāra). Then having imagined that the above Divinities are seated on the fronting Heavens let the worshipper think that he is himself multiplied innumerably. Each of his counterparts should repeat salutation to the Gurus (namogurubhyah) and salutation to the Mandala of Shrī-chakra-sambhāra (Namah Shrī-chakra-sambhāra-mandalebhyah) in honour of the Guru and the Devatās respectively and let each bow down to them.

Then let him offer the offerings in their order. They are Arghya, Pādya, Pushpa, Dhūpa, Āloka, Gandha, Naivedya, and Shabda; [5] saying the following Mantra " Om Sarva-Tathāgata-Shrī-chakra-Sambhāra-

---

(1) " Padma-gargyi-dvang-phyug-ma. The Lady of Dances." (2) Ākāsha. (3) Padmahi-dra-va-can " She who has the net of Lotuses." (4) rDo-rje-chös. (5) Water, flowers, incense, lights, perfume, food, music. See A. Avalon's "Principles of Tantra."

Mandala-Chakra-Sarva-Vīra-Yoginī."[1] This should be repeated before each of the offerings which are as follows :—

Arghyam pratishthāyai svāhā [2] Pādyam pratishthāyai svāhā ; Vajra-pushpam [3] Āh Hūm ; Vajra-Dhūpa [4] Āh Hūm ; Vajra Āloka Āh Hūm ; Vajra Gandha, Āh Hūm ; Vajra Naivedyam, Āh Hūm ; Vajra Shabda [5] Āh Hūm.

Then after the last Mantra [6] having offered music [7] let the worshipper think of every possible object worthy of offering which is not any one's private property. Let his mind create for itself every imaginable article of worship and worship with them.

Then making the Mudrā of the heavenly treasury, he should say :—

" Obeisance by the grace of the Dharma-Dhātu,[8] the Buddhas, Bodhisattvas, Mantras and the power of Mudrā ; by the grace of my own faith and Samādhi and by the power of all my good wishes ; let every kind of offering for worship existing in this world, not held in possession by any one, which is as inconceivably grand and magnificent as the cloud of offering that was offered by the Bodhisattva Samanta Bhadra (Kuntu-Zangpo) appear before my Guru and the Buddhas of the Mandala Chakra and let them be on the grandest scale."

---

(1) *Quaere* Yoginībhyah. (2) The text has "pratitcha ye," which is a mistake for "pratishthāyai," that is that which is truly and firmly established or the Devatā. (3) The flowers and other things are mental offerings. The mind also resolves, " May they be Vajra," that is the embodiment of the great irresistible enduring Vajra. (4) The text has Pushpe Dhupe, etc., ending with Shabda. The nominative form would appear to be correct. (5) Bells, drums, cymbals, conches, etc. (6) See p. 8, note *ante*.

Having uttered this wish he should snap with his fingers and thumb. Again making the Mudrā on the heart, he should repeat this Mantra :—

Om sarvavid pura pura sūra sūra āvarta āvarta ho nama samanta buddha nām abhismaraye spharana immam gagana kham dharmadhātu akashya samantamа sarva tathāgata apari shadhale mandale mama pranite punya jnāna bālena sarva tathāgata balendha bandhasa sthāna balena ca le svāhā.[1]

"Om, all-knowing one, fulfil (my desire), fulfil (my desire) ; come forward, come forward ; be round, and round (the Mandala) ; Salutation to Thee ; I remember the Samanta Buddha ; Let this upper space be clear (of obstacles) ; Let Dharmadhātu the unchanging be everywhere ; May the Tathāgata be in the petalled Mandala which is opposite to, and made by, me. Svāhā to all Tathāgatas who are holy, knowledge and power, who are the fuel of strength (strong as fire issuing from fuel), who are the Power of this Mandala, and who are all mighty."

Snap the fingers and thumb again, and worship with the above Mantra. Then let the worshipper say :—

(1) I seek absolution for the sins which I have committed, or attempted to commit, or in

(1) The Mantra in the text is in corrupt Sanskrit the meaning of which is not clear. The following is perhaps the correct rendering.

Om sarvavit pura pura sara sara āvartasva āvartasva ho namah samanta-buddhanāma abhismare spharanagagana imam kham (astu) dharmadhātuh akshayah samantatah (astu) sarva-tathāgata apare sadale mandale, mama pranīte punya-jnāna-balāya sarvatathāgata valendhanāya bandhasamsthānabalāya balīyase svāhā.

which I have taken pleasure when committed (by others) by body, speech, mind; proceeding from motives of lust, anger, sloth, stupidity during all the states of my previous existences time without beginning. I seek absolution for each and every sin so committed in the presence of my Guru and the Devatās of this holy Mandala:

(2) I will not commit them again (and then he should further say):—

(3) I (naming himself) do hereby seek refuge in the Buddha, Dharma and Sangha from this moment until I attain the glorious state of Shrī-Chakra-Mahāsukha (dPal-khorlo-bDe-mChog):

(4) I vow to continue in the practice and observance of the rules and conditions imposed by Shrī-Chakra-Sambhāra:

(5) I will feel satisfaction and take delight in the merits acquired by laymen, noble Shrāvakas, Pratyeka Buddhas, Bodhisattvas and by all the highest perfect Buddhas:

(6) I will free those persons who yet remain unfreed:

(7) I will give courage to those who are dispirited:

(8) I will help those who have not attained complete Nirvāna to gain the same:

(9) I will entreat those Buddhas of the ten directions who do not set the wheel of truth (Chös-kyi-khorlo) in motion to do so:

(10) I will pray and entreat such of the Tathāgatas who intend passing away into Nirvāna not to pass away into Nirvāna:[1]

(1) So that they may remain to aid others who are not yet liberated from suffering.

(11) I will remain sincerely and earnestly in the two-fold path of Shrī-chakra-Sambhāra. And by the merits of my practice of these resolutions may I and all sentient beings speedily attain the state of Shrī-chakra-Sambhāra.

The worshipper should repeat this clearly and distinctly three times, remembering at each time the deep meaning of the words which he is repeating. Then he should think that the Divine Beings whom he has invoked are addressing him in reply, thus :—

" Oh, son of noble descent,[1] well have you adopted your abode. If you abide therein of a surety you will attain the highest stage.

Then again worship the Devatās with the brief form of worship already given.

The worshipper should repeat the invocation Mantra Vajra-muh[2] and say in his mind " Pray come." These constitute the thirteen means of acquiring merits. Then from the Bīja Mantra Hūm which lies in the heart emanate ten female Devatās (Dākinī) who are the keepers of the doors. There are eight of them in the eight points of the compass and Khanda and Roha are above (zenith) and below (nadir). They are on the east, south, west, north, and then south-east, south-west, north-east, and north-west. Then repeat a syllable (Pada) of the Mantra of the four-faced Devatā and as each Pada is repeated make a snapping noise with the finger and thumb of the left hand. By these means let him think that he has expelled all mischievous Spirits. Then on a

(1) Rigs-kyi-bu. Sanskrit Kula putra. (2) Of the Mandala.

flood of light issuing from the "Hūm" in the heart proceed by stages to make the Vajra-bhūmi (ground); next the wall, ceiling, ceiling curtain with fringes, and net-work of arrows [1] and outside all a fence of divine flames. He should commence this work from within and proceed outward in their order.

Then form the fingers of the left hand into the threatening Mudrā [2] and point it at the ten directions, making the snapping noise abovementioned, repeating solemnly the following Mantras thrice:

(Foundation) Om medinī-vajra bhava vajra-bandhana hūm hūm phat.[3] (Wall) Om Vajra-prākāra Hūm Vam Hūm.[4] (Ceiling) Om Vajra-panjara Hūm Yam Hūm.[5] (Cloth) Om Vajra vitāna Hūm Kham Hūm.[6] (Network) Om Vajra-sharajāla Tram Sham Tram.[7] (Fire-fence) Om Vajra-jvālānalārka Hūm Ram Hūm.[8]

Having concentrated the mind on the above protective circles, create from the "Hūm" in the heart Vajra-daggers [9] with Vajra-hilts, and Vajra-clubs.

Placing these in the left and right hands of the innumerable attendants resembling himself let him centre his mind on the innumerable attendants filling the skies who summon the Spirits, including those powerful ones who guard the four directions of the world-system.

---

(1) There is netting work at the top of the sides of the building in the Mandala. (2) Tarjanī Mudrā: the thumb on the bent middle finger and the index finger raised. (3) Om earth-Vajra worldly Vajra-bondage hum hum Phat (destroy). (4) Om Vajra-fence Hūm Vam Hūm. (5) Om Vajra dome or ceiling Hūm Yam Hūm. (6) Om Vajra ceiling cloth Hūm, Kham, Hūm. (7) Om Vajra net work of arrows Tram (protect), Sham (bliss), Tram. (8) Om vajra fire-fence Hūm Ram Hūm. The word jvālānalārka is not clear but fire-fence is the meaning. (9) The Phurpa.

Those who are white [1] take the refuge and enter the path of righteousness.[2] Think of those who are black as being transfixed with a dagger [3] through the crown of their head.

Then orally recite :—

Om gha gha ghataya ghataya sarva-dukham (in text dukhtan) Phat [4]—Kīlaya kīlaya sarvapāpam hūm phat [5] —Vajra-kilaya vajra-dhara (in text dharod) adya [6] jnāpayati [7] (in text adjnapayatī)—Sarva-vijnāna-(in text bhignan)-kāya-vākya (in text vakka) chitta [8] (in text citta)-kīlaya hūm phat.[9]

At the same time imagine that they are pounded into dust by strokes from the Vajra-Hammer.

Then again repeat the Mantra :—Om vajra-mudgara vajra-kīlaya ākotaya hūm phat.[10]

Concentrate the mind on the absolution of the sins of the mischievous Spirits and imagine that their Vijnāna-principles have been transferred to the Realm of Buddha Akshobhya. Then the attendants take up their position at the outer fence of Vajras. Imagine that they guard the devotee so long as he does not attain Buddhahood. This is the method by means of which one guards against the possibility of being interrupted whilst seeking to acquire wisdom through meditation on the magical protective

---

(1) Righteously inclined. (2) Bodhisattvik mind. (3) The Phurpa. (4) Om: may the dispersal of the dense mass of darkness of delusion of Avidyā (gha = ghanapatalāvidyāmohāndhakāravighātakam) be brought about; may all misery be destroyed. (5) Bind bind (Avidyā): may all sin be destroyed. (6) The text has vajra-dharod-ad. (7) Bind firm; hold firm; now proclaims *sed. qu.* (8) Text has bhignan-kaya-vākka-chitta. (9) Bind all consciousness, body, speech and mind: may all (enemies) be dispersed. (10) Om vajra-clubs hold (under you) firmly, break in pieces Hūm Phat.

fences. This is acquiring of causal merits.[1] Then regarding all outward and inward objects to be illusory like dreams say :—

Om svabhāva-shuddha sarva-dharma-svabhāva-shuddho'ham.[2]

Again, meditating on Māyā (sGyūma, that is the world) as being Shūnyatā (the Void) inconceivable by thought, say —Om : shunyatā-jnāna-vajra-svabhāvātmako'ham.[3]

This is the acquiring of spiritual merits. The two-fold merit is acquired thus :—

Imagine arising from Shūnyatā the Mantra Yam, from which issues the Mandala of Air of the shape of a bent bow (semi-circular) with banners at each end; the Mantra Ram, evolving the Mandala of Fire red in colour and triangular in shape with a flaming gem; the Mantra Vam, from which issues the Mandala of Water round of form and white in colour with a pot; the Mantra Lam, from which evolves the Mandala of Earth square in shape and yellow in colour, with three pointed Vajra (Dorji) at the four angles. Then from the Mantra Sūm imagine Mount Meru the King of Mountains; the four fences of which are of crystal on the East, gold in the North, ruby in the West, and emerald on the South. It is quadrangular in shape with three tiers of squares thereon and eight turrets. Imagine all these to be placed, the

(1) Merits are of two kinds either (a) Causal (Dhātu) rgyu-bsod-nams-kyi tshogs; (b) Resultant (Phala) hbras-bu-yeshes-kyi-tshogs. The first are those which accrue from virtuous acts; and the second is Jnāna. That is wisdom (Prajnā) acquired with energy (Vīrya) and through meditation. (2) Om, I am the pure which is the true nature of all things. (3) I am of the nature of the Void and Vajra knowledge. Māyā in Tibetan is sGyūma, a term applied to the illusive magical show of magicians and conjurers. The phenomenal world is compared (as Shangkara does) to such an illusory exhibition.

one above the other in their order, and on the top of all a multi-coloured, four-headed Vajra, blue on the East, green on the North, red on the West, yellow on the South, and in the Centre dark-blue. On this dark blue ground again place the Mantra Pam from which emanates an eight-petalled lotus. In the centre of the lotus again imagine a ring formed by the sixteen Sanskrit vowels, twice repeated, going from right to the left, thus :—

a, ā, i, ī, u, ū, ri, rī, lri, lrī, e, ai, o, au, am, ah.

Consider these thirty-two letters as constituting the essence of the thirty-two signs of physical perfection :[1] and that from meditation thereon there arises the lunar disc[2] upon which imagine the letters :—

Ka, Kha, Ga, Gha, Nga; Cha, Chha, Ja, Jha, Nya; Ta, Tha, Da, Dha, Na (hard) ; Ta, Tha, Da, Dha, Na (soft) ; Pa, Pha, Ba, Bha, Ma ; Ya, Ra, La, Va ; Sa Sha, Sha, (hard), Ha, Ksha ; Ya, Ra, La, Va, Dha, Ha.[3]

These, when set on the lunar disc going from left to right and duplicated, make the Essence of the eighty exemplary graces[4] the contemplation of which produces the solar disc symbolising the Equality of Wisdom. Imagine, between these two revolving discs, the Mantra " Hūm " white in colour and know it to be the essence of Discriminating Wisdom. On the surface of the solar disc again imagine the Mantras Om, Ā, Hūm the essence of the ordinary physical body, speech, and mind.

---

(1) As regards hair, eyes, teeth, tongue, voice, skin, shoulders, body, etc. The *membrum virile* should be sunk into the body that is not apparent. (2) Typical of the mirror-like aspect of the divine wisdom. (3) In all 40 letters, which are given in Tibetan characters in the text though they are meant to refer to the Sanskrit alphabet. (4) Bodily symmetries and beauties, graceful walk and so forth.

Above all these, meditate upon a Lotus Disc, the pure emblem of the female organ of the Female Deity,[1] and above that on the Lunar Disc, emblem of the male seed of the Male Deity.[1] Over these again meditate upon the Mantra Hūm as the true emblem of the Clear Light of one's own mind.[2] Having meditated upon each of these as being placed the one above the other, imagine that each of the Discs, beginning with the lowest, merges into the next one above it, and all at length into the Mantra Hūm. Then imagine that the Mantra Hūm itself gradually disappears, Ukāra into the body of H or Hakāra, the top [of the latter (Mātrā) into the Nāda, and the latter into the Bindu.[3]

Then concentrate on the fine, light-red waving flame of the Nāda, thinking of it as emitting a sound,[4] humming the Mantra of the twenty-four Heroes (Vīras). Think of it as vibrating very quickly and as giving forth sound. Next imagine that this vibrating wave of sound pierce the Solar Disc. Finally the Mantra Hūm merges into, and is mingled with, the Solar Disc.[5] This is the Consciousness which accomplishes everything

---

(1) The Deities created by the mind, the Male according to the Tantrik Buddhists being the Symbol of Power and the Female of the mind which guides and uses it. (2) Sems-kyi-rang-bZhin-hōd-gSalvahi-ngo-vo. The real clear light which is the nature of the Mind. Its nature is clear light; the clear state of uncognizing super-consciousness undistracted by thoughts which is likened to that of deep sleep. Hūm is the emblem of mind. (3) ཧཱུྃ. First ུ disappears in ཧ; the latter in—; this again in ◡ and the last in o. (4) In the Indian Tantra, Nāda is subtle "sound" (Shakti) which in its more massive form as Māyā produces the universe. (5) The subtle point of this waving current of force, which is Nāda, pierces the Solar Disc. That which waves or bends and quickly moves is the sound (sGra pronounced Da).

(Amogha-Siddhi-Jnāna).[1] All these considered as one, ncluding the objects of worship,[2] and their receptacles,[3] and forming one Mandala is the Consciousness which is Eternal and Immutable (Dharma Dhātu-Jnāna).[4]

Concentrate on the above until it[5] is vividly present to the mind's eye. Then proceed as follows:—Within the magical protective fences, created as above by Mantras imagine a grand temple (Vihāra), quadrangular, with four entrances, built of various precious metals, on the summit of Mount Meru[6] on each of the four sides. Imagine the walls to be five-fold[7] and of five different colours in the following order, black, white, yellow, red, and green. These walls are surmounted by a yellow metal cornice ornamented with moons, to which are suspended bells with half and full loops of jangling metal

---

(1) Bya-va-grub-pahi-ye-shes (pronounced Jawa-ḍubpai Yeshe) *see ante* p. 4, Note 7. Exoterically it is the Dhyāni Buddha of the North, called Las-rab-mdjes-pahi-zhing khams, meaning the Realm of the most beautiful and best works: and esoterically it is the Almighty Attribute or function of the Perfect Buddha—the Wisdom which succeeds in accomplishing acts. (2) The Mandala and the Devatās which constitute the Mandala. (3) The Devatās are the objects of worship, and the places they occupy are the receptacles. (4) Dhārma-dhātu-jnāna is the Sanskrit rendering of the Tibetan " Chös-kyi-dvyings-kyi-yeshes," the changeless Jnāna. At core nothing has absolute independent reality or permanence. They have only a relative truth. (5) That is, the " Chös-kyi-dVyings-kyi-Yeshes"—The Dharma-dhātu-jnāna. (6) Because the Mind has to be exercised in imagining the great, the high, and the exalted; Mount Meru, being the highest thing imaginable, is selected as an object of meditation, as the site of the Vihāra of the God-head or Deity the devotee is going to create and worship with his mind. (7) The four side-walls, each being five-fold, *e.g.*, a black wall, built of some precious material like jet for instance, then conch, then gold, then ruby, and emerald: the ceilings are treated separately.

bells waving in the wind. There are domed-roof towers supported by red corbels, ornamented with the figures of Devīs bearing offerings for worship. Each of the four entrances have pillared porticos, the pillars being surmounted by four-tiered cornices. These again are topped by the Wheel of Dharma, figures of antelopes,[1] umbrellas, banners, as also yak-tail fans with jewelled handles. Imagine [2] a beautiful arrangement of flowers, and gems and decorations and bannerets. The corbels supporting the cornice on the inner side are coloured blue on the east, green on the north, red on the west, and yellow on the south. The fourfold central wheel is surmounted by a dome in the form of a Stūpa (Chorten) [3] with four tiers at the base. Then imagine that outside the Vihāra there are the eight Great Cremation Grounds of the dead as follows:

On the East Tumdrak;[4] on the North Tsang-tsing-Khrigspa;[5] on the West Wur-Wur-Barva;[6] on the South Jig-su-rungva;[7] on the South-East Nags-tshalphun sum-tshogs-pa;[8] on the South-West Münpa-mizadpa;[9] on the North-West Kili-Kili-da-dok-pa;[10] on the North-East Ha-Ha-Gödpa.[11]

In each of the burning grounds respectively meditate upon the following Devatās:

(1) The ancient Vihāras seem to have borne these symbols of the peaceful character of these edifices. (2) On the top of the gates and of the Vihāra. (3) There are four circles one within the other. Over this supported by columns is a stūpa-shaped roof, that is, dome. (4) gTum-drag, *i.e.*, "gruesome;" "awful." (5) Tsang-tsing-hKhrigspa; "dense thicket or jungle." (6) Wūr-Wūr-hBarva; "burning with the Wur Wur sound." (7) hJigs-surungva; "the terrible." (8) The perfectly endowed forest. (9) "The ever gloomy" or "Interminable gloom." (10) Kili-Kili-sgra-sgrog-pa; "Resounding with the cries Kili Kili," that is the shrill notes of eagles and other birds of prey. (11) Ha-Ha rGödpa; "resounding with the wild laughter Ha Ha."

1. Yellow Indra, mounted on an elephant, holding a thunderbolt. 2. Yellow Yaksha, mounted on a horse and holding a mace. 3. White Varuna, mounted on a Makara[1] and holding a noose. 4. Blue Yama, mounted on a buffalo holding a lance. 5. Red Agni, mounted on a goat, four-handed, whose two right hands make the gesture of giving boons, and hold a three-headed mace, and whose two left hands hold a rosary and a vessel containing drops (rilbu : that is of wine). 6. Black Rākshasa, mounted on a resuscitated dead body, holding a sword and a skull. 7. Green Marut, mounted on a deer, holding a banner. 8. White Vang-Dan,[2] mounted on a bull, holding a three-pointed thunderbolt.

All these are beautifully garmented and bedecked with jewels. They are each accompanied on their left by their consorts of the same colour as themselves, and all bow towards the Victorious One (Chom-dan-da).[3]

Again, think of these cemeteries as respectively adorned with the eight kinds of Gigantic Trees, one kind in each as follows:

Shirīsa, Ashvattha, Ankola,[4] Tsuta,[4] Karanja, Latapa-rakati,[4] Partipata, and Bhata.[5] These are eight great trees which adorn the burning grounds. There are eight

(1) A mythical animal in part like an alligator, the vehicle of Varuna the Water God and of Gangā. (2) dVang-lDan = (Mighty, Powerful) Sanskrit, Nāgarāja. They are of two kinds, *viz.* :—(*a*) The ordinary Tiras-chan-Nāga animal-serpent or Snakes ; and (*b*) The Divya-Nāga = Serpent-Spirits which are represented as being half human and half snake, the portion above the waist being human, and when females much more beautiful than human women. The body of, and the portion below, the waist is said to be that of a snake. And these Nāgarājās (King among Nāgas) are decorated with 3, 5, 7 or 9 hooded heads of serpents which appear as a hood over their human head. (3) bCom-lDan-hDas or the " victorious one," who having conquered the host of Māra has passed away from misery. Here Shrī-Chakra-Sambhāra. (4) *Qu.* (5) *Qu.* Pārijāta, Vata. *Cf.* eight Kulavriksha.

Female Devīs, headed by Drag-Tum-mo,[1] who as door-keepers guard these places. Then there are the eight Serpent-spirit-kings,[2] to wit the eight who are Norgyay,[3] Jogpo,[4] Top-kyi-Gyu,[5] Padma,[6] Hulunta,[7] Rigs-Dan,[8] Dung-Kyong,[9] and Mahā-padma.[10]

Then there are eight Clouds; namely, Dra-drag-pa,[11] Mugs-pa,[12] Mun-pa,[13] Kuntu-Khyilva,[14] Gang-pa,[15] Babpa,[16] Dragpo,[17] and Khrigspa.[18] These are the eight clouds. Again there are the eight Rivers, the eight Fires, and the large Stūpas, in each of the great cremation grounds. Then there are in each cemetery and according to each sect of (worshippers) Avatāras,[19] Vīras, Yoginīs, Siddhas, Vidyādharas, Pretas, Rākshasas, Yakshas,[20] Ghouls, Elementals,[21] the male and female "sky-goers"[22] and Jackals. Thinking that each of the cemeteries is full of these, then imagine that these eight burning grounds enclose the Vihāra.

Next imagine within the latter a circle within which again picture an eight-petalled lotus. Let the worshipper think of himself in the centre of the Lotus as being

(1) Drag-gTum-mo, "The greatly angry" (or The Angry and Haughty One). (2) Nāga (Tibetan = Klu [pronounced Loo]. (3) "Increasing wealth" = Nor-rgyas. (4) "The Carpenter" = hJog-po. (5) "The cause of might" = Stobs-kyi-rgyu. (6) Lotus (Padma-nāgarājā). (7) Hulunta = Huludu = a Nāgarājā. (8) Rigs-ldan = Of noble birth. (9) Dung-sKyong = Shangkha-pāla Nāgarājā. (10) Great Lotus = Mahā Padma. (11) sGra-grag-pa, The noisy (Thunder clouds). (12) rMugs-pa = the misty (Mists). (13) Kuntu-hKhyilva = the dark or gloomy (fogs). (14) The wreathing (clouds). (15) The filling; those which envelope the whole sky or landscape. (16) hBab-pa = the descending (Rain clouds). (17) The fierce (Fast drifting clouds which move before the storms). (18) hKhrigspa—The enshrouding. (19) That is each of the sects such as Karma-kargyuts, Dugpa-Kargyut, Nying-mapa, etc., have their own Siddhas, etc., and these are in each of the cemeteries. (20) Giving the Sanskrit equivalents for the Tibetan in text. (21) hByung-po. (22) mKhah-hgro-dang-mKhah-hgro-mas.

the Chief Devatā, Khorlo-Demchog (Chakra-Mahāsukha) with four faces symbolising the four Purified Elements,[1] the four Boundless Wishes,[2] the four Emancipations,[3] and the four Acts.[4]

The face in front is blue, that on the left green, that at the back red, and that on the right yellow. To symbolise that he does not change from the Dharma-dhātu-jnāna,[5] the body is of a blue colour. To show that all the three Lokas[6] are under His vision and that He knows the Three Times[7] each Face has three eyes. To show that He knows the process of the evolution and involution of the twelve Nidānas[8] (categories bound together by the chain of mutual dependence,) and that

---

(1) hByung-va-bzhi (pronounced jung-va), that is, earth (sa); water (choo); fire (mé); air (rlung). (2) Tshad-med-bzhi or dNying-rje (compassion); dGah-va (affection); and Byams-pa (Love) bTang-sNyoms (equal regard or impartiality). (3) rNampar-tharpa-bzhi. These are: (*a*) dNgös-po-sTong-pa-nyid (Bhāva-shūnyatā); (*b*) dNgös-po-med-pa-sTongpa-nyid (Abhāva-shūnyatā); (*c*) Dön-dam-sTongpa-nyid (Paramārtha-shūnyatā); (*d*) gZhan-gyi-dNgös-pohi-sTongpa-nyid (the voidness of others that is all objectivity). Emancipation is the realization of these four truths. (4) hPhrin-las-bzhi. That is the peaceful (Zhi-va) the grand upholding (zGyas-pa) the fascinating and producing (dVang-va) and the fierce, stern and destructive (dragpo). (5) *See ante*, pp. 4, 5. (6) The three Lokas are Kāmaloka or sensual world, Rūpaloka where there is form without sensual craving, and Arūpaloka the formless spiritual world. There are six of the first, *viz.*:—Deva, Asura, Human, Preta, Tiraschan, Naraka: seventeen of the second or Brahmalokas, and four of the Arūpalokas. (7) Past, present and future. (8) The twelve Nidānas: the chain of causation, *i.e.*, causes of existence: (1) Avidyā, (2) Samskāra, (3) Vijnāna, (4) Nāmarūpa, (5) The six Āyatanas, (6) Sparsha, (7) Vedanā, (8) Trishnā, (9) Upādāna, (10) Bhava, (11) Jāti, (12) Jarā Marana; that is, (1) Ignorance, (2) Impression, (3) Cognition, (4) Name and form, (5) The six senses, (6) Touch, (7) Sensation, (8) Desire or Attachment or Craving, (9) Enjoyment, (10) Existence (11) Birth, (12) Old Age and Death. The first five are the Avidyā, Sangskāra, Buddhi, Ahangkāra, Manas and five senses of Hindu philosophy.

He knows the twelve Projections [1] thoroughly, He is represented as with twelve hands.

To show that the Perfect Mind [2] is both the Void [3] and Compassion [4] he holds in the upper hands a Dorje and a Bell.[5] To show that Power [6] and Wisdom [7]

(1) Phowa or projections. This is a very secret science, known to adepts in the Demchog-Tantra, in itself one of the most advanced doctrines. Such adepts, it is said, may be found in the Monastery of Punakha and in Tsari and Khams in Thibet. One form of it is taught publicly to those who desire to practice it. It enables a person to project his Consciousness (Vijnāna-skandha) just before his death into some other form. (2) Byang-chub-kyi-sems. The mind is the source of both good and evil thoughts, so the Text says not merely mind (sems) but well-trained or perfected mind (Byang-chub-sems). This is Bodhi or the purified mind. Hence the term Byang-chub-sems dPah for a Bodhisattva or one aspiring and next to Buddhahood. (3) sTong-pa-nyid or Shūnyatā. *See* p. 2, Note (1), *ante.* (4) sNying-rje—Karunā. The goal of the Mahāyāna Buddhist is expressed in the wish " May I attain Buddhahood in Dharmakāya and for the good of others may I empty the very last pits of Sangsāra (worldly existence) by the acquisition of indestructible compassion." Again it is said " Not erring in existence (Sangsāra) nor remaining inactive in the tranquil state (zhiva = the passive state of Nirvāna); May I be able to emancipate sentient beings as infinite as the Heavens." The Mahāyāna Buddhist seeks not mere tranquillity, but working for the benefit of all so as to attain the state which is both Void (Shūnyatā) and Compassion (Karunā). (5) That is, these are symbols of Shūnyatā (for Vajra is ultimately this) and Karunā. (6) Thabs; the Power to do and the Means (Upāya) or method by which anything is done as compared with Shes-rab the wisdom (Prajnā) which guides and utilises it. According to Tantrik Buddhism the first is a male and the second a female principle. This is mere symbolism for worship. Such and other statements are not mere Dogmas but a means of training the mind to reach Shūnyatā which in its essence is Compassion or Love for all. The Buddhist Tantra does not so much say " Here is the answer or theory, train your mind to believe so," but " Here are the problem and the means, work out the answer for yourself." (7) Shes-rab = Prajnā. She utilises the former in order that Nirvāna may be obtained. Thabs is associated as phenomenal objects, (sNangva = Rūpa) bliss

are ever in union the first or uppermost two hands embrace His Spouse.[1] The next two hands hold the raw elephant-hide, emblem of ignorance, over the upper part of the body.[2] The third (right) hand holds a drum (Damaru), to signify that He proclaims the most joyous tidings. The fourth (right) hand brandishes a battle-axe, to signify that he cuts off births and deaths, root and trunk. The fifth (right) hand holds a dagger[3] to show that He cuts off pride and the six sins.[4] The sixth (right) hand holds a trident, to signify that He destroys the sins pertaining to the three Lokas.[5]

To show that Perfect Mind[6] is endowed with supreme bliss, the third left hand holds a staff (surmounted by a Dorji). To signify that He does away with all ideas which regard things as material or immaterial,[7] the fourth left hand holds a skull filled with blood. To

(bDeva), clearness (gSalva), pure intellect (Rigpa), Shūnyatā. The two are inseparable. The above are systematic stages of progress. The essence of this Buddhistic doctrine is Thabs or the great Compassion and Shunyatā are ever associated with it as the supremely Pure Experience which is beyond all worlds. (1) The hands embrace the spouse to show that Thabs and Shes-rabs are ever in union. *See* Notes, *ante.* (2) In the Tibetan Tantras, the Īshtadevatā (Yidam) is the Ideal at which the worshipper aims. His form, colour, hands, implements, etc., are particular means of attainment. The key to these symbols is provided in the explanation given. As He tears the elephant of ignorance asunder, He holds the raw elephant-hide aloft with His two next hands to clothe the upper part of his body. (3) Gri-gūg, a knife, dagger and scraper combined. (4) (*a*) Pride = Nga-rgyal. (*b*) Dis-belief = Ma-dad. (*c*) Want of serious devotion = Dön-du-gNyer-va-med-nyid. (*d*) Distraction = rNamg-gYengs. (*e*) Inattention = Nang-sdud. (*f*) Boredom = skyo-vas-nyan-pa. (5) That is the root sins, Anger, Sloth and Lust. (6) Byang-chub-kyi-sems-bde-va-chenpo-dang-ldan-pa, that is, Bodhi-chit. (7) dNgös-po-dang-dNgös-po-med-pahi-rnam-par-rtog-pa-bcad-pa = As He destroys the notion of substance and no-substance. By contemplation on the Heruka, Samyag-jnāna is attained.

show that knowledge holds the nature of sentient beings, the fifth left hand holds a Vajra-noose. To show that He has shaken off all Samsaric delusions,[1] the sixth left hand holds the head of the four-faced Brahmā. To signify that out of His great Compassion He still lives in the world of sentient beings, He treads with the out-stretched right leg the prostrate body of an emaciated red figure of time [2] holding a curved dagger and skull, who represents the extreme of Nirvāna, being a state of utter passing away.[3]

To show that to His great Consciousness there is neither subject nor object,[4] His bent left leg treads the form of a Black Destroyer [5] lying stretched (face downwards) holding in His two right hands a drum (Damaru) and curved dagger, and in His two left hands a staff (Khaṭvanga) and a skull symbolising the extreme of eternal Sangsāra.[6] To signify that merits have been acquired in the fullest measure, He (the Heruka) ties His hair in a knot on the crown of His head, which is adorned with a gem which grants all desires.[7] To denote that the Bodhisattvik mind attains higher and higher degree, the left side of His knotted hair is surmounted by the

(1) gTimug (Stupidity); Moha—Skt. (2) Düs-mtshan-ma; literally having the sign of time, a Devī representing time. She lives and is therefore coloured red; she is emaciated, for she does not produce. The posture and the figures symbolise the extremes of various doctrines. Here the Devī is the type of belief in the extreme of passive Nirvāna, and the Black Destroyer the type of belief in an eternal action Sangsāra. (3) That is of all phenomenality, or the belief that Nirvāna is the sole eternal reality—a belief to be also, as an extreme, avoided. (4) To show that to His great wisdom (Shes-rab-chenpo=Mahā-Prajnā) there is no Pudgala (gang-zag) and Dharma (chös) subject and object, or enjoyer and enjoyment. (5) hJig-byed, translated by Csoma de Koros as Vidhvangsaka. (6) *See* Note 2, *ante*. (7) Yid-bZhin-norbu, *i.e.*, Chintāmani denoting that He grants all wishes of those who ask Him.

first-day phase of the moon.[1] To show that His various acts serve the purpose of all sentient beings, the top of His head is adorned with a multi-coloured Vajra (Dorji) having four points.[2] To signify that the five kinds of wisdom are in Him perfectly developed, each of the heads is adorned with a crown of five dry skulls.[3] To denote that the fifty letters have been purified, He wears a garland of fifty freshly severed heads.[4] To signify that Māra and all heresy are overcome, His faces frown and His teeth are set. His earrings stand for fortitude, necklace for charity, bracelets for chastity, girdle for energy, and the wheel of bone on the crown of His head for Dhyāna.

Ashes from the cremation ground (rubbed on His body) and worshipping objects borne outside[5] denote Wisdom.[6] Thus He is adorned with the six bone ornaments symbolising the six Pāramitās.[7]

Being heroic in His destruction of Māra and having cast aside all belief in the reality of matter and mind,[8] He wears round His middle a Tiger's skin loosened,[9]

(1) The first day after new moon. (2) These point to East, South, West and North which are coloured white, yellow, red, and green respectively. (3) The bones of the head, with the skin taken off, quite clean and dry. (4) The letters of the Sanskrit alphabet are fifty in number and the heads stand as the gross manifestations of them. *See* Arthur Avalon's "Shakti and Shākta": Chapters on Origin of Mantra and Varnamālā. (5) The text reads Thal-chengyi-rgya-dang-mchod-ph yir-thogs-shes-rabs-ste. The seal of the Cremation ground Ashes, and worshipping objects borne outside (represent) Prajnā (Shes-rab). (6) Prajnā=Shes-rab. (7) Charity, Chastity, Fortitude, Energy, Tranquillity, Wisdom. (8) gZung-hDzin is put aside. gZung-hDzin-spangs-pas = to denote that He has forsaken the holding of certain things to be permanent and such notions or beliefs. (9) The tiger skin denotes gZung-hDzin and His wearing it loose denotes casting off. gZung=outward object. hDzin = inner perceiving subject.

showing that the virtue of His three principles [1] are fully developed and that He graciously follows after and saves erring beings overpowered and maddened by obscuring passions. His body has symmetry and grace, His visage is heroic, stern and severe, He is full of energy and awe-inspiring, and yet He is compassionate and His features of a peaceful cast.[2] These are the nine different aspects or grades of His splendour and magnificence.

He embraces Vajra Vārāhī who clings to Him [3] and who is red [4] of colour [5] because She is devoted to the service of all sentient beings. She has only one face to denote that all things have but one taste [6] in the "That."[7] To signify that She comprehends both Truths, apparent

---

(1) Skū = Body = (Kāyā). gSungs = Speech (Vāk). Thugs = Mind=(Chitta). (2) This Devatā (Demchog) is depicted as being of a semi-wrathful type: neither terrible like the Krodha-Bhairavas nor yet wholly peaceful. He is serious, energetic and stern. (3) He is standing. She is in sexual union clinging to Him with the legs passed round the Devatā's back, as represented in the Tangkas. (4) She is red because red is the colour of love. She loves all beings in the Sangsāra and would save them. Therefore She is coloured red and clings to the Male who is emblematic of the Method (Thabs) to save, *e.g.*, Sādhanā and Dhyāna. (5) She is represented Red—the colour of Love—to show that She is Love and actuated by Love to the service of all sentient beings. (6) Ro = rasa. That is, all are at base one considered as the "That" the bliss of which has been compared by Kāmalasila to the virgin's bliss in love. (7) Chös-thams-cad-de-bzhin-nyid-du-ro-gcig-pas zhal-gcig-pas. In the "That" everything. The "That" (De-bzhin-nyid or De-Khona-nyid, or Ji-bzin-nyid) is thus explained. The ether or Ākāsha (nam-mKhah) is that which offers no resistance to motion and therefore induces no feeling of touch. So that which can only be described by saying "not that" "not that" when every picture of everything is presented to the mind and is yet Itself indescribable is called the "That." Has it form, touch, smell or any other thing? No; and so on with the rest. Then there is nothing? No. There is something which to us is nothing since it cannot be named. It is the ultimate Mysterious "That."

and real,[1] She has two hands. With the left holding a human skull full of blood, She embraces the Male, denoting that She confers Supreme Bliss. The right hand holds a curved dagger with a Vajra hilt symbolising that Wisdom-Consciousness which cuts away every thought[2] and destroys all sinful obscuring passions and Māras, She thrusts this dagger menacingly in all the ten directions. To show that She has untied the knot which holds all things as they appear, Her hair is loose and flowing. To denote Her freedom from the obscuring veil of evil passion She is naked. She is three-eyed, garlanded with fifty, and crowned with five dried skulls. She wears five bone ornaments.[3] To show that She is inseparate from Method,[4] She encircles the body of the Bhagavān with Her limbs and embraces Him. Appearance,[5] Method[6] and Great Compassion[7] are the Male Deity whilst the Void,[8] Prajnā,[9] Tranquillity[10] and Great Bliss[11] are the Female Deity.[12]

---

(1) bDen-pa-gNyis—the two truths. They are Drang-don apparent or vyavahārika truth and Nges-don or real or pāramārthika truth. The first is the world-experience of the phenomenal world. The second is noumenal truth or Shūnyatā, the wisdom which knows in actual experience that all things exist only in the mind but have no independent reality either as mental or external objects. (2) rTog-pa-thams-cad-bCad-pahi-yeshes, the Jnāna which cuts away all rTog-pa that is Kalpanā, Vitarka. In Dhyāna (or Meditation on the Supreme) the simplest notions "yes" or "no," "is" or "is not" not to speak of such qualifications as "is good," "is bad," etc., are obstructions to and interceptions of the Dhyāna. All such thoughts are rTogpa, that is Kalpanā, something by which the mind is arrested and prevented from flowing on. Her Sādhaka is freed from all these. (3) She has not the ashes which are the Sixth. (4) *Vide ante*, p. 23, Note 6. (5) Snang-va—that is, the phenomenal universe. (6) Thabs. See *ante*, p. 23. (7) sNying-rje-chenpo = (Mahā-Karunā) Lhag-mthong = A super conscious state in Dhyāna. (8) Shūnyatā = sTongpa. (9) Shes-rab = Prajnā. (10) Tranquillity = Zhi-gnas. (11) bDeva = Bliss. (12) She thus represents Shūnyatā or the Great Void.

To show that these two must be in union,[1] They are depicted as in sexual union touching at all points of contact. To denote that the fire of Supreme Wisdom[2] burns up all obstacles and (the influence of) malignant Spirits within or without (the two Devatās) should be meditated upon as in union in the midst of a halo of flames emitted by the Supreme Wisdom.[3]

Passing to the four petals of the Lotus, blue Khandoma[4] is on the Eastern petal, green Lāma[5] on the Northern petal, red Khanda-Rohe[6] on the Western petal, yellow Zugs-chen-ma[7] on the Southern petal.

Each of these has one head but four hands.

The two right hands of each hold a drum (Damaru) and a curved dagger. The two left hands of each hold a skull filled with blood and a staff. They are quite naked with their right legs outstretched. On the four intervening points (of the compass) that is, South-East, North-East, North-West, and South-West are four urns made of precious metals and filled with the water of wisdom.[8] On the top of these there are the five nectars in skull-bowls, thus making

---

(1) In the XVIIth Chapter on Prajnā-pāramitā of the Dvags-po-thar-rgyan by Dvags-Lha-sGampo rJe-btsün, Mila's foremost disciple it is said that Prajnā separated from Method binds to Nirvāna and method without Prajnā to Sangsāra. (2) Yeshes-Chenpohi-mes. (3) Yeshes-kyi-me. The aura which is surrounding these energising Deities manifests as flames. She clings to Him with the left hand which holds the Cup of Blood. (4) That is, mKhah-hGro-ma (Dākinī). "She who moves through the sky." (5) Not a Tibetan priest but a female Devatā so named. (6) This is as in text: probably the corruption of some Sanskrit name. (7) gZugs-chen-ma meaning "she having body"=Rūpinī. (8) Yeshes-kyi-chu: literally, "water of wisdom" but it is generally meant to signify the wine which is the nectar of wisdom, *i.e.*, Jnānāmrita. In the Indian Tantra Wine is known as Causal Water (Kāranavāri).

the Chakra of great bliss. Outside these are fences, pillars, beams, rafters, and ceilings, made up of curved daggers each having the half of a Dorje as their hilt. Outside these is the blue Mandala of the Mind [1] with eight points. [2]

In the eastern point thereof lies Pulira-Malaya [3] where abide Khanda-Kapālī and Rab-Tummo. [4] In the northern point thereof lies Jalandhara where abide Mahākāmakala and Tumpahi-mig-chen-ma. [5] In the western point thereof lies Ugyen where abide Kāmakalā and Wod-dan-ma. [6] In the southern point thereof lies Arputa where abide Chewa-nampar-tsegma [7] and Na-chen-ma. [8] In the south-east point thereof lies Godavari where dwell Sura-vairi and Tanpai-lo-chen-ma. [9] In the south-west point thereof lies Ramesvari where abide O-pa-me [10] and Mihū-thūng-ma. [11] In the north-western point thereof lies Devikota where abide Dorje-wöt [12] and Lankai-Wang-Chūgma. [13] In the north-eastern point thereof lies Malava where abide Dorje-yi-ku [14] and Shing-dib-ma. [15] The blue Mandala of Mind [16] is in the sky and enjoying there. They (the Devatās of the Mandala) purify the spaces above the surface of the

(1) Thugs—Sanskrit = Chitta. (2) rTsibs: literally, ribs or spokes. (3) Puliramalaya—These are twenty-four Tīrtha-Sthānas. (4) Rab-gTummo: meaning "The furious or very angry." (5) gTumpahi-mig-can-ma—She with fierce eyes. (6) Höd-lDan-ma: meaning "The effulgent" = Prabhāvatī. (7) mCheva-rNampar-bTsegma: meaning "She who has her teeth ever set on end." (8) sNa-chen-ma: meaning "She with a large nose." (9) bTan-pahi-blo-can-ma—"She with the firm mind." (10) Höd-dPag-med = "Boundless light." (11) That is, the "Dwarfish lady." (12) rDo-rje-up Höd—Vajra-prabhā; vajra light or brilliance. (13) Lan-Kahi-dVang-Phyūg-ma = Lankeshvarī. (14) rDorje-hi-sKu = Vajrakāya. (15) Shing-grib-ma = "Shadow of the trees." (16) Thugs-kyi-kyil-khor.

Earth.[1] This Mandala is surrounded by a fence of Vajras and pillars, beams, rafters and ceiling made of Vajras. This constitutes the very self of the incomprehensible secret of the Mind.[2]

Outside the above there is the red Mandala of Speech with eight points. At the eastern point is Kāmarūpa where abide Angūri and Airāvati. At the northern point lies Otre where abide Dorje-Ralpachen[3] and the Great Destructress.[4] In the western apex lies Trisha-kun[5] where abide Pa-wo-chenpo[6] and Lungi-shug-chen-ma.[7] At the southern point lies Kosala where abide Dorje-hung-zad[8] and Chang-thung-ma.[9] In the south-east lies Kalinga where abide Rabtu-zangpo[10] and Shamadevī.[11] In the south-west lies Lampaka where abide Dorje-zangpo[12] and Shintu-zangmo.[13] In the north-east lies Kantsi where live Jig-jed-chempo[14] and Ta-na-ma.[15] In the north-east lies Himalaya where abide Mig-mi-Zang[16] and Khagana.

---

(1) Probably the Mind is trained to think of the Devatās as being in the sky because the sky being unobstructed by other objects offers no impediment to the forming of a complete mental picture. By being in the sky they purify it. (2) The Vihāra, its occupants and surroundings denote the mysterious forces which are the Devatā and Chitta. The Sādhaka begins by endowing the mind principle of the Devatā with virtues and functions so that he does not meditate upon an un-thinking form alone. (3) He who has the Vajra—matted hair = Vajra-jātā. (4) hJigs-byed-chen-mo—Destructress. (5) Trishakune (one of the twenty-four Tīrthasthānas or places of pilgrimage). (6) dPah-vo-chenpo: Mahāvīra: great hero. (7) rLung-gi-shugs-can-ma—"She of the force of the Wind." (8) Vajra-hūng-kāra. (9) Chhang-hThung-ma—"She who drinks wine." (10) Rabtu-bZangpo—Sūbhadra. (11) *Qu.* Shyāma-Devī. (12) rDorje-bZangpo—Vajrabhadra. (13) Shintu-bZangmo—"She who is very good." (14) hJig-Jed-Chenpo—"The great Destroyer." (15) rTa-rNa-ma—"She with the horse's ears." (16) Mig-mi-bZang (Virupaksha):—the slanting eye attributed to the Shivamūrti.

These which constitute the red wheel of speech dwell upon the surface of the Earth and purify it. It is surrounded by a fence of Lotuses, and by pillars, beams, rafters and ceiling of Lotuses. It is the very Self [1] of the incomprehensible secrets of Speech.[2]

Outside the Mandala there lies again the white eight-petalled Mandala of the body (Kāyā). At the eastern point Pretapuri dwell Top-po-che [3] and Khorlohi-shugs-chenma.[4] At the northern point Grihadeva dwell Rinchendorji [5] and Khanda Roha, at the western point Sourakhta dwell Tamdin [6] and Shondini. At the southern point Suvarna-dvīpa [7] dwell Ṅamkhai-Nyingpo [8] and Khorloi-go-chama.[9]

At the south-eastern point Nagara dwell Shrī Heruka [10] and Shintu-pah-mo.[11] At the south-western point Sindhu dwell Padma-gargyi-wangchuk [12] and Tops-chen-ma.[13] At the north-western point Maro dwell

---

(1) Ngo-vo—that is, the true self. (2) Vāk (gSūng); having thus dealt with the Mandalas of Mind (Chitta) and Speech (Vāk) the text proceeds to the description of the Mandala of the Body (Kāyā). (3) sTobs-po-che—Mahābala; the mighty. There are twenty-four Tīrthasthānas (gnas-yül) in Jambudvīpa which are sacred to the Hindus and Tantrik Bauddhas. As regards the latter, see Arthur Avalon's "Origin of the Vajrayāna Devatās." (4) hKhorlohi-shugs-chenma—"She who has the force of the Chakra. (5) Rinchen-rDorje—Ratnavajra=gem-vajra. (6) rTa-mGrin—Hayagrīva; horse's neck. Though the paintings denote him with a horse's head, yet the name refers to the neck denoting connection with "Vāk" (speech). (7) In text Suverna. (8) Nam-Khahi-sNyinghpo—Ākāsha-garbha. (9) hKhorlohi-go-chama—She who has the armour of Chakra. (10) dPal-Heruka. (11) Shintu-dPah-mo—She who is very heroic or the great heroine. (12) Padma-gargyi-dVang-phyug—Padma Nateshvara; Padma Lord of dances. (13) sTops-chen-ma=Mahābalī; She of great might.

Nampar-nang-dzad[1] and Khorlo-gyurma[2]. At the north-eastern point Kūlūta dwell Dorje-Sempah[3] and Tsön-dü-chen-mo[4].

This Mandala is white in colour. These enjoy beneath the earth and purify the nether-world. This Mandala is surrounded by a fence of Chakras[5]. It is the very self of the incomprehensible mystery of the Body[6]. All the male Heroes[7] have each one head and four hands. The right and left upper hands hold a Dorje and a bell respectively and hold their Spouses in embrace[8]. The lower right hand holds a drum (Damaru) and the left hand a staff surmounted by a Dorje (Khatvanga)[9]. Some Lamas say that this hand holds a skull-bowl whilst the staff is held in the inner bend of the elbow.

In dress, ornaments and pósture they resemble Dorje Phagmo[10]. Outward of this is the circle or conclave of the

---

(1) rNampar-sNang-mDzad—Vairochana. (2) hKhorlo-sGyurma—The wielder of the Chakra. (3) sDorje-sems-dPah = Vajrasattva. (4) brTsön-hGrus-chen-mo=Mahāvīryā: She of great energy. (5) Discus: hKhorlo. The offensive weapon used by the Sikhs in battle and the ancient Mahābhārata heroes. (6) Sku-hi-gSangva-bSamgyis-Mikhyabs-pahi-ngo-vo-ho. This is the real incomprehensible mystery of the Body of the Bhagavān or Shrī Heruka made up of an aggregate of other Devatās or the purified and deified constituent principles which have been enumerated. (7) dPah-bo=Vīras. (8) Kha-sByor-chenpohi-tshül-gyi-bzhugs-pa-ho; that is, they are in the condition of the great coupling, *i.e.*, coitus. (9) Shiva's Khatvanga is, according to Indian iconography, surmounted by a skull. Here the Khatvanga is surmounted by a trident. The Khatvanga is variously surmounted by a trident (Dorje) skull or gem according to the Devatā—Thus the Dākinī Vārāhī has a Khatvanga surmounted by a Dorje on a triple head; the lowest being a fresh bleeding head, the next one in decay and the topmost a dry skull; the Dākinī Singhamukhī's Khatvanga bears a trident (Trisūla) and so does that of Guru Padma-sambhava. (10) rDorje-Phagmo=Vajravārāhī. They are each in contact at all points—that is, in the act of coition.

sacred devotion[1]. The northern entrance is guarded by the crow-headed guardian[2], the southern by the owl-headed guardian[3], the eastern by the sow-headed guardian[4], and the western by the dog-headed guardian[5]. In the southern entrance dwells Shinje-tanma[6] the right half of whose body is blue and the left half yellow. In the south-west dwells Shin-je-pho-nya-ma[7] the right half of whose body is yellow and the left red, in the north-west Shin-je-cheva-ma[8] is on guard. The right side of her body is red and the left green. The guardian on the north-east is Shin-je-jom-ma[9] whose body is green on the right and blue on the left. All these resemble the Chief Devatā Vajra-yoginī as regards the number of faces and hands and the different implements which they hold. All the Virās and Yoginīs[10] have features of the wrathful type. They are themselves filled with great bliss. Their brows are crowned with a garland of Dorje[11] from which shoot forth miraculous rays. In particular the guardians of

---

(1) The Deities created by the Mind are of two classes, *viz.* :—Jnānī (Yeshes-pa) and Bhakta (Damtshig-pa). The latter are those first imagined and they invite the Jnānī-devatās, wait upon, serve, and worship Them. At length the Jnānīs are absorbed in the Bhaktas; the latter in the Mantras; these into the Bīja and finally all disappear in Shūnyatā. It is the conclave of the Bhakta Devatās which is here meant. (2) Kha-gDong = Kāka-mukhī; Kakāsye, etc., is the Mantra of this door-keeper and so with the rest. (3) Hug-gDong = Ulūka-mukhī; Ulūkāsye etc. (4) Phag-gDong = Varāha-mukhī; Shūkarā-sye, etc. (5) Khyi-gDong = Kukkura-mukhī; Shvanāsye, etc., (6) gShin-rje-brTanma = She who is the Pillar of Yama. (7) gSin-rje-pho-ña-ma = Female messenger of Yamarāja (skt = Yamadūtī). (8) gSin-rje-mchevama. (9) gSin-rje-hJoms-ma. The mantras are set out in another fascicule of the Tantra. (10) rNal-hByor-ma. (11) Vajra-mālā: rDo-rje-Phrengva. Not fierce but terrible on account of the awful glory and beauty so that men can scarcely look upon them.

the doors are seated on Pretas[1] and are very fierce and blazing of mien. Thus meditate upon them. Various drugs, rich and nutritious aliments and nectar fill the angles and corners in the space between the Devatās. There are also eight urns of gems the necks of which are adorned with knots and bows of celestial silk and surmounted by wish-granting trees[2] laden with flowers and fruit. There are pillars, beams, rafters and ceilings ornamented with vari-coloured, four-pointed Vajras. The worshipper should meditate upon all this Mandala consisting of the dwellings and their inmates quite clearly and distinctly and without any vagueness and dimness. They should be meditated upon as being the Dual-Unity which is, as appearance, form and in itself the formless Void or Shūnyatā[3].

With a view to avoid differences in the regard with which mind-created and self-existing Devatās are held one should think thus[4]. These

---

(1) Pretas: unhappy spirits or ghosts. Each Deity has one Preta. (2) dPag-bsam-shing: Kalpataru. (3) Literally appearances (sNang-va-dang) and Shūnyatā (sTongpa) united of (zungdu-hjugpahi) the selfness (bdag-nyid)—having—in—do, meditate (can-du-bSgom-par-byaho.) That is:—meditate (upon it) as being the very self of the united being of Āloka (appearance) and Shūnyatā. That is Form (Rūpa) and the formless Void (Shūnyatā) united in One: what in other schemes is called the phenomenal and the real or spiritual. Shangkarāchāryya if (as western critics allege) he lived after the development of Buddhist philosophy may have borrowed from it substituting Ātmā for Shūnyatā which it resembles but asserting that this Ātmā was eternal substance. (4) The meaning of this is:—We are generally in the habit of underrating the products of our own mind as being not divine, which however ought not to be so. One should regard these products of one's own mind—the sixty-two Devatās who constitute the Mandalas—as being the very Devatās, incarnated for the benefit of the Jambu-dvīpa. Or, in other words, as an artist regards the

Beings[1] which are made to appear by means of Mantras which constitute the Mandala of one's mind are in truth the Devatās who inhabit the twenty-four sacred places in Jambu-dvīpa. And these same Devatās are the (Nirmāna-kāya[2]) manifest forms of the perfect Sambhogakāya[2] Beings who inhabit the pure Wogmin[3]. And these again are in no wise different from the Dharmakāya[2]. In this way one should dispel the notion that they are in any way inferior on account of their being mind-evolved images which may be regarded with indifference; and one should know that these sixty-two Mandala Devatās, which appear in one's mind, to be none other than the manifest (Nirmāna-kāya) Devatās existent in Jambu-dvīpa who in turn are no other than the Sambhoga-kāya Devatās existing in Wogmin who again are not

---

product of his mind and brush or pencil with adoration and fondness, so should the Sādhaka adore the Devatās produced by his mind and regard them as the real manifestation of the Deities of the Jambu-dvīpa. And these again as not only wielding influence in the Jambu-dvīpa, but throughout the whole universe, being the concentrated rays or manifestations of the Sambhogakāya and who reside in the Akanishta Heavens. This Sambhoga-kāya in its turn is not any other thing than the Dharmakāya. Ordinary people regard the Devatās as objectively existing and venerate them because of this supposed objectivity. Here the Sādhaka is led to guard himself against such notions. They are of the mind and as such one with the Devatās of the Wogmin. (1) Pho-nyas = Messengers. (2) Chos-kyi-sku. The bodies here referred to are as follows :—(*a*) Dharmakāya (The body of Dharma or ultimate reality). That which is free from inherent obscuration and accidental obscuration is said to be Dharmakāya. (*b*) The embodiment of all that is wise, merciful and loving in the Dharmakāya—as clouds on the surface of the heavens or a rainbow on the surface of clouds—is said to be Sambhoga-kāya = Longs-sku. (*c*) The still more concentrated ray from the Sambhoga-kāya which is shot forth to affect any particular person, place or time is the Nirmānakāya (Sprül-sku). (3) A state (Akanishta Loka) from which there is no falling back into Sangsāra.

separate from the Dharmakāya[1]. In this way one should dispel the notion that they are in any respect inferior to mind-evolved images upon which one looks with indifference ; and should know these sixty-two Mandala Devatās which appear in one's mind to be none other than the Manifest (Nirmānakāya) Divinities existent in Jambu-dvīpa who in turn are no other than the Sambhogakāya Devatās existing in Wogmin [2] who again are not separate from the Dharmakāya. So should one accustom the mind to regard the Divinities as superior beings[3]. This entire Mandala[4] is subject of meditation by a highly developed mind. Each

---

(1) Chos-kyi-sku. (2) v. *ante* p. 36 n[3]., Hog-min—Akanishta Heavens. (3) When we create images of Devatā with our mind we are apt to regard them with indifference because they are mind-evolved. But this is not right. They are equal in all respects to the actually existing images Devatās in Hogmin. If we merely think to ourselves " I am creating with my mind " no more advancement is made than by solving any merely intellectual problem. But the Sādhaka's occupation is not merely mental. He should train his mind to regard these exercises with exalted regard, veneration and devotion looking upon the Devatās as real, holy and divine. They are none the less so because mind-produced, for the mind ultimately is That and its ideas forms of That. (4) The Mandala may be drawn as follows :— Draw a circle within which is the Principal Devatā Shrī-chakra-Sambhāra. Give it eight petals in the N, E, S and W, which are Lama, mKhah-hGro-ma, Rūpinī, Khanda-Rohe. Outside these eight petals draw eight other larger ones. This is the inner Mandala of Chitta in which are Maha Kamkala and others. Outside this, draw again eight larger petals to form the red middle Mandala fenced with lotuses called Vāk Mandala, containing in each petal Otre, Sthāna, and Devatās rDorje-Ralpachan and other Sthānas and Devatās. Outside this again draw eight larger petals which is the Kāya Mandala fenced by Chakras containing Griha Deva, Rinchen—rDorje and others. Outside this last is the fourth circle (Phag-gDongma, called the Damtshig-hKhorlo) containing in its eight divisions the gate-keeper and warders who guard the good faith and worshipping female Devatās Hug-gDong-ma and others. Then draw the outermost circle of flames enclosing and guarding all.

Mandala and its petal with its particular Devatā must be meditated upon with special veneration and faith. In the Mūla-Tantra[1] it is said that The three classes of Devatās when well known confer boons on the devotee. This is the mode of acquiring practical knowledge. Then with a view to dispel doubts about the Devatās and the Path[2] identify the thirty-seven Devatās created by, and meditated upon by, the mind with the thirty-seven branches of the Dharma[3] which leads to Buddhahood and these again must be thought of as being within the worshipper himself in the form of the thirty-seven Devatās. This practice is for men of the highest intellect. Men of middling and lower intelligence should identify the recollection of the body to be Khando-ma[4]; the recollection of the

---

(1) rTs-a-vahi-rGyud—The fourteenth of the fifteen parts of the last volume of the Tantra section of the Kah-gyur. (2) The Sādhaka may doubt whether the Devatās are real and efficacious for the purpose invoked: whether they exist independently of the Sādhaka's belief, in which case what about non-ego or Shūnyatā? So with a view to dispel such doubts the Sādhaka is enjoined to identify the Devatās with the saving Dharma; so that he may realise the truth that enlightenment and liberation are to be obtained from himself and by himself through his own effort and not from any external help or favour. The thirty-seven Devatās are previously enumerated, the chief being dPal Heruka (Shrī Chakra-Sambhāra). The two principal Devatās are Sambhāra and Vārāhī; the attendants Khanda Rohe, etc., are four: the Deities of the Sthānas are twenty-four, each couple being taken as one: the door-keepers are four; and four others are Shinje Tanma, Shinje-phonyama, Shinje Chewamo, Shinje-jom-ma. (3) The thirty-seven branches of the Dharma in Pali are:—(*a*) Cattaro Satipatthang 4; (*b*) Cattaro Sammappadhana 4; (*c*) Cattaro Iddhipada 4; (*d*) Panca Indrayani 5; (*e*) Panca Balani 5; (*f*) Satta-Bhojanga 7; (*g*) Atthanga-Magga 8 = 37. (4) Khah-hGro-ma: Dākinī, *i.e.*, to be represented by the Devatā. To recollect that one's body (Kāyasmriti upasthāna) is made up of several elements, ingredients, parts, functions, etc. This recollection regarding the body is to be identified with mKhah-hGro-ma.

nature of things[1] to be Khanda-rohe; the recollection of the mind to be Zūchen-ma[2]; the miraculous feet of good and strong motive to be Khanda-Kapālī [3] and Rab-tum-ma[4], the miraculous feet of energy to be Maha-Kam-kala and Tum-pai-Mig-chen-ma[5]; the miraculous feet of investigation[6] to be Kam-kala and Wö-dan-ma[7]; the miraculous feet of the mind to be Cheva-nampar-tsigpa[8] and Na-chen-ma[9]; the faculty of faith to be Suravairi and Tanpai-lo-chen-ma[10]; the organ of endeavour to be Wö-pa-me[11] and Mihu-thung-ma[12]; the organ of memory to be Dorje-Wöd[13] and Lankayi-wang-chugma[14]; the faculty of deep meditation to be Dorjehi-sKu[15]; the faculty of wisdom to be Anguri and Eravati; the power of faith to be Dorje Ralpachan[16] and the Great Destructress; the power of strength and endeavour to be Pawo-chenpo[17] and Lungi-Shu-chan-ma[18]; the strength of memory to be Dorje-Hung-zad[19] and Chang-thungma; strength of deep meditation to be Rab-tu-Zangpo[20] and Shyāmā Devī[21]; and the strength of wisdom to be Dorji-zangmo[22].

---

(1) Chös—Dharma. (2) gZugs-canma (Rūpinī or—Rūpavatī.) (3) Khanda-kapālī—The "miracle" which can be accomplished by good motive and perseverance by the mind as a whole. (4) Rab-gTum-ma. (5) gTumpai-mig-canma v *ante*. (6) dPyöd-pa-Vichâra. (7) Höd-lDan-ma. (8) mCheva-rNampar-gTsigspa. (9) "He who shows his teeth fiercely". sNa-chen-ma—big nosed. (10) bTan-pahi-bLo-canma—She of firm intellect. (11) Amitābha. (12) The dwarfish lady. (13) rDorjihi-Höd—Light of Dorje or Vajra. (14) Langka-hi-dVang-phyugma=Lankeshvarī. (15) rDorjehi-sku-Vajrakāya. (16) rDorje-ralpachan—having mane of Dorje. (17) dPah-vo-chenpo—Mahāvīryya. (18) rLungi-sugs-can-ma—She who has the might of the wind. (19) rDorge-hum-mdZad=Vajra-hūng-kāra. (20) Rab-tu-bZangpo-(Subhadra). (21) In text—Shyama Devi. (22) rDorje-bZangmo—the good Dorje and the very good Lady.

The seven Bodhyangas are (the aspects of the Perfect Experience), namely, Pure Wisdom as Ecstasy[1] represented by Jig-jed-chenpo[2] and Ta-na ma[3], Pure Wisdom as Energy[4] represented by Migmi-zang[5] and Khagana,[6] Pure Wisdom as Love[7] represented by Tob-po-che[8] and Khor-loi-shug chen-ma[9], Pure Wisdom as Action[10] represented by Rinchen-Dorje[11] and Khanda-Roha[6], Pure Wisdom as Dharma [12] represented by Tamdin [13] and Shondini, [14] Pure Wisdom as Clear Memory[15] represented by Nam-khayi-Nyning-po [16] and Khorlohi-gochama [17], Pure Wisdom as Detachment [18] represented by Heruka and Shintu-Pahmo[19].

The eight branches of the Noble Path are: Right-view [20] represented by Padma-gargyi-Wang-chug [21] and Tob chen-ma[22]; Rightmindedness or Right resolve [23] by Nampar-Nang-zad [24] and-Khorlo-Gyurma [25]; Right speech [26] represented by Dorje-Sem-pa [27] and Tson-du-chenmo [28]; Right Action [29] represented by Khva-dong-

(1) Ting-nge-hdzin-yang-dag-byang-chub-kyi yan-lag = Samādhi—Sambodhyanga. (2) hJigs-byed-chenpo. (3) rTa-snama. (4) brTsön--Grüsyang-dag-byang-chub-kyi-yanlag = Vīryya-Sambodhyanga. (5) Virupaksha. (6) In Text-Khanda-Roha. (7) dGah-va-yang-dag-byang-chub-kyi-yanlag. = Priti-sambodhyanga. (8) sTobs-po-che. (9) hKorlohi-sugs-can-ma. (10) Sintu-sbyangspa-yang-dag-byang chub-kyi-yanlag—Prasrabdhi-sambodhyanga. (11) Rinchen-rDorje. (12) Dharma, Chös-rab-tu-rnam-par-hbyed-pa-yang-dag-byang - chub-kyi-yan-lag = Dharma-pravichaya-Sambodhyanga. (13) Hayagriva : rTa-mgrin. (14) In Text. (15) Dran-pa-yang-dag-pa-byang-chub-kyi-yan-lag—Smriti-sambodhyanga. (16)Nam-mKhahi-snyingpo.(17) hKhorlohi-go-chama. (18) bTang-snyoms-yang-dag-byang chub-kyi-yan-lag= Upeksha-Sambodhyanga. (19) Shintü-dpah-mo. (20) Samyag-drishti or Right belief=Yang-dag-pahi-lTa-va. (21) Padma-gargyi-dVang-phyug. (22) sTob-chen-ma. (23) Samyak-samkalpa or Right aim.=Yang-dag-pahi-rTog-pa. (24) rNampar-sNang-mZad. (25) hKhorlös-sGyurma. (26) Samyag—vāk ; Yang-dag-pahi-ngag. (27) rDorje-sems-dpah. (28) brTsön-hGrüs-chen-mo. (29) Samyak-Karmanta = Yang-dag pahi-las-kyi-mthah.

ma[1]; Right Living[2] represented by Wug-dong-ma[3]; Right Endeavour[4] represented by Khyi-dong-ma[5]; Right Mindfulness[6] represented by Phag-dong-ma[7]; and Right Meditation[8] represented by Pal-Heruka[9] and Dorje Phagmo[10].

The production of unborn meritorious acts is represented by Yamadhadi. The careful guarding of meritorious principles, when produced, is represented by Shin-jehi-Pho-nya-mo[11]; avoidance of irreligious principles which have been produced is represented by Shin-jehi-cheva-ma[12]; prevention of the birth of unborn religious acts is represented by Shin-je-Jom-ma[13].

Having uttered these let the Sādhaka remember all these Devatās are but symbols representing the various things which occur on the Path such as the helpful impulses and the stages attained by their means.

Should doubts arise as to the divinity of these Devatās, one should say " the Dākinī is only the recollection of the body " and remember that the Deities constitute the Path. One should meditate on the pure and sacred outer Mandala of the Nirmāna-kāya[14] as the first step on the Path. Thus

---

(1) Khva-gDong-maī : her mantra Kākāsye, etc. (2) Samyag-jīvanam; including right means of livelihood : Yang-dag-pahi-hTsho-va. (3) Hug-gDong-ma ; her mantra Hūluka-sye. (4) Samyag-vyāpāra or cheshtā=Yang-dag pahi-rTsol-va. (5) Khyi-gDong-ma ; her mantra Shvanāsye or Shvānamukkhī. (6) Samyak-smriti=Yangdag-pahi-dranpa. (7) Phag-gDong ma ; her mantra Shūkarāsye. (8) Samyag-dhyānam: Yang-dag-pahi-Ting-Nge-hdzin. (9) dPal-Heruka. (10) rDorje-Phagmo or Vajravārāhī. (11) gShin-rJehipho-nya-mo. (12) gShin-rJehi-mCheva-ma. (13) gShin—Je-hJoms-ma. (14) Sprul-pahi-sku=One of the three bodies of Buddha namely, Dharma-kāya the essential formless Bodhi which is true experience free of all error ; Sambhoga-kāya the reflected body of glory of the same ;

all who reside in such Mandala must be clearly brought before the mind. This mental movement, together with the lower and upper Vāyu [1] in motion, cause the Ham [2] sound at the crown of the head to hum, and the A-shaped [3] vital principle [4] to pass through the Sūkshma-nādi [5] where both the Vāyus meet in the heart and unite in one.

From the gradual combination of residence and residents [6] into one, vividly impressed upon the mind, there evolves the many-coloured Vajra [7] at the crown of the head. Meditate upon the heels as the Vajra foundation, the ribs as Vajra-fence, the skin as dome, ceiling cloth and curtains of Vajra and on the downy hair in the body as a net-work [8] of arrows. Think of the hair of the head and on the nails as a fence of divine magical fire protecting the whole. Think of the heels as being air, the trijunction [9] as fire, the stomach as water, the heart as earth, and the vertebral column as Mount Meru [10]. Think upon the head as being the upper portion (of Mount Meru). Imagine the body, one fathom in length and the same in breadth, to be the square-shaped Vihāra [11] of which the four doors are the four airs of the four elements issuing from the heart; the eyes to be the ornaments of the Vihāra; the legs its pillars.

Nirmāna-kāya the transformed body of the human Buddhas. The first is the essential, the second the reflected, and the third the practical aspects of the one Wisdom. See Foreword. (1) The Apāna Vāyu the seat of which is below the abdomen and the Prāna Vāyu which is above it in the region of the chest and throat. (2) The Mantra (3) The Akàra. (4) lTe-vahi-A-tshul. (5) dVūma. (6) rTen-dang-rTenpahi-dKyil—hKhor = the Mandala. (7) Sna-Tshogs-rdo-rje. (8) Mdah-hi-dra-va. (9) Possibly the junction (gsum-mdo) of Idā, Pinggalā and Sushumnā below the navel centre or the Mūlādhāra. (10) In Sanskrit the spine is called Merudanda, *i.e.*, Meru axis. (11) Temple-gZhal-yas-khang. The Text gives the head as the upper part of Meru.

Meditate upon the whole Mandala consisting of the residence and the " Hūm" which dwells in the heart as the Divine Heruka and His Consort as above explained.

Meditate upon His twelve hands as follows[1]:—The uppermost right hand—Mam, Khah-gro-ma.[2] The next uppermost right hand—Lam, Lama. The uppermost left hand—Pam, Khanda-rohe. The next uppermost left hand—Tam, Zug-chan-ma.[3]

The other eight hands as eight long Hūms.

Of these, the four right hands are the crow-faced, the owl-faced, the dog-faced and the sow-faced Dākinīs. The four left hands are (the female Devatās) Shin-je-Tan-ma[4] Pho-nyama [5], Cheva-ma [6], Jom-ma [7]; and in the twenty-four sacred places, including the crown of the head imagine the twenty-four letters, Pu, Jā, Ū, Ā, Go, Ra, De, Ma, Ka, Ō, Trī, Ko, Kā, Lā, Ka, He, Pre, Grī, Sō, Sū, Na, Si, Ma, Kū,[8] to be the twenty-four Vīras [9] and Yoginīs [10].

---

(1) Here the true signification of the Shrī Heruka's twelve hands is explained. (2) Khah-hgro-ma = Dākinī. (3) gZugs-chan-ma = Rūpinī. (4) gShin-r Je-brTan-ma, meaning the anvil or firm post of Yama. (5) Meaning messenger of Yama (Yamadūti). (6) mCheva-ma meaning fangs of Yama (Yama-danta). (7) hJoms-ma meaning Destructress. (8) These stand for the names of the twenty-four Sthānas given later. (9) dPah-vo. (The Heroes.) (10) rNal-hjormas. Vīras and Yoginīs are exalted Mahā-Siddhas worthy of special veneration. They have attained Siddhi through the four Vajra-sādhanās. The body is purified of gross material substance. Language is purified of all useless utterances and becomes efficacious Mantra. The thought is purged of the notions begotten of the contact of the internal senses and external objects displayed as likes and dislikes. Mind is tranquillised and filled with exalted clearness and wisdom. Thus is obtained the undecaying body, speech, mind and knowledge, Vajra-kāya, Vajra-vāk, Vajra-chitta, Vajra-jnāna (sku-rDorje, gSungs-rDorje, Thugs-rDorje, Yeshes-rDorje.) These are the four Vajras of the four Chakras. The Chakras are the beings and the Vajras are the results of the Siddhi obtained by them.

Thus (1) in Puliramalaya[1] (the crown of the head) reside Khanda-Kapali and Rabtu-Tummo[2]. (2) In Jālandhara, the centre of the crown—reside Mahākamkala[3] and Tumpahi-mig-chan-ma[4]. (3) in Udyāna, the right ear, reside Kamkala[5] and Wöd-Danma[6]. (4) In Arputa, the nape of the neck, reside Cheva-Nampar-tsig-pa[7] and Na-chen-ma[8]. These are the sacred places[9]. (5) In Godāvari, the left ear, reside Suravairi and Tan-pahi-lochan-ma[10]. (6) In Rameshvari, the spot between the eye-brows[11], reside Wöd-pag-me[12] and Miwa-Thūng-ma[13]. (7) In Devikota, the two eyes reside Dorje-yi-wöd[14] and Lang-kai-Wang-chugma[15]. (8). In Malava, the two shoulders reside Dorji-yi-sku[16] and Shing-dib-ma[17]. These are the secondary[18] sacred places. These belong to the blue Mandala of the mind which occupies the Heaven.

(9) In Kamarupa, the two arm-pits, reside Amkuri and Erapati. (10) In Otre, the two breasts, reside Dorje-Ralpachen[19] and Jigjed-chen-mo[20]. These four are the Realms[21].

(1) (In the Text) on the head = Spyivo—the crown of the head. (2) Rabtu-gTum-mo. (3) Sic: Kam-kala. (4) gTumpahi-mig-chan-ma. Her Mantra seems to be Om-Tsanda-akshi-ye-Hūm-Hūm Phat. (5) Sic: Kam-kala. (6) Hod-lDanma = Prabhāvatī. (7) mCheva-rNampar-gtsigs-spa = Grinning fangs. The Mantra seems to be: Om-Tra-sa-ya Tra-sa-ya Hūm-hūm-phat. (8) sNa-chen-ma = Big-nosed or She with big nose. Her Mantra: Om-Ksho-bha-ya, Ksho-bha-ya, Hūm hūm phat. (9) Sthānas = gnas. (10) brTtan pahi-bLo chan-ma = Vīra-mati. (11) What the Hindus call the Ājnā Chakra. (12) Hod-dpag-med whose Mantra is Om-Rhoum Rhoum, etc. (13) The dwarfish lady = Om kharba-ri-ye, etc. (14) rDorje-hi-höd = Vajra-Prabhā. The Mantra: Om-Rha, Rha Hūm Hūm, Phat. (15) Lang-kahi-dVang-chug-ma = Lankeshvarī. The Mantra in Text is: Om-Lankeshvarī ye, etc. (16) rDorje-hi-sku. Mantra: Om Phem, Phem, etc. (17) Shing-grib-ma. Mantra: Om Druma-Tshaye Hūm- Hūm-Phat. (18) Nye-vahi-gnas = Literally, "nearer." (19) rDorje-Ralpachan: Having mane of Vajra. The Mantra of this Devatā is: Om-da-ha-da-ha-hūm-hūm-phat. (20) hJigs-byed-chen-mo = The great Destructress. Mantra: Om Maha-Bhai-ra-vi-ye Hūm-Hūm-Phat. (21) Zhing = field = realm.

(11) In Trisha-kune, the naval, reside Pah-ho-chenpo[1] and Lungi-shug-chan-ma[2]. (12) In Kosala, the nose-tip, reside Dorje-hum-zad[3] and Chang-thung-ma[4]. These form the nearer realms of sacred places, second in importance. (13) In Kalinga, the mouth, reside Rabtu-Zangpo[5] and Shyama Devī. (14) In Lampaka, the neck, reside Dorje-Zangpo[6] and Shintu-Zangmo[7]. These are the warm regions[8]. (15) In Kantsi, the heart, reside Jig-Jed-chen-po[9] and Ta-na-ma[10]. (16) In Himalaya, the private abdominal regions which form the warm regions of the second grade, dwell Mig-mi-zang[11] and Khagana.

These belong to the red Mandala of speech.

(17) In Pretapuri, the sexual organs, dwell Tob-po-che[12] and Khorlohi-shug-chan-ma[13]. (18) In Grihadeva, the

---

(1) dPah-ho - chen-po = Mahā - vīra (Great hero). His Mantra : Om-Patsa-Patsa, etc. (2) rLungi-shugs-chan-ma. = "She who has the strength of the wind" whose Mantra is : Vāyu-bege-hūm, etc. (3) rDorje-Hūm -mdZad = Vajra-hūm-kāra. His Mantra : Om-Baksha-Baksha-basaru-dira-āntra-māla-balambi-ni-ye-hūm-hūm-phat. (4) Chang-hThung-ma = She who drinks wine. Om-sūra-bakshi-ye-Hūm-Hūm-Phat. (5) Rabtu-bZangpo = Very-good. His Mantra : Om-grihana-grihana-sapta-pātāla-gatāma-bhujanga sarvam-va-tapjāya-tapjāya. (6) rDorje-bZangpo = Vajra-Bhadra : The righteous or good Vajra. The Mantra is : Om-Ā-Katdya-Katdya. (7) Shintu-bZangmo. Whose mantra is = Om-sū-bhadre. (8) The body is likened to Jambudvīpa wherein are warm and cold places. Here the neck is said to be a warm region. (9) hJigs-byed-chenpo = The great Destroyer. Mantra is = Om-Rhini-Rhini-Hūm-Hūm-Phat. (10) rTa-sNa-ma = The horse-nosed lady. The Mantra Om-Jnyōm-Jnyom-Hūm-Hūm-Phat. (11) Migmi-bZang = Virupāksha. (12) sTobs-po-che = Very mighty (Mahābala). His Mantra seems to be : Om-Kshmām Hūm-phat. (13) hKhorlohi-shugs-chan-ma = She having the force of the wheel.

anus, dwell Rinchen-dorje[1] and Khanda Rohe. These are the junctions[2]. (19) In Suvarnadvīpa, the two calves of the legs, dwell Nam-khahi-Nyingpo[3] and Khorlohi Gochama[4]. These are the nearer (or secondary) junctions[5]. (20) In Sourakhta, the two thighs, dwell Tam-dim[6] and Shondini. These are the junctions[7]. (21) In Nagara, the sixteen fingers[8], reside Heruka and Shintu-Pah-mo[9]. (22) In Sindhu, the ankles, dwell Padma-gargyi-Wang-chug[10], and Tob-chen-ma[11]. These are the cremation grounds[12]. (23) In Maro, the four thumbs[13], dwell Vairochana[14] and Korlohi-gyurma[15]. (24) In Kuluta, the two knees, dwell Vajra-Sattva[16] and Tson-Dubs-chen-mo[17]. These are the nearer cremation grounds of the second order. These occupy the whole Mandala of the body beneath the surface of the earth. The nature of these Devatās have been above described.

Having thus vividly brought the outer and inner Deities before the mind, repeat the Mantra *Om* and think that the outer and inner Chakras, the Nirmānakāyas, the Sambhogakāyas, which make the four Chakras, and those (mentioned hereunder) are vividly present and inseparably

---

(1) Rinchen-rDorje = Ratna-vajra, Precious Vajra. (2) hDu-va. (3) Nam-mKhahi-sNingpo = Akāsha-garbha. (4) hKhorlohi-gochama = She wearing the armour of the wheel. Om-cakra varmīnī-ye-Hūm-Hūm-Phat. (5) Nyevahi hDu-va. (6) rTamgriṇ = Hayagrīva. (7) hDu-va. (8) Sormo-bcu-drug. That is, fingers and toes excluding thumbs and big toes. (9) Shintu-dPah-mo. The great heroine. (10) Padma-gargyi-dVang-phyug = Padma Natakeshvara, Lord of Dancers. (11) sTob-chen-ma = Mahābalā or Lady of great strength. Her Mantra is: Om Mahābale Hūm Hūm Phat. (12) Dur-khröd. (13) That is, two thumbs and big toes. (14) rNampar-sNang-mdZad = Vairochana. (15) hKorlohi-sGyurma = She who turns the wheel or rules. (Om-cakra Vartinī ye-Hūm-Hūm-Phat.) (16) The heroic Vajra mind = rDor-rje-semsdPah. (Om-Dhili Dhi-li-ye.) (17) bTson-hGrus-chen-mo = She of great perseverance. The Mantra is: Om-Mahā-vīrye-Hūm-Hūm-Phat.

one. Similarly when repeating the Mantra " A " one should meditate upon the four-fold Mandala of speech (Vāk) ; and when repeating Hūm one should think of the four-fold Mandala of the mind (Chitta).

Then repeating Sarva-vīra-yoginī one should think of the twenty-five heroes (Vīra) and of the thirty-seven Yoginīs. Repeat " Kāya " (Body) thinking of the Body of all. Repeat " Vāk " (Speech) thinking of the Speech of all. Repeat " Chitta " (Mind) thinking of the Mind of all, and that these are inseparable the one from the other. After thus meditating well say—" Om-vajra-svabhāva ātmakoham[1]," thinking at the same time that all the above are of the nature of Vajra[2]. Then repeat—Om vajra-shuddha-sarva-dharma-vajra shuddhoham [3]—and think " every thing is of the nature of the pure, indestructible (Vajra-like) Shūnyatā and that is Myself[4]." Repeat this three times (with thought clearly fixed).

This is the first branch[5], when one meditates on the sacred word[6], by which one obtains the Sambhoga-kāya through the physical body owing to its development by the grace and power of the Mantra[7]. Lord Naropa has said that the imagined Devatā and Mandala should be absorbed into the Devotee's self, that one may thus clearly understand their true nature. But [8] in the Tantras it is

---

(1) " I am of the true nature of Vajra." (2) That is Body, Speech and Mind are manifestations of Vajra. (3) I am pure Vajra ; that pure Vajra which all things are. (4) Thams-cad-kyang sTong-pa-nyid-rdo-rje-hi-Rang-bZhin-du-rNam-par-Dag-pahi-Ngovo-bDag-yin sNyampa-lan-gSūm-dū-Bya-ho. Everything is in the nature of the Pure Void which is the real nature of the Sādhaka himself. (5) That is the first process in the course of this devotional exercise. (6) By the Japa of which the body is divinised. (7) At first one is only aware of the physical body. This by Sādhanā is transformed into Sambhogakāya. (8) Indicating some difference of technical detail.

said " Having mastered the two armours[1] think particularly of the Divine Chakra. Having mastered the combination of Mantras and symbols, quickly enter into the Chakra of devotion[2]. Thus it is said and in the Guru Lohipa's works also the same is said. By that it is meant that in those portions called Sthānas[3], meditation is made on lunar thrones[4] upon which the white letters "Om-Ha[5] " are placed.

On the head is the Mantra " Nama-hi[6] " the letters of which are yellow and represent Vairochana. On the crown of the head are the red letters " Sa Ha Hu " representing Padma-Gargyi-Wang-chuk[7]. On the two shoulders are the black letters Pou-khat-he[8] representing the black Heruka. In the two eyes are the orange letters Hum, Hum, Ho which represent Dorje-Nyima. In all the limbs are the green letters Phat-Ham which represent the green Hayagrīva.

The above constitute the armour of the Vīra the male Deity.

---

(1) The clear vivid mental pictures of the various letters in the various parts of the body, representing the male and female Devatās, are the armours which render the Sādhaka unassailable. (2) Damtshig-hKorlo: Bhakti-chakra which is essentially the Sādhaka's own personality meditated upon as Devatā as contrasted with the Yeshes-hKhorlo, the Chakra of knowledge meditated upon as being without. The Devotee imagines his own body to be the Mandala included in the chief Devatā. This is the Bhakti-chakra. Next he imagines a Jnāna-chakra without himself of Devatās who are worshipped with obeisance and offerings by the Bhakti-chakra and finally the former is absorbed into the latter. (3) The sacred places which are the heart, etc. (4) The white basis on which the Devatā or Mantra rests. The colour of the seat of the Devatā indicates whether it is solar or lunar, the former being an orange-coloured disk. (5) = Vajrasattva. (6) In Text Nama-hi. *quære* namah (7) Padma-gargyi-dVang-phyug. (8) Bīja Mantras.

In the navel are the red letters Om-Vam which represent Vajra-Vārāhī.[1] In the heart are the blue letters Ham-Yom which stand for Shin-je-ma.[2] In the mouth are the white Hrim-Mom representing Mong-jed-ma.[3] In the head are the yellow Hrim Hrim standing for Kyöd-jed-ma.[4] On the crown of the head are the green " Hūm Hūm " standing for Tag-jed-ma.[5] In all the limbs are the smoky coloured " Phat Phat " standing for Chandikā.

Then think that the Male and the Female are inseparably one and not two, and know that meditation on the letters of the Mantras as different Devatās is merely for the sake of clearly defining the armour[6] which consists of different Devatās. This is the second branch (of the process of meditation). Then making with the hands on the forehead the sign of the flaming gem[7] and turning the hands round[8] say " Phem "[9], imagining that the Hūm in the heart emits rays whereby worship[10] is done of the whole self-existing conclave of Devatās consisting of the Buddhas surrounded by the Bodhisattvas who

---

(1) rDorje-Phagmo. Here the armour of the female Devatā commences. (2) gShin-rJe-ma = Yamī. (3) rMongs-byed-ma = The stupefier. (4) bsKyod-byed-ma = She who causes movements. (5) Skrag-byed-ma = She who frightens. (6) It is called Armour because meditation on the Bījas of the Devatās on the different parts of the body protects it from the attacks of Māra. The feeling of exaltation with which it is endowed by such exercise fortifies it against the temptation to abuse the body or to employ it in wicked and unworthy actions. (7) That is the jewel Chintāmani mentioned in the Tantras. (8) This is called the Mani Mudrā (Norbuhi-phyag-rgya). Put the thumbs and first two fingers together and turn them in a circle going left to right over the head. (9) A Bīja mantra. (10) The Sādhaka imagines the "Hūm" in the heart. The Hūm emits Rays. These are the objects with which worship is done. These rays are Rays of adoration. They vibrate and cause answering vibrations of compassion and love to vibrate back to the Sādhaka from the Jnāna-chakra Devatās.

are brought to mind as being in the Heavens which are in front of the worshipper.

Then say " Ja, Hum, Bam,[1] Ho " and think that all the Devatās are absorbed into oneself. Repeat Om yoga-shuddha-sarva-dharma-yoga-shuddhoham. (I am pure through that Yoga which purifies all things.)

In saying this mantra the worshipper should think that the Devatās and himself are inseparably (indivisibly) one and not two. This is the third Branch (of the meditative process).

Again after invoking the sixty-two Devatās constituting the Mandala surrounded by Buddhas, Bodhisattvas, Krodha-devas and Krodha-devīs,[2] all surrounded by hosts of countless worshipping Devīs, worship them as before and pray that all the Tathāgatas [3] may grant you power.

Imagine then that the Devatās utter this verse :—

" Just as the Buddha was born
All the Devatās bathed him with holy water."
So with holy celestial water
Do I also confer Power on thee.

Think then that the Devatā says the mantra " Om sarva-tathāgata abishekha-samaye[4] Shrī Hūm." (Om let there be all auspiciousness at the time of the sprinkling given by all Tathāgatas, Hūm.)

---

(1) Come, be present, stay, Ho (interjection). (2) Terrific male and female Devatās (Khrovo-dang-Khromo). (3) Those who had " gone before." That is the Buddhas of which varying numbers are given and who preceded the Buddha Sakya Muni. He who has gone the same way, *e.g.*, as the previous Buddhas have gone, and future Buddhas will go. (4) In text it runs. Om-sarva-Tathā-gata-abhi-kshe-kata-samaya-Shri-Hūm.

Repeating the above let him think that the Tathāgatas have conferred the power, amidst auspicious songs and hymns. Imagine that worship is offered and all evil Spirits are exorcised. Then think that the holy and divine water fills the whole body and cleanses it of all impurities and that then the remainder of the water surges up to the crown of the head, where it becomes the five chief blissful Devatās[1] of the five orders;[2] and then that all the divinities of devotion are embodied in Buddha Vajrasattva; in the Mandala of the mind Akshobhya; in the Mandala of speech Amitābha; in the Mandala of the body Vairochana.[2] This is the fourth Branch (of the process) wherein the seals of the chiefs of the orders are set impressively.[3]

This is how the meditation is done in detail. Having clearly defined the above Devatās in detail the Devotee should repeat the refuge formula and the good-wishes formula.[4] Having meditated upon the three joys[5] and the full conclave of the protecting Mandala let him think that his Guru, or at least his two hands, are held over his head and that the Guru embodies

---

(1) That is Vajra (Vajra sattva: rDorje-Sems-dPah). Ratna (Ratnasambhava: Rinchen-hByun-gNaś). Padma (Amitābha: sNang-va-mThah-yas). Karma: Dön-yöd-Grub-pa (Amogha-siddhi). Dharma (Vairochana; rNampar-sNang-mdZad.) (2) These five Dhyāni Buddhas personify each onc of the Yeshes (Jnāna) of a Perfect Buddha—thus Vajra, the mirror-like wisdom: Ratna, the equalising wisdom: Padma, the distinguishing wisdom: Karma, the wisdom which accomplishes all works: and Dharma, the Dharmadhātu. (3) That is where the Chiefs are clearly defined in imagination. (4) I take refuge in the Buddha-Dharma and the Sangha (the best of all assemblies) until I obtain trained perfection. May all the good that I do enable me to obtain Buddhahood for the benefit of sentient beings. (5) Meditation on the ordinary body as the spiritual body of the Devatā; on the speech as Mantra; on the mind as the compassionate mind of the Devatā.

in himself all the virtues of the three gems (Triratna).[1] Then exerting to his utmost his faith let him think that the Guru's body has been absorbed in his own whereby the person of the devotee becomes the same as that of the Guru. This is the middle course of meditation (neither too brief nor too detailed).

The shortest method is that in which the worshipper without meditating on the protective Chakra at once sets to meditate upon the inner Mandala only; and, without binding himself with the armour above described, recites the Mantras which confer blessings upon the Mandalas.

This is the method wherein one meditates upon oneself as Buddha.[2] Then worship the Buddha with the prescribed Mantras, external ritual, nectar,[3] pleasures[4] and mental products[5] and, chanting the two verses of eight feet,[6] fix the mind on the apparent yet unsubstantial[7] forms of the Devatās of the Mandala and put oneself into the quiescent state.

Then, according to the four kinds of effects desired[8] one imagines that the Mantras assume the under

(1) Buddha, his word, and the assembly. (2) Worship the self as Buddha. (3) Wine which is offered is nectar. (4) All that pleases and gratifies the senses, etc., scents for the nose, form for the eye, praise for the mind, etc. (5) Meru, the four continents, and eight continents. All which is mentioned, amounting to thirty-seven, is imagined as offerings to the self as Buddha. (6) Given in another book the bDe-mchog mChod-hPhreng. (7) dKyil-hKhor-gyi-sKu-snang-la-rang bzhin med-pa-la-yid-gtad-de-sems-mayeng-par gzhag-go. The bodies of the Devatās of the Mandala, though visible, have no reality (or natural existence = rang-bzhins) in themselves. Fix the mind on that fact and put the mind in the quiescent state. (8) That is, Peaceful (Zhiva. Shānti = Health, long life and good fortune), Grand (rgyaspa = Pushti = followers, name, fame and wealth), Fascinating (dvangva = vashī-karana = love and influence), and Destructive (dragpo = mārana = power to destroy or hurt).

mentioned colours and shapes as they issue from the seed-mantra (Bīja) in the hearts of the Devatās. (1) For peaceful results the Mantras issue in a dazzling white string shooting forth with the speed of arrows.[1] (2) For grand results the Mantras, assuming a bright yellow-colour and the shape of bunches of feathers, go forth and along with a whirling motion.[2] (3) For fascinating effects the Mantras appear in colour to be red and in shape linked together like a chain.[3] (4) For destructive effects the Mantras are black in colour and in a line like a spinning thread darting with a quick motion.[4]

In each case the colours must be like that of the Devatās themselves and bright and glorious.

The rosary of Mantra-letters[5] is produced from the seed-mantras (Bīja) of the male and female Deities issuing from their mouths and re-entering the male and female organs of the male and female Devatās, thus passing up in a circle to the Bījas in their hearts.

---

(1) In the first imagine oneself to be the Devatā with the Bīja-Mantra vividly seen in the heart. This is not seen flat like a written letter but upright like a flame. The Bīja gradually shines brighter and shoots out rays of white Mantras in a fine line so swiftly as to be like an arrow. These also are each separate upright figures. The rays shot forth from the Sādhaka's Mantra-chakra, excite the Jnāna Devatā's Mantra-chakra which also throws back similar white rays which, shining on the Sādhaka, purify him and being thus freed of evil Karmic results endow him with health, life and good fortune. (2) Similar observations apply here, only the rays are yellow, form bunches and produce a different result. (3) In Vashī-karana the rays are red and in links like a chain. For in Vashī-karana one imagines oneself as binding up the beings whom one wishes to fascinate and overpower. (4) The rays are black and shoot with a spinning motion. In all the cases the colours are not the ordinary ones but as the text says celestial, that is, something extraordinarily bright and luminous. (5) That is, the Mantras previously described.

The Mantras are :—

(1) Om Shrī-vajra-He-He-Rū-Rū-Kam-Hūm-Hūm-Phat. (2) Dākinī-Jala-Sambhāra[1] Svāhā. (3) Om Vajra-Vairocāni-Ye-Hūm-Hūm-Phat Svāhā. (4) Om Hri-Ha-Ha-Hūm-Hūm-Phat. (5) Om Sarva-Buddha-Dākinī-Ye ; Vajra-Varnani-Ye-Hūm-Hūm-Phat-Svāhā.

These are the chief Mantras of the male and female Devatās and their secondary Mantras. Thirty thousand essential Mantras of both the chief male and female Devatās, five thousand five hundred for each of the twelve Yoginīs, and twenty thousand for each of the Devatās of the three Chakras should be recited.

This renders one competent and capable to engage in the various duties[2] of this Mandala. This is the productive[3] stage wherein Mantras are recited (and the mind is engaged in meditation on certain objects).

Should one then wish to meditate in the advanced stage let him contemplate as follows :—

Imagine in one's navel a white eight-petalled lotus. In the centre of this white lotus is a lunar disc. Upon this disc there are the forms of Vajra-sattva[4] and His Spouse[5] in close embrace,[6] the Mantra Hūm being in their hearts.

---

(1) *Quaere.* In text Sam-Vara. (2) The general meaning is that the Sādhaka may henceforth without the assistance of his Guru perform the rites, periodical Pūjās, and perhaps confer the initiation to others or receive Chelas. (3) bsKyed-rim or bskyed-pahi-rimpa ; the stage where the mind produces pictures of Devatās, Mantras and actions, and concentrates itself upon these. 'Productive' refers to the producing of the pictures, etc., etc., which are the "objects." This term is used relatively to the other and final process of meditation, which is called rDzogs-rim (dJog-rim), perfecting or completing stage, which consists in resolving all the mental pictures of objects into Shūnyatā (the void). (4) rDorje-Semspah. (5) rDorje-sNyems-ma. (6) To indicate—

Then imagine that rays of light issue from the "Hūm" in all directions, vividly defining in the mind both the chief Devatā and the surrounding space as the vessel, and the other Devatās and Beings occupying it as the vessel's content. Fix the attention on this mental picture. Then imagine that the rays of light emitted from the "Hūm" excite all these into activity. The process is like that of a magnet exciting movement of particles of iron dust (filings). Then as the rays are gradually drawn back imagine that all the external space and its contents are drawn inwards and absorbed into the form of the principal external Deity (Heruka and His consort). This process is likened to the absorption of mercury by cow-dung. Next of the two principal Devatās the female is absorbed in the male and the two into one face and two hands. This process is likened to that of a tortoise contracting its limbs.[1]

Then the consort of the external Heruka is absorbed in the male and this into Vajra-sattva in the navel. The consort of this Deity, too, sinks into the male. Then gradually the male figure itself sinks back into the "Hūm" in the heart and the "Hūm" gradually resolves itself into the Bindu.[2] This process is likened to that of meteoric lights dissolving into each other. Then finally even the Bindu itself gradually becomes fainter and fainter until it fades away and disappears altogether; a process which is likened to salt dissolving in water. Such are the five principal processes of meditation illustrated by what are called the five radical similies.

---

their inseparable union. (1) A well known Indian simile applied to Mūlaprakriti and the extension of its Vikriti. (2) Thigle: the point such as the Anusvāra breathing.

In the uncurtailed or unabridged process the mental pictures[1] are like dresses, light rays, waves of water; but in themselves and according to their own true nature they are like dancers, the sun and ocean.[2] The final process of absorption and absence of all thoughts is likened to that of a bubble sinking back into water, or a rainbow melting away into the skies.

So the process is illustrated in various manners by various similies.

Finally the keeping of the mind in a state of tranquillity devoid of objects is called the process of concentration on Vajra-sattva.[3]

Again[4] imagine a four-petalled lotus in the navel, the petals of which, going leftward from the East, are earth and air; on the North water and air; on the West fire and air and on the South air and air; represented by the yellow La, white Va, red Ra, and green Ya[5] respectively. In the centre think of a blue-point as standing for the ether.[6] Having visualised[7] these clearly, next imagine that when you are breathing outward a ray of light as thick as a medium-sized thread issues outwards from La through the left nostril going to a distance of sixteen finger

---

(1) sNang-va = that which appears = that which is visible. (2) That is, the dancers put on and off the dress. The sun emits and withdraws its rays of light. The ocean throws up waves which again sink into it. (3) Dorje-Sems-dPah. De-ltar-mi-rtog-pahi-ngang-la-mnyam par-bzhag pa-ni-rDorje-Semsdpah-bsDu-vaho. The putting of the mind in quiescence is the concentration or contraction on Vajra-sattva because the mental image of Vajra-sattva is made to dissolve into Shūnyatā or the Void. (4) Here follows concentration on Mantras and the Bindu (the shape of which is a point). (5) Here are the Bīja Mantras of earth, water, fire and air. (6) Literally "air of the skies." (7) Literally "having brought these clearly and vividly before the mind's eye."

breadths[1], and again when re-entering sinking into the La thus making a pair of breaths.[2] Then with constant meditation the imagined ray of Light assumes a misty appearance.[3] When this happens sink the La into the Va.[4] Then imagine that a white ray issues from the Va, and proceed as aforementioned until one sees the image or reflection.[5] When this happens sink the Va into the Ra and meditate as abovementioned changing the colour of the ray from white to red which issues and re-enters Ra until the ray is seen as a firefly.[6] When this happens sink the Ra into the Ya. Then follow the same process with a green ray of light until one sees a burning altar lamp.[7] When this is seen sink the Ya into the blue point in the centre. Then drop meditation on the rays, their issue and re-entrance, and concentrate the mind on the blue point itself and meditate upon these two-fold airs until the sign of a cloudless sky is seen. This is the wisdom of the path of vision.[8] This is concentration on letters (Mantras). Thinking that all these letters are really the point (Bindu) and meditating as aforementioned is called concentration on the Point. It is necessary to concentrate the mind on

---

(1) Anguli; sormo. (2) Literally "airs." (3) Assumes a misty appearance or "sees the sign of smoke" is the literal meaning of the text. The imagined line of yellow light begins to appear smoky or misty; (4) That is earth into water, the Bhūta next above it. (5) sMig-rGyu is the Tibetan word meaning an optical illusion, visionary mirage, also reflection. The reflection must be of the white ray of light issuing from Va. The reflection or mirage-like appearance of a bright white ring would be a sign of having reached a certain point in the meditation where one has to change. (6) Literally "sees the sign of firefly." (7) Literally "until one sees the sign of a burning ghee-lamp," that is such a lamp as is used for an altar lamp. (8) mThong-vahi-lam = Drishti-mārga.

Dorjesempa at the conclusion of every mental exercise of the productive meditation.[1]

The two latter processes may be practised according to one's own faith.[2] Thus it has been said. This is called the final or perfect stage where the Yogī practises the putting of the mind into the quiescent state.

Then meditate on one's self as embodying the united Deities Shrī Heruka and His consort suddenly issuing from the midst of the Void (Shūnyatâ). In Their heart is the "Hūm" from which rays of light issue and resolve themselves into the Deities of the outer and inner Mandalas. Having fixed these vividly in your mind then imagine that your own teeth and nails are Khanda-Kapali, that the hairs of the head and the body are Mahakamkala ;[3] that the skin and the sweat thereon is Kamkala ; that the flesh is Cheva-Nampar-tsigspa ;[4] that the arteries and tendons are Suravaeri ;[5] that the bones are Wöd-pa-me ;[6] that the kidneys are Dorje-yi-wöd ;[7] that the heart is Dorje-yi-sku ;[8] that the eyes are Amkuri ; that the bile is Dorje-yi-ralpachen ;[9] that the lungs are Pawo-chempo ;[10] that the intestines are Dorje-hum-zad;[11] that the great gut is Dorje-zangpo ;[12] that

---

(1) Productive meditation or the "Creative Stage" (bsKyed-rims) literally.— It means the state in which the mind produces or creates pictures of the Devatās, etc., etc. (2) 'According to one's faith' or 'as one believes.' This is ambiguous. It may mean, 'as earnestly as possible,' or it may mean, 'according to the special teaching inculcated by one's special line of Gurus' ; probably the former. (3) In text Maha-Kamkala and Kam-Kala. (4) mCheva-rNampar-gTsigspa (He who shows his fangs with a terrible grin). (5) Sic. (6) Höd-dPag-Med ; Amitābha. (7) rDorje-hi-Hod ; "lustre of Vajra." (8) rDorje-hi-sku—"body of Vajra." (9) rDorje-hi-Ralpachen "Having Vajra-mane." (10) dPah-vo-Chenpo. "The great Hero" Mahāvīra. (11) rDorje-Hum-mdZad.—Vajra Hūngkāra. (12) rDorje-bZangpo—Vajrabhadra.

the bladders are Jig-jed-chenpo;[1] that the secret parts between the thighs are Mig-mi-zang;[2] that the phlegm is Tob-po-che;[3] that the mucus is Vajraratna;[4] that the blood is Hayagriva;[5] that the perspiration is Dorje-rinchen;[6] that the fat is Vajra Heruka;[7] that the liver is Padma-gargyi-Wang-chyug;[8] that the spittle is Vairochana;[9] that the rheum[10] is Vajra-sattva.[11] Having so imagined then proceed as follows.[12]

Meditate on the teeth and nails as being adorned with the Mantra " Om Kara-Kara Hūm Hūm Phat " whereby all which compose them[13] become identified with the Vīras and the dependents thereon are the twenty-four Yoginīs. The Mūla-mantra of the Male Deity becomes on repetition, the Heruka adorned with the six bone ornaments which are symbols for the six Kulas.[14] On repeating Om Ha and so forth they become the six ornaments including the wheel and so forth. These are for the six Vīras.[15] The Mūla-mantra of the Yoginīs[16] becomes the necklace adorned Vajra-Varāhī.[17] The principal mantras[18] of the

(1) hJigs-byed-chenpo " the great Destroyer." (2) Mig-mi-bZang—Virupaksha (slanting eyed). (3) sTob-po-che=Mahābala. (4) Rinchen-rDo-rje=Vajra-Ratna. (5) rTa-mGrin Tamdin. (6) (Akāshagarbha—Nam-mKhah-hi sNyingpo). (7) rDorje Heruka. (8) Padma-Gargyi-dVang-phyug=Padma-nateshvara. (9) rNampar-SNang-mdZad. (10) Nasal excretion. (Snabs—the running humour from the nose.) (11) rDorje-Sems-dPah. (12) Here follow Mantras for different parts of the body. (13) That is those above enumerated which constitute the person's personality. (14) Here Lokas—(Rigs-drug=six kinds of beings, meaning here the six lokas of the universe or the five Dhyāni Buddhas with Vajradhara as the sixth.) (15) That is Heroes (dPah-vo). (16) Heroines (dPahmo also called rNalhbyor-ma.) (17) rDorje-Phagmo. (18) Mantras are of four kinds, namely, Sabön or Bīja; sTsa-sNgags or Mūla-mantras; Snyingpo or Hridaya; that is seed, root and (primary) principal. There are also secondary principal (Nye-sNying). Of these the first are generally single syllables or letters; the second long; the third conveniently short and

male Deity form the garland of human heads; and the secondary mantras[1] form the ear ornaments. The heart mantras[1] of the female Deity form the Elephant and Tiger skins. From the Mantras " Om Vam " and so forth, springs a waist girdle formed by the six Yoginīs. The Mūla-mantra of the chief female Deity and of the thirty Heroines form the weapons and other emblems and the four skulls[2] in the four intervening directions (S-E, S-W, N-E, N-W). Let the female Deity's secondary mantra[3] form the tiara for Her head, and let it be thought of as being in fact the (surrounding) Deities. The long vajra-mounted staff is the body[4] of the Deity. The sound of the drum (Damaru) is His wisdom.[5] During the day it is Bhagavān Vajra-dhara[6] and at night it is the Yoginī.[7] Call these clearly to mind and then repeat the armours of the Vīras and Yoginīs as well as their mantras of worship. Then imagine that the Devatās sink each into His or Her own respective place. By this protection is gained for oneself.

Having so done then repeat the Sumbhani[8] Mantra above given and make secure all the directions. Then

---

used in Japa in the Sādhanā of a Devatā whose Mantra it is. The fourth is generally short and is the Mantra of the surrounding (āvarana) Devatās which are around the chief Devatā. (1) See *ante*, p. 59, note, 18. (2) or Kapāla. (3) The secondary essential Mantras of the female Devatā form the tiara of skulls for Her head. They are the surrounding Devatās (female) and the Mantras themselves personified. (4) Lhahi-sku, that is the person of the Divinity. (5) Prajnā (in text Shes-rab). (6) lCom-lDan-rDorje-hchhang. (7) The Sādhaka should imagine himself to be the male Devatā by day and as the female Devatā by night. It may also mean that the competent Guru may expound male Devatā texts by day and female Devatā texts by night. (8) The Mantra is " Om Sumbhani Sumbha Hūm Hūm Phat." From this the Eastern and zenith door-keepers are produced, namely, Kaka-sye and Khanda Rohe; from " Om-grihana grihana Hūm Hūm Phat " meditate on oneself and every visible object as constituting the Deity and His Mandala and on every audible sound to be Mantra and lastly upon every thought of the mind as a miraculous display of the great Divine Wisdom.[1] Then repeat " Hūm " and the eight-syllabled Mantra of the Male Devatā. Then having said " Hūm " and sanctified all with Mantra, every object of enjoyment[2] should be enjoyed without either undue relish and attachment or disgust. Every visible object is to be regarded as a Deity whose real nature is Shūnyatā. Then both are always united. And in recollection of the union[3] one should preach, read, recite, and listen to religious discourses and books; and make water-ablutions,[4] Stupas, Chaityas, ceremonies for the consecration of such, and Hōmas.

In short every one should be incessantly engaged in doing what is of spiritual benefit for oneself and others, and which will of a surety help one in the path. This is the

---

comes Ulluka-sye keeper of the northern gate; from " Om Grihana-paya-grihana-paya Hūm Hūm Phat " issues the western door-keeper Shvana-sye and the guardian of the Nadir Khanda-rohe. From " Om anaya-ho-Bhagavān-Vajra-raja-Hūm-Hūm Phat " issues the warden of the southern gate—Sukara-sye; and so on for all the ten directions. (1) Sems-Kyi-rTog-pahi-hDu-hPhro-thams-cad-yeshes-chenpo—hi-cho-hPhrül-du-bsGoms-nas. The divine wisdom (yeshes-chenpo) is embodied in the chief Devatā invoked here and is the Dharmakāya wisdom. (2) Probably the food and other offerings on the altar. (3) Thams-cad-du-sNang-va-Lhahi- rNampa - dang-Rang- bZhin - sTong-pa - dang, gNyis-Ka hang-zung-hJug-tu-shes-pahi-Ngang-las; that is whilst conscious of the union of forms and Shūnyatā the Sādhaka should, etc. (4) Every pious Lama makes a gift of water to the ghosts (Pretas) every morning as these suffer from hunger and thirst, particularly the latter. A Lama pronouncing mantra on the water so given makes it available for, and enjoyable to, them. Otherwise the water which seems to us pure would appear to them as dirty, muddy, with blood, pus, and rotting organisms in it and therefore they could not use it.

Yoga of the conduct Path.[1] Then having recited the Sumbhani Mantra on the offerings [2] which have been laid on the altar and censed them with spiritual incense[3] and having transformed them into the Void (Shūnyatā) by the Svabhāva Mantra, imagine that from the midst of the Void springs forth the Mantra " Yam " from which comes air ;[4] and " Ram " from which comes fire ; and upon these is a skull as extensive as the firmament springing from the letter " A ".[5] Inside this skull again imagine another A from which issues a lunar disc. Upon this latter (disc) place (working from left to right) the letters Go for beef in the centre, Ku in the East for dog-flesh, Da in the South for horse-flesh, Ha in the West for Elephant-flesh, and Na in the North for human-flesh.[6] On these again imagine the letters Bi, Mu, Shu, Ma, Ra (placed in the same order as above beginning with " Bi " in the centre), which stand for excreta, urine, semen and human-flesh and blood respectively.[7] Then upon these imagine the Mantras " Hūm, Bhrūm Am, Dzrim Kham " which respectively represent the Dharmadhātu[8]

---

(1) Yoga of the Chārya Path = Spyod-lam-gyi-rNal-hByor : Spyodlam = Chārya-mārga or Path of conduct or practice or enjoyment: rNal-hByor = Yoga = or finding of resting place or Finding Rest or Peace. (2) Such as rice, cakes, fruit, wine and meat. (3) By means of the Mantras. " Om Sumbhani" is recited whilst the real fumigation is being done with incense (Dhūpa) and the Svabhāva Mantra transforms the material offerings into Shūnyatā. (4) " Yam " is the Bīja of air (Vāyu). (5) The rounded sphere of universal space appears and is filled with the first sound A which stands for speech which manifests knowledge. (6) These are the five uneatable meats ; " essence of human flesh " (sha-chen-gyi-dangs-ma) the best essence of great flesh (Mahā-māngsa) that is human flesh. (7) These stand for the Sanskrit words for excreta, etc. (8) Chos-kyi-dVyings.

Mirror-like[1], Equalising[2], Distinguishing[3] and All-powerful[4] aspects of the Divine Wisdom.[5]

Then on the top of these imagine a dazzling white "Om" in an inverted position and upon that again another "A" from which comes a Lunar Disc. On this there is a "Hūm" which transforms into a four-headed Vajra of four different colours bearing in the centre a Hūm. This Hūm emits rays downwards which excite and set the air in motion which causes fire to blaze up, thus making the above ingredients melt and boil. The steam from this rises upward causing the "Om" and the Lunar Disc and the vari-coloured Vajra to drip nectar and emit rays of light. These rays and steam fill the ten directions with glorious rays of light which attract the Tathāgatas and cause them to send down from their hearts, skulls[6] filled with the nectar of knowledge. These skulls along with the varied-coloured Vajra the "Om" and the Lunar Disc are absorbed in the rice-cake which then assumes a glorious colour, emits a delicious fragrance and is of a delicious taste besides possessing other untold virtues. It then becomes an immense ocean of nectar. Having imagined all these, repeat the Mantra "Om, A, Hūm, Ha, Ho, Hri" several times and bless the offerings with them. Then bring vividly to view in the heavens fronting you all the sixty-two Devatās[7] with their mansions of residence as afore-described; and imagine that the Chief Devatā emits rays from the Hūm in His heart which fall upon (and thus light up) the eight cemeteries.

---

(1) Melong-lta-bu. (2) mNyam-pa-nyid. (3 Sosor-rTog-pa. (4) Bya-va-Grub-pahi Yeshes. (5) See *ante*, pp. 4,5, notes. (6) Tantrik offerings (particularly wine) are made in skulls which denote and remind one of the transiency of forms and symbolise the Dharmakāya which, like the skull, is the basis on which the rest (flesh, skin, hair, etc. are and from which they proceed. (7) They are the 25 Vīras, and the 37 Dākinīs or Yoginīs.

These eight then resolve themselves into eight perfect Mandalas consisting of mansions and their residents. Then all the Devatās become the same as the Chief Devatā.[1]

They emit rays of light from their mouths and drink of the nectar through the tubes of these rays. Having imagined all this, join the hands with open palms and repeat the following Mantras :—" Om Vajra, Araliho Dza, Hūm Vam, Ho, Om, A, Hūm, Ho, Vajra-Dākini Samaya-stvam Drikshya.[2]

These must be repeated as many times as there are Devatās (*i.e.*, 62 times) or according to the number of Chakras (eight). Also make offerings, reciting the Mantras of the twenty-four Vīras, and worship with every imaginable object created by the mind whether external or internal. Then praise the Devatās by repeating twice over the verses of eight feet[3] and pray for whatever you wish. Finally repeat the Mantras of a hundred letters and pray for forgiveness of all errors and sins. Then say Vajra-Mū and entreat the worshipped Devatās[4] to go, and then absorb the worshipping Devatās into your own self.[5] Give offerings to the Laukika Devatās[6] by repeating the general

(1) This means that all the Devatās become one in nature—they are Wisdom Yeshes-pa. (2) *Sic* in text. (3) This shloka of praise is not in this text, but is given in another. (4) The Devatās invoked for worship (Yeshes-pa). (5) The Devatā whom the worshipper has imagined himself to be is the Bhakta or Dam-tschig-pa. The Sādhaka imagines his own body to be a conclave of Devatās called Bhakta Devatās who keep and guard the rules and faith ; in short the faith of the Sādhaka personified as Devatā. From their heads, fore-heads and throats they emit rays which create similar Devatās in the heavens fronting them. These are the worshipped Devatās (Jnāna or Yeshes Devatā). These are entreated to pass away into the region of External Shūnyāta ; whilst the former are drawn into the Inner Shūnyāta of the mind. (6) hJig-rtenpa : that is of the world such as Brahmā, Lokapālas and all others who have not attained the Akanishta Realms. But such Devatās as Vajra-Vārāhī and His Consort, Tārā, etc., are Lokottara=beyond Sangsāra, and in the Akanishta Heavens.

Mantra of the Dākinī. This is the Yoga relating to the rice-cake offerings.[1]

Then again bless the foods. In the same way, as already done in the case of the rice-cake, imagine the self to be the Heruka in whose navel burns the fire of vital heat. This fire fills the whole body. In the midst of this fire set all the Deities of the Mandala around the Guru as the Presiding Deity. Imagine that there are in the stomach the Deities who reside in the great cremation grounds and all the sentient beings of the three worlds. Then having worshipped the Deity of the hands by manual worship [2] imagine that the two hands are the Homa spoon, the mouth the triangular fire-hearth for Homa, and the food to be the ingredients of the Homa sacrifice; and then partake of the food with notice of the taste and flavour but without undue relish. Then the remains should be given to the Spirits[3] with the mantra " Om-u-tsik-ta-ba-lim-ta-bakshyasi svāhā. This is the Yoga pertaining to the partaking of food.

The conclave of Devatās invoked in the Cariyamārga[4] in which they[5] are produced from the Mantras and the Realms; those constituting the Bhakta-chakra;[6] and those in the outer Mandala; the apparent truth

---

(1) gTorma. (2) Sprinkling holy water and wine. (3) hByungpo=Half-mischievous, half-helpful beings, that exist in the Air, and who have command over the elements to some extent. These can be coaxed to help, or excited to injure. (The word hByungva means—' becoming,' as well as ' elements '—as we say hByungva-bzhi—the four elements—and so the four Bhūtas. Thus hByungpo means Bhūtas or spirits. 4) Path of conduct or practice above described. (5) Literally " Messengers " (Pho-nya) or Angels. The Sanskrit term Devatā has been employed. (6) Dam-tshig-hKhorlo: See *ante*, p. 64, note 5.

aspect (world of objects); the physical body with its gestures—all these constitute the Nirmānakāya.[1]

The conclave of Devatās produced by the mind during the productive (or creative) stage;[2] the Deities[3] who exist along with oneself; the three Chakras; the body transformed into a conclave of Devatās; and the united aspect (of form and Shūnyatā in union); along with the mantras—all these constitute the Sambhogakāya.

Then in the final or perfecting stage, the real truth as to the three kinds of Devatās; the Chakra of great Bliss; the wisdom;[4] the void;[5] the mind together with ecstasy;[6] all these constitute the Dharmakāya.

As these produce realization of the Dharmakāya, this process of summarising the various elements of devotion under the three headings of the three Kāyas is regarded as the process of utilising the three bodies (Kāya) on the Path.[7] By this method and constant application to the four Yogas[8] with their branches given above, one may attain (perfection) in the three Kāyas.

One gradually attains the power of successfully carrying out the four kinds of acts[9] as also the eight great Siddhis.[10]

---

(1) Manifest incarnate body: See *ante*, Introduction. (2) bsKyed-rims: See *ante*, p. 58, note 1. (3) Literally " Messengers " (Pho-nya) or Angels. The Sanskrit term Devatā has been employed. (4) bDe chen-Gyi-hkhorlo and Yeshes. (5) Shūnyatā. (6) Samādhi. (7) Where at length all preceding mental exercises merge into the state of tranquillity. (8) The four Yogas:—(*a*) Equalising or tranquillising the Mind; (*b*) The Yoga of the Path of Conduct; (*c*) gTorma; and (*d*) Of Food. (9) That is the peaceful (zhiva), the grand (rGyas-pa), the fascinating (dVang), and the stern (Dragpo). (10) Animā, Mahimā, etc.

From the two-fold stages of Meditation[1] are produced two kinds of Samādhi[2]—that which is produced by mental effort, and that which is devoid of mental effort. Then by constant practice in the last, one becomes firmly established therein and gains that knowledge which transcends all worldly knowledge.[3] By practising Sādhanā of Samanta-Bhadra [4] for the sake of others one gradually advances and attains twelve degrees in the stages of Bodhisattva. These secondary causes assist towards attainment of the Divine body and the forms of knowledge[5] (in their entirety) which enables one to fulfil every act beneficial to oneself and others. One becomes endowed with great Compassion and acquires every form of miraculous power. Finally one attains the divine state of Vajradhara[6] who exists as long as the Sangsāra[7] endures.

The state of vividly impressing the Mandala (on one's mind) consists in (picturing) the residence or mansions and the occupants thereof.[8] That being so I have first described the Mandala of the residence and the Devatās who reside therein.

---

(1) Creative or speculative (bsKyed-rim-dang-rdZogs-rim) and perfect or final (rDzogs-rim). In the first the Sādhaka creates mental pictures of the Mandala and the Devatās and in the second they are absorbed. (2) Ecstasy (Ting-nge-hDzin or Samādhi). The two kinds here spoken of are—artificial (sprös-bcas), and natural (sprös-med). (3) Alaukika Jnāna or Lokottara-Jnāna (mJig-rten-las-hdas-pahi-ye-shes). (4) Kuntu-bzangpo; by mastering His doctrine and putting it into practice. (5) Yeshes or Jnāna. (6) Dorje-chang (rDorje-hChang or Vajradhara). (7) The transmigrating world of births and deaths (Sangsāra) which had no beginning and will have no end (hkhorva-la-thog-mthah-med). Therefore He is eternal. If it ever came to an end then there would be no need of rDorje-hChang as such. All would be one and the same. (8) Sthāna and Devatā.

With a view however to make quite clear the real meaning of the objects (here Devatās) meditated upon—and to render oneself familiar with the steps of meditation one ought to refer to every work bearing on the subject written by the Precious Lord.[1]

The book has been completed by the venerable one[2] at the oft repeated request of Ji-big-Demur[3] who is blest by the possession of the right and best knowledge which truly enlightens ; who is further endowed with the beauty of the desire to obtain the highest aim.[4] May the merit of my contribution tend to enable every sentient being speedily to attain the highest state of the Divine Teacher[5] beyond whom higher there is none.

Part II.

This contains the prescribed form of Sādhanā of the Demchog Mandala, and is the same (except for a few particulars) and a repetition of Part I, extending from the 28th to the 45th folio.

---

(1) rJe-bTsün-Rinpoche. This must be the Famous Sakya Panchen rJe-bTsun-Rinpoche born 1233 A.D. (2) hPhagspa means Noble or Venerable or Reverend. The author of this work may possibly be Sakya hGro-mGon-hPags-pa, a great Hierarch of Sakya during whose time the whole of Thibet was given to him by the Chinese Emperor in 1251 A.D. (3) hJi-big-Demur ; evidently a Newar Prince (or a Tartar Prince) as seen from the book. The Newars were Buddhists, earlier than the Tibetans. But the name is not a Tibetan one but foreign. But probably Ji-big-Demur is a Newar Prince from the fact that the work is written at Svayambhu Nath in Nepal, called by the Sikkhimese hPagspa-Shingkün. (4) That of obtaining Buddhahood for the benefit of the world. (5) rDorje-hChang or Vajradhara.

PART III.

Contains only two folios under the Title "Looyipa's prayer in seven branches passed down through Naropa (Naropa-las rgyüd-pahi-Looyipahi-Yan-Lag-bDünpa)."

In the first verse obeisance is made to the Guru, in the second to Dharmadhātu Mahājnāna (Yeshes-chenpo), to Vārāhī, to the Vīras and Yoginīs, to the Lords of the Sangsāra and to Nirvāna. In the third offerings are made of every imaginable object, infinite as the expanse of the heavens ; in the fourth absolution is sought of sins committed by body, speech or mind. The fifth verse contains the Refuge Formula and refuge is sought in the Ishtadevatā. In the sixth resolution is made to observe the Yidam laws of the Mandala. The seventh speaks of the joy felt in the acquirement of merit and of the emulation of the wishes and the acts of the noblest amongst men and Devatās, Bodhisattvas and Buddhas. It ends with the prayer that Siddhi may be attained and happiness found.

At the close it is written that this is the truth. Mother above whom there is none. The Tantra of Chakra-Sambhāra (hKhorlo-sDompa), as practised according to Looyipa handed down through Naropa. The prayer was reduced to metrical form by bLo-grös-rGyal-mTshan-dPal-bzangpo (pronounced—Lodoigyaltsan Pal-zangpo), a disciple of the great Sakya Pandit. The composer or compiler is a Sramanera (dGetsül), and Vajradhara (rDorje-hdZinpa), who presides at the rites. This bears the date—" Water Mouse, 1st month—8th day" ; and the place is called Limju-tsi on the Northern route. The writer does not give his name, but the hand appears the same as that of the writer whose name is elsewhere given as Achara.

PART IV.

Contains the high praise of the Mandala of Shrī Chakra Sambhāra (dPal-hKhorlo-bDe-mchoggi dkyil-hkhor-gyi-bstöd-pahi-rabtu-byedpa-zhes-bya-va).

Obeisance to the feet of the Sacred Gurus evolved from the glorious two-fold merit Shūnyatā and Karunā (compassion) inseparably embodied in the Great Bliss of incomprehensible mystery. Obeisance to the Heruka!

This part consists of 48 verses or stanzas in metrical praise of the Deities. It extends from the front page of the 48th folio to the second line of the back page of the 52nd folio. The first thirty-five verses are addressed to the Deities thus :—In a number of stanzas (each of four lines), the first is addressed to Heruka, the second to Phagmo (Vārāhī) and Demchog, the third to Phagmo or Vārāhī, the fourth to mKhah-hGroma, the fifth to Lāma, the sixth to Dūm-skyes-ma or Kapāli, the seventh to gZugs-chan-ma (Skt. Rupinī), the eighth to bDemchog-hKhorlo (Mahā-Sukha-Chakra), and so on. During Sādhanā the Sādhaka has to repeat this and bow down by which means he identifies different parts of his own body with different Devatās, certain functions of his body with other Devatās and so forth.

The note at the end of this part says that the author (hPhags-pa) composed this at the request of one sTönpa Shesrab in the Iron Sheep year (full 20 years after the previous part in the Nag-pa month = 3rd Tib. month = April or May, and the day is given as the 24th midday). The place is given as the Great Palace of Chengto (possibly Chengtu in China ?). The writer is Achara.

PART V.

Begins :—Om-Svasti-Siddham.

This part deals with the dVang rites (Abhisheka), which means the rites of conferring power on the Sādhaka to undertake the Sādhanā. This only proceeds for two folios, *viz.*, 53rd and 54th folios, and describes in brief metre the rite. This MS. does not give any date or place but only the author's name which is hPhags-pa.

PART VI.

bDe-mChog-Lüs-dKyil, Mahā Sukkha-Kāya Mandala.

The title of this part runs in the text :—dPal-hKhorlo-bDemchog-gi-lüskyi-dkyil hkhordu-bDag-nyid-hjug-Cing-dVang bLang-Vahi-Choga-Zhes-bya-va : that is, " This is called the rite of taking Abhisheka, (dVang or power), by entering into the Mandala of Srī-Chakra-Sambhāra (or Mahāsukha)."

This part extends from the 56th folio, back page, to the 77th folio, back page—twenty-two folios in all. It begins :—" Obeisance to the Guru, and to Shrī Heruka. To gain the fruits by the power of the initiation to acquire which the highest of initiation has been granted by the best of Gurus, to whom having bowed down the method of making (use of) initiation as the path is herein explained."

Having obtained initiation into the Bodily Mandala of the Highest Bliss (Chakra Mahāsukha), and accustomed oneself to meditation thereon till one has attained firmness of mind, one should set about to acquire Bodhi Chit by means of Samādhi. In a quiet place, set up the object of worship (either a picture or an image), the outer and inner offerings used in worship, and three rice-cakes, two holy waterpots, a bell and a rDorje. Having got together these objects necessary for the rite, then seek a friend or assistant who has been accustomed to putting himself into the quiescent state of Yoga and then proceed.

First give to the local spirits and elementals who may be gathered there, the Torma (rice-cakes), with the general Mantras used in offering to the Dākinīs, so that they may be appeased. Exorcise those spirits who are not authorised to be present during the mystic rites, entreat those who are so authorised to be present to befriend the performance and to remain in the state of communion (Yoga = rNal-hByor). Then repeat the mantra of the hundred letters (syllables) to cleanse one's own nature. Meditate, repeat the mantras and imagine one's self to be the Devatā and worship one's self. Then fumigate the (objects of) offering by repeating the Sumbhani mantra and purify them by the Sva-bhava mantra; then from the midst of these, imagine an A from which issues a skull, from inside of which there come the seven objects of offerings in worship such as Arghya, Pādya, Pushpa. These are offered with the appropriate mantras, imagining them to be of the best and purest imaginable (ingredients) and on the grandest scale of profusion (literally, as illimitable as the expanse of the heavens). Then imagine, in the space fronting the Sādhaka, Mount Meru, on the top of which, within the charmed circle, there are the eight great cemeteries and in the centre a Vihāra (grand hall), four-sided with four entrances, adorned and embellished with every kind of ornament. The inside of this Vihāra is divided into five concentric circles (one within the other), the innermost of which is occupied by hKhorlo-bDe-mChog inseparably united with Vajra-Vārāhī surrounded by the Devatās, numbering sixty-two in all, who constitute the Mandala. The next outer circle is the Mahāsukha (great Bliss circle—bDechen), the third that of the mind, then that of speech (Vāk), and lastly that of the body (Kāya-Chakra). The outer lower storey or foundation is occupied by the door-keepers. Then seal the whole by the members of the various kūlas (classes), as was done when imagining one's own self to be the Devatā. Worship again as before with outer and inner offerings. Then the two holy water jars (which should be in perfect accordance with the prescribed forms) should next be fumigated and sanctified as above. One is in the inner circle of the altar, and the other on the outer and lower platform of the altar for use during the rite. The inner pot is called rNam-rGyal Būm-pa (the Vijaya jar). The outer one for use is called the Las-thāms-cad-pahi-bumpa—the holy water jar for all purposes (Sarvakarma). The Vijaya jar is to be thought of as containing the entire Mandala of Devatās, and the Las-boom (the Karma pot) to contain only the Deities of the Mahāsukha-Chakra.

Both are imagined to contain the vowels and consonants. The Vijaya (rNam-rGyal = Namgyal bumpa) contains the 62 Devatās. Having imagined these vividly, let the Sādhaka worship these as before till he comes to the hymn of praise (stotra). Recite mantras, imagine threads of moving light to be issuing from the heart and attached to the Vijaya jar exciting the Devatās, from whom in turn issue streams of Amrita. (The mantras are the same as those given before.) Then having poured the water into the conch vessel, imagine that all the Devatās are merged therein.

(3rd.—Folio 58th).—This is the rite pertaining to the holy water jars. Then imagine one's self to be absorbed into the outer Heruka. With two hands take the dVang (Power-abhisheka) from the Guru who is the same with the Supreme (Devatā). Think that you perform those functions which the Guru has to perform. The assistant's functions are to be performed by a two-handed Heruka produced from the heart. The Chela's (disciple's) functions are to be performed by one's self. Then the Chela offers the flowers and other offerings and joins his palms together, and the Guru says—" All objects (Dharma) are like reflections in a mirror. They are clear, pure and not confused. They cannot be seized and cannot be expressed. They are born purely from the cause (Hetu), and Karma. Thus is the ' That ' (De-nyid) actually produced. May all you Chelas see the Mandala of That Truth in the vivid and clear forms without any obscurations." This is repeated thrice, then the mantra "A kham-bhira hūm " is repeated and the veil is tied over the face of the Chela and a flower is put into his hands sprinkled with water from the Las-boom (the outer Karma jar), and a drop of Amrita (wine) is put on his tongue—blessed with the mantra "Om-A-Hūm." He is asked "O Son! what do you delight in?" In answer he says—"O, you of Noble Destiny (Skal-bZang), I desire Great Bliss." "What would that do to you?" to which he replies: "It is the Sacred Word of the highest Buddhas." Then the Guru places the rDorje on the head of the Chela with certain mantras and says: "All the Tathāgatas confer their blessings on you henceforth. This holy secret of the Tathāgatas you must not divulge to those who have not entered the Mandala of the Tathāgatas, nor to those who are unbelievers."

60th folio begins.—Then the recipient must imagine that he is being led out of the circle by the door-keepers (the Female Devatās). This is the outer form of entering. Then come the prayers and the injunctions by the Guru and the vows of the Chela which are twenty in number.

62nd folio.—Then the Guru repeats the exorcism mantra, burning incense and scattering mustard seeds. Then follows the washing of sins with water from the Las-boom with appropriate mantras.

63rd folio.—Folio 64th of the Original MS.

The Abhisheka (or initiation) rites extend to the 77th folio of the Original MS. It ends with the injunction not to confer the Abhisheka rites on those who are not ripe enough for it. It is said to be the highest and most glorious (possession) of the venerable line of the Sakya Hierarchs. It is compiled by hPhags-Pa (Skt.—Ārya) at the repeated request of Du-Khal-

Dur-Mis. It is the teachings of the Indian Guru rDorje-Drilbupa (he who held the rDorje and the Bell). It is dated Water-Fowl Year, 4th month, 27th day, and at Shingkün. The writer is again Achara.

Part VII.

78th folio of Original Text, 86th page of Printed Text, contains dPal-hKhorlo-sDom-pahi-rimpa-lNga-hi-man-ngag-ces-bya-va :

This is called the five stages of the practical teachings of the Shrī Sambhāra-Chakra. Obeisance to dPal-rDorje-mKhah-hGro Shrī-Vajra-Dākinī. Having bowed down to the feet of the Guru, by whose gracious kindness one obtains the Advaita-jnāna (gNyis-med-yeshes), I proceed to describe here the different stages or gradual processes (rim-pa) thereof. A properly accomplished Guru having initiated the disciple into the mysteries of the outer and inner circles of hKhorlo-sDompa (Chakra Sambhāra), and having caused him to be thoroughly developed by means of the blessings of this Mandala, the latter should set himself to the meditation on forms, wherein he must attain steadfastness to some extent; then should he wish to enter upon the final meditation—the rDzogs-rim—the stage of Perfection by meditating on the formless, he must seat himself in an easy posture cross-legged, and begin by meditating on forms as prescribed herein. Imagine the Hūm in one's heart to be emitting rays and to gather all external objects into one's own body. Even the Female (the Mother) is to be gathered into one's heart (the Male Devatās) through the nostrils. During this worship the Male Devatā is the form with only two hands. Think of one's own Guru as being seated on the crown of one's head. Exert faith and humility as much as possible and pray that the best and purest kind of Samādhi may be produced in one's mind.

Having bowed down to the feet of the Guru by whose mercy is gained the light of the Advaita (non-dual or literally "not-two") Yeshes (Jnāna) speedily, the author explains the process of meditation (gNyis-med sGompa-hi-rimpa).

Having been duly initiated into the outer and inner Mandalas, which constitute the very self of Chakra Sambhāra by a competent (perfect) Guru, and having been further developed by its (the Mandala's) own grace or blessing, one speedily sets forth to obtain the special teachings, and to learn their practical results. Assuming that he has attained to the stage of firm concentration of the mind and that he wishes to proceed further in the perfect or final stage (meditation on the formless) he should proceed thus :—Either in the morning (or any other time) let him take an easy position, cross-legged, and go through as a preliminary step the previously described stage of meditation on Forms (bsKyed-rims). Let him imagine that the Hūm inside his heart sheds out rays of light on all outer space and the objects therein. They are all gathered within the body. The Female Devatā, too, is drawn in through the nostrils into one's own heart. Having thought of oneself as the two-handed (Heruka), imagine the Guru on one's head. Put forth intense faith in him, and pray

"I beseech thee, cause pure Samādhi to grow in my mind." Then imagine on the letter "A" a lunar disc, red and white, about the size of the half of a pea inside one's heart. Upon the lunar disc imagine a light-point (a zero or Bindu) about the size of a mustard seed which is the concentrated form of one's Mind. Fix the mind on that and regulate the breath gently (literally, "make it a gentle pair"). When one is well practiced, the mind is held and does not run astray but remains fixed. Then one attains the blissful and clear (bDe-gSal) Samādhi. When one attains stability or firmness in that (Samādhi), then transfer the imagination to another of the sense organs (Tib. dVangpo = Skt. Indriyas). Go through the preliminary step described above. For the actual method: imagine within the two pupils of the Eyes, that there are two very fine bright white points, one in each eye. Close the eyes and imagine in your mind that the points are there. When the mind gets accustomed to that, then look on various objects. Whilst all the while keeping the points before the mind, let it stray upon other objects. On being well practised the point is constantly and vividly present to the mind's eye. No matter on whatever object the eye may fall, Samādhi is produced. Having attained stability in that, draw in the Point within the heart, and imagine that the latter gains greater brilliancy and clearness, and keep the mind tranquil (literally at a level: mNyam-bzhag); this will produce Samādhi of the most excellent kind, or the state of Tranquillity. (That is when the mind concentrates upon an object of sight and endeavours to understand what that object is, it discovers the empty character of such apparition. The dawning of this truth fills the Sādhaka with a feeling of certainty and of inexpressible joy and peace. It is realised that all visible objects are the Void (Shūnyatā). One gets more and more used to regarding things from the true standpoint, and this true experience is not impeded or disturbed by thought of fresh objects. The deeper the insight into the unreality of things as mere expressions of the Void behind and in them the more profound is the peace which ripens into full Samādhi.)

After this transfer the imagination to the Ears. The preliminary steps are as described before. For the actual meditation :—Imagine two blue Points or Dots upon two lunar discs the size of a half-pea inside each ear and meditate upon them, in a place free from noise. When you have succeeded in fixing the mind upon them, listen to sounds, at the same time keeping the mind fixed upon the two Points and not letting it stray away from them. On being practised in that, one attains vividness of the mind-picture and Samādhi follows on hearing sound. When one has gained stability in this, withdraw the Points inside the heart and imagine that the Points have gained blazing brilliancy and vividness. From this the excellent Samādhi or Tranquillity (state of mental level) is produced. (When the mind is deeply concentrated on sound and its nature as the Void (Shūnyatā) is realised the same thing happens as in the exercise of the sense of sight upon objects. One discovers the empty nature of sound. When that is seen sweetness, harshness, melody, harmony, discord, all lose their meaning. For what is all this but Shūnyatā, the full apprehension of which fills the Sādhaka with rapture. This is Samādhi produced by means of the gates of hearing.) Then transfer the imagination to the Nose. The preliminaries same as above :—Imagine a yellow Point on a lunar disc in the cavity of each nostril in a place free from any odour, and concentrate your mind on that. When the mind is fixed, smell various odours, keeping the mind fixed on the yellow Points, not letting the mind stray away. When one gets used to that, on perception of odours there is produced Samādhi. (The same process as regards the sense of smell and the object of it or odour which are analysed into and realised as Shūnyatā. Samādhi is thus produced by means of the gate of the sense of smell.) When firmness is gained in this, draw the Points in to the heart. By this, brilliancy and vividness of the Point is produced, and practice in this produces Samādhi. Next transfer the imagination to the Tongue. Preliminaries the same as above :—Imagine a red Point on a lunar disc at the root of the tongue, and meditate on it without tasting any flavour. Concentrate your mind on it, do not let it stray. Then, when the mind is fixed on the Point, taste various flavours, keeping your mind concentrated on the Point. Then draw it inside the heart. When the Point attains brilliancy and vividness, Samādhi is produced through the sense of taste. Then transfer your imagination to the Body. Preliminaries the same as above. Either at the root of the secret parts (that is, the junction of the penis and the scrotum), or on your forehead, imagine a green Point on a lunar disc, and fix your mind on it without touching anything. When your mind has attained some degree of fixity on that spot (Bīja), try concentration, touching various things and keeping the mind from straying. When vividness of the Point is obtained, practise until it is quite firm, then draw the Point in the place of touch into the Point within the heart, and meditate upon that, until great brilliance and vividness is obtained, which will produce Tranquillity or excellent Samādhi. Then after that, transfer the imagination to the Mind, which moves everywhere. Preliminaries same as above. Actual process :—Imagine a very small pink Point on the top of that already imagined as being within the heart. Try the meditation in a very quiet place at first. When you have succeeded in concentrating your mind, try the meditation in company where you are sure that some evil passions will be excited, such as lust or the like. Then imagine that the chief passion—Moha (infatuation)—which accompanies all other evil passions is concentrated in it. Think that it is absorbed into a blue Point. Fix the mind on that. On getting accustomed in that (practice), passions will not arise; or should they do so, they are controlled by the mind. When one has attained firmness in that, sink the blue Point into the pink Point, and that into the white and red Point below it. Then the last sinks into the moon-disc ; which in its turn is dissolved or disappears in the sky like a cloud (which has disappeared). Then there remains only Emptiness (Shūnyatā or sTongpa), in which the mind is to be kept at a level. This will produce the profound tranquil state Samādhi called Zhi-gNas (literally, Resting-in-peace). Then rising from the state of Tranquillity (Samādhi), again imagine the lunar discs and the Points to be present or springing-forth simultaneously : and that one's ownself, too, is at once transformed into the Heruka. Regard external objects as being only visible and apparently true, but having no independent and absolute reality in themselves. Meditating thus till each stage has shown its sign of perfection or proficiency, one at last attains proficiency or perfection in the whole, as a result of which one obtains profound Tranquillity (Zhi-gNas), which is realisation of the Shūnyatā, which is bliss and clarity. Continuation in these practices produces the knowledge of the path (mThong-Lam), from which is produced Buddha-hood. This is the stage of conferring grace and blessing (bdag-byin-brlabs-pahi) on oneself, accompanied by Bīja (Sabön) (that is by means of meditation on the various sense organs).

This extends to the end of the 89th folio. In the 90th folio the composer says "These five stages of meditation" are very clearly defined.

"Though done by the venerable Guru, being found too brief, being requested by one who wishes to have it more clearly explained, I have contributed this, in which (if there be any shortcomings) forgive."

"Let the merit of this work tend to confer the blessings which comes of practising these for myself and for all sentient beings. Let all avoid the extremes of worldly existence and selfish quiescence attaining success in the two ends. Let all become the Heruka Himself."

" Being desired by Prince hJi-big-Demur and at the special request of Dügal Durmis (Tugal Turmi ?) (I) Sharamana Mantradhara named Ārya (hPhags-pa) have done this at the noble Monastery of Shākya on the 25th of the 1st Summer month of the Earth-Tiger year."

The writer's name is given as Yeshes-Senge, a priest of gNas-rNying.

K. D.

sMon-lam-sTobs-po-che.

"The Powerful Good Wish."

༄༅། །སྨོན་ལམ་སྟོབས་པོ་ཆེ་བཞུགས་སོ།།

EDITED BY

DAWASAMDUP KAZI.

༄༅།། ཨོཾ་ཧཱུྃ་ཨཱཿ༔ དེ་ནས་ཐོག་མའི་སངས་རྒྱས། ཀུན་ཏུ་བཟང་པོས་འཁོར་བའི་སེམས་ཅན་རྣམས་འཚང་མི་རྒྱ་བའི་དབང་མེད་པའི་སྨོན་ལམ་ཁྱད་པར་ཅན་འདི་གསུངས་སོ།།

༄༅། ཧོ་སྣང་སྲིད་འཁོར་འདས་ཐམས་ཅད་ཀུན། གཞི་གཅིག་ལམ་གཉིས་འབྲས་བུ་གཉིས། རིག་དང་མ་རིག་ཆོ་འཕྲུལ་ཏེ། ཀུན་ཏུ་བཟང་པོའི་སྨོན་ལམ་གྱིས། ཐམས་ཅད་ཆོས་དབྱིངས་ཕོ་བྲང་དུ། མངོན་པར་རྫོགས་པར་སངས་རྒྱས་ཤོག། ཀུན་གྱི་གཞི་ནི་འདུས་མ་བྱས། རང་བྱུང་ཀློང་ཡངས་བརྗོད་དུ་མེད། འཁོར་འདས་གཉིས་ཀྱི་མིང་མེད་དེ། དེ་ཉིད་རིག་ན་སངས་རྒྱས་ཏེ། མ་རིག་སེམས་ཅན་འཁོར་བར་འཁྱམས། ཁམས་གསུམ་སེམས་ཅན་ཐམས་ཅད་ཀྱིས། བརྗོད་མེད་གཞི་དོན་རིག་པར་ཤོག། ཀུན་ཏུ་བཟང་པོ་ང་ཡིས་ཀྱང་། རྒྱུ་རྐྱེན་མེད་པ་གཞི་ཡི་དོན། དེ་ཉིད་གཞི་ལ་རང་བྱུང་རིག། ཕྱི་ནང་སྒྲོ་སྐུར་སྐྱོན་མ་ཧྲིག། དྲན་མེད་སྨུན་པའི་ དྲི་མ་མེད། དེ་ཕྱིར་རང་སྣང་སྐྱོན་མ་གོས། རང་རིག་ས་ལ་གནས་པ་ལ། སྲིད་གསུམ་འཇིགས་ཀྱང་དངངས་སྐྲག་མེད། འདོད་ཡོན་ལྔ་ལ་ཆགས་པ་མེད། རྟོག་མེད་ཤེས་པ་རང་བྱུང་ལ། རྫས་པོའི་གཟུགས་དང་དུག་ལྔ་མེད། རིག་པའི་གསལ་ཆ་མ་འགགས་པའི། ངོ་བོ་གཅིག་ལ་ཡེ་ཤེས་ལྔ། ཡེ་ཤེས་ལྔ་པོ་སྨིན་པ་ལ། ཐོག་མའི་སངས་རྒྱས་རིགས་ལྔ་བྱུང་། དེ་ལ་ཡེ་ཤེས་མཐར་རྒྱས་པའི། སངས་རྒྱས་བཞི་བཅུ་རྩ་གཉིས་བྱུང་། ཡེ་ཤེས་ལྔ་ཡི་རྩལ་ཤར་བས། ཁྲག་འཐུང་དྲུག་ཅུ་ཐམ་པ་བྱུང་། དེ་ཕྱིར་གཞི་རིག་འཁྲུལ་མ་མྱོང་། ཐོག་མའི་སངས་རྒྱས་ང་ཡིན་པས། ང་ཡི་སྨོན་ལམ་བཏབ་པ་ཡི། ཁམས་གསུམ་འཁོར་བའི་སེམས་ཅན་གྱིས། རང་བྱུང་རིག་པ་ངོ་ཤེས་ནས། ཡེ་ཤེས་ཆེན་པོ་མཐར་རྒྱས་ཤོག།། ང་ཡི་སྤྲུལ་པ་རྒྱུན་

སྨོན་ལམ་སྟོབས་པོ་ཆེ།

མི་ཆད། བྱེ་བ་ཕྲག་བརྒྱ་བསམ་ཡས་འགྱེད། གང་ལ་གང་འདུལ་སྣ་ཚོགས་སྟོན།

ང་ཡི་ཐུགས་རྗེའི་སྨོན་ལམ་གྱིས། ཁམས་གསུམ་འཁོར་བའི་སེམས་ཅན་ཀུན།

རིགས་དྲུག་གནས་ནས་མཐར་བར་ཤོག། དང་པོ་སེམས་ཅན་འཁྲུལ་པ་རྣམས།

གཞི་ལ་རིག་པ་མ་ཤར་བས། ཅི་ཡང་དྲན་མེད་ཐེབས་སེ་བ།

དེ་མ་རིག་འཁྲུལ་པའི་རྒྱུ། དེ་ལ་ཧད་ཀྱི་བརྒྱལ་བ་ལས།

དངངས་སྐྲག་ཤེས་པ་ཟ་ཟིར་འགྱུས། དེ་ལ་བདག་གཞན་དགྲ་འཛིན་སྐྱེས།

བག་ཆགས་རིམ་གྱིས་བརྟས་པ་ལས། འཁོར་བ་ལུགས་སུ་འཇུག་པ་བྱུང་།

དེ་ལ་ཉོན་མོངས་དུག་ལྔ་རྒྱས། དུག་ལྔའི་ལས་ལ་རྒྱུན་ཆད་མེད།

དེ་ཕྱིར་སེམས་ཅན་འཁྲུལ་པའི་གཞི། དྲན་མེད་མ་རིག་ཡིན་པའི་ཕྱིར།

སངས་རྒྱས་ང་ཡི་སྨོན་ལམ་གྱིས། ཀུན་གྱིས་རིག་པ་རང་ཤེས་ཤོག།

ལྷན་ཅིག་སྐྱེས་པའི་མ་རིག་པ། ཤེས་པ་དྲན་མེད་ཡེང་བ་ཡིན།

ཀུན་ཏུ་བརྟགས་པས་མ་རིག་པ། བདག་གཞན་གཉིས་སུ་འཛིན་པ་ཡིན།

ལྷན་ཅིག་ཀུན་བརྟགས་མ་རིག་གཉིས། སེམས་ཅན་ཀུན་གྱི་འཁྲུལ་གཞི་ཡིན།

སངས་རྒྱས་ང་ཡི་སྨོན་ལམ་གྱིས། འཁོར་བའི་སེམས་ཅན་ཐམས་ཅད་ཀྱིས།

དྲན་མེད་ཐིམ་པའི་མུན་པ་སངས། གཉིས་སུ་འཛིན་པའི་ཤེས་པ་དྭངས།

རིག་པའི་རང་ངོ་ཤེས་པར་ཤོག། གཉིས་འཛིན་བློ་ནི་ཐེ་ཚོམ་ཟ།

ཞེན་པ་ཕྲ་མོ་སྐྱེས་པ་ནས། བག་ཆགས་འཐུག་པོ་རིམ་གྱིས་བརྟས།

ཟས་ནོར་གོས་དང་གནས་དང་གྲོགས། འདོད་ཡོན་ལྔ་དང་བྱམས་པའི་གཉེན།

ཡིད་འོང་འདོད་པའི་ཆགས་པ་བྱུང་། དེ་དག་འཇིག་རྟེན་འཁྲུལ་པ་སྟེ།

བྱང་འཛིན་ལས་ལ་ཟད་མཐའ་མེད། ཞེན་པས་འབྲས་བུ་སྨིན་པ་ཡིས།
བསམ་ཆགས་གདུངས་པའི་ཡི་དྭགས་སུ། སྐྱེས་ན་བཀྲེས་སྐོམ་ཡ་ར་ང་།
སངས་རྒྱས་ང་ཡི་སྨོན་ལམ་གྱིས། འདོད་ཆགས་ཞེན་པའི་སེམས་ཅན་རྣམས།
འདོད་པ་གདུང་བ་ཕྱིར་མ་སྤངས། འདོད་ཆགས་ཞེན་པ་ཕྱིར་མ་བླང་།
ཤེས་པ་རང་གཟོ་གློད་པ་ཡིས། རིག་པ་རང་ས་ཟིན་གྱུར་ནས།
ཀུན་རྟོག་ཡེ་ཤེས་ཐོབ་པར་ཤོག། ཕྱི་རོལ་ཡུལ་གྱི་སྣང་བ་ལ།
འཇིགས་སྐྲག་ཤེས་པ་ཕྲ་མོ་འགྱུས། སྡང་བའི་བག་ཆགས་བརྟས་པ་ལས།
དགྲ་འཛིན་བདག་གསོད་རགས་པ་སྐྱེས། ཞེ་སྡང་འབྲས་བུ་སྨིན་པའི་ཚེ།
དམྱལ་བའི་གཅོ་བསྲེག་སྡུག་རེ་བརྟལ། སངས་རྒྱས་ང་ཡི་སྨོན་ལམ་གྱིས།
འགྲོ་དྲུག་སེམས་ཅན་ཐམས་ཅད་ཀྱི། ཞེ་སྡང་དྲག་པོ་སྐྱེས་པའི་ཚེ།
སྤང་བླང་མ་བྱེད་རང་སར་གློད། རིག་པ་རང་ས་ཟིན་གྱུར་ནས།
གསལ་བའི་ཡེ་ཤེས་ཐོབ་པར་ཤོག། རང་སེམས་ཁེངས་པར་གྱུར་པ་ལས།
གཞན་ལ་འགྲན་སེམས་སྨད་པའི་བློ། ང་རྒྱལ་དྲག་པོའི་སེམས་སྐྱེས་པས།
བདག་གཞན་འཐབ་རྩོད་དུ༔ཁ་སྡུར། ལས་དེའི་འབྲས་བུ་སྨིན་པའི་ཚེ།
ཕོ་ལྟུང་སྤྱོད་པའི་ལྷ་རུ་སྐྱེས། སངས་རྒྱས་ང་ཡི་སྨོན་ལམ་གྱིས།
ཁེངས་སེམས་སྐྱེས་པའི་སེམས་ཅན་རྣམས། དེ་ཚེ་ཤེས་པ་རང་སོར་གློད།
རིག་པ་རང་སོ་ཟིན་གྱུར་ནས། མཉམ་པ་ཉིད་ཀྱི་དོན་རྟོགས་ཤོག།
གཉིས་འཛིན་འཕེལ་བའི་བག་ཆགས་ཀྱིས། བདག་བསྟོད་གཞན་སྨོད་སྡུག་རྩའི་ལས།
འཐབ་རྩོད་མགྲན་སེམས་བརྟས་པ་ལས། གསོད་གཅོད་ལྷ་མིན་གནས་སུ་སྐྱེས།

འབྲས་བུ་དམྱལ་བའི་གནས་སུ་ལྷུང་། སངས་རྒྱས་ང་ཡི་སྨོན་ལམ་གྱིས།
འཁྲུན་སེམས་འཐབ་རྩོད་སྐྱེས་པ་རྣམས། དགྲ་འཛིན་མི་བྱ་རང་སོ་གློད
ཤེས་པ་རང་སོ་ཐེན་གྱུར་ནས། འཕྲིན་ལས་ཐོགས་མེད་ཡེ་ཤེས་ཤོག
དྲན་མེད་བཏང་སྙོམས་གཡེངས་པ་དང་། འཐིབ་དང་རྨུགས་དང་བརྗེད་པ་དང་།
བརྒྱལ་དང་ལེ་ལོ་གཏི་མུག་ཡིན། འབྲས་བུ་སྐྱབས་མེད་བྱོལ་སོང་འཁྱམས།
སངས་རྒྱས་ང་ཡི་སྨོན་ལམ་གྱིས། གཏི་མུག་བྱིང་བའི་མུན་པ་ལ།
དྲན་པ་གསལ་བའི་མདངས་ཤར་ནས། རྟོག་མེད་ཡེ་ཤེས་ཐོབ་པར་ཤོག
ཁམས་གསུམ་སེམས་ཅན་ཐམས་ཅད་ཀུན། ཀུན་གཞི་སངས་རྒྱས་ང་དང་མཉམ།
དྲན་མེད་འཁྲུལ་པའི་གཞི་རུ་སོང་། ད་ལྟ་དོན་མེད་ལས་ལ་སྤྱོད།
ལས་དྲུག་རྨི་ལམ་འཁྲུལ་པ་འདྲ། ང་ནི་སངས་རྒྱས་ཐོག་མ་ཡིན།
འགྲོ་དྲུག་སྤྲུལ་པ་འདུལ་བའི་ཕྱིར། ཀུན་ཏུ་བཟང་པོའི་སྨོན་ལམ་གྱིས།
སེམས་ཅན་ཐམས་ཅད་མ་ལུས་པ། ཆོས་ཀྱི་དབྱིངས་སུ་སངས་རྒྱས་ཤོག

༈ ཨེ་མ་ཧོ།།

ཕྱིན་ཆད་རྣལ་འབྱོར་སྟོབས་ཆེན་གྱིས།
འཁྲུལ་མེད་རིག་པ་རང་གསལ་ནས། སྨོན་ལམ་སྟོབས་ཆེན་འདི་བཏབ་པས།
འདི་ཐོས་སེམས་ཅན་ཐམས་ཅད་ཀུན། སྐྱེ་བ་གསུམ་ནས་མངོན་འཚང་རྒྱ།
ཉི་ཟླ་གཟའ་ཡིས་ཟིན་པ་འམ། སྒྲ་དང་ས་གཡོས་བྱུང་བ་ནའང་ཉི་ལྡོག་དུས།
རང་ཉིད་ཀུན་ཏུ་བཟང་པོར་བསྐྱེད། ཉི་མ་ལྡོག་འགྱུར།
ཀུན་གྱིས་ཐོས་སར་འདི་བརྗོད་ན། ཁམས་གསུམ་སེམས་ཅན་ཐམས་ཅད་ཀུན།

རྣལ་འབྱོར་ང་ཡི་སྨན་ལམ་གྱིས། སྡུག་བསྔལ་རིམ་གྱིས་གྲོལ་ནས་ཀྱང་།

མཐར་ཕྱུག་སངས་རྒྱས་ཐོབ་པར་ཤོག། ཅེས་སྨན་ལམ་སྟོབས་པོ་ཆེ་རྫོགས་སོ།།

རྗོར་གླིང་གཞུང་གི་པར་ཁང་དུ་པར་དུ་བསྐྲུན་པའོ།། སན་མནྡ་ལམ།

བོད་ལུགས་ས་ཕོ་རྟ་ལོ་དང་། ཡི་ཤུའི་འདས་ལོ—༡༩༡༨ ལོ་ཁམས

G. B. P. D.—827—500—27-11-1918.

TANTRIK TEXTS

EDITED BY

ARTHUR AVALON.

VOL. XI.

DEM-CHOG TANTRA

༄༅། དཔལ་འཁོར་ལོ་བདེ་མཆོག། རྡོ་རྗེ་རྣལ་འབྱོར་མ།

དཔལ་སྒྱུ་མ་ཆེན་མོ། སྒྲོལ་མ་རྣམས་བཞུགས་སོ༎

dPal-hKhorlo-bDe-mChog (Pal Khorlo-Dem-Chog); rDo-rje-rNal-hByor-ma (Dorje-Naljorma); dPal-sGyuma-Chen-mo (Pal-Gyuma-Chemo); sGrol-ma (Dolma).

Shri-Chakra-Sambhara
Vajra-Yogini, Shri Maha-Maya and Tara.

EDITED BY

KAZI DAUSAMDUP.

DARJEELING:
DARJEELING BRANCH PRESS.

1918.

༄༅ སྦྲུ་ནི་གཉིས་མེད་ཡེ་ཤེས་ཏེ། ཧ་ནི་རྒྱུ་སོགས་སྤང་པ་ཉིད། རུ་ནི་ཚོགས་དང་བྲལ་བ་སྟེ། ཀ་ནི་གང་དུའང་མི་གནས་པ། ཅེས་པའི་དོན་དང་ལྡན་པ་བདག་ཉིད་ཡིན་སྙམ་དུ་བསམ་པ་ནི་ངག་ཐུགས་སུ་བྱིན་གྱིས་བརླབ་པ་གསུང་གི་དགའ་བའོ། །རང་གི་སྙིང་གི་ནང་དུ་ཨ་རྣམ་པར་མི་རྟོག་པའི་ཡེ་ཤེས་ལས་བྱུང་བ། ཟླ་བའི་དཀྱིལ་འཁོར་དག་པ་འཇིག་རྟེན་པའི་ཡེ་ཤེས་ཀྱི་སྙིང་དུ། གཟུང་འཛིན་དང་བྲལ་བའི་སེམས་ཧཱུྃ་དུ་དམིགས་པའི་ཞབས་ཀྱུ་བྱ་བ་གྲུབ་པ། ཕོག་པ་སོ་སོར་རྟོག་པ། མགོ་བོ་མཉམ་པ་ཉིད། ཟླ་ཚེས་མེ་ལོང་ལྟ་བུ། ཐིག་ལེ་ཆོས་ཀྱི་དབྱིངས་ཏེ་ཡེ་ཤེས་ལྔར་བསྒོམ་པ་ནི་སེམས་ཡེ་ཤེས་སུ་བྱིན་གྱིས་བརླབ་པ་ཐུགས་ཀྱི་དགའ་བ་སྟེ་སྔོན་དུ་འགྲོ་བའོ།། ཧཱུྃ་དེ་ལས་འོད་ཟེར་སྔོན་པོ། ལྗང་ཁུ། དམར་པོ། སེར་པོ་རྣམས་ཞལ་བཞི་ནས་རིམ་པ་བཞིན་འཕྲོས་པས་འཇིག་རྟེན་གྱི་ཁམས་ཐམས་ཅད་གང་བས། སེམས་ཅན་ཐམས་ཅད་བདེ་བ་དང་བདེ་བའི་རྒྱུ་དང་ལྡན་པ་དང་། སྡུག་བསྔལ་དང་སྡུག་སྡུག་བསྔལ་གྱི་རྒྱུ་དང་བྲལ་བ་དང་། བདེ་བ་སྡུག་མེད་པ་དང་མི་འབྲལ་བ་དང་། ཆགས་པ་དང་སྡང་བ་མེད་ཅིང་། འཇིག་རྟེན་གྱི་ཆོས་བརྒྱད་སྙོམས་པར་གྱུར་པ་རྣམས་རིམ་པ་བཞིན་བསྒོམ་པ་དང་། ལུས་ཀྱིས་ལག་པ་གཡོན་པའི་འཛུབ་མོ་ཕྱུགས་བཅུར་བསྒོམ་ཞིང་སེ་གོལ་གཏོགས་པ་དང་། ངག་ཏུ་སུ་ཁི་ཧཱ་ཝན་དུ་ཞེས་བརྗོད་པས་བྱིན་གྱིས་བརླབ་པ་ནི་སོག་པར་འགྱུར་བའི་དགེ་བའི་རྩ་བ་ཐམས་ཅད་གཞན་དོན་དུ་འགྱུར་བར་བྱ་བའི་ཕྱིར། ཚངས་པའི་གནས་བཞི་བསྒོམ་པའོ།། སྔར་ཡང་། ཧཱུྃ་ལས་ཁ་མདོག་སྣ་ཚོགས་པའི་འོད་ཟེར་འཕྲོས་པས་རང་གི་ལུས་ཐམས་ཅད་གང་བས་བདག་ཉིད་དང་ཕྱི་རོལ་དུ་འཕྲོས་པས་སེམས་ཅན་ཐམས་ཅད་ཀྱི་སྡིག་པ་དང་སྒྲིབ་པ་བག་ཆགས་དང་བཅས་པ་སྦྱངས་ནས། ཐམས་ཅད་ཀྱང་འཁོར་ལོ་བདེ་

༄༅། མཆོག་ཏུ་གྱུར་ཏེ། འོད་ཟེར་རྣམས་སྡུར་འདུས་ནས་རང་ལ་ཐིམ་པས་རང་གི་གཟུགས་ཀྱི་ཕུང་པོ་རྣམ་པར་སྣང་མཛད། ཚོར་བ་རྡོ་རྗེ་ཉི་མ། འདུ་ཤེས་པད་མ་གར་གྱི་དབང་ཕྱུག། འདུ་བྱེད་རྡོ་རྗེ་རྒྱལ་པོ། རྣམ་པར་ཤེས་པ་རྡོ་རྗེ་སེམས་དཔའ་དེ་བཞིན་གཤེགས་པ་ཐམས་ཅད་ཉིད་དུ་གྱུར་བ་ནི་དཔལ་ཧེ་རུ་ཀ། མིག་གཏི་མུག་རྡོ་རྗེ། རྣ་བ་ཞེ་སྡང་རྡོ་རྗེ། སྣ་སེར་སྣ་རྡོ་རྗེ། ཁ་འདོད་ཆགས་རྡོ་རྗེ། ལུས་ཕྲག་དོག་རྡོ་རྗེ། སྐྱེ་མཆེད་ཐམས་ཅད་དབང་ཕྱུག་རྡོ་རྗེ། སའི་ཁམས་ལྷུང་བར་བྱེད་མ། ཆུའི་ཁམས་གསོད་པར་བྱེད་མ། མེའི་ཁམས་འཁྲུགས་པར་བྱེད་མ། རླུང་གི་ཁམས་གར་གྱི་དབང་ཕྱུག། ནམ་ཁའི་ཁམས་པད་མའི་དྲ་བ་ཅན་དུ་གྱུར་པར་བསམ་པ་ནི་ཚོགས་སོག་པ་ལ་རྟེན་འབྲུད་པར་ཅན་ཞིག་དགོས་པས། [illegible]ཕུང་པོ་ཁམས་དང་སྐྱེ་མཆེད་གཞི་སྣང་ཞིང་བསྒྱུར་བའོ། ཡང་སྙིང་ཁའི་ཧཱུྃ་ལས་འོད་འཕྲོས་པས་མདུན་གྱི་ནམ་མཁའི་སྟེང་གི་ཆ་ལ། རང་གི་བླ་མ་རྡོ་རྗེ་ཆོས་ཀྱི་རྣམ་པ་ལ། བླ་མ་བརྒྱུད་པ་ཐམས་ཅད་ཀྱིས་བསྐོར་བ་དང་། འོག་གི་ཆ་ལ་འཁོར་ལོ་བདེ་མཆོག་ལྷ་དྲུག་བཅུ་རྩ་གཉིས་ཀྱི་དཀྱིལ་འཁོར་ལ་སངས་རྒྱས་དང་བྱང་ཆུབ་སེམས་དཔའ་ཐམས་ཅད་ཀྱིས་བསྐོར་བ་སྤྱན་དྲངས་ལ། རང་གི་ལུས་དཔག་ཏུ་མེད་པར་སྤྲུལ་ནས། ན་མོ་གུ་རུ་བྷྱས་བླ་མ་དང་། ན་མ། ཤྲཱི་ཙཀྲ་སཾ་བ་ར་མཎྜལ་བྷྱས་དཀྱིལ་འཁོར་ལ་ཕྱག་འཚལ་ལོ། དེ་ནས་མཆོད་པ་རྣམས་ཀྱིས་རིམ་པས་མཆོད་པར་བསམ་ཞིང་། ཨོཾ་སརྦ་ཏ་ཐཱ་ག་ཏ་ཤྲཱི་ཙཀྲ་སམ་བྷ་ར་ཙཀྲ་སརྦ་ཏྲཻ་ར་ཡོ་གི་ནི་ཞེས་ཀུན་ལ་སྦྱར་ལ། ཨརྒྷཾ་པྲ་ཏཱི་ཙྪ་ཡེ་སྭཱཧཱ་ཡིས་མཆོད་ཡོན། པཱ་དྱཾ་པྲ་ཏཱི་ཙྪ་ཡེ་སྭཱཧཱ་ཡིས་ཞབས་བསིལ། བཛྲ་པུ་ཥྤེ་ཨཱཿ ཧཱུྃ་གིས་མེ་ཏོག། བཛྲ་དྷཱུ་པེ་ཨཱཿ ཧཱུྃ་གིས་བདུག་སྤོས། བཛྲ་ཨཱ་ལོ་ཀེ་ཨཱཿ ཧཱུྃ་གིས་མར་མེ། བཛྲ་གནྡྷེ་ཨཱཿ ཧཱུྃ་གིས་དྲི་ཆབ། བཛྲ་

༈ ནཻ་ཝེ་དྱ་ཨཱཿ ཧཱུྃ་གིས་ཞལ་ཟས། བཛྲ་ཤབྡ་ཨཱཿ ཧཱུྃ་གིས་རོལ་མོ། གིས་རོལ་མོ་ ཕུལ་ནས། བདག་པོས་ཡོངས་སུ་མ་བཟུང་བ་དང་། སྤྲོས་སྤྲུལ་པའི་མཆོད་པས་མཆོད་ པར་བསམ་ཞིང་། དབྲལ་བར་ནམ་མཁའ་མཛོད་ཀྱི་ཕྱག་རྒྱ་བྱས་ལ། ན་མོ་ཆོས་ཀྱི་ དབྱིངས་ཀྱི་བྱིན་གྱིས་བརླབས་དང་། སངས་རྒྱས་དང་། བྱང་ཆུབ་སེམས་དཔའ་ཐམས་ ཅད་ཀྱི་ཐུགས་རྗེ་རྣམ་པར་དག་པའི་བྱིན་གྱིས་བརླབས་དང་། གསང་སྔགས་དང་། ཕྱག་རྒྱའི་ མཐུ་དང་། བདག་གི་མོས་པ་དང་། ཏིང་ངེ་འཛིན་དང་སྨོན་ལམ་གྱི་དབང་གིས་འཇིག་ རྟེན་གྱི་ཁམས་ན་བདག་པོས་ཡོངས་སུ་མ་བཟུང་བའི་མཆོད་པའི་བྱེ་བྲག་ཇི་སྙེད་པ་དང་། གཞན་ཡང་བྱང་ཆུབ་སེམས་དཔའ་ཀུན་ཏུ་བཟང་པོའི་རྣམ་པར་ཐར་པ་ལས་བྱུང་བའི་མཆོད་ པའི་སྤྲིན་གྱི་ཕུང་པོ་ལྟ་བུ་བསམ་གྱིས་ཁྱབ་པ་ཞིག། བླ་མ་དང་། དཀྱིལ་འཁོར་གྱི་ འཁོར་ལོ འི་སངས་རྒྱས་དང་། བྱང་ཆུབ་སེམས་དཔའ་ཐམས་ཅད་ཀྱི་སྤྱན་ལམ་དུ་ འབྱུང་ཞིང་རྒྱས་པར་གྱུར་ཅིག། ཅེས་བརྗོད་ལ་སེ་གོལ་གཏོགས། ཡང་སྙིང་ཁར་ཕྱག་ རྒྱ་བཅས་ལ། ཨོཾ་སརྦ་བིད་པུ་ར་པུ་ར། སུ་ར་སུ་ར། ཨཱ་བརྟ་ཨཱ་བརྟ་ཧོ། ན་མ། ས་མནྟ་བུདྡྷ་ནཱ་མ། ཨ་ཧྲྀཤྨ་ར་ཨེ་སྨ་ར་ཎ་ཨཱི་མམ་ག་ག་ན་ཁཾ། ཧྲཱཾ་ཧ་ཏུ་ཨ་ཀ་ཤུ་ ས་མནྟ་མ། སརྦ་ཏ་ཐཱ་ག་ཏ་ཨ་པ་རི་ཤུདྡྷ་ལེ། མཏྱ་ལ་ལི་མ་མ་བྲ་ཥ་ཏེ། པུ་ཏྲ་ཧྲཱུཾ་ན་བྲ་ ལི་ན། སརྦ་ཏ་ཐཱ་ག་ཏ་བ་ལེན་དྲ། བན་དྷ་ས་སྨྲ་ན། བ་ལི་ན་ཙ་ལི་སྭ་ཧཱ། ཞེས་ བརྗོད་ནས་སེ་གོལ་བརྡབས་ལ་མཆོད་པར་བྱའོ།། དེ་ནས་བདག་གིས་ཚེ་ཐོག་མ་མེད་པ་ ནས་འདོད་ཆགས་དང་། ཞེ་སྡང་དང་། གཏི་མུག་གི་དབང་གིས། ལུས་དང་། ཡིད་ ཀྱི་སྒོ་ནས། སྡིག་པའི་ལས་བགྱིས་པ་དང་། འགྱིད་དུ་སྩལ་བ་དང་། བགྱིད་པ་ལ་རྗེས་སུ་ ཡིད་རང་བ་དེ་ཐམས་ཅད་བླ་མ་དང་དཀྱིལ་འཁོར་གྱི་ལྷ་ཚོགས་ཀྱི་སྤྱན་སྔར་སོ་སོར་

༄༅ བཤགས་ཤིང་ཡང་མི་བགྱིད་དོ། ཅེས་པ་དང་། བདག་མིང་འདི་ཞེས་བགྱི་བས་དུས་འདི་ནས་བཟུང་ནས། ཇི་སྲིད་དཔལ་འཁོར་ལོ་བདེ་མཆོག་གི་གོ་འཕང་མ་ཐོབ་ཀྱི་བར་དུ། སངས་རྒྱས་ལ་སྐྱབས་སུ་མཆིའོ། ཆོས་ལ་སྐྱབས་སུ་མཆིའོ། དགེ་འདུན་ལ་སྐྱབས་སུ་མཆིའོ། ཞེས་པ་དང་། བདེ་མཆོག་གིས་དཔལ་འཁོར་ལོ་བདེ་མཆོག་གི་དམ་ཚིག་དང་། སྡོམ་པའི་ཚོགས་བླང་ཞིང་བསྲུང་བར་བགྱིའོ། ཞེས་པ་དང་། སོ་སོའི་སྐྱེ་བོ་དང་། འཕགས་པ་ཉན་ཐོས་དང་།རང་སངས་རྒྱས་དང་། བྱང་ཆུབ་སེམས་དཔའ་དང་། བླ་ན་མེད་པ་ཡང་དག་པར་རྫོགས་པའི་སངས་རྒྱས་ཐམས་ཅད་ཀྱི་དགེ་བའི་རྩ་བ་ཐམས་ཅད་ལ་དགའ་ཞིང་རྗེས་སུ་ཡིད་རང་བར་བགྱིའོ་ཞེས་པ་དང་། བདག་གིས་སེམས་ཅན་མ་བསྒྲལ་བ་རྣམས་བསྒྲལ་བར་བགྱིའོ། མ་གྲོལ་བ་རྣམས་དགྲོལ་བར་བགྱིའོ། དབུགས་མ་ཕྱུང་བ་རྣམས་དབུགས་དབྱུང་བར་བགྱིའོ། ཡོངས་སུ་མྱ་ངན་ལས་མ་འདས་པ་རྣམས་ཡོངས་སུ་མྱ་ངན་ལས་ཟླ་བར་བགྱིའོ་ཞེས་པ་དང་ཕྱོགས་བཅུའི་དེ་བཞིན་གཤེགས་པ་ཆོས་ཀྱི་འཁོར་ལོ་བསྐོར་བར་མི་མཛད་པ་དེ་དག་ཐམས་ཅད་ལ་ཆོས་ཀྱི་འཁོར་ལོ་བསྐོར་བའི་ཕྱིར་བསྐུལ་བར་བགྱིའོ། ཞེས་པ་དང་། དེ་བཞིན་གཤེགས་པ་ཡོངས་སུ་མྱ་ངན་ལས་འདའ་བར་བཞེད་པ་དེ་དག་ཐམས་ཅད་ལ་མྱ་ངན་ལས་མི་འདའ་བར་གསོལ་བ་འདེབས་སོ། ཞེས་པ་དང་། བདག་གིས་དཔལ་འཁོར་ལོ་བདེ་མཆོག་གི་ལམ་རིམ་པ་གཉིས་ལ་ཡང་དག་པར་གནས་པར་བགྱིའོ། ཞེས་པ་དང་། བདག་གིས་དེ་ལྟར་བགྱིས་པའི་དགེ་བའི་རྩ་བ་དེ་དག་གིས་བདག་དང་སེམས་ཅན་ཐམས་ཅད་ཀྱིས་འཁོར་ལོ་བདེ་མཆོག་གི་གོ་འཕང་མྱུར་དུ་ཐོབ་པར་གྱུར་ཅིག། ཅེས་པ་རྣམས་དོན་དྲན་བཞིན་པས་ལན་གསུམ་དུ་བརྗོད་པར་བྱའོ།། དེ་ནས་ཚོགས་ཀྱི་

༄༅། དཔལ་འཁོར་ལོ་བདེ་མཆོག།

༄༅། ཞིང་དེ་རྣམས་ཀྱིས་རིགས་ཀྱི་བུ་ཁྱོད་ཀྱི་གནས་པ་འདི་ནི་ལེགས་པར་གནས་པ་ཡིན་གྱིས། གནས་པ་འདི་ལ་གནས་ན་མཆོག་གི་གོ་འཕང་ཐོབ་པར་འགྱུར་རོ། ཞེས་གནང་བ་ནོད་པར་བསམ་མོ། སླར་ཡང་མཆོད་པ་བསྡུས་པ་ཙམ་གྱིས་ཀྱང་མཆོད་ནས། ཨོཾ་བཛྲ་མུཿ ཞེས་བརྗོད་པས་གཤེགས་སུ་གསོལ་བ་ནི་ཚོགས་བསག་པ་དངོས་དང་འབྲེལ་བ་ཚོགས་བསག་བཅུ་གསུམ་གྱིས་ཚོགས་བསག་པའོ།། དེ་ནས་ཡང་། རང་གི་སྙིང་ཁའི་ཧཱུྃ་ལས་སྙིང་རོག་ཏུ་ཁཊྭཱ་ངོ་ གཉིས་དང་བཅས་པའི་སྒོ་མཚམས་བཅད། ཤར་ནས་རིམ་པ་དང་། ཤར་ལྷོ་ནས་རིམ་པ་ལས་བཟློག་པའི་རྩལ་གྱིས་ཕྱོགས་བཅུར་སྤྲོ་བར་བསམ། ངག་ཏུ་ཞལ་བཞི་པའི་སྔགས་ཀྱི་ཀང་པ་རེ་རེ་བརྗོད་ལུས་ཀྱིས་གཡོན་པའི་སེ་གོལ་བརྡབས་པ་སྦྱར་ཞིང་། བགེགས་ཐམས་ཅད་བསྒྲད་པར་བསམ་མོ། དེ་ནས་སྙིང་ཁའི་ཧཱུྃ་ལས་འོད་འཕྲོས་པས་རྡོ་རྗེའི་ས་གཞི། ར་བ་དྭ་བ་གུར། བླ་བྲེ། མདའི་དྭ་བ་དང་། ཡེ་ཤེས་ཀྱི་མེ་འབར་བ་རྣམས་སུ་རིམ་པ་བཞིན་དུ་གྱུར་པར་བསམ་མོ།། ལུས་ཀྱིས་གཡོན་པའི་སྡིགས་འཛུབ་ཕྱོགས་བཅུར་བསྐོར་ལ་སེ་གོལ་བརྡབ། ངག་ཏུ།།

ཨོཾ་ཨཻ་ཧྲི་ཉེ་བཛྲ་ཧྲ་བ་བན་ཧྲ་ཧཱུྃ་ཧཱུྃ་ཕཊ། ཨོཾ་བཛྲ་ཙྲ་ཀ་ར་ཧཱུྃ་བཾ་ཧཱུྃ། ཨོཾ་བཛྲ་པཉྫ་ར་ཧཱུྃ་བཾ་ཧཱུྃ། ཨོཾ་བཛྲ་བི་ཏ་ན་ཧཱུྃ་ཁཾ་ཧཱུྃ། ཨོཾ་བཛྲ་ཤྭ་ར་ཛྭ་ལ་ཧཾ་སཾ་ཧཾ། ཨོཾ་བཛྲ་ཛྭ་ལ་ཨ་ན་ལཱརྐ་ཧཱུྃ་རཾ་ཧཱུྃ།།

ཅེས་པ་རྣམས་ལན་གསུམ་གསུམ་བརྗོད་པ་དང་། རིམ་པ་བཞིན་སྦྱར། བསྲུང་བའི་འཁོར་

༄༅ ལོ་འཇུག་པར་བསྒོམ་མོ། ཡང་ཧཱུྃ་ལས་རྡོ་རྗེ་ཕྲེང་བུའི་ཚོགས་དང་། རྡོ་རྗེ་ཐོ་བའི་ཚོགས་སྤྲོས་པ་པོ་ཉ་རྣམས་ཀྱི་ལག་པ་གཡོན་པ་དང་གཡས་པར་གཏད་ནས། པོ་ཉ་རྣམས་རང་དང་འདྲ་བའི་སྤྲུལ་པ་དཔག་ཏུ་མེད་པས་ནམ་མཁའ་གང་བར་གྱུར་པས། ཕྱོགས་སྐྱོང་པ་རྣམས་ཀྱིས་གཙོ་བྱས་པའི་བགེགས་རྣམས་བཀུག། དཀར་པོའི་ཕྱོགས་རྣམས་སྐྱབས་སུ་འགྲོ་བ་དང་། བྱང་ཆུབ་ཀྱི་སེམས་ལ་བཀོད། ནག་པོའི་ཕྱོགས་རྣམས་ཀྱི་སྤྱི་བོར་ཕུར་བུས་བཏབ་པར་བསྒོམ་ཞིང་། ངག་ཏུ།།

ཨོཾ་ཛ་ཛ། ཛ་ཏ་ཡ་ཛ་ཡ། སརྦ་དུ་ཥྚཱན་ཕཊ། ཀཱི་ལ་ཡ་ཀཱི་ལ་ཡ། སརྦ་པཱ་པཾ་ཧཱུྃ་ཕཊ། བཛྲ་ཀཱི་ལ་ཡ་བཛྲ་དྷ་རོ་ད་ཨཱ་ཛྙཱ་པ་ཡ་ཏི། སརྦ་ཝིགྷ་ནཱན་ཀཱ་ཡ་ཝཱཀ་ཙིཏྟ་ཛ་ཀཱི་ལ་ཡ་ཧཱུྃ་ཕཊ།། ཅེས་བརྗོད་རྡོ་རྗེ་ཐོ་བས་བརྡུངས་ནས་རྡུལ་དུ་བརླག་པར་བསམ་ཞིང་། ཨོཾ་བཛྲ་མུད་ག་ར་བཛྲ་ཀཱི་ལ་ཡ་ཨ་ཀོ་ཊ་ཡ་ཧཱུྃ་ཕཊ། ཞེས་བརྗོད་པས་བགེགས་རྣམས་ཀྱི་སྡིག་པ་ཕྱུངས་ནས་རྣམ་ཤེས་མི་བསྐྱོད་པའི་ཞིང་དུ་སྐྱེས་པར་བསམ་ཞིང་། པོ་ཉ་རྣམས་རྡོ་རྗེའི་ར་བའི་ཁ་ཕྱིར་ལ་འཁོད་ནས། བསྒྲུབ་པ་པོ་སངས་མ་རྒྱས་ཀྱི་བར་སྲུང་བར་བཞེ་པ་ནི་ དོན་ཆེན་པོ་ཡེ་ཤེས་ཀྱི་ཚོགས་སོག་པ་ལ་བར་ཆད་མི་འབྱུང་བར་བྱ་བའི་ཕྱིར་བསྲུང་བའི་འཁོར་ལོ་བསྒོམ་པ་སྟེ། བསོད་ནམས་ཀྱི་ཚོགས་བསག་པའོ།། དེ་ནས་ཕྱི་ནང་གི་ཆོས་ཐམས་ཅད་སྒྱུ་མ་རྨི་ལམ་ལྟ་བུར་བསམ་ནས། ཨོཾ་སྭ་བྷཱ་ཝ་ཤུདྡྷ་སརྦ་དྷརྨཱ་སྭ་བྷཱ་ཝ་ཤུདྡྷོ྅ཧཾ། ཞེས་པ་དང་། སྒྱུ་མ་མི་དམིགས་པའི་སྟོང་པ་ཉིད་དུ་བསྒོམས་ནས། ཨོཾ་ཤུ་ནྱ་ཏཱ་ཛྙཱ་ན་བཛྲ་སྭ་བྷཱ་ཝ་ཨཏྨ༔ ཀོར་ཧཾ། ཞེས་བརྗོད་པ་ནི་ཡེ་ཤེས་ཀྱི་ཚོགས་བསག་པ་སྟེ་

༄༅ རྒྱུ་ཚོགས་གཉིས་བསག་པའོ༎ སྟོང་པའི་ངང་ལས་ཡཾ་ལས་རླུང་གི་དཀྱིལ་འཁོར་
གཞུ་བཞུངས་པ་ཧྲ་ཏུ་བ་དན་གྱིས་མཚན་པ། རཾ་ལས་མེའི་དཀྱིལ་འཁོར་གྲུ་གསུམ་དམར་
པོ་འབར་བས་མཚན་པ། བཾ་ལས་ཆུའི་དཀྱིལ་འཁོར་དཀར་པོ་ཟླུམ་པོ་བུམ་པས་མཚན་
པ། ལཾ་ལས་སའི་དཀྱིལ་འཁོར་གྲུ་བཞི་སེར་པོ་གྲྭ་བཞིར་རྡོ་རྗེ་རྩེ་གསུམ་པས་མཚན་པ།
སུཾ་ལས་རིའི་རྒྱལ་པོ་རི་རབ། ཤར་ཤེལ། བྱང་གསེར། ནུབ་པདྨ་ར་ག།
ལྷོ་བཻ་ཌཱུརྻའི་རང་བཞིན་ལས་གྲུབ་པ། གྲུ་བཞི་པ། བང་རིམ་བཞི་པ། ཙོག་བརྒྱད་
དང་ལྡན་པ་རྣམས་བརྩེགས་པའི་སྟེང་དུ། ཧཱུྃ་ལས་སྣ་ཚོགས་རྡོ་རྗེ་ཤར་སྔོ། བྱང་
ལྗང་། ནུབ་དམར། ལྷོ་སེར། ཕྱི་བ་མཐིང་ནག་ཅན་གྱི་སྟེང་དུ་པཾ་ལས་པདྨ་འདབ་མ་
བརྒྱད་པའི་དབུས་སུ། ཨ་ཨཱ། ཨི་ཨཱི། ཨུ་ཨཱུ། རྀ་རཱྀ། ལྀ་ལཱྀ། ཨེ་ཨཻ།
ཨོ་ཨཽ། ཨཾ་ཨཿ ཅེས་པ་ཕྲག་གཉིས་གཡོན་སྐོར་དུ་བཀོད་པས་མཚན་བཟང་པོ་སུམ་
བཅུ་སོ་གཉིས་ཀྱི་ངོ་བོར་བསྒོམས་པ་ལས་བྱུང་བའི་ཟླ་བའི་དཀྱིལ་འཁོར་མེ་ལོང་ལྟ་བུའི་
ཡེ་ཤེས་སུ་མོས་པའི་སྟེང་དུ། ཀ་ཁ་ག་གྷ་ང་། ཙ་ཚ་ཛ་ཛྷ་ཉ། ཊ་ཋ་ཌ་ཌྷ་ཎ།
ཏ་ཐ་ད་དྷ་ན༎ པ་ཕ་བ་བྷ་མ། ཡ་ར་ལ་ཝ། ཤ་ཥ་ས་ཧ་ཀྵ། ཡ ···· ར་ལ་ཝ་ཧྣ་
ཧ། ཞེས་པ་ཕྲག་གཉིས་གཡས་སྐོར་དུ་བཀོད་པ་དཔེ་བྱད་བཟང་པོ་བརྒྱད་ཅུའི་ངོ་བོར་
དམིགས་པ་ལས་བྱུང་བའི་ཉི་མའི་དཀྱིལ་འཁོར་མཉམ་པ་ཉིད་ཀྱི་ཡེ་ཤེས་སུ་བསམ། དེ་
གཉིས་ཀྱི་བར་དུ་ཧཱུྃ་དཀར་པོ་སོ་སོར་རྟོག་པའི་ཡེ་ཤེས་ཀྱི་ངོ་བོར་བསྒོམ། ཉི་མའི་
སྟེང་དུ་ཐ་མལ་གྱི་ལུས་ངག་ཡིད་གསུམ་གྱི་ངོ་བོ་ཨོཾ་ཨཱཿ ཧཱུྃ་དང་། ཡུམ་གྱི་མཁའ་
དག་པའི་ངོ་བོ་པདྨ། ཁུ་བ་ཀྱི་བྱང་ཆུབ་ཀྱི་སེམས་ཀྱི་ངོ་བོ་ཟླ་བ། སེམས་ཀྱི་རང་
བཞིན་འོད་གསལ་བའི་ངོ་བོ་ཧཱུྃ་ཡིག་རྣམས་རིམ་གྱིས་བརྩེགས་པ་རྫོགས་ནས། མས་

༄༅ ཡར་རིམ་པ་བཞིན། ཧཱུྃ་གི་བར་དུ་ཐིམ་ཞིང་། ཧཱུྃ་གིའང་ཞབས་ཀྱུ། ཐིག་ལ། མགོ་བོ། ཟླ་ཚེས། ཐིག་ལེ་རྣམས་རིམ་གྱིས་ན་ད་ལ་ཐིམ་ནས། ན་ད་དམར་སྐྱ། ཤིན་ཏུ་ཕྲ་ཞིང་ཕྲེད་པ། དཔའ་བོ་ཉི་ཤུ་རྩ་ལྔའི་ཐུགས་ཀྱི་སྒྲ་སྒྲོགས་བཞིན་པ། འཁྲུག་ཅིང་སྨུར་དུ་བབས་པ་ནི་སྒྲ་ཡིན་ལ། དེས་ཉི་མའི་དཀྱིལ་འཁོར་ཐུག་ནས། ཧཱུ་གི་ཡི་གེ་རྐྱལ་ལ་ཐིམ་ནས་ཐམས་ཅད་གཅིག་ཏུ་འདྲེས་པ་བྱ་བ་གྲུབ་པའི་ཡེ་ཤེས་སུ་བསྒོམས་ལ། དེ་ཡོངས་སུ་གྱུར་པ་ལས་རྟེན་དང་རྟེན་པར་བཅས་པའི་དཀྱིལ་འཁོར་གྱི་འཁོར་ལོར་གཅིག་ཆར་གྱུར་པ་ནི། ཆོས་ཀྱི་དབྱིངས་ཀྱི་ཡེ་ཤེས་ཀྱི་ངོ་བོ་འོ། དེ་ཉིད་ཀྱི་རིམ་གྱིས་གསལ་གདབ་པར་བྱ་སྟེ། རི་རབ་ཀྱི་སྟེང་བསྲུང་བའིའཁོར་ལོའི་ནང་དུ་རིན་པོ་ཆེ་སྣ་ཚོགས་ལས་གྲུབ་པའི་གཞལ་ཡས་ཁང་གྲུ་བཞི་སྒོ་བཞི་པ། ནང་ནས་ནག་པོ། དཀར་པོ། སེར་པོ། དམར་པོ། ལྗང་ཁུའི་རྩིག་པ་རིམ་པ་ལྔ་དང་ལྡན་པ། དེའི་སྟེང་དུ་རིན་པོ་ཆེའི་པ་གུ་སེར་པོའི་ཁ་ཁྱེར་དང་། དེའི་སྟེང་དུ་མདའ་ཡབ་ལ་ཟླ་བ་རྒྱུང་གིས་བསྐྱོད་པ་དང་དྲིལ་བུ་གཡེར་ཁ་དང་བཅས་པའི་དྲྭ་བ་དང་དྲྭ་ཕྱེད་པ་འཕྱང་བ། མདའ་ཡབ་ཀྱི་སྟེང་དུ་རིན་པོ་ཆེའི་དྲྭ་བ་སེང་མའི་ཕུ་ཤུས་བཀར་བ། ཕྱི་རོལ་འདོད་ཡོན་གྱི་སྣམ་བུ་དམར་པོའི་སྟེང་དུ་ཕྱོགས་རེར་རབ་ཏུ་མཛེས་ཤིང་ཡིད་དུ་འོང་བའི་ལྷ་མོ་བཞིས་མཆོད་རྫས་དཔག་ཏུ་མེད་པ་ཐོགས་ནས་མ ཆོད་པ་བྱེད་པ་བྲིམ་པ་ལྟར་ཐོ་ཐུར་དུ་གྱུར་བའི་སྒོ་བཞི་དེའི་སྟེང་གི་ཐད་སོར་ཀ་བ་བཞི་བཞིས་བཏེག་པའི་རྟ་བབས་བང་རིམ་བཞི་པའི་སྟེང་དུ། ཆོས་ཀྱི་འཁོར་ལོ་དང་། རི་དྭགས་དང་། གདུགས་དང་ལྡན་པ། གཞན་ཡང་ཛ་ཡབ་ནོར་བུའི་ཕུ་བ་ཅན་དང་། རིན་པོ་ཆེ་དང་། མེ་ཏོག་གི་ཕྲེང་བ་དང་། གོས་དང་འཕན་ལ་སོགས་པའི་རྒྱན་རྣམས་ཀྱིས་མཛེས་པར་བྱས་པའོ།། ནང་གི་ལྷ་སྣམ་ཤར་རྡོ། བྱང་

༄༅ ཞུང་། ནུབ་དམར་ལྷོ་སེར་བའི་དབུས་ན་འཁོར་ལོ་རིམ་པ་བཞི། མཆོད་རྟེན་ཐང་རིམ་བཞི་པའི་རྩལ་དུ་གནས་པ། གཞལ་ཡས་ཁང་གི་ཕྱི་རོལ་དུ་ཤར་ཕྱོགས་སུ་གཏུམ་དྲག། བྱང་དུ་ཙང་ཚེང་འཁྲིགས་པ། ནུབ་ཏུ་ཙུར་ཙུར་འབར་བ། ལྷོར་འཇིགས་སུ་རུང་བ། ཤར་ལྷོར་ནགས་ཚལ་དྲུན་སུམ་ཚོགས་པ། ལྷོ་ནུབ་ཏུ་སྨུན་པ་མི་ཟད་པ། ནུབ་བྱང་དུ་ཀི་ལི་ཀི་ལིའི་སྒྲ་སྒྲོགས་པ། བྱང་ཤར་དུ་ཧ་ཧ་ཀ ད་པའི་དུར་ཁྲོད་རྣམས་སུ་རིམ་པ་དེ་ཉིད་ཀྱིས་བརྒྱ་བྱིན་སེར་པོ་གླང་པོ་ཆེ་ལ་ཞོན་པ་རྡོ་རྗེ་འཛིན་པ། གནོད་སྦྱིན་སེར་པོ་རྟ་ལ་ཞོན་པ། དབྱུག་ཐོ་འཛིན་པ། ཆུ་ལྷ་དཀར་པོ་ཆུ་སྲིན་ལ་ཞོན་པ། སྦྲུལ་ཞགས་འཛིན་པ། གཤིན་རྗེ་སྔོན་པོ་མ་ཧེ་ལ་བཞོན་པ། བེ་ཅོན་འཛིན་པ། མེ་ལྷ་དམར་པོ་ར་སྐྱེས་ལ་ཞོན་པ། ཕྱག་བཞི་པ་གཡས་པ་གཉིས་ཀྱིས་མཆོག་སྦྱིན་དང་། དབྱུག་གུ་གསུམ་པ། གཡོན་པ་གཉིས་ཀྱིས་བགྲང་ཕྲེང་དང་རིལ་བ་སྤྱི་བླུགས་འཛིན་པ། སྲིན་པོ་ནག་པོ་རོ་ལངས་ལ་ཞོན་པ། རལ་གྲི་དང་ཐོད་པ་འཛིན་པ། རླུང་ལྷ་ལྗང་ཁུ་ཤྭ་བ་ལ་ཞོན་པ་བ་དན་འཛིན་པ། དབང་ལྡན་དཀར་པོ་གླང་ལ་ཞོན་པ་རྡོ་རྗེ་རྩེ་གསུམ་འཛིན་པ། ཐམས་ཅད་ཀྱང་རྒྱན་གྱིས་བརྒྱན་ཞིང་རང་དང་འདྲ་བའི་རིག་མས་གཡོན་ནས་བརྟེན་པ། སྤྱི་བོས་བཅོམ་ལྡན་འདས་ལ་འདུད་པའོ།། དེ་བཞིན་དུ་ཤི་རི་ཤ། ཨ་ཤྭཏྠ། ཨཾ་ཀོ་ལ། ཙཱུ་ཏ། ཀ་རན་ཛ། ལ་ཏ་པར་ཀ་ཊི། པར་ཊི་པ་ཏྲ། ཧྲ་ཊ་སྟེ་ཤིང་ཆེན་པོ་བརྒྱད་དང་། དེ་རྣམས་ལ་བརྟེན་པའི་སྐྱོ་མཚམས་མ་རྣམས་ཀྱི་གཟུགས་འཛིན་པའི་དྲག་གཏུམ་སྐྱོངས་བ་ལ་རྩོགས་པའི་ཞིང་སྐྱོང་བརྒྱད་དང་། ནོར་རྒྱུས། འཛོག་པོ། སྟོབས་ཀྱི་རྒྱུ། པད་མ། ཏུ་ལུན་ཏ། རིགས་ལྡན། དུང་སྐྱོང་། པད་མ་ཆེན་པོ་སྟེ་ཀླུ་བརྒྱད་དང་། སྒྲ་གྲག་པ། རྨུགས་པ། སྨུན་པ་ཅན། ཀུན་དུ་འཁྱིལ་པ། གང་བ།

༄༅། འབབ་པ། དྭག་པོ། འཁྲིགས་པ་སྟེ་སྤྲིན་ཆེན་པོ་བརྒྱད་དང་།། གཞན་ཡང་རྩ་བོ་ཆེན་པོ་བརྒྱད། མེ་ཆེན་པོ་བརྒྱད། མཆོད་རྟེན་ཆེན་པོ་བརྒྱད་གནས་ཤིང་། རྨུལ་པ་དང་། རང་རྒྱུད་པའི་དཔའ་བོ་དང་། རྣལ་འབྱོར་མ་དང་། གྲུབ་པ་དང་། རིག་པ་འཛིན་པ་དང་། མཁའ་འགྲོ་དང་མཁའ་འགྲོ་མ་དང་། འདྲེ་དང་། སྲིན་པོ་དང་། གནོད་སྦྱིན་དང་། ཤ་ཟ་དང་། འབྱུང་པོ་དང་། ལྷ་སྲུང་ལ་སོགས་པས་ཡོངས་སུ་གང་བའི་དུར་ཁྲོད་ཀྱིས་བསྐོར་བའོ། གཞལ་ཡས་ཁང་གི་ནང་དུ་འཁོར་ལོའི་དངོས་སུ་

པད་མ་འདབ་མ་བརྒྱད་པའི་ལྟེ་བར་ཉི་མའི་དཀྱིལ་འཁོར་གྱི་སྟེང་དུ་རང་ཉིད་འཁོར་ལོ་བདེ་མཆོག། འབྱུང་བ་བཞི་དག་ཅིང་། ཚད་མེད་པ་བཞི་དང་། རྣམ་པར་ཐར་པ་བཞི་དང་། འཕྲིན་ལས་བཞིའི་ངོ་བོ་ཞལ་བཞི་པ།། རྩ་བའི་ཞལ་སྔོ། གཡོན་ལྗང་། རྒྱབ་དམར། གཡས་སེར་བ།། ཆོས་ཀྱིས་དབྱིངས་ལས་མི་འགྱུར་བས་སྐུ་མདོག་སྔོན་པོ། ཁམས་གསུམ་ལ་གཟིགས་ཤིང་ དུས་གསུམ་གྱི་ དངོས་ པོ་ མཁྱེན་ པས་ ཞལ་ རེ་ རེ་ ཞིང་ སྤྱན་གསུམ་གསུམ་པ།། རྟེན་ཅིང་ འབྲེལ་བར་འབྱུང་བ་བཅུ་ གཉིས་ ལུགས་འབྱུང་དང་ ལུགས་ལས་བཟློག་པ་ཐུགས་སུ་ཆུད་ཅིང་། འཕོ་བ་བཅུ་གཉིས་རྣམ་པར་དག་པས་ཕྱག་བཅུ་གཉིས་པ། བྱང་ཆུབ་ཀྱི་སེམས་སྟོང་པ་དང་སྙིང་རྗེ་མཚོན་པས། རྡོ་རྗེ་དང་དྲིལ་བུ་འཛིན་པའི་ཕྱག་དང་པོ་གཉིས་ཀྱིས་ཐབས་དང་ཤེས་རབ་ཟུང་དུ་འཇུག་པའི་ཕྱིར་ཡུམ་ལ་འཁྱུད་པ སྨྲོངས་པའི་གླང་པོ་དྲལ་བས་དེའི་འོག་མ་གཉིས་གླང་པོ་ཆེའི་ཀོ་རློན་གོས་སུ་གྱོན་པ། མཆོག་ཏུ་དགའ་བའི་སྒྲ་སྒྲགས་པས་གསུམ་པ་ན་ཌཱ་མ་རུ། སྐྱེ་ཤི་རྩ་བ་ནས་གཅོད་པས་བཞི་པས་དགྲ་སྟ། ང་རྒྱལ་ལ་སོགས་པའི་སྐྱོན་དྲུག་གཅོད་པས་ལྔ་པས་གྲི་གུག། སྲིད་པ་གསུམ་གྱི་ཉེས་པ་འཇོམས་པས་དྲུག་པས་མདུང་རྩེ་གསུམ་པ། བྱང་ཆུབ་ཀྱི་སེམས་བདེ་བ་ཆེན་

༄༅ པོ་དང་ལྡན་པས་གཡོན་གྱི་གསུམ་པས་རྡོ་རྗེས་མཚན་པའི་ཁ་ཊྭཱཾ་ག། དངོས་པོ་དང་དངོས་པོ་མེད་པའི་རྣམ་པར་རྟོག་པ་བཅད་པས་བཞི་པས་ཁྲག་གིས་གང་བའི་ཐོད་པ། ཡང་དག་པའི་ཡེ་ཤེས་སེམས་ཅན་གྱི་རྒྱུད་ལ་འཆིང་བས། ལྔ་པས་རྡོ་རྗེ་ཞགས་པ། གཏི་མུག་སྤངས་པས་དྲུག་པས་ཚངས་པའི་མགོ་བོ་གདོང་བཞི་པ་བསྣམས་པ། ཐུགས་རྗེ་ཆེན་པོས་སེམས་ཅན་གྱི་ཁམས་ལ་བཞུགས་པའི་ཕྱིར་ཞབས་གཡས་པ་བརྐྱང་པས་མྱ་ངན་ལས་འདས་པའི་མཐའ་དུས་མཚན་དམར་མོ་ཞིང་དུ་རིད་པ་གྲི་གུག་དང་ཐོད་པ་འཛིན་པ་གན་རྒྱལ་དུ་མནན་པ། ཤེས་རབ་ཆེན་པོས་གང་ཟག་དང་ཆོས་སུ་མི་འཛིན་པས་ཞབས་གཡོན་པ་བསྐུམ་པས་འཁོར་བའི་མཐའ་འཇིགས་བྱེད་ནག་པོ་ལག་པ་བཞི་པ་གཡས་པས་ཌ་མ་རུ་དང་། གྲི་གུག་གཡོན་པས་ཁ་ཊྭཱཾ་ག་དང་། ཐོད་པ་འཛིན་པ་ཁ་སྦྱར་དུ་མནན་པ།། ཚོགས་ཡོངས་སུ་རྫོགས་པས་རལ་པའི་ཐོར་ཚུགས་སྤྱི་བོར་བཅིངས་པའི་རྒྱུར། དགོས་འདོད་ཐམས་ཅད་ཡིད་བཞིན་དུ་སྩོལ་བས། ཡིད་བཞིན་གྱི་ནོར་བུ་རིན་པོ་ཆེས་བརྒྱན་པ། བྱང་ཆུབ་ཀྱི་སེམས་གོང་ནས་གོང་དུ་འཕེལ་བས་གཡོན་ན་ཆོས་གཅིག་གི་ཟླ་བ་དང་། འཕྲིན་ལས་སྣ་ཚོགས་པས་སེམས་ཅན་གྱི་དོན་མཛད་པས་འཚོགས་མའི་སྟེང་དུ་སྣ་ཚོགས་རྡོ་རྗེས་མཚན་པ། ཡེ་ཤེས་ལྔའི་ཡོན་ཏན་ཡོངས་སུ་རྒྱས་པས། དབུ་རེ་རེ་མི་མགོ་སྐམ་པོ་ལྔ་ལྔའི་དབུ་རྒྱན་དང་། ཨ་ལི་ཀཱ་ལི་ལྔ་བཅུ་དག་པས་མི་མགོ་རློན་པ་ལྔ་བཅུའི་དོ་ཤལ་ཅན། བདུད་དང་ལོག་པར་ལྟ་བ་འཇོམས་པས་ཞལ་རྣམ་པར་འགྱུར་ཞིང་མཆེ་བ་གཙིགས་པ། ན་རྒྱན་བཟོད་པ། མགུལ་རྒྱན་སྦྱིན་པ་གདུ་བུ་ཚུལ་ཁྲིམས། སྐ་རགས་བརྩོན་འགྲུས། སྤྱི་བོར་རུས་པའི་འཁོར་ལོ་བསམ་གཏན། ཐལ་ཆེན་གྱི་རྒྱ་དང་མཆོད་ཕྱིར་ཐོགས་ཤེས་རབ་སྟེ་ཕ་རོལ་དུ་ཕྱིན་པ་དྲུག་གི་ངོ་བོ་རུས་པའི་རྒྱན་དྲུག་གིས་བརྒྱན་པ། བདུད་འཇོམས་པ་ལ

༄༅ དཔའ་ཞིང་། གཟུང་འཛིན་གྲངས་པའི་རྟག་གི་ལྷུགས་པའི་ཤམ་ཐབས་གྲོལ་བ། སྐུ་
གསུང་ཐུགས་ཀྱི་ཡོན་ཏན་རྒྱས་ཤིང་། ཉོན་མོངས་པས་གཟིར་བའི་གདུལ་བྱ་རྣམས་རྗེས་སུ་འཛིན་
པ་ལ་མ་ཁས་པས། སླེག་པ། དཔའ་བ་མི་སྡུག་པ། གོད་པ་དྲག་ཤུལ་འཇིགས་སུ་རུང་། སྙིང་
རྗེ་ཏམ་དང་ཞི་བ་སྟེ། གར་དགུའི་རོ་དང་ལྡན་པ་ཉིད། དེའི་པང་ན་ཡུམ་རྡོ་རྗེ་ཕག་མོ་
སེམས་ཅན་གྱི་དོན་ལ་རྗེས་སུ་ཆགས་པའི་སྐུ་མདོག་དམར་མོ། ཆོས་ཐམས་ཅད་དེ་བཞིན་ཉིད་
དུ་རོ་ཅིག་པས་ཞལ་གཅིག་པ། བདེན་པ་གཉིས་ཐུགས་སུ་ཆུད་པའི་ཕྱག་གཉིས་ཀྱི་གཡོན་
པས་བདེ་བ་ཆེན་པོ་ཡོངས་སུ་སྐྱོང་བའི་ཐོད་པ་ཁྲག་གིས་གང་ བ་འཛིན་པས་ཞབ་ལ་འཁྱུད་པ།
གཡས་པས་རྟོག་པ་ཐམས་ཅད་བཅད་པའི་ཡེ་ཤེས་ཀྱིས་ བདུད་དང་ཉོན་མོངས་པ་ཐམས་ཅད་
འཇིག་པར་བྱེད་པས་རྡོ་རྗེས་མཚན་པའི་གྲི་གུག་དང་བཅས་པའི་སྡིག་འཛུབ་ཀྱིས་ཕྱོགས་
ཐམས་ཅད་དུ་སྡིགས་པར་བྱེད་པ། ཀུན་དུ་འཛིན་པའི་མདུད་པ་གྲོལ་བས་སྐྲ་གྲོལ་བ། ཉོན་
མོངས་པའི་སྒྲིབ་གཡོགས་དང་བྲལ་བས་གཅེར་བུ། སྤྱན་གསུམ་པ། མི་མགོ་སྐམ་པོ་ལྔའི་
དབུ་རྒྱན་དང་། རློན་པོ་ལྔ་བཅུའི་དོ་ཤལ་ཅན། རུས་པའི་རྒྱན་ལྔ་དང་ལྡན་པ། ཐབ་
དང་མི་བྲལ་བའི་ཕྱིན་པ་གཉིས་ཀྱིས་བཅོམ་ལྡན་འདས་ལ་འཁྱུད་པ། སྣང་བ་དང་། ཐབས་དང་།
ལྷག་མཐོང་དང་། སྙིང་རྗེ་ཆེན་པོ་འི་ངོ་བོ་ནི་ཡབ་ཡིན་ལ། སྟོང་པ་དང་ཤེས་རབ་དང་
ཞི་གནས་དང་། བདེ་བ་ཆེན་པོའི་ངོ་བོ་ཡུམ་ཡིན་ཞིང་། ཟུང་དུ་འཇུག་པའི་ཕྱིར་ཀུན་དུ་
ཁ་སྦྱར་བ། ཡེ་ཤེས་ཆེན་པོ་འི་མེས་ཕྱི་ནང་གི་གདོན་ཐམས་ཅད་སྲེག་པར་བྱེད་པས་
ཡེ་ཤེས་ཀྱི་མེ་འབར་བའི་དབུས་ན་བཞུགས་པར་བསམ་མོ། པད་མའི་འདབ་མ་
བཞི་ལ་ཤར་དུ་མཁའ་འགྲོ་མ་སྔོན་མོ། བྱང་དུ་ལ་མ་ལྗང་ཁུ། ནུབ་ཏུ་ཁཎྜ་རོ་ཧེ་དམར་མོ།
ལྷོར་གཟུགས་ཅན་མ་སེར་མོ། ཐམས་ཅད་ཀྱང་ཞལ་གཅིག་ཕྱག་བཞི་མ། གཡས་གཉིས་

༄ ཀྱིས་གྲི་གུག་དང་ཌཱ་མ་རུ་དང་། གཡོན་གཉིས་ཀྱིས་ཐོད་པ་ཁྲག་གིས་གང་བ། ཁ་ཊཱ། ག་འཛིན་པ་གཅེར་བུ་གཡས་བརྐྱང་པས་བཞུགས་པའོ།། མཚམས་བཞིར་རིན་པོ་ཆེའི་བུམ་པ་ཡེ་ཤེས་ཀྱི་རྫས་གང་བ་ནོས་ཀྱི་སྙིང་དུ་བདུད་རྩི་ལྔས་ཡོངས་སུ་གང་བའི་ཐོད་པ་གནས་པའི་བདེ་བ་ཆེན་པོའི་འཁོར་ལོའོ།། གྲི་གུག་གི་ར་བ་དང་། ཀ་བ་དང་། གདུང་དང་། ཐོག་ཕུབས་ཅན། རྡོ་རྗེ་ཕྱེད་པའི་ཏོག་གིས་མཛེས་པར་བྱས་པའོ།། དེའི་ཕྱི་རོལ་ཐུགས་ཀྱི་འཁོར་ལོ་ཁ་དོག་སྔོན་པོ་རྩིབས་བརྒྱད་པའི་ཤར་ཕྱོགས་སུ་པུ་ལི་ར་མ་ལ་ཡར་ཁཎྜ་ཀ་པ་ལི་དང་རབ་ཏུ་གཏུམ་མོ།། བྱང་ཕྱོགས་ཛ་ལན་དྷ་རར་མ་ཧཱ་ཀཾ་ཀ་ལ་དང་། གཏུམ་པའི་མིག་ཅན་མ། ནུབ་ཕྱོགས་ཨོ་རྒྱན་དུ་ཀཾ་ཀ་ལ་དང་། འོད་ལྡན་མ་ལྷོ་ཕྱོགས་ཨར་བུ་དར་མཆེ་བ་རྣམས་པར་གཙིགས་མ་དང་། སྐ་ཆེན་མ།། ཤར་ལྷོ་གོ་ད་བ་རིར་སུ་ར་བཱི་རི་དང་། བརྟན་པའི་བློ་ཅན་མ།། ལྷོ་ནུབ་ར་མི་ཤ་རིར་ འོད་དཔག་མེད་དང་། མིའུ་ཐུང་མ། ནུབ་བྱང་དེ་ཝཱི་ཀོ་ཊར་རྡོ་རྗེའི་འོད་དང་། ལང་ཀའི་དབང་ཕྱུག་མ།། བྱང་ཤར་མ་ལ་བར་རྡོ་རྗེའི་སྐུ་དང་ཤིང་གྲིབ་མ་སྟེ། ཐུགས་ཀྱི་འཁོར་ལོ་ཁ་དོག་སྔོན་པོ་རྣམས་མཁའ་ལ་སྤྱོད་པའི་ཚུལ་གྱིས་བཞུགས་ཤིང་ས་བླ་སྟེང་བ། རྡོ་རྗེ་འི་ར་བ་དང་། ཀ་བ་དང་གདུང་དང་། ཐོག་ཕུབས་དང་བཅས་པ། ཐུགས་ཀྱི་གསང་བ་བསམ་གྱིས་མི་ཁྱབ་པའི་ངོ་བོའོ།། དེའི་ཕྱི་རོལ་དུ་གསུང་གི་འཁོར་ལོ་ཁ་དོག་དམར་པོ་རྩིབས་བརྒྱད་པའི་ཤར་ཕྱོགས་ཀ་མ་རུ་པར་ཨཾ་ཤུ་རི་དང་ཨཻ་ར་བ་ཏི། བྱང་ཕྱོགས་ཨོ་ཏྲར་རྡོ་རྗེ་རལ་པ་ཅན་དང་འཇིགས་བྱེད་ཆེན་མོ།། ནུབ་ཕྱོགས་ཏྲི་ཤ་ཀུ་ནེར་དཔའ་བོ་ཆེན་པོ་དང་། རླུང་གི་ཤུགས་ཅན་མ། ལྷོ་ཕྱོགས་ཀོ་ས་ལར་རྡོ་རྗེ་ཧཱུྃ་མཛད་དང་ཆང་འཐུང་མ། ཤར་ལྷོ་ཀ་ལིང་ཀར་རབ་ཏུ་བཟང་པོ་དང་། ཤྱ་མ་དེ་བཱི།། ལྷོ་ནུབ་ལམ་པ་ཀར། རྡོ་རྗེ་བཟང་པོ་དང་། ཤིན་ཏུ་བཟང་མོ།།

༄༅། ཀྱབ་བྱང་ཀུན་ཅོར་འཇིགས་བྱེད་ཆེན་པོ་དང་། ཏ་ན་མ། བྱང་ཤར་ཏི་མ་ལ་ཡར་མིག་མི་བཟང་དང་། ཁ་ག་ན་སྐྱེ་གསུང་གི་འཁོར་ལོ་ཁ་དོག་དམར་པོ་ས་ལ་སྤྱོད་པའི་ཚུལ་གྱིས་བཞུགས་ཤིང་ས་སྙིང་སྤྱོད་བ་པར་མའི་ར་བ་དང་། ཀ་བ་དང་། གདུང་དང་། ཐོག་ཕུབས་དང་བཅས་པ། གསུང་གི་གསང་བ་བསམ་གྱིས་མི་ཁྱབ་པའི་ངོ་བོ་འོ།། དེའི་ཕྱི་རོལ་སྐུའི་འཁོར་ལོ་ཁ་དོག་དཀར་པོ་ཅི་བས་བརྒྱུད་པའི་ཤར་ཕྱོགས་བྲེ་ཏ་པུ་རིར་སྟོབས་པོ་ཆེ་དང་འཁོར་ལོའི་ཤུགས་ཅན་མ། བྱང་ཕྱོགས་ཀྲི་ཏ་དེ་བར་རིན་ཆེན་རྡོ་རྗེ་དང་། ཁནྡྷ་རོ་ཧི།། རྒྱབ་ཕྱོགས་སོཽ་རཥྚ་ར་རྟ་མགྲིན་དང་། ཤོན་ཊ་ནི། ལྷོ་ཕྱོགས་སུ་ཝརྣ་དྭི་པར་ནམ་མཁའི་སྙིང་པོ་དང་། འཁོར་ལོའི་གོ་ཆ་མ།། ཤར་ལྷོ་ན་ག་རར། དཔལ་ཧེ་རུ་ཀ་དང་། ཤིན་ཏུ་དཔའ་མོ། ལྷོ་རྒྱབ་སིནྡྷུ་ར་པད་མ་གར་གྱི་དབང་ཕྱུག་དང་། སྟོབས་ཆེན་མ། རྒྱབ་བྱང་མ་རོར་རྣམ་པར་སྣང་མཛད་དང་། འཁོར་ལོ་སྒྱུར་མ།། བྱང་ཤར་ཀུ་ལུ་ཏར་རྡོ་རྗེ་སེམས་དཔའ་དང་། བརྩོན་གྲུས་ཆེན་མོ་སྐྱེ་སྐུའི་འཁོར་ལོ་སྐུ་མདོག་དཀར་པོས་འོག་ན་སྤྱོད་པའི་ཚུལ་གྱིས་བཞུགས་ཤིང་ས་འོག་སྤྱོང་བ། འཁོར་ལོའི་རབ་དང་། ཀ་བ་དང་། གདུང་དང་། ཐོག་ཕུབས་དང་བཅས་པ་སྐུའི་གསང་བ་བསམ་གྱིས་མི་ཁྱབ་པའི་ངོ་བོ་འོ།། དཔའ་བོ་རྣམས་ཞལ་ཅིག་ཕྱག་བཞི་པ། དང་པོ་གཉིས་ཀྱིས་རྡོ་རྗེ་དང་དྲིལ་བུ་འཛིན་པས་ཡུམ་ལ་འཁྱུད་པ། གཡས་ཀྱིས་གཉིས་པས་ཌཱ་མ་རུ་དང་། གཡོན་གྱི་གཉིས་པས་ཁ་ཊྭཱཾ་ག་འཛིན་པའོ།། ཡང་ན་སྒྲུ་མོ་ནཱ་ཁ་ཊྭཱཾ་ཀ་དང་། གཡོན་གྱི་གཉིས་པར་ཀ་པ་ལ་ཞེས་བླ་མ་འགའ་ཞིག་གསུང་ངོ་།། རྒྱན་དང་ཆ་ལུགས་དང་བཞུགས་ཚུལ་རྡོ་རྗེ་ཕག་མོ་དང་འདྲ་བ། ཁ་སྦྱོར་ཆེན་པོའི་ཚུལ་གྱིས་བཞུགས་པའོ།། དེའི་ཕྱི་རོལ་དམ་ཚིག་གི་འཁོར་ལོ་ལྷ་སྣམ་གྱི་གཞིའི་ཤར་སྒོར། ཁ་གདོང་མ་སྔོན་མོ། བྱང་སྒོར་

༄༅ འུག་གདོང་མ་ལྗང་ཁུ། ནུབ་སྒོར་ཁྱི་གདོང་མ་དམར་མོ།། ལྷོ་སྒོར་ཕག་གདོང་མ་སེར་མོ།། ཤར་ལྷོར་གཤིན་རྗེ་བརྟན་མ་གཡས་སྔོ་གཡོན་སེར། ལྷོ་ནུབ་ཏུ་གཤིན་རྗེ་ཕོ་ཉ་མ་གཡས་སེར་གཡོན་དམར། ནུབ་བྱང་དུ་གཤིན་རྗེ་མཆེ་བ་མ་གཡས་དམར་གཡོན་ལྗང་། བྱང་ཤར་དུ་གཤིན་རྗེ་འཇོམས་མ་གཡས་ལྗང་གཡོན་སྔོ་བ།། ཞལ་དང་ཕྱག་དང་ཕྱག་མཚན་ལ་སོགས་པ་སྙིང་པོ་འི་རྣལ་འབྱོར་མ་རྣམས་དང་མཚུངས་པའོ།། དཔའ་བོ་དང་རྣལ་འབྱོར་མ་ཐམས་ཅད་ཁྲོ་ཞལ་འབར་བའི་སྐུ་བདེ་བ་ཆེན་པོས་ལོངས་སུ་གང་བ། དབྱལ་བར་རྡོ་རྗེའི་ཕྲེང་བས་བསྐོར་ཞིང་སྤྲུལ་པའི་འོད་ཟེར་དུ་མ་འཁྲོ་བ། ཁྱད་པར་དུ། སྒོ་མཚམས་མ་རྣམས་ནི་ཡིད་བཏགས་ཀྱི་གདན་ལ་བཞུགས་པ། ཤིན་ཏུ་དྲག་གཅིང་འབར་བའི་གཟུགས་སུ་བསྒོམ་པར་བྱའོ།། ལྷ་རྫས་ཀྱི་གྲྭ་རྣམ་སྦྱ་སྨན་དང་བཅུད་སྣ་ཚོགས་དང་། བདུད་རྩི་ས་གང་ཞིང་། ལྷ་རྫས་ཀྱི་གོས་ཀྱིས་མཁྲུལ་པ་གཡོགས་པ། མེ་ཏོག་དང་འབྲས་བུས་ཁྱུང་པའི་དཔག་བསམ་གྱི་ཤིང་གིས་ཁ་བརྒྱན་པའི་རིན་པོ་ཆེའི་བུམ་པ་བརྒྱད་དང་ལྡན་ཞིང་། སྣ་ཚོགས་རྡོ་རྗེས་མཚན་པའི་ཀ་བ་དང་། གདུང་དང་ཐོག་ཕུབས་དང་བཅས་པ་སྟེ། རྟེན་དང་བརྟེན་པར་བཅས་པའི་དཀྱིལ་འཁོར་ཐམས་ཅད་གསལ་ཞིང་སྒྲིབ་པ་མེད་ལ། སྣང་བ་དང་། སྟོང་པ་ཟུང་དུ་འཇུག་པའི་བདག་ཉིད་ཅན་དུ་བསྒོམ་པར་བྱའོ།། དེ་ལྟར་རང་གིས་བསྒོམས་པའི་ལྷ་དང་། རང་བཞིན་གྱིས་གྲུབ་པའི་ལྷ་ལ་ཐ་དད་དང་མཆོག་དམན་དུ་ལྟ་བ་སྤང་བའི་ཕྱིར། བདག་གི་བློ་ལ་སྣང་བའི་ཕོ་ཉ་སྔགས་སྐྱེས་ཀྱི་རྟེན་གྱི་དཀྱིལ་འཁོར་འདི་ཉིད་འཛམ་བུའི་གླིང་ན་བཞུགས་པའི་ཕོ་ཉ་ཞིང་སྐྱེས་སྤྲུལ་པའི་སྐུའི་གནས་ཡུལ་ཉི་ཤུ་རྩ་བཞི་ལ་སོགས་པ་ཡིན་ཞིང་། དེ་ཉིད་ལོངས་སྤྱོད་རྫོགས་པའི་སྐུ་ཕོ་ཉ་ལྷན་སྐྱེས་ཀྱི་གནས་འོག་མིན་གྱི་ཞིང་ཁམས་རྣམ་པར་དག་པ་ཡིན་ལ།

༄༅ དེ་ཉིད་ཆོས་ཀྱི་སྐུ་ལས་གཞན་མ་ཡིན་ནོ་ཞེས་ཡུལ་ལ་ཡུལ་གྱི་ཞེན་པ་དང་། བདག་གི་བློ་ལ་སྣང་བའི་རྟེན་པ་ལྷ་དྲུག་བཅུ་རྩ་གཉིས་པོ་འདི་ཉིད་འཛམ་བུའི་གླིང་ན་བཞུགས་པའི་སྤྲུལ་པའི་སྐུ་རྣམས་ལས་གཞན་མ་ཡིན་ཞིང་། དེ་ཉིད་འོག་མིན་གྱི་ལོངས་སྤྱོད་རྫོགས་པའི་སྐུ་ལས་གཞན་མ་ཡིན་ལ། དེ་ཉིད་ཆོས་ཀྱིས་སྐུ་ལས་གཞན་མ་ཡིན་ནོ་ཞེས་ལྷ་ལ་ལྷའི་ཞེན་པ་བྱའོ།། འདི་ནི་བློ་མཆོག་གི་དབང་དུ་བྱས་པ་ཡིན་ལ་འཁོར་ལོ་རེ་རེ་དང་རྩ་བས་རེ་རེ་ནས་བསྒྲི་བརང་བློ་དང་མོས་པའི་བྱེ་བྲག་དང་སྦྱར་ནས་བསྒོམ་པར་བྱ་སྟེ།། ཙ་བའི་རྒྱུད་ལས། ཕོ་ཉ་རྣམ་གསུམ་ཞགས་འཛིན་ནས། སྒྲུབ་པ་པོ་ལ་དངོས་གྲུབ་སྟེར། ཞེས་གསུངས་པའི་ཉམས་སུ་བླང་བའི་ཚུལ་ཡིན་ནོ། །དེ་ནས་ལྷ་དང་ལམ་ལ་སོམ་ཉི་ཐུངས་པའི་ཕྱིར་བདག་གི་བློ་ལ་དམིགས་པའི་ལྷ་སུམ་བཅུ་སོ་བདུན་པོ་འདི་ཉིད་བྱང་ཆུབ་ཀྱི་ཕྱོགས་ཀྱི་ཆོས་སུམ་བཅུ་སོ་བདུན་གྱི་ངོ་བོ་ཉིད་ཡིན་ལ། བྱང་ཆུབ་ཀྱི་ཕྱོགས་ཀྱི་ཆོས་སུམ་བཅུ་སོ་བདུན་ཡང་ལྷ་སུམ་བཅུ་སོ་བདུན་གྱི་རྣམ་པར་གནས་པའོ་ཞེས་པ་ནི། བློ་མཆོག་གི་དབང་དུ་བྱས་པ་ཡིན་ལ། བློ་འབྲིང་དང་ཐ་མ་ནི་ལམ་ལ་སོམ་ཉི་ཐུངས་པའི་ཕྱིར་ལུས་རྗེས་སུ་དྲན་པ་ནི་མཁའ་འགྲོ་མ། ཚོར་བ་རྗེས་སུ་དྲན་པ་ལ་མ། ཆོས་རྗེས་སུ་དྲན་པ་ཁཎྜ་རོ་ཧེ།། སེམས་རྗེས་སུ་དྲན་པ་གཟུགས་ཅན་མ། འདུན་པའི་རྫུ་འཕྲུལ་གྱི་རྐང་པ་ནི་ཁཎྜ་ཀ་པ་ལི་དང་རབ་ཏུ་གཙུ་མོ།། བརྩོན་འགྲུས་ཀྱི་རྫུ་འཕྲུལ་གྱི་རྐང་པ་ནི་མ་ཧཱ་ཀཾ་ཀ་ལ་དང་གཏུམ་པའི་མིག་ཅན་མ། དཔྱོད་པའི་རྫུ་འཕྲུལ་གྱི་རྐང་པ་ནི་ཀཾ་ཀ་ལ་དང་འོད་ལྡན་མ། སེམས་ཀྱི་རྫུ་འཕྲུལ་གྱི་རྐང་པ་ནི་མཆེ་བ་རྣམ་པར་གཙིགས་པ་དང་། སྣ་ཆེན་མ། དད་པའི་དབང་པོ་ནི་སུ་ར་བྷཻ་རི་དང་། བརྟན་པའི་བློ་ཅན་མ། །བརྩོན་འགྲུས་ཀྱི་དབང་པོ་ནི་འོད་དཔག་མེད་དང་མིཙྪ་ཐུང་མ། །དྲན་པའི་དབང་ནི་ཧཱ་ཧཱའི་འོད་དང་། །ཡང་ཀའི་

༄༅ དབང་ཕྱུག་མ། །ཏིང་ངེ་འཛིན་གྱི་དབང་པོ་ནི་རྡོ་རྗེའི་སྐུ་དང་ཞིང་གྲིབ་མ། །ཤེས་རབ་ཀྱི་དབང་པོ་འི་ཨཾ་ཀུ་རི་དང་། ཨོ་ར་བ་ཏི། །དད་པའི་སྟོབས་ནི་རྡོ་རྗེ་རལ་པ་ཅན་དང་། འཇིགས་བྱེད་ཆེན་མོ།། །བརྩོན་འགྲུས་ཀྱི་སྟོབས་ནི་དཔའ་བོ་ཆེན་པོ་དང་། རླུང་གི་ཤུགས་ཅན་མ། །དྲན་པའི་སྟོབས་ནི་རྡོ་རྗེ་ཧཱུྃ་མཛད་དང་། ཆང་འཐུང་མ། ཏིང་ངེ་འཛིན་གྱི་སྟོབས་ནི་རབ་ཏུ་བཟང་པོ་དང་། །ཤུ་མ་དེ་ཝི། །ཤེས་རབ་ཀྱི་སྟོབས་ནི་རྡོ་རྗེ་བཟང་པོ་དང་ཤིན་ཏུ་བཟང་མོ།། །ཏིང་ངེ་འཛིན་ཡང་དག་བྱང་ཆུབ་ཀྱི་ཡན་ལག་ནི་འཇིགས་བྱེད་ཆེན་པོ་དང་རྟ་རྣམ། །བརྩོན་འགྲུས་ཡང་དག་བྱང་ཆུབ་ཀྱི་ཡན་ལག་ནི་མིག་ཡི་བཟང་དང་ཁ་ག་ན། །དགའ་བ་ཡང་དག་བྱང་ཆུབ་ཀྱི་ཡན་ལག་ནི་སྟོབས་པོ་ཆེ་དང་འཁོར་ལོའི་ཤུགས་ཅན་མ། །ཤིན་ཏུ་སྦྱངས་པ་ཡང་དག་བྱང་ཆུབ་ཀྱི་ཡན་ལག་ནི་རིན་ཆེན་རྡོ་རྗེ་དང་། ཁཎྜ་རོ་ཧ། །ཆོས་རྣམ་པར་འབྱེད་པ་ཡང་དག་བྱང་ཆུབ་ཀྱི་ཡན་ལག་ནི་རྟ་མགྲིན་དང་། ཤཽཎ་ཌི་ནི། །དྲན་པ་ཡང་དག་བྱང་ཆུབ་ཀྱི་ཡན་ལག་ནི་ནམ་མཁའི་སྙིང་པོ་དང་། འཁོར་ལོ་འི་གོ་ཆ་མ། །བཏང་སྙོམས་ཡང་དག་བྱང་ཆུབ་ཀྱི་ཡན་ལག་ནི་ཧེ་རུ་ཀ་དང་། ཤིན་ཏུ་དཔའ་མོ། །ཡང་དག་པའི་ལྟ་བ་ནི་པདྨ་གར་གྱི་དབང་ཕྱུག་དང་སྟོབས་ཆེན་མ། ཡང་དག་པའི་རྟོག་པ་ནི་རྣམ་པར་སྣང་མཛད་དང་། འཁོར་ལོས་སྒྱུར་མ། ཡང་དག་པའི་ངག་ནི་རྡོ་རྗེ་སེམས་དཔའ་དང་། བརྩོན་འགྲུས་ཆེན་མོ།། །ཡང་དག་པའི་ལས་ཀྱི་མཐའ་ནི་ཁྭ་གདོང་མ། །ཡང་དག་པའི་འཚོ་བ་ནི་འུག་གདོང་མ། །ཡང་དག་པའི་རྩོལ་བ་ནི་ཁྱི་གདོང་མ། །ཡང་དག་པའི་དྲན་པ་ནི་ཕག་གདོང་མ། །ཡང་དག་པའི་ཏིང་ངེ་འཛིན་ནི་དཔལ་ཧེ་རུ་ཀ་དང་རྡོ་རྗེ་ཕག་མོ།། །དགེ་བའི་ཆོས་མ་སྐྱེས་པ་རྣམས་སྐྱེད་པ་ལ་མ་ཧཱ་ཏུ། །དགེ་བའི་ཆོས་སྐྱེས་པ་རྣམས་ཡང་དག་པར་སྡུང་བ་ནི་ག་ཤིན་

༄༅ ཧྲེ་རི་ཝོ་ཉ་མ། །མི་དགེ་བའི་ཆོས་སྐྱེས་པ་རྣམས་ཡང་དག་པར་སྤོང་བ་ནི་གཤིན་རྗེ་མཆེ་བ་མ། །མི་དགེ་བའི་ཆོས་མ་སྐྱེས་པ་རྣམས་མི་སྐྱེད་པ་ནི་གཤིན་རྗེ་འཇོམས་མའོ། །ཞེས་བརྗོད་ཅིང་། ལམ་གྱི་ཆོས་རྣམ་ལྔའི་རྣམ་པར་དྲན་པར་བྱའོ།། ལྷ་ལ་སེམས་ཉི་སྒྲོང་ན། མཁའ་འགྲོ་མ་ནི་ལུས་རྗེས་སུ་དྲན་པའོ་ཞེས་པ་ལ་སོགས་པའི་ཚུལ་གྱིས་བརྗོད་ཅིང་ལྷ་རྣམས་ལམ་གྱི་ངོ་བོར་དྲན་པར་བྱའོ།། །སྤྲུལ་པའི་སྐུ་ལམ་དུ་བྱེད་པ་ཕྱིའི་དཀྱིལ་འཁོར་དག་པ་དང་བཅས་པ་བསྒོམ་པའོ། དེ་ལྟར་ཕྱིའི་རྟེན་དང་རྟེན་པའི་དཀྱིལ་འཁོར་གསལ་བར་དམིགས་པའི་མཐུ་དང་འོག་རླུང་དང་། ལྷག་པའི་རླུང་གཡོས་པས་སྤྱི་གཙུག་གི་ཧཾ་སྐྱ་དང་། ལྟེ་བའི་ཨ་ཚུལ་རྐྱ་དབུ་མའི་ལམ་ནས་སྙིང་ཁར་འདྲེས་པས་རྐྱེན་བྱས་ནས་ལུས་ཀྱི་དཀྱིལ་འཁོར་རྟེན་དང་རྟེན་པར་ཅིག་ཆར་གྱུར་ནས་རིམས་ཀྱིས་གསལ་གདབ་པར་བྱ་སྟེ། སྤྱི་བོ་སྣ་ཚོགས་རྡོ་རྗེ། རྐང་མཐིལ་རྡོ་རྗེའི་ས་གཞི། རྩིབ་ལོག་རྡོ་རྗེའི་ར་བ། ཕྲགས་པ་རྡོ་རྗེའི་གུར་དང་བླ་བྲེ། བ་སྤུ་མདའི་དྲྭ། སྣ་སེན་ཡེ་ཤེས་ཀྱི་མེ་འབར་བའི་བསྲུང་འཁོར་དང་། རྐང་མཐིལ་རླུང་། སུམ་མདོ་མེ། ལྟོ་བ་ཆུ། སྙིང་ཁ་ས། རུས་ཚིགས་རི་རབ། མགོ་བོ་རི་རབ་ཀྱི་སྟོད་ཀྱི་ཆ། །ལུས་འདོམ་གང་གྲུ་བཞི་གཞལ་ཡས་ཁང་གྲུ་བཞི། །སྙིང་ཁ་ནས་འབྱུང་བ་བཞིའི་རླུང་རྒྱུ་བ་སྒོ་བཞི། །མིག་ལ་སོགས་པ་གཞལ་ཡས་ཁང་གི་རྒྱན། རྐང་རྣམས་ཀ་བའི་ཚོགས་ཏེ། རྟེན་གྱི་དཀྱིལ་འཁོར་དང་སྙིང་གི་ནང་གི་ཧཱུྃ་ཉིད་དཔལ་ཧེ་རུ་ཀ་ཡུམ་དང་བཅས་པར་སྔར་བཤད་པ་བཞིན་གསལ་གདབ་བོ། དེའི་ཕྱག་བཅུ་གཉིས་ཀྱི་གཡས་ཀྱི་དང་པོར་ཨཾ་མཁའ་འགྲོ་མ། གཉིས་པར་ཡཾ་ལ་མ། གཡོན་གྱི་དང་པོར་ཁཾ་ཁཎྜ་རོ་ཧཱ། གཉིས་པར་ཧཾ་གཟུགས་ཅན་མ། ཕྱག་ལྷག་མ་བརྒྱད་ལ། ཧཱུྃ་རིང་པོ་བརྒྱད་ཀྱི་གཡས་ཀྱི་བཞི་ཁྲ་གདོང་། འུག་གདོང་། ཁྱི་གདོང་མ། ཕག་གདོང་མ་དང་། །གཡོན་

ༀ ཀྱི་བཞི་གཤིན་རྗེ་བརྟན་མ། ཕོ་ཉ་མ། མཆེ་བ་མ། འཇོམས་མ་རྣམས་དང་།། སྤྱི་བོ་ལ་སོགས་པའི་གནས་ཉི་ཤུ་རྩ་བཞིར། པུ་ཛྲ་ཨུ་ཨ་གོ་ར་དེ་མ། ཀ་ཨོ་ཏྲི་ཀོ་ཀ་ལ་ཀ་ཧི། པྲེ་གྲི་ས་སུ་ན་སི་མ་ཀུ། །ཁམས་དང་བཅས་པ་རྣམས་དཔའ་བོ་དང་དཔའ་མོ་རྣམས་སུ་གྱུར་པ་ནི། སྤྱི་བོ་པུ་ལི་ར་མ་ལ་ཡར་ཁཊྭཱ་ཀ་པ་ལི་དང་རབ་ཏུ་གནས་སོ། །སྤྱི་གཙུག་ཛཱ་ལན་དྷ་རར་མ་ཧཱ་ཀཾ་ཀ་ལ་དང་། གཏུམ་པའི་མིག་ཅན་མ། ཉ་བ་གཡས་པ་ཨུ་ཌི་ཡཱ་ན་དུ་ཀཾ་ཀ་ལ་དང་། འོད་ལྡན་མ། ལྟག་པ་ཨར་བུ་ཏར་མཆེ་བ་རྣམ་པར་གཙིགས་པ་དང་། སྣ་ཆེན་མ་སྐྱེ་གནས། །ཉ་བ་གཡོན་པ་གོ་ད་བ་རིར་སུ་ར་བེ་རི་དང་། །བརྟན་པའི་སྒོ་ཅན་མ། །སྨིན་མའི་དབུས་ར་མི་ཤ་རིར་འོད་དཔག་མེད་དང་། མིའུ་ཐུང་མ། མིག་གཉིས་དེ་བི་ཀོ་ཊར་རྡོ་རྗེའི་འོད་དང་ལང་ཀའི་དབང་ཕྱུག་མ། ཕྲག་པ་གཉིས་མ་ལ་བར་རྡོ་རྗེའི་སྐུ་དང་། ཤིང་གྲིབ་མ་སྐྱེ་ཉེ་བའི་གནས། ཐུགས་ཀྱི་འཁོར་ལོ་སྔོན་པོ་ནམ་མཁའ་ལ་སྤྱོད་པའོ།། །མཆན་ཁུང་གཉིས་ཀ་མ་རུ་པར་ཨཾ་ཀུ་རི་དང་། ཨོ་ར་པ་ཏྲི། ནུ་མ་གཉིས་ཨོ་ཏྲེར་རྡོ་རྗེ་རལ་པ་ཅན་དང་། འཇིགས་བྱེད་ཆེན་མོ་སྐྱེ་ཞིང་། ལྟེ་བ་ཏྲི་ཤ་ཀུ་ནིར་དཔའ་བོ་ཆེན་པོ་དང་། རླུང་གི་ཤུགས་ཅན་མ། །སྣ་རྩེ་ཀོ་ས་ལར་རྡོ་རྗེ་ཧཱུྃ་མཛད་དང་ཆང་འཐུང་མ་སྐྱེ་ཉེ་བའི་ཞིང་། །ཁ་ཀ་ལིང་ཀར་རབ་ཏུ་བཟང་པོ་དང་ཤ་མ་དེ་བཱི།། །མགྲིན་པ་ལཾ་པ་ཀར་རྡོ་རྗེ་བཟང་པོ་དང་། ཤིན་ཏུ་བཟང་མོ་སྐྱེ་ཚན་དོ། །སྙིང་ཁ་ཀན་ཙིར་འཇིགས་བྱེད་ཆེན་པོ་དང་རྟ་རྣ་མ། འདོམས་བར་ཧི་མ་ལ་ཡར་མིག་མི་བཟང་དང་། ཁ་ག་ན་སྐྱེ་ཉེ་བའི་ཚནྡོ་རྣམས། །གསུང་གི་འཁོར་ལོ་ཁ་དོག་དམར་པོ་ས་ལ་སྤྱོད་པའོ།། །མཚན་མ་པྲེ་ཏ་པུ་རིར་སྟོབས་པོ་ཆེ་དང་། འཁོར་ལོའི་ཤུགས་ཅན་མ། བཤང་ལམ་གྲི་ཧ་དེ་བར། རིན་ཆེན་རྡོ་རྗེ་དང་། ཁཎྜ་རོ་ཧ་ཧེ

༄༅ འདུ་བ། །བཛྲ་གཉིས་སོཙུ་རཏྣ་ཧ་མགྲིན་དང་། སཾ་པུ་ཊ་ནི། །ཕྱིན་པ་གཉིས་ཞུ་ཙཀྲ་དྭི་པར། ནམ་མཁའི་སྙིང་པོ་དང་། འཁོར་ལོའི་གོ་ཆ་མ་སྡེ་ཉེ་བའི་འདུ་བ། །སོར་མོ་བཅུ་དྲུག་ན་གར་རར་དཔལ་ཧེ་རུ་ཀ་དང་། ཤཱིན་དུ་དཔའ་མོ། །ངོལ་གོང་སེན་ཧྲུར་པད་མ་གར་གྱི་དབང་ཕྱུག་དང་སྟོབས་ཆེན་མ་སྡེ་དུར་ཁྲོད། །མཐེ་བོང་བཞི་མ་རོར་རྣམ་པར་སྣང་མཛད་དང་། འཁོར་ཡོས་སྐྱུར་མ། །བྱུས་མོ་གཉིས་ཀུ་ལུ་ཏར་རྡོ་རྗེ་སེམས་དཔའ་དང་། བརྟེན་འགྲུས་ཆེན་མོ་སྡེ་ཉེ་བའི་དུར་ཁྲོད་རྣམས་སྐུའི་འཁོར་ལོ་ཁ་དོག་དཀར་པོ་ས་འོག་ན་སྤྱོད་པའོ།། །ལྷ་དེ་རྣམས་ཀྱི་ཚུལ་ནི་གོང་དུ་བཤད་པ་བཞིན་ནོ།། །དེ་ལྟར་ཕྱི་ནང་གི་ལྷ་ཐམས་ཅད་གསལ་བར་དམིགས་ནས། ཨོཾ་ཞེས་བརྗོད་པས། བདག་གིས་བསྒོམས་པའི་ཕྱི་ནང་གི་སྐུའི་འཁོར་ལོ་གཉིས་དང་། རྫུལ་པའི་སྐུ་དང་ལོངས་སྤྱོད་རྫོགས་པའི་སྐུ་སྡེ་སྐུའི་འཁོར་ལོ་བཞི་དང་། །དེ་བཞིན་དུ་ཨཱཿཞེས་བརྗོད་པས་གསུང་གི་འཁོར་ལོ་བཞི་དང་། ཧཱུྃ་ཞེས་བརྗོད་པས་ཐུགས་ཀྱི་འཁོར་ལོ་བཞི་དང་། །སརྦ་ཀྲིར་ཡོ་གི་ནི་ཞེས་པས་དཔའ་བོ་ཉི་ཤུ་ཙ་བཞི་དང་། །རྣལ་འབྱོར་མ་སུམ་བཅུ་སོ་བདུན་དྲན་པར་བྱ། །ཀཱ་ཡ་ཞེས་བརྗོད་པས་ཐམས་ཅད་ཀྱི་སྐུ་དང་། ཝཱཀྐ་ཡིས་གསུང་དང་། ཙིཏྟ་ཡིས་ཐུགས་རྣམས་དབྱེར་མི་ཕྱེད་པར་བསམས་ནས། ཨོཾ་བཛྲ་སྭ་བྷཱ་ཝ་ཨཏྨ་ཀོ་ཧཾ་ ཞེས་བརྗོད་པས་ཐམས་ཅད་ཀྱི་ངོ་བོ་རྡོ་རྗེའི་རང་བཞིན་བདག་ཡིན་སྙམ་དུ་བསྒོམས་ནས། ཨོཾ་བཛྲ་ཤུདྡྷ་སརྦ་དྷརྨ་བཛྲ་ཤུདྡྷོ་ཧཾ་ ཞེས་བརྗོད་པས། ཐམས་ཅད་ཀྱང་སྟོང་པ་ཉིད་རྡོ་རྗེའི་རང་བཞིན་དུ་རྣམ་པར་དག་པའི་ངོ་བོ་བདག་ཡིན་སྙམ་པ་ལན་གསུམ་དུ་བྱའོ།། ལོངས་སྤྱོད་རྫོགས་པའི་སྐུ་ལམ་དུ་བྱེད་པ་ལུས་ཀྱི་དཀྱིལ་འཁོར་རྟགས་ཀྱིས་བྱིན་གྱིས་བརླབས་པ་དང་བཅས་པ་སྟེ་དམ་ཚིག་གི་དཀྱིལ་

༄༅ འཁོར་སྐྱིད་པ་ཡན་ལག་དང་པོ་ནི༎ །རྗེ་བཙུན་ན་རོ་པའི་དགོངས་པས་དམ་ཚིག་པ་ལ་ཡེ་ཤེས་ཀྱི་དཀྱིལ་འཁོར་བསྐྱེམས་ནས་མི་འབྲལ་བར་བྱ་བའི་ཕྱིར་སྒོ་ཆའི་ལྷ་རྣམས་གདབ་པར་བྱའོ་ཞེས་གསུངས་ཡང་། རྒྱུད་དག་ལས། །དེ་ནས་སྒོ་ཆ་གཉིས་ཤེས་ནས། ཡེ་ཤེས་འཁོར་ལོ་རྣམ་པར་བསྒོམ། ཐུགས་དང་ཕྱག་རྒྱའི་སྦྱོར་ཤེས་ནས། དམ་ཚིག་འཁོར་ལོ་ལ་སྦྱར་གཞུག། ཅེས་འབྱུང་ཞིང་། །སློབ་དཔོན་ལོ་ཡི་པའི་གཞུང་ལས་ཀྱང་དེ་ལྟར་བཤད་པས། །ཐོག་མར་སྒོ་ཆ་དགོད་པར་བྱ་སྟེ། དེ་ཡང་གནས་རྣམས་སུ་ཟླ་བའི་གདན་ལ། སྙིང་ཁར་ཨོཾ་ཧ། རྡོ་རྗེ་སེམས་དཔའ་དཀར་པོ༎ མགོ་བོར་ན་མ་ཧི། རྣམ་པར་སྣང་མཛད་སེར་པོ། སྤྱི་གཙུག་ཏུ་སྭཱ་ཧཱ་ཧུ། པད་མ་གར་གྱི་དབང་ཕྱུག་དམར་པོ༎ ཕྲག་པ་གཉིས་སུ་བཽ་ཥཊ་ཧེ། ཧེ་རུ་ཀ་ནག་པོ༎ མིག་གཉིས་སུ། ཧཱུཾ་ཧཱུཾ་ཧོ༎ རྡོ་རྗེ་ཉི་མ་དམར་སེར། ཡན་ལག་ཐམས་ཅད་ལ་ཕཊ་ཧཾ། ཧ་ མཆོག་ལྷུང་ ཁྲུ་ སྟེ་ དཔའ་བོའི་ སྒོ་ཆ་དང་། །ཕྱི་བར་ཨོཾ་བཾ་རྡོ་རྗེ་ཕག་མོ་དམར་མོ༎ སྙིང་ཁར་ཧཾ་ཡོཾ༔ གཤིན་རྗེ་མ་སྔོན་མོ༎ ཁར། ཧྲིཾ་མོཾ། རྨོངས་བྱེད་མ་དཀར་མོ། མགོ་ལ་ཧྲིཾ་ཧྲིཾ་བསྐྱོད་བྱེད་མ་སེར་མོ༎ སྤྱི་གཙུག་ཏུ། ཧཱུཾ་ཧཱུཾ། སྐྲག་བྱེད་མ་ལྗང་ཁུ། ཡན་ལག་རྣམས་ལ་ཕཊ་ཕཊ། ཙཎྜ་ཀ་དུད་ཀ་སྟེ་དཔའ་མོའི་སྒོ་ཆ་བཀོད་ལ། །ཡབ་ཀྱི་གནས་སུ་ཡུམ་དང་ཡུམ་གྱི་གནས་སུ་ཡབ་གཉིས་མེད་པར་བསམ་སྟེ། ཡི་གེ་རེ་རྣམ་པ་ཉིད་ལྷའི་ངོ་བོར་བསྒོམ་པ་ནི་སྒོ་ཆ་དགོད་པ་སྟེ། ཡན་ལག་གཉིས་པའོ༎ དེ་ནས་འབར་བའི་ཕྱག་རྒྱ་དབྲལ་བའི་དབྱིབས་སུ་བཀོར་ཞིང་ ཛཿ ཞེས་བརྗོད་པས་སྙིང་ཁ་ཧཱུཾ་ལས་འོད་འཕྲོས་པས་རང་བཞིན་གྱིས་གྲུབ་པའི་དཀྱིལ་འཁོར་སངས་རྒྱས་དང་བྱང་ཆུབ་སེམས་དཔའ་ཐམས་ཅད་ཀྱིས་བསྐོར་བ་མདུན་དུ་སྤྱན་དྲངས་པ་ལ་ཇ་མ་ལྟར་མཆོད་ནས། ཛཿ་ཧཱུཾ་བཾ་ཧོཿ ཞེས་བརྗོད་པས་རང་ལ་བསྟིམས་ནས༎

༄ ཨོཾ་ཡོ་ག་ཤུད་དྷ་སརྦ་དྷརྨ་ཡོ་ག་ཤུད་དྷོ་ཧཾ ཞེས་བརྗོད་པས་གཉིས་སུ་མེད་པར་སྒྱུར་པར་བསམ་པ་ནི་ཡེ་ཤེས་ཀྱི་འཁོར་ལོ་གཅུག་པ་སྟེ་ཡན་ལག་འཁྱུམ་པའོ།། །ཡང་དབང་གི་ལྷ་དྲུག་བཅུ་རྩ་གཉིས་ཀྱི་དཀྱིལ་འཁོར་ལ་སངས་རྒྱས་དང་བྱང་ཆུབ་སེམས་དཔའ་དང་། ཁྲོ་བོ་དང་ཁྲོ་མོ་དང་། མཆོད་པའི་ལྷ་མོའི་ཚོགས་དཔག་ཏུ་མེད་པ་དང་བཅས་པ་སྤྱན་དྲངས་པ་ལ་སྔར་བཞིན་མཆོད་ནས། །དེ་བཞིན་གཤེགས་པ་ཐམས་ཅད་ཀྱིས་བདག་ལ་མངོན་པར་དབང་བསྐུར་དུ་གསོལ་ཞེས་གསོལ་བ་བཏབ་པས། །ལྷ་རྣམས་ཀྱིས། །ཇི་ལྟར་བལྟམས་པ་ཙམ་གྱིས་ནི། ལྷ་རྣམས་ཀྱིས་ནི་ཁྲུས་གསོལ་ལྟར། ལྷའི་ཆུ་ནི་དག་པ་ཡིས། དེ་བཞིན་བདག་གིས་དབང་བསྐུར་རོ།། ཨོཾ་སརྦ་ཏ་ཐཱ་ག་ཏ་ཨ་བྷི་ཥེ་ཀ་ཏ་ས་མ་ཡ་ཤྲཱི་ཡེ་ཧཱུཾ། ཞེས་གསུང་ཞིང་དབང་བསྐུར་ནས། བཀྲ་ཤིས་ཀྱི་གླུ་དང་། བགེགས་བསྐྲད་པ་དང་། མཆོད་པ་མཛོད་པས་ཡེ་ཤེས་ཀྱི་ཆུས་ལུས་ཐམས་ཅད་གང་། དྲི་མ་ཐམས་ཅད་དག། ཆུའི་ལྷག་མ་སྤྱི་བོར་ལུད་པས་རིགས་ཀྱི་བདག་པོར་གྱུར་པ་ནི་བདེ་བ་ཆེན་པོའི་ལྷ་ཁྱུ་དང་། དམ་ཚིག་གི་ལྷ་རྣམས་ལ་རྡོ་རྗེ་སེམས་དཔའ། ཐུགས་ཀྱི་འཁོར་ལོ་ལ་མི་བསྐྱོད་པ། གསུང་གི་འཁོར་ལོ་ལ་འོད་དཔག་མེད། སྐུའི་འཁོར་ལོ་ལ་རྣམ་པར་སྣང་མཛད་ཀྱིས་དབུ་བརྒྱན་པར་བསམ་པ་ནི་དབང་བསྐུར་ནས་རིགས་ཀྱི་བདག་པོས་རྒྱས་གདབ་པ་སྟེ་ཡན་ལག་བཞི་པའོ།། རྒྱས་པར་བསྒོམ་པའི་ཚུལ་ལོ།། སྐྱབས་སུ་འགྲོ་བ་དང་། སེམས་བསྐྱེད་པ་དང་། དཀའ་བ་གསུམ་སྔོན་དུ་སོང་ནས་བསྲུང་བའི་འཁོར་ལོ་རྫོགས་པར་བསྒོམས་ནས། སྤྱི་བོར་བླ་མའི་ཕྱག་གཉིས་སམ་བླ་མ་དངོས་དཀོན་མཆོག་གསུམ་གྱི་རང་བཞིན་དུ་བསྒོམ་པ་ལ་མོས་པ་དྲག་པོ་བྱས་པས་ལུས་ལ་ཐིམ་པའི་རྐྱེན་གྱིས་ནང་གི་སླ་ཚུལ་འདྲེས་པས་ལུས་ཀྱི་དཀྱིལ་འཁོར་གསལ་བར་བྱས་པ་མན་ཆད་སྔ་མ་ལྟར་བསྒོམ་པ་ནི་འབྲིང་གི་ཚུལ་ལོ།། །སྔོན་དུ་བསྲུང་བའི་འཁོར་ལོ་ཡང་

༄༅ མི་སློམ་ཞིང་། །ནང་གི་དཀྱིལ་འཁོར་བསྒོམ་པ་འབའ་ཞིག་ལམ་དུ་བྱེད་པའི་ཕྱིར། གོ་ཆ་བཅིང་བ་མན་ཆད་ཀྱང་མི་བྱེད་པར་སྔ་མའི་ཚུལ་གྱིས་ལུས་ཀྱི་དཀྱིལ་འཁོར་གསལ་བཏབ་ནས། སྔགས་ཀྱིས་བྱིན་གྱིས་བརླབས་ལ་དེ་ཉིད་ལ་ཡིད་མཉམ་པར་འཇོག་པ་ནི་བསྡུས་པའི་ཚུལ་ཏེ་བདག་ཉིད་སངས་རྒྱས་སུ་བསྐྱེད་པའོ།། དེ་ལ་སྔགས་དང་། ཕྱི་དང་། བདུད་རྩི་དང་། ཉ་ཉེས་པ་དང་། ཡིད་ལས་བྱུང་བས་མཆོད་ནས། ཁང་པ་བརྒྱད་པ་གཉིས་ཀྱིས་བསྟོད་ལ་དཀྱིལ་འཁོར་གྱི་སྐུ་སྣང་ལ་རང་བཞིན་མེད་པ་ལ་ཡིད་གཏད་དེ་སེམས་མཉམ་པར་གཞག་གོ།། དེ་ནས་ལྷ་རྣམས་ཀྱི་ཐུགས་ཁའི་ས་བོན་ལས་སྔགས་ཞི་བ་ལ་དཀར་པོ་ཕྲེང་དུ་དངར་ཞིང་མདའི་ཤུགས་ཀྱིས་རབ་ཏུ་འགྲོ་བ་དང་། རྒྱས་པ་ལ་སེར་པོ་གཟི་བརྗིད་འབར་བ་སྒོའི་ཆུན་པོ་ལྟར་འགྲོ་བ་དང་། དབང་ལ་དམར་པོ་མཐུད་པ་ཞགས་ཀྱོག་ལྟ་བུ་དང་། དྲག་པོ་ལ་ནག་པོ་སྨུར་དུ་འགྲོ་བ་སྤར་བུ་ལྟ་བུ་དང་། མངོན་ལ་ལྷའི་མངོན་ལྟ་བུའི་ཕྲེང་བ་ཡབ་ཀྱི་ཞལ་དང་། ཡུམ་གྱི་ཞལ། ཐུགས་ཁའི་ས་བོན། ཧ་ག་རོ་ཛེ། །ཐུགས་ཁའི་ས་བོན་རྣམས་ནས་འཁོར་བ་ལ་དམིགས་ཏེ་ཨོཾ་ཤྲཱི་བཛྲ་ཧེ་ཧེ་རུ་རུ་ཀཾ་ཧཱུཾ་ཧཱུཾ་ཕཊ་ཌཱ་ཀི་ནཱི་ཛཱ་ལ་སམྦ་ར་སྭཱཧཱ། ཨོཾ་བཛྲ་བཻ་རོ་ཙ་ནཱི་ཡེ་ཧཱུཾ་ཧཱུཾ་ཕཊ་སྭཱཧཱ། ཨོཾ་ཧྲི། ཧ༔ཧ༔ཧཱུཾ་ཧཱུཾ་ཕཊ། ཨོཾ་སརྦ་བུདྡྷ་ཌཱ་ཀི་ནཱི་ཡེ། བཛྲ་ཝརྞ་ནཱི་ཡེ་ཧཱུཾ་ཧཱུཾ་ཕཊ་སྭཱ་ཧཱ།། ཞེས་ཡབ་ཡུམ་གྱི་སྙིང་པོ་དང་། ཉེ་སྙིང་ལ་སོགས་པ་བཟླའོ།། གཙོ་བོ་ཡབ་ཡུམ་གྱི་སྙིང་པོ་ལ་ཁྲི་ཕྲག་གསུམ་དང་། ཉལ་འབྱོར་མ་བཅུ་གཉིས་ལ་ཁྲི་སྟོང་དང་། ཁྲི་བརྒྱ་པ་རེ་རེ་དང་། འཁོར་ལོ་གསུམ་གྱི་ལྷ་རྣམས་ལ་ཁྲི་ཕྲག་གཉིས་གཉིས་བཟླས་པས་དཀྱིལ་འཁོར་གྱི་ལས་ལ་སོགས་པ་ལ་དབང་དུ་རུང་ངོ་།། སྔགས་ཀྱི་བཟླས་པས་བསྙེན་བ་སྟེ་བསྐྱེད་པའི་རིམ་པའོ།།

༄༅ རྫོགས་པའི་རིམ་པ་བསྒོམ་པར་འདོད་པས། །རང་གི་ལྟེ་བར་པད་མ་འདབ་

༄ མ་བཀྲུད་པའི་སྙིང་པོར་ཟླ་བའི་སྙིང་དུ་རྡོ་རྗེ་སེམས་དཔའ་རྡོ་རྗེ་སྙེམས་མ་དང་གཉིས་སྐུ་མེད་པའི་ཐུགས་ཁར་ཧཱུྃ་བསམ་པ་ལས་འོད་འཕྲོས་པས་གཙོ་བོ་ནས་རིམ་པས་དཀྱིལ་འཁོར་དང་སྟོད་བཅུད་ཐམས་ཅད་གསལ་བཏབ་པ་ལ་དམིགས་པ་གཏད་པས་ཐམས་ཅད་གཡོ་བར་བསྒོམ་པ་ནི་རྡོ་རྗེ་ཁབ་ལེན་གྱིས་ལྕགས་ཕྱེ་གཡོ་བ་ལྟ་བུའོ། །དེ་ནས་འོད་ཟེར་ཚུར་བསྡུས་པའི་དབང་གིས་ཐམས་ཅད་རིམས་ཀྱིས་ཕྱི་འི་ཧེ་རུ་ཀ་ལ་ཐིམ་པ་ནི་ཆུ་བས་དངུལ་ཆུ་འཇུད་པའི་དཔེ།། དེའི་ཡང་ཡུམ་ཡབ་དང་། །ཡབ་ཀྱང་ཞལ་གཅིག་ཕྱག་གཉིས་པར་བསྡུ་བ་ནི་དུས་སྦྲལ་ཡན་ལག་འཁུམ་པ་ལྟ་བུའོ།། །དེ་ནས་ཕྱི་འི་ཧེ་རུ་ཀ་འང་ཐིམ་པའི་རྡོ་རྗེ་སེམས་དཔའ་དང་། དེའི་ཡུམ་ཡབ་དང་། །ཡབ་ཀྱང་ཐུགས་ཁའི་ཧཱུྃ་དང་། །དེའང་རིམ་གྱིས་ཐིག་ལེ་ལ་ཐིམ་པ་ནི། སྐར་མདའ་གཅིག་ལ་གཅིག་ཐིམ་པ་ལྟ་བུའོ།། །དེའང་ཇེ་ཕྲར་གྱུར་ནས་མཐར་ཡལ་བར་བསྒོམ་པ་ནི···ལག་ཆྭ་ཆུ་ལ་ཐིམ་པ་ལྟ་བུ་སྟེ་རྩོ་བའི་དཔེ་ལུས་མཆོད་པའོ།། །མ་བསྡུས་པའི་གནས་སྐབས་ཀྱི་སྣང་བ་རྣམས་ཆ་ལུགས་དང་། འོད་ཟེར་དང་། ཐ་རླབས་ལྟ་བུ་ཡིན་པ། རང་བཞིན་ནི་གར་མཁན་དང་། ཉི་མ་དང་། རྒྱ་མཚོ་ལྟ་བུ་ཡིན་ཞིང་། ཐིམ་ནས་མི་དམིགས་པར་གྱུར་བ་ནི་ཆུ་བུར་ཆུ་ལ་ཐིམ་པ་འམ་ནམ་མཁའ་ལ་གཞའ་ཚོན་ཡལ་བ་ལྟ་བུ་སྟེ། ཡན་ལག་གི་དཔེ་དུ་མས་མཚོན་པར་བྱའོ།། དེ་ལྟར་མི་རྟོག་པའི་ངང་ལ་མཉམ་པར་བཞག་པ་ནི་རྡོ་རྗེ་སེམས་དཔའ་བསྡུ་བའོ།། ཡང་རང་གི་ལྟེ་བར་པད་མ་འདབ་མ་བཞི་པའི་ཤར་ནས་གཡོན་སྐོར་གྱིས་ས་རླུང་། ཆུ་རླུང་། མེ་རླུང་། རླུང་གི་རླུང་གི་རང་བཞིན། ལ་སེར་པོ།། ཝ་ཀར་པོ། ར་དམར་པོ།། ཡ་ལྗང་ཁུ་དང་། དབུས་སུ་ནམ་མཁའི་རླུང་གི་རང་བཞིན་ཐིག་ལེ་སྔོན་པོ་རྣམས་དམིགས་ནས། །དབུགས་ཕྱིར་རྒྱུ་བའི་ཚེ་ལ་ལས་འོད་ཟེར་སྤྲུད་པ་འཕྲིང་པོའི་ཚད་ཙམ་སྣ་བུག་གཡོན་ནས་མདུན་དུ་ཐད་ཀར་སོར་བཅུ་དྲུག་གི་བར་དུ་བྱུང་ཞིང་།

༄༅ ནང་དུ་འཇུག་པའི་ཚེ། ལ་ཉིད་ལ་སླར་ཐིམ་པར་བསམས་ནས་རླུང་ཁ་སྦྱོར་བྱའོ།། དེ་ལྟར་རྟག་ཏུ་བསྒོམས་པས། དུ་བའི་རྟགས་མཐོང་བའི་ཚེ་ལ་ཛ་ལ་བསྐྱིམས་ནས། དེ་ལ་འོད་ཟེར་དཀར་པོའི་ལྡང་འཇུག་དང་རླུང་གི་རྣལ་འབྱོར་སྔ་མ་ལྟར་བསྒོམས་པས་སྨིག་རྒྱུའི་རྟགས་མཐོང་བའི་ཚེ་ཡ་ར་ལ་བསྐྱིམས་ནས། དེ་ལས་འོད་ཟེར་དམར་པོའི་ལྡང་འཇུག་དང་རླུང་གི་རྣལ་འབྱོར་སྔ་མ་ལྟར་བསྒོམས་པས། མེ་ཁྱེར་གྱི་རྟགས་མཐོང་བའི་ཚེར་ཡ་ལ་བསྐྱིམས་ནས། དེ་ལས་འོད་ཟེར་ལྗང་ཁུའི་ལྡང་འཇུག་དང་རླུང་གི་རྣལ་འབྱོར་སྔ་མ་ལྟར་བསྒོམས་པས་མར་མེ་འབར་བའི་རྟགས་མཐོང་བའི་ཚེ་ཡའང་དབུས་ཀྱི་ཐིག་ལེ་ལ་བསྐྱིམས་ནས་དེ་ལས་འོད་ཟེར་ལྡང་འཇུག་གི་དམིགས་པ་མི་བསྒོམ་པར་ཐིག་ལེ་ཉིད་ལ་ཡིད་གཏད་དེ་རླུང་ཁ་སྦྱོར་བསྒོམས་པས། ནམ་མཁའ་སྤྲིན་མེད་ལྟ་བུའི་རྟགས་འབྱུང་ལ་དེའི་མཐར་མཐོང་བའི་ལམ་གྱི་ཡེ་ཤེས་སྐྱེ་བར་འགྱུར་རོ།། ཡི་གེ་བཅུ་བའོ།། །ཡི་གེ་དེ་དག་གི་སྟེང་དུ་ཐིག་ལེ་དམིགས་ནས་སྔ་མ་ལྟར་བསྒོམ་པ་ནི་ཐིག་ལེ་བཅུ་བའོ།། །རྡོ་རྗེ་སེམས་དཔའ་ང་ཛྙ་བ་ནི་བསྐྱེད་རིམས་ཀྱི་མཐར་ཅི་ནས་ཀུང་བསྒོམ་ལ། འོག་མ་གཉིས་པོ་ནི་ཇི་ལྟར་འོས་པ་བཞིན་བསྒོམ་མོ་ཞེས་གསུང་ངོ་།། རྫོགས་པའི་རིམ་པ་སྒོ་མཉམ་པར་བཞག་པའི་རྣལ་འབྱོར་རོ།།

༄༅ དེ་ནས་སྟོང་པ་ཉིད་ཀྱི་ངང་ལས་སྐད་ཅིག་གིས་རང་ཉིད་ཧེ་རུ་ཀ་ཡབ་ཡུམ་དུ་དམིགས་པའི་ཐུགས་ཁའི་ཧཱུྃ་ལས་འོད་འཕྲོས་པས་ནང་དང་ཕྱིའི་དཀྱིལ་འཁོར་དང་། སྣོད་བཅུད་ཐམས་ཅད་གསལ་བར་དམིགས་ནས། སོ་དང་སེན་མོ་ནི་ཁཎྜ་ཀ་པ་ལི། སྐྲ་དང་སྤུ་ནི་མ་ཧཱ་ཀ་ཀ་ལ། ལྤགས་པ་དང་དྲི་མ་ནི་ཀཾ་ཀ་ལ། ཤ་ནི་མཆེ་བ་རྣམ་པར་གཙོགས་པ། རྩ་རྒྱུས་ནི་སུ་ར་བྷ་ཀྵི། རུས་པ་ནི་འོད་དཔག་ཏུ་མེད་པ། མཁལ་མ་ནི་རྡོ་རྗེའི་འོད། སྙིང་ནི་རྡོ་རྗེའི་སྐུ། མིག་ནི་ཨོཾ་ཀུ་རི། མཁྲིས་པ་ནི་རྡོ་རྗེ་རལ་པ་ཅན། སློ་བ་ནི་དཔའ་བོ་

ཆེན་པོ།། རྒྱ་མ་ནི་རྡོ་རྗེ་ཧཱུཾ་མཛད། གཉིས་མ་ནི་རྡོ་རྗེ་བཟང་པོ།། ཕྲང་པ་ནི་འཇིགས་བྱེད་ཆེན་པོ།། འདོམས་བར་ནི་མིག་མི་བཟང་། བད་ཀན་ནི་སྟོབས་པོ་ཆེ། ནག་ནི་རིན་ཆེན་རྡོ་རྗེ། ཁྲག་ནི་རྟ་མགྲིན། རྡུལ་ནི་ནམ་མཁའི་སྙིང་པོ། ཚིལ་ནི་རྡོ་རྗེ་ཧེ་རུ་ཀ། མཆི་མ་ནི་པད་མ་གར་གྱི་དབང་ཕྱུག། མཆིལ་མ་ནི་རྣམ་པར་སྣང་མཛད། སྣབས་ནི་རྡོ་རྗེ་སེམས་དཔའོ་ཞེས་པ་དང་། །སོ་དང་སེན་མོ་ལ། ཨོཾ་ཀ་ར་ཀ་ར་ཧཱུཾ་ཧཱུཾ་ཕཊ། ཅེས་པ་ལ་སོགས་པས་ཁམས་རྣམས་དཔའ་བོ་དང་། དེ་དག་གི་རྟེན་རྣམས་རྣལ་འབྱོར་མ་ཉེ་ཤུ་རྩ་བཞིར་དྲན་པར་བྱའོ།། །ཡབ་ཀྱི་རྩ་སྔགས་ཀྱིས་དུས་པའི་རྒྱུན་དྲུག་རིགས་དྲུག་གི་ངོ་བོ་དཔལ་ཧེ་རུ་ཀ་དང་། ཨོཾ་ཧ་ ལ་སྟོགས་པས་འཁོར་ལོ་ལ་སོགས་པའི་རྒྱན་དྲུག། དཔའ་བོ་དྲུག་དང་། ཡུམ་གྱི་རྩ་སྔགས་ཀྱིས་མགྲིན་པའི་ཕྲེང་བ་རྡོ་རྗེ་ཕག་མོ་དང་། ཡབ་ཀྱི་སྙིང་པོས་མི་མགོའི་རྡོ་ཤལ་དང་། ཉེ་སྙིང་གིས་རྣ་རྒྱན་དང་། ཡུམ་གྱི་སྙིང་པོས་གླང་པོ་དང་སྟག་གི་ལྤགས་པ་དང་། ཨོཾ་བཾ་ ལ་སོགས་པས་སྐ་རགས་དཔའ་མོ་དྲུག་དང་། གཙོ་མོའི་སྙིང་པོ་ལ་སོགས་པ་དཔའ་མོ་སུམ་བཅུ་རྩ་བདུན་གྱི་སྔགས་ཀྱིས་ཕྱག་མཚན་དང་། མཚམས་བཞིའི་ཐོད་པ་དང་། ཡུམ་གྱི་ཉེ་སྙིང་གིས་མགོའི་དབུ་རྒྱན་རྣམས་སྔགས་དང་ལྷ་དེ་དག་གི་ངོ་བོར་དྲན་པར་བྱ་ཞིང་། ཁ་ཊྭཾ་ཀ་ནི་ལྷའི་སྐུ་ཤེས་རབ་ཌ་མ་རུའི་སྐུ། ཉིན་མོ་བཅོམ་ལྡན་རྡོ་རྗེ་རན། རྣལ་འབྱོར་མ་ནི་མཚན་མོར་ངེས།། ཅེས་དག་པ་རྗེས་སུ་དྲན་པར་བྱའོ།། དེ་ནས་དཔའ་བོ་དང་དཔའ་མོ་དང་། ཕྱུ་རྡེ་ལ་སོགས་པའི་གོ་ཆ་ཆེན་པོ་རྣམས་བརྗོད་ཅིང་། ལྷ་རྣམས་སོ་སོའི་གནས་སུ་ཐིམ་པས་བདག་ཉིད་བསྲུངས་ནས། གོང་བཞིན་སུམ་རྡ་བའི་སྔགས་ཀྱིས། ཕྱོགས་མཚམས་རྣམ་པར་བཅིངས་ལ། བདག་དང་སྣང་བ་ཐམས་ཅད་ལྷའི་དཀྱིལ་འཁོར་དང་། བརྗོད་པ་

དང་། གྲགས་པའི་སྒྲ་ཐམས་ཅད་ཐུགས་དང་། སེམས་ཀྱི་རྟོག་པའི་འདུ་འཕྲོ་
ཐམས་ཅད་ཡེ་ཤེས་ཆེན་པོའི་ཆོ་འཕྲུལ་དུ་བསྒོམས་ནས་རིམ་བཞིན་ཧཱུྃ་དང་། ཡབ་ཀྱི་ཁང་
པ་བརྒྱད་པ་དང་། ཧཱུྃ་ཞེས་བརྗོད་པས་བྱིན་གྱིས་བརླབས་ཏེ། ཡུལ་རྣམས་ལ་ཆགས་
པ་དང་། སྡང་བ་མེད་པར་ཡོངས་སྤྱོད་དོ།། །ཐམས་ཅད་དུ་སྣང་བ་ལྷའི་རྣམ་པ་དང་།
རང་བཞིན་སྟོང་པ་དང་། གཉིས་ཀའང་ཟུང་འཇུག་ཏུ་ཤེས་པའི་ངང་ལས་ཆོས་བཤད་པ་
དང་། ཉན་པ་དང་། སྒོམ་པ་དང་། ཁ་ཐོན་དང་། ཆུ་སྦྱིན་དང་མཆོད་རྟེན་
བརླབས་ལ་རབ་གནས་དང་། སྦྱིན་སྲེག་དང་། རང་དང་གཞན་གྱི་དོན་སྒྲུབ་པ་སྟེ་ཀུན་
དུ་སྤྱོད་པ་ཐམས་ཅད་ལམ་དུ་འགྱུར་བར་བྱ་བ་ནི་ སྤྱོད་ལམ་གྱི་རྣལ་འབྱོར་རོ།། །དེ་
ནས་མཚོན་པར་བཤམས་པའི་གཏོར་མ་སུམ་ཧྲཱ་བས་བསང་། སྭ་བྷཱ་བས་སྟོང་པར་སྦྱངས་
པའི་དང་ངང་ལས་ཡཾ་ལས་རླུང་དང་། རཾ་ལས་མེའི་སྟེང་དུ་ཨ་ལས་ཐོད་པ་ཡངས་པར་
ཨ་ལས་ཟླ་བའི་སྟེང་དུ། །ཤར་ནས་གཡས་སྐོར་དང་། དབུས་སུ། གོ་ཀུ་ད་ཧ་ན། ལས་བ་
གླང་། ཁྱི། རྟ། གླང་པོ་ཆེ། མིའི་ཤ་དང་། དེའི་སྟེང་དུ། བི། མུ། ཤུ། མ། ར་ལས་དྲི་
ཆེན་དྲི་ཆུ་བྱང་ཆུབ་ཀྱི་སེམས། ཤ་ཆེན་གྱི་དངས་མ། རཀྟ།། །དེའི་སྟེང་དུ། ཧཱུྃ་བྷྲཱུྃ་
ཨཾ་ཛྲཱིཾ་ཁཾ་ རྣམས་ཆོས་ཀྱི་དབྱིངས། མེ་ལོང་ལྟ་བུ། མཉམ་པ་ཉིད། སོ་སོར་རྟོག་པ།
བྱ་བ་གྲུབ་པའི་ཡེ་ཤེས་སུ་བསམ་པའི་སྟེང་དུ་ཨོཾ་དཀར་པོ་མགོ་ཐུར་དུ་ལྟ་བ། དེའི་སྟེང་
དུ། ཨ་ལས་ཟླ་བའི་སྟེང་དུ་ཧཱུྃ་ལས་སྣ་ཚོགས་རྡོ་རྗེ་ཧཱུྃ་གིས་མཚན་པ་ལས་འོད་ཟེར་འོག་
ཏུ་འཕྲོས་པས་རླུང་གཡོས་ཤིང་མེ་སྦར་བས། རྫས་རྣམས་བཙོ་ཞིང་བསྐོལ་བའི་རླངས་པ་
གྱེན་ལ་སོང་བས་བསྐུལ་ནས་ཨོཾ་དང་། ཟླ་བ་དང་། སྣ་ཚོགས་རྡོ་རྗེ་ལས་ཀྱང་བདུད་རྩི་
བབས་ཤིང་འོད་ཟེར་རླངས་པ་དང་བཅས་པ་ཕྱོགས་བཅུར་འཕྲོས་པས་དེ་བཞིན་གཤེགས་

པ་ཐམས་ཅད་ཀྱི་ཐུགས་ཁ་ནས་ཡེ་ཤེས་ཀྱི་བདུད་རྩི་ས་གང་བའི་འོད་པ་དཔག་ཏུ་མེད་པ་སྤྲིན་ཕྲངས་པ་དང་། སྣ་ཚོགས་རྡོ་རྗེ་དང་། ཟླ་བ་དང་། ཨོཾ་དང་བཅས་པ་རྣམས་གཏོར་མ་ལ་ཐིམ་པས། ཁ་དོག་དང་། དྲི་དང་། རོ་དང་། ནུས་པ་ཕུན་སུམཚོགས་པའི་བདུད་རྩི་འི་རྒྱ་མཚོ་ཆེན་པོར་བསམས་ལ། ཨོཾ༔ ཨཱཿ༔ ཧཱུཾ༔ ཧ༔ ཧོ༔ ཧྲཱིཿ༔ ཞེས་ཡང་ཡང་བརྗོད་པས་བྱིན་གྱིས་བརླབ་བོ།། དེ་ནས་མདུན་གྱི་ནམ་མཁར་སྐད་ཅིག་གིས་རྟེན་དང་རྟེན་པར་བཅས་པའི་ལྷ་དྲུག་བཅུ་རྩ་གཉིས་ཀྱི་དཀྱིལ་འཁོར་དམིགས་ལ་གཙོ་བོ འི་ཐུགས་ཁའི་ཧཱུྃ་ལས་འོད་འཕྲོས་པས་དུར་ཁྲོད་བརྒྱད་ལ་ཕོག་པས་དཀྱིལ་འཁོར་ཡོངས་སུ་རྫོགས་པ་བརྒྱད་དུ་གྱུར་ཏེ། ཡེ་ཤེས་པ་དང་རོ་གཅིག་ཏུ་བྱས་པའི་ལྷ་རྣམས་ཀྱི་ཞལ་ནས་བྱུང་བའི་འོད་ཀྱི་སྦུ་གུའི་ལམ་ནས་གསོལ་བར་བསམ་ཞིང་། རྡོ་རྗེ་ཐལ་མོ་ཁ་ཕྱེ་ལ། ཨོཾ་བཛྲ་ཨ་ར་ལི་ཧོ་ཛཿ༔ ཧཱུཾ་བཾ་ཧོ༔ བཛྲ་ཌཱ་ཀི་ནི་ས་མ་ཡ་སྟྭཾ་དྲི་ཤ་ཧོ༔ ཨོཾ་ཨཱཿཧཱུཾ༔ ཞེས་ལྷ་འམ་འཁོར་ལོ འི་གྲངས་དང་མཉམ་པ་དང་། དཔའ་བོ་ཉི་ཤུ་རྩ་བཞིའི་ཕྲེང་སྔགས་ཀྱིས་ཀྱང་ཕུལ་ནས། ཕྱི་ནང་ཡིད་ལས་བྱུང་བས་མཆོད་ནས། ཤང་པ་བརྒྱད་པ་གཉིས་ཀྱིས་བསྟོད་དེ། འདོད་པའི་དོན་གསོལ་བ་བཏབ་ལ། ཡི་གེ་བརྒྱ་པ་བརྗོད་ཅིང་ནོངས་པ་བཟོད་པར་གསོལ་ནས། བཛྲ་མུཿ ཡེ་ཤེས་པ་གཤེགས་སུ་གསོལ་ལ་དམ་ཚིག་པ་བདག་ལ་བསྡུའོ།། འཇིག་རྟེན་པ་ལ་ནི་མཁའ་འགྲོ་སྤྱི་འི་གཏོར་མས་འབུལ་ལོ།། གཏོར་མའི་རྣལ་འབྱོར་རོ།། ཁ་ཟས་གཏོར་མ་ལྟར་བྱིན་གྱིས་བརླབས་ནས་རང་ཉེ་དུ་གར་དམིགས་པའི་ལྟེ་བར་གཏུམ་མོ་འི་མེ་འབར་བས་ཞུས་ཡོངས་སུ་གང་བའི་ཁྲོད་ན། དཀྱིལ་འཁོར་གྱི་ལྷ་ཚོགས་དང་། ནང་གི་ཙོ་བོ་ལ་བླ་མ་རིགས་བདག་གི་ཚུལ་དུ་བཞུགས་ཤིང་། ལྟོ་བར་དུར་ཁྲོད་ན་གནས་པའི་ལྷ་རྣམས་དང་། ཁམས་གསུམ་གྱི་སེམས་ཅན་ཐམས་ཅད་གནས་པར་བསམས་ལ། ལག་པའི་པའི་མཆོད་པས་ལག་པའི་

ལྷ་ཚོགས་ནས། ལག་པ་གཉིས་དགང་བླུགས། ཁ་རྟེམ་ཁྲུང་། ཁ་ཟས་བསྲེག་རྫས་སུ་དམིགས་ཏེ་ཤིན་ཏུ་ཞེན་པར་མི་བྱ་ཞིང་། རོ་ཕྱིན་པར་ཟོས་ནས། ལྷག་མ། ཨོཾ་ཨུ་ཙྪིཥྚ་བ་ལིམ་ཏ་བཀྵ་ས་སི་སྭཱ་ཧཱ། ལྷག་མ་ལ་དབང་པའི་འབྱུང་པོ་ལ་སྦྱིན་ནོ།། ཁ་ཟས་ཀྱི་རྣལ་འབྱོར་རོ།།

སྤྱོད་ལམ། །པོ་ཉ་སྔགས་དང་ཞིང་ལས་སྐྱེས་པ། དམ་ཚིག་གི་འཁོར་ལོ། ཕྱིའི་དཀྱིལ་འཁོར་སྣང་བའི་ཆ་ལུས་ཕྱག་རྒྱ་དང་བཅས་པ་རྣམས་སྤྲུལ་པའི་སྐུ། །བསྐྱེད་པའི་རིམ་པ། པོ་ཉ་ལྷན་སྐྱེས། འཁོར་ལོ་གསུམ། ལུས་ཀྱི་དཀྱིལ་འཁོར། །ཟུང་འཇུག་གི་ཆ་རྟགས་དང་བཅས་པ་རྣམས་ལོངས་སྤྱོད་རྫོགས་པའི་སྐུ། །རྫོགས་པའི་རིམ་པ། །པོ་ཉ་གསུམ་གྱི་ཆོས་ཉིད། བདེ་ཆེན་གྱི་འཁོར་ལོ། ཡེ་ཤེས། སྟོང་པའི་ཆ། ཡིད་ཏིང་ངེ་འཛིན་དང་བཅས་པ་རྣམས་ཆོས་ཀྱི་སྐུ་དང་རྗེས་སུ་མཐུངས་པའི་ཕྱིར་ཚུལ་འདི་སྐུ་གསུམ་ལམ་དུ་བྱེད་པར་དགོངས་སོ།། །དེ་ལྟར་རྣལ་འབྱོར་བཞི་ཡན་ལག་དང་བཅས་པ་ལ་ཤིན་ཏུ་གོམས་པས་ཞི་བ་ལ་སོགས་པའི་འཕྲིན་ལས་དང་། གྲུབ་པ་ཆེན་པོ་བརྒྱད་ཀྱི་དངོས་གྲུབ་གནས་སྐབས་སུ་འགྲུབ་ཅིང་། །རིམ་པ་གཉིས་ལས་སྐྱེས་པའི་ཏིང་ངེ་འཛིན་སྤྲོས་བཅས་དང་སྤྲོས་མེད་དང་། ཤིན་ཏུ་སྤྲོས་མེད་ཀྱི་སྤྱོད་པས་བརྟན་པར་བྱས་པས་འཇིག་རྟེན་ལས་འདས་པའི་ཡེ་ཤེས་སྐྱེས་པ་དང་། །གཞན་གྱི་དོན་དུ་ཀུན་ཏུ་བཟང་པོའི་སྤྱོད་པ་སྤྱད་པས་བྱང་ཆུབ་སེམས་དཔའི་ས་བཅུ་གཉིས་བགྲོད་དེ། ཉེ་བའི་རྒྱུ་མཚམས་སྦྱར་ནས་སྐུ་དང་ཡེ་ཤེས་ཟུང་གྱིས་གྲུབ་ཅིང་། རང་དང་གཞན་གྱི་དོན་ཕུན་སུམ་ཚོགས་པ། སྙིང་རྗེ་ཆེན་པོ་དང་། རྫུ་འཕྲུལ་གྱི་ཚོགས་ཀྱིས་རྣམ་པར་རྩེན་ཞིང་། འཁོར་བ་སྲིད་དུ་བཞུགས་པའི་རྡོ་རྗེ་འཆང་ཆེན་པོའི་གོ་འཕང་མྱུར་དུ་ཐོབ་པར་གྱུར་བ་ཉིད་དོ།། དཀྱིལ་འཁོར་གསལ་འདེབས་པའི་རིམ་པ་ནི། རྟེན་དང་རྟེན་པ་ཡིན་པའི་ཕྱིར། ཁོ་བོས་རྟེན་གྱི་དཀྱིལ་འཁོར་གསལ་གདབ་པ་ཐོག་མར་

༄ སྨྲས་སོ།། བསྒོམ་བྱའི་དོན་དང༌། བསྒོམ་པའི་གོ་རིམས་ལ། བློ་གྲོས་ངེས་པར་བྱ་བའི་ཕྱིར། རྗེ་བཙུན་རིན་པོ་ཆེའི་ཞལ་སྔ་ནས་མཛད་པའི་མངོན་པར་རྟོགས་པའི་གཞུང་ཅི་ནས་ཀྱང་བལྟ་ཞིང༌། འདྲིས་པར་བྱའོ།། འདི་ལ་འདུན་པའི་འདུན་པ་རྣམ་དག་རྣམ་པར་མཛེས་པའི་སྐུ་མངའ་ཞིང༌། ཚུལ་བཞིན་མཁྱེན་པའི་མཁྱེན་པ་རབ་གསལ་རབ་ཏུ་འབྱོར་པའི་དཔལ་འབྱོར་ཅན། འཛི་ཤིག་དེ་སྐུར་དེ་ཡིས་བསྐུལ་ནས་བསྐུལ་བའི་ཞལ་ངོར་འཕགས་པས་སྨྲས། དགེ་བས་འགྲོ་ཀུན་འགྲོ་བའི་བླ་མ་བླ་མེད་གོ་འཕང་ཐོབ་པར་ཤོག། ||

༄ སློབ་དཔོན་རྣལ་འབྱོར་གྱི་དབང་ཕྱུག་ལོ་ཡི་པས་མཛད་པའི་གཞུང་ཉམས་སུ་བླང་པའི་ཚུལ། དཔལ་འཁོར་ལོ་བདེ་མཆོག་གི་བསྒྲུབ་པའི་ཐབས། རིམ་པ་གསལ་བ་ཞེས་བྱ་བ། དགེ་སློང་འཕགས་པས། ཕྱུགས་མོ་ལུག་གི་ལོ།། སྨིན་དྲུག་གི་ཟླ་བའི་ཚེས་བཅུ་ལ། ཤིང་ཀུན་མཁར་དུ་སྦྱར་བའི་ཡི་གེ་པ་ནི་ཨ་ཙ་རའོ།།

ལེའུ་དང་པོ་རྫོགས་སོ།།

DEM-CHOG TANTRA.

Fascicule II.

༄༅། །དཔལ་འཁོར་ལོ་བདེ་མཆོག །རྡོ་རྗེ་རྣལ་འབྱོར་མ།

དཔལ་སྒྲུ་མ་ཆེན་མོ། སྒྲོལ་མ་རྣམས་བཞུགས་སྭོ།།

གཉིས་པ།།

དཔལ་འཁོར་ལོ་བདེ་མཆོག། རྡོ་རྗེ་རྣལ་འབྱོར་མ། དཔལ་སྒྲུ་མ་ཆེན་མོ། སྒྲོལ་མ་རྣམས་བཞུགས་སོ༎

༄༅། དཔལ་འཁོར་ལོ་བདེ་མཆོག་གི་དཀྱིལ་འཁོར་གྱི་འཁོར་ལོ་བསྒྲུབ་པའི་ཐབས་ཞེས་བྱ་བ་བླ་མ་མཆོག་དང་ཧེ་རུ་ཀའི། ཞབས་ཀྱི་པད་མོར་ཕྱག་འཚལ་ནས། ཕྱུང་ཞིང་གསང་བའི་ངག་གིས་ནི། འཁོར་ལོ་སྡོམ་པའི་སྒྲུབ་ཐབས་བཤད། དཀྱིལ་འཁོར་འདིར་དབང་བསྐུར་བ་ཐོབ་ཅིང་བླ་མ་ལ་གནང་བ་ཐོབ་པའི་རྣལ་འབྱོར་པས། སྟན་བདེ་བ་ལ་ཁ་ལྷོ་ཕྱོགས་སུ་བལྟས་ཏེ་འདུག་ལ། བདུད་རྩི་རི་རིལ་བུ་མྱངས་ནས། རང་ཧེ་རུ་ཀ་ཡབ་ཡུམ་དུ་བསྒོམས་ཤིང་། ཤྲཱི་ཧེ་རུ་ཀ་ཨ་ཧཾ་ཞེས་བརྗོད་ལ། ཤྲཱི་ནི་གཉིས་མེད་ཡེ་ཤེས་ཏེ། ཧེ་ནི་རྒྱུ་སོགས་སྟོང་པ་ཉིད། རུ་ནི་ཚོགས་དང་བྲལ་བ་སྟེ། ཀ་ནི་གང་དུ་འང་མི་གནས་པའི་དོན་དང་ལྡན་པ་བདག་ཡིན་སྙམ་དུ་བསྒོམས་པའི་སྙིང་གི་ནང་དུ། ཨ་རྣམ་པར་མི་རྟོག་པའི་ཡེ་ཤེས་ལས་བྱུང་བའི་ཟླ་བ་དག་པ། འཇིག་རྟེན་པ་དང་ཐུན་མོང་པའི་ཡེ་ཤེས་ཀྱི་སྙིང་དུ་གཟུང་འཛིན་དང་བྲལ་བའི་སེམས་ཧཱུྃ་དུ་དམིགས་པ་ཡེ་ཤེས་ལྔའི་ངོ་བོར་བསྒོམ་པ་ལས་འོད་ཟེར་སྔོན་པོ། ལྗང་ཁུ། དམར་པོ། སེར་པོ་རྣམས་ཞལ་བཞི་ནས་རིམ་པ་བཞིན་འཕྲོས་པས་འཇིག་རྟེན་གྱིས་ཁམས་ཐམས་ཅད་གང་བས། སེམས་ཅན་ཐམས་ཅད་བདེ་བ་དང་བདེ་བའི་རྒྱུ་དང་ལྡན་པ་དང་། སྡུག་བསྔལ་དང་། སྡུག་བསྔལ་གྱི་རྒྱུ་དང་བྲལ་བ་དང་། བདེ་བ་བླ་ན་མེད་པ་དང་མི་འབྲལ་བ་དང་། ཆགས་སྡང་མེད་ཅིང་འཇིག་རྟེན་གྱི་ཆོས་བརྒྱད་ཉམས་པར་གྱུར་པའི་ཚད་མེད་བཞི་

༄༅ རིམ་པ་བཞིན་བསྒོམ་ཞིང་། ལག་པ་གཡོན་པའི་མཐེབ་མོ་ཕྱོགས་བཙུར་བསྐོར་ནས། སེ་གོལ་བརྡབ་པ་དང་། སུ་ཁི་ཧྲ་ཕཊ་དུ་ཞེས་བརྗོད་པས་བྱིན་གྱིས་བརླབ་བོ། ཡང་ཧཱུྃ་ལས་འོད་ཟེར་སྣ་ཚོགས་འཕྲོས་པས། བདག་དང་སེམས་ཅན་ཐམས་ཅད་ཀྱི་སྡིག་སྒྲིབ་སྦྱངས་ནས། སེམས་ཅན་ཐམས་ཅད་ཧེ་རུ་ཀར་གྱུར་ཏེ་སླར་འདུས་ནས་རང་ལ་ཐིམ་པས་རང་གི་གཟུགས་ཀྱི་ཕུང་པོ་རྣམ་པར་སྣང་མཛད། ཚོར་བ་རྡོ་རྗེ་ཉི་མ། འདུ་ཤེས་པདྨ་གར་གྱི་དབང་ཕྱུག། འདུ་བྱེད་རྡོ་རྗེ་རྒྱལ་པོ། རྣམ་པར་ཤེས་པ་རྡོ་རྗེ་སེམས་དཔའ། དེ་བཞིན་གཤེགས་པ་ཐམས་ཅད་ཉིད་དུ་གྱུར་པ་དཔལ་ཧེ་རུ་ཀ། མིག་གཏི་མུག་རྡོ་རྗེ། རྣ་བ་ཞེ་སྡང་རྡོ་རྗེ། སྣ་སེར་སྣ་རྡོ་རྗེ། ཁ་འདོད་ཆགས་རྡོ་རྗེ་ལུས་ཕྲག་དོག་རྡོ་རྗེ། སྐྱེ་མཆེད་ཐམས་ཅད་དབང་ཕྱུག་རྡོ་རྗེ། སའི་ཁམས་ལྷུང་བར་བྱེད་མ། ཆུའི་ཁམས་གསོད་པར་བྱེད་མ། མེའི་ཁམས་འགུགས་པར་བྱེད་མ། རླུང་གི་ཁམས་གར་གྱི་དབང་ཕྱུག། ནམ་མཁའི་ཁམས་པད་མའི་དྲྭ་བ་ཅན་དུ་གྱུར་བར་བསམ་མོ། ཡང་ཧཱུྃ་ལས་འོད་འཕྲོས་པས་སྟེང་གི་ཆར་རང་གི་བླ་མ་རྡོ་རྗེ་ཆོས་ཀྱི་རྣམ་པ་ལ་བླ་མ་བརྒྱུད་པ་ཐམས་ཅད་ཀྱིས་བསྐོར་བ་དང་། འོག་གི་ཆར་འཁོར་ལོ་བདེ་མཆོག་གི་དཀྱིལ་འཁོར་ལ་སངས་རྒྱས་དང་བྱང་ཆུབ་སེམས་དཔའ་ཐམས་ཅད་ཀྱིས་བསྐོར་བ་སྤྱན་དྲངས་པ་ལ། ན་མོ་གུ་རུ་བྷྱས་བླ་མ་དང་། ནམཿ ཤྲཱི་ཙཀྲ་སཾ་བྷ་ར་མཎྜལ་བྷྱས་དཀྱིལ་འཁོར་ལ་ཕྱག་བྱས་ནས། ཕྱི་དང་ཕྲོས་སྤྲུལ་པས་མཆོད་ལ། སྡིག་པ་ཐམས་ཅད་སོ་སོར་བཤགས། དཀོན་མཆོག་གསུམ་ལ་བདག་སྐྱབས་མཆི། འཁོར་ལོ་སྡོམ་པའི་དམ་ཚིག་ཀུན། གཟུང་ཞིང་ཡོངས་སུ་སྐྱོང་བར་བགྱི། འགྲོ་བའི་དགེ་ལ་རྗེས་ཡིད་རང་། མ་བསྒྲལ་བ་རྣམས་བདག་གིས་བསྒྲལ། མ་གྲོལ་བ་རྣམས་བདག་གིས་དགྲོལ། དབུགས་མ་ཕྱིན་པ་དབུགས་དབྱུང་ཞིང་། སེམས་ཅན་མྱ་ངན་འདས་ལ་

༄༅ དགོད། ཕྱོགས་བཅུའི་སངས་རྒྱས་ཐམས་ཅད་ལ། ཟབ་མོའི་ཆོས་ནི་ཉན་པ་དང་། རྟག་ཏུ་བཞུགས་པར་གསོལ་བ་འདེབས། འཁོར་ལོ་སྒོམ་པ་ལམ་གྱི་མཆོག། རིམ་པ་གཉིས་ལ་གནས་པར་བགྱི། དགེ་བས་བདག་གཞན་མ་ལུས་པ། ཧེ་རུ་ཀ་དཔལ་ཐོབ་པར་ཤོག། ཅེས་ལན་གསུམ་བརྗོད་པ་དང་། ཚོགས་ཀྱིས་ཞིང་རྣམས་ཀྱིས་རིགས་ཀྱི་བུ་ཁྱོད་ཀྱི་གནས་པ་འདི་ནི་ལེགས་པར་གནས་པ་ཡིན་གྱིས། གནས་པ་འདིས་གནས་ན་མཆོག་གི་གོ་འཕང་ཐོབ་པར་འགྱུར་རོ་ཞེས་གནང་བ་བྱིན་པ་ལ་སྨྲར་ཡང་མཆོད་ནས། ཨོཾ་བཛྲ་མུཿ་གཤེགས་སུ་གསོལ་ལོ། དེ་ནས་ཨོཾ་སུམྦྷ་ནི་སུམྦྷ་ཧཱུཾ་ཧཱུཾ་ཕཊ། ཅེས་བརྗོད་ནས་སྙིང་ཁའི་ཧཱུཾ་ལས། ཤར་དུ་ཁྭ་གདོང་། སྙིང་དུ་ཁཎྜ་རོ་ཧ་དང་། ཨོཾ་གྲྀཧྞ་གྲྀཧྞ་ཧཱུཾ་ཧཱུཾ་ཕཊ། བྱང་དུ་འུག་གདོང་། ཨོཾ་གྲྀཧྞ་པ་ཡ་གྲྀཧྞ་པ་ཡ་ཧཱུཾ་ཧཱུཾ་ཕཊ། ནུབ་ཏུ་ཁྱི་གདོང་དང་། འོག་ཏུ་ཁཎྜ་རོ་ཧ། ཨོཾ་ཨཱ་ན་ཡ་ཧོ་བྷ་ག་ཝན་བཛྲ་ཧཱུཾ་ཧཱུཾ་ཕཊ། ལྷོར་ཕག་གདོང་། དེ་བཞིན་ཤར་ལྷོར་གཤིན་རྗེ་བརྟན་མ། ལྷོ་ནུབ་ཏུ་ཕོ་ཉ་མ། ནུབ་བྱང་དུ་མཆེ་བ་མ། བྱང་ཤར་དུ་འཇོམས་མ་རྣམས་རིམ་པ་བཞིན་སྤྲོས་པས་བགེགས་ཐམས་ཅད་བསྐྲད་པར་བསམ་མོ། ཡང་ཧཱུཾ་ལས་འོད་འཕྲོས་པས་རྡོ་རྗེའི་ས་གཞི། ར་བ། དྲ་བ། གུར། བླ་བྲེ། མདའི་དྲ་བ་དང་། ཡེ་ཤེས་ཀྱི་མེ་འབར་བ་རྣམས་སུ་གྱུར་པར་བསམ་པ་དང་། གཡོན་པའི་སྡིགས་འཛུབ་ཕྱོགས་བཅུར་བསྐོར་ཞིང་སོ་གོལ་བརྡབ་པ་དང་། ཨོཾ་མེ་དི་ནི་བཛྲཱི་བྷ་ཝ་བནྡྷ་ཧཱུཾ་ཧཱུཾ་ཧཱུཾ་ཕཊ། ཨོཾ་བཛྲ་པྲ་ཀཱ་ར་ཧཱུཾ་བཾ་ཧཱུཾ། ཨོཾ་བཛྲ་པཉྫ་ར་ཧཱུཾ་ཡཾ་ཧཱུཾ། ཨོཾ་བཛྲ་བི་ཏཱ་ན་ཧཱུཾ་ཁཾ་ཧཱུཾ། ཨོཾ་བཛྲ་ཤ་ར་ཛཱ་ལ་ཧཱུཾ་ཤཾ་ཧཱུཾ། ཨོཾ་བཛྲ་ཛྭཱ་ལ་ཨ་ན་ལཱ་ཀ་ཧཱུཾ་རཾ་ཧཱུཾ། ཞེས་རེ་རེ་ལ་འང་ལན་གསུམ་གསུམ་བརྗོད་པ་དང་། རིམ་པ་བཞིན་སྤྱར་ཞིང་། སྲུང་བའི་འཁོར་ལོ་བསྒོམ་མོ།། ཡང་ཧཱུཾ་ལས་རྡོ་རྗེ་ཕུར་བུ་དང་། རྡོ་རྗེ་ཐོ་བའི་ཚོགས་སྤྲོས་པ་ཕོ་ཉ་རྣམས་ཀྱི་ལག་པ་གཡོན་པ་

༄༅ ངང་གསལ་སྲུ་གནོད་པ་ཉིད་སྤྲུལ་དུ་མ་དང་བཅས་པས་ཕྱོགས་སྐྱོང་རྣམས་ཀྱིས་གཙོ་བྱས་པའི་བགེགས་རྣམས་བཀུག་ནས་དཀར་པོའི་ཕྱོགས་རྣམས་ཡཾ་ལ་བགོད། ནག་པོའི་ཕྱོགས་རྣམས་ཀྱི་སྤྱི་བོར་ཕུར་བུ་བཏབ་པར་བསྒོམ་ཞིང་། ཨོཾ་ཛྷ་ཛྷ་ཛྷ་ཧ་ཡ་ཛྷ་ཧ་ཡ་སརྦ་དུཥྚཱན་ཕཊ། ཀཱི་ལ་ཡ་ཀཱི་ལ་ཡ་སརྦ་པཱ་པཾ་ཧཱུཾ་ཕཊ། བཛྲ་ཀཱི་ལ་ཡ་བཛྲ་དྷ་རོ་ཨཱ་ཛྙཱ་པ་ཡ་ཏི། སརྦ་བིགྷ་ནཱན་ཀཱ་ཡ་ཝཱཀ་ཙིཏྟ་བཛྲ་ཀཱི་ལ་ཡ་ཧཱུཾ་ཕཊ། ཅེས་པ་དང་། ཐོ་བས་བྲིག་བརྡུངས་བར་བསྒོམ་ཞིང་། ཨོཾ་བཛྲ་མུད་ག་ར་བཛྲ་ཀཱི་ལ་ཡ་ཨཱ་ཀོ་ཊ་ཡ་ཧཱུཾ་ཕཊ། ཅེས་བརྗོད་པས་ལུས་ཐལ་བར་བརླགས་ནས་རྣམ་ཤེས་མི་བསྐྱོད་པའི་ཞིང་དུ་སངས་རྒྱས་པར་བསྒོམ་ཞིང་། ཕོ་ཉ་རྣམས་རྡོ་རྗེའི་ར་བའི་ཁ་ཕྱིར་ལ་འཁོད་ནས་སྒྲུབ་པ་པོ་སངས་མ་རྒྱས་ཀྱི་ངར་དུ་བསྲུང་བར་བསམ་མོ།། དེ་ནས་ཆོས་ཐམས་ཅད་སེམས་ཙམ་དང་དེ་འང་རང་བཞིན་མེད་པར་བསམས་ནས༔ ཨོཾ་སྭ་བྷཱ་ཝ་ཤུདྡྷ་སརྦ་དྷརྨཱ་སྭ་བྷཱ་ཝ་ཤུདྡྷོ྅ཧཾ༔ ཨོཾ་ཤཱུ་ནྱ་ཏཱ་ཛྙཱ་ན་བཛྲ་སྭ་བྷཱ་ཝ་ཨཱཏྨ་ཀོ྅ཧཾ། ཞེས་བརྗོད་པས་ཕྱི་ནང་གི་ཆོས་ཐམས་ཅད་སྟོང་པར་བསམ་པ་ནི་རྒྱུ་ཚོགས་གཉིས་བསགས་པའོ། སྟོང་པའི་ངང་ལས་ཡཾ་ལས་རླུང་གི་དཀྱིལ་འཁོར་ལྗང་ཁམ་གཞུ་ཁྱུ། རཾ་ལས་མེའི་དཀྱིལ་འཁོར་གྲུ་གསུམ་དམར་པོ།། བཾ་ལས་ཆུའི་དཀྱིལ་འཁོར་ཟླུམ་པོ་དཀར་པོ། ལཾ་ལས་སའི་དཀྱིལ་འཁོར་གྲུ་བཞི་སེར་པོ། སུཾ་ལས་རི་རབ༔ ཤར་ཤེལ། བྱང་གསེར། ནུབ་པདྨ་ར་ག། ལྷོ་བཻ་ཌཱུརྻ་ལས་གྲུབ་པ་གྲུ་བཞི། བང་རིམ་བཞི་ཅན། བརྒྱད་དང་ལྡན་པ་རྣམས་བརྩེགས་པའི་སྟེང་དུ་ཧཱུཾ་ལས་སྣ་ཚོགས་རྡོ་རྗེའི་ལྟེ་བར་ པཾ་ལས་སྣ་ཚོགས་པདྨ་འདབ་མ་བརྒྱད་པའི་སྟེང་ ཡོར་མཚན་བཟང་པོ་སུམ་བཅུ་རྩ་གཉིས་ཀྱི་ངོ་བོ་ཨཱ་ལི་ཕྲག་གཉིས་ལས་ཟླ་བའི་དཀྱིལ་འཁོར་མེ་ལོང་ལྟ་བུའི་ཡེ་ཤེས་སུ་བསྒོམས་པའི་སྟེང་དུ་དཔེ་བྱད་བཟང་པོ་བརྒྱད་ཅུའི་ངོ་བོ་ ཨ་ར་ལ་ཁ་ཊ་ཀྵ་ དང་བཅས་པའི་ཀཱ་ལི་ཕྲག་གཉིས་ལས་ཉི་མའི་དཀྱིལ་

༄༅། འཁོར་མཉམ་པ་ཉིད་ཀྱི་ཡེ་ཤེས་སྦུ་བསམ་པའི་བར་དུ་སོ་སོར་རྟོག་པའི་ཡེ་ཤེས་ཀྱི་ངོ་བོ་ཧཱུྃ་དཀར་པོ་བསྒོམ། ཉི་མའི་སྟེང་དུ་ལུས་ངག་ཡིད་གསུམ་དང་ཡུམ་གྱི་མཁའ་དང་། ཡབ་ཀྱི་བྱང་ཆུབ་ཀྱི་སེམས་དང་། སེམས་ཀྱི་རང་བཞིན་འོད་གསལ་བའི་ངོ་བོ། ཨོཾ་ཕཊཿཧཱུྃ། དང་ཿ པད་མ་དང་། བྷ་བ་དང་། ཧཱུྃ་རྣམས་བསྟིགས་པ་བསྒོམ་ལ། ཨོཾ་ནས་བཙོམས་ཏེ་མས་ཡར་རིམ་གྱིས་ཧཱུྃ་གི་བར་དུ་ཐིམ་ཞིང་། ཧཱུྃ་ཡང་ན་དའི་བར་དུ་ཐིམ་ནས་ན་ད་དམར་སྐྱ་ཤིན་དུ་ཕྲ་ཞིང་ལྡིད་པ། དཔའ་བོ་ཉི་ཤུ་རྩ་བཞིའི་ཐུགས་སྒྲོགས་བཞིན་པ། ཁྲིག་གཅིག་སྨུར་དུ་བབས་པ་ནི་སྣ་ཡིན་ལ། དེས་ཉི་མ་ཞུག་ནས་ཆུལ་ཧཱུྃ་ལ་ཐིམ་ནས། ཐམས་ཅད་གཅིག་ཏུ་འདྲེས་པ་བྱ་བ་གྲུབ་པའི་ཡེ་ཤེས། དེ་ལས་རྟེན་དང་རྟེན་པའི་དཀྱིལ་འཁོར་དུ་གཅིག་ཆར་གྱུར་པ་ནི་ཆོས་ཀྱི་དབྱིངས་ཀྱི་ཡེ་ཤེས་སོ།། དེ་རིམ་གྱིས་གསལ་གདབ་སྟེ། རི་རབ་ཀྱི་སྟེང་དུ་སྲུང་བའི་འཁོར་ལོ འི་ནང་དུ་རིན་པོ་ཆེ་སྣ་ཚོགས་ལས་གྲུབ་པའི་གཞལ་ཡས་ཁང་གྲུ་བཞི། སྒོ་བཞི། ནང་ནས་ནག་པོ། དཀར་པོ། སེར་པོ། དམར་པོ། ལྗང་ཁུའི་རྟེག་པ་རིམ་པ་ལྔ་པའི་སྟེང་དུ་རིན་པོ་ཆེ འི་ཕ་གུ་སེར་པོ འི་ཁ་ཁྱེར་དང་། དེའི་སྟེང དུ་མདའ་ཡབ་ལ་དྲ་བ་ཕྲུང་གིས་བསྐྱོད་པ་དང་། དྲིལ་བུ་གཡེར་ཁ་དང་བཅས་པའི་དྲ་བ་དང་དྲ་ཕྱེད་པ་འཕྱང་བ། མདའ་ཡབ་ཀྱི་སྟེང་དུ་རིན་པོ་ཆེ འི་དྲ་བ་སེང་མའི་པུ་ཤུས་བསྐོར་བ། ཕྱི་རོལ་འདོད་ཡོན་གྱི་སྣམ་བུ་དམར་པོ་ལ་མཆོད་རྫས་དུ་མ་ཐོགས་པའི་ལྷ་མོ་བཅུ་དྲུག་གནས་པ། ཁྲིམས་པ་ལྟར་སྒོ་འབུར་དུ་གྱུར་པའི་སྒོ་བཞི འི་སྟེང་གི་ཐད་སོར་ཀ་བ་བཞི་བཞིས་བཏེག་པའི་རྟ་བབས་བང་རིམ་བཞི་པའི་སྟེང་དུ་པདྨ་ལ་གནས་པའི་ཆོས་ཀྱི་འཁོར་ལོ་དང་། རི་དྭགས་དང་། གདུགས་དང་ལྡན་པ། གཞན་ཡང་རྔ་ཡབ་ནོར་བུའི་ཡུ་བ་ཅན་དང་། རིན་པོ་ཆེ་དང་། མི་རྟག་གི་ཕྲེང་བ་དང་། གོས་དང་འཕན་ལ་སོགས་པའི་རྒྱན་གྱིས་རྣམ་པར་མཛེས་པར་བྱས་པའི་

༄༅ ནང་གི་ལྷ་རྣམ་ཤར་སྔོ། བྱང་ལྗང་། ནུབ་དམར། ལྷོ་སེར་བའི་དབུ་སུ་མཆོད་རྟེན་བང་རིམ་བཞི་པ་ལྷ་བུའི་འཁོར་ལོ་རིམ་པ་བཞི་པའི་ལྟེ་བར་པད་མ་འདབ་མ་བརྒྱད་པ་བསམ་མོ།། གཞལ་ཡས་ཁང་གི་ཕྱི་རོལ་དུ། ཤར་དུ་གཏུམ་དྲག། བྱང་དུ་ཚང་ཚིང་འཁྲིགས་པ། ནུབ་ཏུ་ཨུར་ཨུར་འབར་བ། ལྷོར་འཇིགས་རུང་བ། ཤར་ལྷོར་ནགས་ཚལ་ཕུན་སུམ་ཚོགས་པ་ལྷོ་ནུབ་ཏུ་སྨུན་པ་མི་བཟད་པ། ནུབ་བྱང་དུ་ཀི་ལི་ཀི་ལིའི་སྒྲ་སྒྲོགས་པ། བྱང་ཤར་དུ་ཧ་ཧ་ཀད་པའི་དུར་ཁྲོད་རྣམས་སུ་རིམ་པ་དེ་ཉིད་ཀྱིས་བརྒྱ་བྱིན། གནོད་སྦྱིན། ཆུ་ལྷ། གཤིན་རྗེ། མེ་ལྷ་བསྲིན་པོ།། རླུང་ལྷ། དབང་ལྡན་ཏེ་ཕྱོགས་སྐྱོང་བ་དང་།། དེ་བཞིན་དུ། ཤི་རི་ཤ། ཨ་ཤྭད་ཐ། ཀཾ་ཀ་ལ། ཙཱུ་ཏ། ཀ་རན་ཛ། ལ་ཏ་པར་ཀ་ཊི། པར་ཊི་པ་ཏ། ཝ་ཊ་སྟེ་ཤིང་ཆེན་པོ་བརྒྱད་དང་། དེ་རྣམས་ལ་རྟེན་པའི་སྐྱོ་འཚམས་མ་རྣམས་ཀྱི་གཟུགས་འཛིན་པའི་དྲག་གཏུམ་སྐྱོང་བ་ལ་སོགས་པའི་ཞིང་སྐྱོང་བ་བརྒྱད་དང་། ནོར་རྒྱས། འཇོག་པོ།། སྟོབས་ཀྱི་རྒྱ། པདྨ། ཧུ་ལུན་ཏ། རིགས་ལྡན། དུང་སྐྱོང་། པད་མ་ཆེན་པོ་སྟེ་ཀླུ་བརྒྱད་དང་། སྤྲི་གྲག་པ། རྨུགས་པ། སྨུན་པ་ཅན། ཀུན་དུ་འཁྱིལ་བ། གང་བ། འབབ་པ། དྲག་པོ།། འཁྲིགས་པ་སྟེ་སྤྲིན་ཆེན་པོ་བརྒྱད་དང་། གཞན་ཡང་རྩ་ཆེན་པོ་བརྒྱད། མེ་ཆེན་པོ་བརྒྱད། མཆོད་རྟེན་ཆེན་པོ་བརྒྱད་གནས་ཤིང་། རྒྱལ་པ་དང་། རང་རྒྱུད་པའི་དཔའ་བོ་དང་རྣལ་འབྱོར་མ་དང་། གྲུབ་པ་དང་། རིག་པ་འཛིན་པ་དང་། མཁའ་འགྲོ་དང་། མཁའ་འགྲོ་མ་དང་། འདྲེ་དང་། སྲིན་པོ་དང་། གནོད་སྦྱིན་དང་། ཤ་ཟ་དང་། འབྱུང་པོ་དང་། ཕྱི་སྲུང་ལ་སོགས་པས་ཡོངས་སུ་གང་བའི་དུར་ཁྲོད་ཀྱིས་བསྐོར་བའོ།། ནང་གི་པད་མའི་ལྟེ་བར་ཉི་མའི་སྟེང་དུ་རང་ཉིད་འཁོར་ལོ་བདེ་མཆོག་ཞལ་བཞི། ཕྱག་བཅུ་གཉིས་པ། ཙོ་བའི་ཞལ་སྔོ།། གཡོན་ལྗང་། རྒྱབ་དམར། གཡས་སེར་བ། ཞལ་རེ་རེ་ལ་སྤྱན་གསུམ་གསུམ་དང་ལྡན་ཞིང་།

༄༅ ཞལ་རྣམ་པར་འགྱུར་བ། མཆེ་བ་གཙིགས་པ། ཕྱག་དང་པོ་གཉིས་ཀྱིས་རྡོ་རྗེ་དང་དྲིལ་བུ་འཛིན་པས་ཡུམ་ལ་འཁྱུད་ཅིང་། འོག་མ་གཉིས་ཀྱིས་གླང་པོ་ཆེ འི་ཀོ་རློན་གོས་སུ་གྱོན་པ། གཡས་ཀྱི་གསུམ་པས་ཌ་མ་རུ། བཞི་པས་དགྲ་སྟ། ལྔ་པས་གྲི་གུག། དྲུག་པས་མདུང་རྩེ་གསུམ་པ། གཡོན་གྱི་གསུམ་པས་རྡོ་རྗེས་མཚན་པའི་ཁ་ཊྭཱཾ་ག། བཞི་པས་ཁྲག་གིས་གང་བའི་ཐོད་པ། ལྔ་པས་རྡོ་རྗེ འི་ཞགས་པ། དྲུག་པས་ཚངས་པའི་མགོ་བོ་གདོང་བཞི་པ་བསྣམས་པ། ཞབས་གཡས་བརྐྱང་པས་དུས་མཚན་དམར་མོ འི་ནུ་མའི་སྙིང་དང་། གཡོན་བསྐུམ་པས་འཇིགས བྱེད་ནག་པོ འི་མགོ་ལྟབ་ནས་མནན་པ། རོལ་པའི་ཐོར་ཚུགས་བཅིངས་པའི་རྩེར་ཡིད་བཞིན་གྱི་ནོར་བུ་རིན་པོ་ཆེ་དང་། གཡོན་ན་ཆོས་གཅིག་གི་ཟླ་བ་དང་། འཚོགས་མའི་སྟེང་དུ་སྣ་ཚོགས་རྡོ་རྗེས་མཚན་པ། མི་མགོ་སྐམ་པོ་ལྔ་ལྔའི་དབུ་རྒྱན་དང་། རློན་པ་ལྔ་བཅུའི་དོ་ཤལ་ཅན། འཁོར་ལོ། རྣ་ཆ། མགུལ་རྒྱན། གདུ་བུ། སྐ་རགས། ཐལ་ཆེན་གྱི་ཀྱུ་སྟེ། རུས་པའི་རྒྱན་དྲུག་གིས་བརྒྱན་ཞིང་། སྟག་གི་ལྤགས་པའི་ཤམ་ཐབས་གྱོན་པ། སྒེག་པ། དཔའ་བ། མི་སྡུག་པ། རྒོད་པ། དྲག་ཤུལ། འཇིགས་སུ་རུང་། སྙིང་རྗེ་རྔམ་དང་ཞི་བ་སྟེ། གར་དགུའི་ཉམས་དང་ལྡན་པའོ།། དེའི་པང་ན། ཡུམ་རྡོ་རྗེ་ཕག་མོ། སྐུ་མདོག་དམར་མོ།། ཞལ་གཅིག་ཕྱག་གཉིས་མ། གཡོན་པས་ཐོད་པ་ཁྲག་གིས་གང་བ་འཛིན་པས་ཡབ་ལ་འཁྱུད་ཅིང་། གཡས་རྡོ་རྗེས་མཚན་པའི་གྲི་གུག་དང་བཅས་པའི་སྡིགས་འཛུབ་ཀྱིས་ཕྱོགས་བཅུར་སྡིགས་པ། སྤྱན་གསུམ་པ། གཅེར་བུ་སྐྲ་གྲོལ་བ། མི་མགོ་སྐམ་པོ་ལྔའི་དབུ་རྒྱན་དང་། སྐམ་པོ་ལྔ་བཅུའི་དོ་ཤལ་ཅན། རུས་པའི་རྒྱན་ལྔས་བརྒྱན་ཞིང་བྱིན་པ་གཉིས་ཀྱིས་བཅོམ་ལྡན་འདས་ལ་འཁྱིལ་བའོ། སྣང་བ་དང་ཐབས་དང་ལྷག་མཐོང་དང་། སྙིང་རྗེ་ཆེན་པོ འི་ངོ་བོ་ཉི་ཡབ་ཡིན་ལ། སྟོང་པ་དང་ཤེས་རབ་

༄ དང་། ཞི་གནས་དང་། བདེ་བ་ཆེན་པོའི་ངོ་བོ་ཡུམ་ཡིན་ཞིང་། ཟུང་དུ་འཇུག་པའི་ཕྱིར་ཀུན་དུ་ཁ་སྦྱོར་བ། ཡེ་ཤེས་ཀྱི་མེ་འབར་བའི་དབུས་ན་བཞུགས་པར་བསམ་མོ། པད་མའི་ཤར་དུ་མཁའ་འགྲོ་མ་སྔོན་མོ། བྱང་དུ་ལ་མ་ལྗང་གུ། ནུབ་ཏུ་ཁཎྜ་རོ་ཧ་དམར་མོ། ལྷོར་གཟུགས་ཅན་མ་སེར་མོ། ཐམས་ཅད་ཀྱང་ཞལ་གཅིག་ཕྱག་བཞི་མ། གཡས་གཉིས་ཀྱིས་གྲི་གུག་དང་ཌ་མ་རུ། གཡོན་གཉིས་ཀྱིས་ཐོད་པ་ཁྲག་གིས་གང་བ་དང་། ཁ་ཊྭཱཾ་ག་འཛིན་པ། གཅེར་བུ་གཡས་བརྐྱང་བས་བཞུགས་པའོ།། མཚམས་བཞིར་ཡེ་ཤེས་ཀྱི་ཆུས་གང་བའི་བུམ་པའི་སྟེང་དུ་བདུད་རྩི་ལྔས་གང་བའི་ཐོད་པ་གནས་ཏེ། བདེ་བ་ཆེན་པོའི་འཁོར་ལོའི་ཕྱི་གུག་གིར་བ་དང་། ཀ་བ་དང་། གདུང་དང་། ཐོག་ཕུབས་ཅན་རྡོ་རྗེ་ཕྱེད་པའི་ཏོག་གིས་མཛེས་པར་བྱས་པའོ།། དེའི་ཕྱི་རོལ་དུ་ཐུགས་ཀྱི་འཁོར་ལོ་སྔོན་པོ་རྩིབས་བརྒྱད་པའི་ཤར་རྩིབས་པུ་ལི་ར་མ་ལ་ཡར་ཁཎྜ་ཀ་པ་ལི་དང་། རབ་ཏུ་གཏུམ་མོ།། བྱང་ཛཱ་ལན་དྷ་ར་ར་མ་ཧཱ་ཀཾ་ཀ་ལ་དང་། གཏུམ་པའི་མིག་ཅན་མ། ནུབ་ཨུ་རྒྱན་དུ་ཀཾ་ཀ་ལ་དང་། འོད་ལྡན་མ། ལྷོ་ཨར་བུ་ཏར་མཆེ་བ་རྣམ་པར་གཙིགས་པ་དང་། སྐྲ་ཆེན་མ། ཤར་ལྷོ་གོ་ད་ཝ་རི་ར་སུར་བཱི་རི་དང་། བརྟན་པའི་བློ་ཅན་མ། ལྷོ་ནུབ་ར་མེ་ཤྭ་རིར་འོད་དཔག་མེད་དང་། མིའུ་ཐུང་མ། ནུབ་བྱང་། དེ་ཝཱི་ཀོ་ཊར་རྡོ་རྗེའི་འོད་དང་། ལང་ཀའི་དབང་ཕྱུག་མ། བྱང་ཤར་མ་ལ་ཝར་རྡོ་རྗེའི་སྐུ་དང་། ཤིང་གྲིབ་མ་སྟེ། ཐུགས་ཀྱི་འཁོར་ལོ་ནམ་མཁའ་ལ་སྤྱོད་པའི་ཚུལ་གྱིས་བཞུགས་ཤིང་། ས་བླ་སྟོང་བ། རྡོ་རྗེའི་ར་བ་དང་། ཀ་བ་དང་། གདུང་དང་། ཐོག་ཕུབས་དང་བཅས་པའོ།། དེའི་ཕྱི་རོལ་དུ་གསུང་གི་འཁོར་ལོ་དམར་པོ་རྩིབས་བརྒྱད་པའི་ཤར་རྩིབས་ཀ་མ་རུ་པར་ཨང་ཀུ་རི་དང་། ཨེ་ར་པ་ཏི། བྱང་ཨོ་ཊྲར་རྡོ་རྗེ་རལ་པ་ཅན་དང་འཛིགས་བྱེད་ཆེན་མོ།། ནུབ་ཏྲི་ཤ་ཀུ་ནེར་དཔའ་བོ་ཆེན་པོ་དང་། རླུང་གི་ཤུགས་

༄ ཙཎ་མ།། ལྷོ་ཀོ་ས་ལར་རྡོ་རྗེ་ཧཱུྃ་མཛད་དང་། ཚང་འབྱུང་མ།། ཤར་ལྷོ་ཀ་ལིང་ཀར་རབ་ཏུ་བཟང་པོ་དང་། ཤུ་མ་དེ་ཤྲི། ལྷོ་ནུབ་ལམ་པ་ཀར་རྡོ་རྗེ་བཟང་པོ་དང་། ཤིན་ཏུ་བཟང་མོ།། ནུབ་བྱང་ཀན་ཙིར་འཇིགས་བྱེད་ཆེན་པོ་དང་། ཏ་ཎ་མ། བྱང་ཤར་ཧི་མ་ལ་ཡར་མིག་མི་བཟང་དང་། ཁ་ག་ན་སྟེ། གསུང་གི་འཁོར་ལོ་དམར་པོ་ས་ལ་སྤྱོད་པའི་ཚུལ་གྱིས་བཞུགས་ཤིང་། ས་སྟེང་སྤྱོད་བ། པད་མའི་ར་བ་དང་། ཀ་བ་དང་། གདུང་དང་། ཐོག་ཕུབས་དང་བཅས་པའོ།། དེའི་ཕྱི་རོལ་དུ་སྐུའི་འཁོར་ལོ་དཀར་པོ་རྩིབས་བརྒྱད་པའི་ཤར་རྩིབས་བྲེ་ཏ་པུ་རིར་སྟོབས་པོ་ཆེ་དང་། འཇོར་ལོའི་ཤུགས་ཅན་མ། བྱང་གྲི་ཧ་དེ་ཕར། རིན་ཆེན་རྡོ་རྗེ་དང་། ཁྲ་རོ་ཏ། ནུབ་སྲུའ་རཀྟར། རྟ་མགྲིན་དང་ཤོན་ཊི་ཀི། ལྷོ་སྲུ་བཙ་དྭི་པར། ནམ་མཁའི་སྙིང་པོ་དང་། འཁོར་ལོའི་གོ་ཆ་མ། ཤར་ལྷོ་ན་ག་རར་དཔལ་ཧེ་རུ་ཀ་དང་། ཤིན་ཏུ་དཔའ་མོ། ལྷོ་ནུབ་སིན་དྷུ་ར་པད་མ་གར་གྱི་དབང་ཕྱུག་དང་། སྟོབས་ཆེན་མ། ནུབ་བྱང་མ་རོར་རྣམས་པར་སྣང་མཛད་དང་། འཁོར་ལོ་སྒྱུར་མ། བྱང་ཤར་ཀུ་ལུ་ཏར་རྡོ་རྗེ་སེམས་དཔའ་དང་། བརྩོན་འགྲུས་ཆེན་མོ་སྟེ། སྐུའི་འཁོར་ལོ་དཀར་པོ། ས་འོག་ན་སྤྱོད་པའི་ཚུལ་གྱིས་བཞུགས་ཤིང་། ས་འོག་སྤྱོད་བ་འཁོར་ལོའི་ར་བ་དང་། ཀ་བ་དང་། གདུང་དང་། ཐོག་ཕུབས་དང་བཅས་པའོ།། དཔའ་བོ་རྣམས་ཞལ་ཅིག་ཕྱག་བཞི་པ། དང་པོ་གཉིས་ཀྱིས་རྡོ་རྗེ་དང་དྲིལ་བུ་འཛིན་པས་ཡུམ་ལ་འཁྱུད་ཅིང་། གཡས་ཀྱི་གཉིས་པས་ཌ་མ་རུ་དང་། གཡོན་གྱི་གཉིས་པས་ཁ་ཊྭཱཾ་ག་འཛིན་པའོ།། གྲུ་མོར་ཁ་ཊྭཱཾ་ག་དང་། གཡོན་གྱི་གཉིས་པར་ཀ་པཱ་ལ་འཛིན་པ་ཞེས་བླ་མ་འགའ་ཞིག་གསུང་ངོ་། རྒྱན་དང་ཆ་ལུགས་ཧེ་རུ་ཀ་དང་མཚུངས་པའོ།། རྣལ་འབྱོར་མ་རྣམས་ཞལ་གཅིག་ཕྱག་གཉིས་པ། ཕྱག་མཚན་དང་། ཆ་ལུགས་རྡོ་རྗེ་ཕག་མོ་དང་མཚུངས་ཤིང་། གཉིས་

༄༅ སྤུ་མེད་པའི་སྦྱོར་བ་ལ་བརྩོན་པའོ།། དེའི་ཕྱི་རོལ་དམ་ཚིག་གི་འཁོར་ལོ འི་ཤར་སྒོར་ཁ་གདོང་མ། བྱང་སྒོར་འུག་གདོང་མ། ནུབ་སྒོར་ཁྱི་གདོང་མ། ལྷོ་སྒོར་ཕག་གདོང་མ་རྣམས་ཕྱོགས་ཀྱི་མདོག་ཅན། ཤར་ལྷོར་གཤིན་རྗེ་བརྟན་མ་གཡས་སྔོ། གཡོན་སེར།། ལྷོ་ནུབ་ཏུ་གཤིན་རྗེ་ཕོ་ཉ་མ་གཡས་སེར། གཡོན་དམར། ནུབ་བྱང་དུ་གཤིན་རྗེ་མཆེ་བ་མ་གཡས་དམར། གཡོན་ལྗང་།། བྱང་ཤར་དུ་གཤིན་རྗེ་འཇོམས་མ་གཡས་ལྗང་། གཡོན་སྔོ་བ།། ཡིད་བཏགས་ཀྱི་གདན་ལ་བཞུགས་པ། དྲག་མོ འི་གཟུགས་ཅན། ཕྱག་མཚན་དང་། ཆ་ལུགས་སྙིང་པོ འི་རྣལ་འབྱོར་མ་ལྟ་བུ་སྟེ།། དཔའ་བོ་དང་རྣལ་འབྱོར་མ་ཐམས་ཅད་ཀྱི་དབྲལ་བར་རྡོ་རྗེའི་ཕྲེང་བས་བསྐོར་བའོ།། ལྷ་རྣམ་གྱི་ཐྲུ་རྣམས་སུ་བཅུད་སྣ་ཚོགས་ཀྱིས་གང་བའི་རིན་པོ་ཆེའི་བུམ་པ་བརྒྱད་དང་ལྡན་ཞིང་། སྣ་ཚོགས་རྡོ་རྗེས་མཚན་པའི་ཀ་བ་དང་། གདུང་དང་། ཐོག་ཕུབས་དང་བཅས་པ་སྣང་ལ་རང་བཞིན་མེད་པར་བསྒོམ་མོ།། དེ་ནས་བདག་གི་བློ་ལ་སྣང་བ་ཕོ་ཉ་སྔགས་སྐྱེས་ཀྱི་རྟེན་དང་རྟེན་པར་བཅས ..... པའི་དཀྱིལ་འཁོར་འདི་འཛམ་བུའི་གླིང་ན་བཞུགས་པའི་ཕོ་ཉ་ཞིང་སྐྱེས་སྤྲུལ་སྐུའི་ བདག་ ཉིད་ཡིན་ལ། དེ་ཉིད་འོག་མིན་གྱི་ཕོ་ཉ་ལྷན་སྐྱེས་ལོངས་སྐུའི་དཀྱིལ་འཁོར་ཡིན་ཞིང་། དེ་ཉིད་ཆོས་ཀྱི་སྐུ་ལས་གཞན་མ་ཡིན་ཞེས་ཕོ་ཉ་གསུམ་གཅིག་ཏུ་བསྲེས་ནས། ཡང་བདག་གི་བློ་ལ་སྣང་བའི་ལྷ་སུམ་བཅུ་སོ་བདུན་པོ་འདི་ཉིད་བྱང་ཆུབ་ཀྱི་ཕྱོགས་ཀྱི་ཆོས་སུམ་བཅུ་སོ་བདུན་གྱི་ངོ་བོ་ཡིན་ལ། བྱང་ཆུབ་ཀྱི་ཕྱོགས་ཀྱི་ཆོས་སུམ་བཅུ་རྩ་བདུན་པོ་ཉིད་ཀྱང་ལྷ་སུམ་བཅུ་སོ་བདུན་གྱི་ངོ་བོར་རྣམ་པར་དག་པའོ། ཞེས་དག་པ་དྲན་པར་བྱ་བ་ ནི་ཕྱིའི་དཀྱིལ་འཁོར་བསྒོམ་པའོ།། དེ་ལྟར་དཀྱིལ་འཁོར་གྱི་རྣམ་པ་དེ་དག་ལ་གསལ་བར་དམིགས་པའི་མཐུས་སྲོག་རླུང་དང་། ལྷག་པའི་རླུང་གཡོས་པས་སྤྱི་གཙུག་གི་ཧཾ་དང་ལྟེ་བའི་ཨ། ཟླ་དང་ཚུལ་སྙིང་ཁར་འདྲེས་པའི་ ཀུན་གྱིས་ལུས་ ཀྱི་དཀྱིལ་འཁོར་

༄ གཅིག་ཆར་བསྐྱེད་ནས། རིམ་གྱིས་གསལ་གདབ་སྟེ། སྤྱི་བོ་སྣ་ཚོགས་རྡོ་རྗེ། ཀང་མཐིལ་རྡོ་རྗེ་འི་ས་གཞི། རྩིབ་ལོགས་རྡོ་རྗེ་འི་ར་བ། ཕྱོགས་པ་རྡོ་རྗེ་འི་གུར་དང་བླ་བྲེ། བ་སྤུ་མདའི་དྲྭ་བ། སྣ་སེན་ཡེ་ཤེས་ཀྱི་མེ་འབར་བའི་བསྲུང་འཁོར་དང་། ཀང་མཐིལ་རླུང་། སུམ་མདོ་མེ། ལྟེ་བ་ཆུ་སྙིང་ཁ་ས། ཀལ་ཚོགས་རི་རབ། མགོ་བོ་རི་རབ་ཀྱི་སྟོད་ཀྱི་ཆ། ལུས་འཛོམ་གང་གྲུ་བཞི་གཞལ་ཡས་ཁང་གྲུ་བཞི། སྙིང་ཁ་ནས་འབྱུང་བ་བཞིའི་རླུང་རྒྱ་བ་སྣོ་བཞི། མིག་ལ་སོགས་པ་གཞལ་ཡས་ཁང་གི་རྒྱན། ཀང་རྣམས་ཀ་བའི་ཚོགས་ཏེ་རྟེན་གྱི་དཀྱིལ་འཁོར་དང་། སྙིང་གི་ནང་གི་ཧཱུྃ་ཉིད་དཔལ་ཧེ་རུ་ཀ་ཡུམ་དང་བཅས་པར་སྔར་བཞིན་གསལ་གདབ་བོ། ཧེ་རུ་ཀའི་ཕྱག་བཅུ་གཉིས་ཀྱི་གཡས་ཀྱི་དང་པོ་ལ་ཨྃ་མཁའ་འགྲོ་མ། གཉིས་པར་ཡམ་ལ་མ། གཡོན་གྱི་དང་པོར་ཕཾ་ཁཎྜ་རོ་ཧེ། གཉིས་པར་ཧཾ་གཟུགས་ཅན་མ། ཕྱག་ལྷག་མ་བརྒྱད་ལ་ཧཱུྃ་རིང་པོ་བརྒྱད་ཀྱི་གཡས་ཀྱི་བཞི། ཁ་གདོང་། ཙུག་གདོང་། ཁྲི་གདོང་། ཕག་གདོང་མ་དང་། གཡོན་གྱི་བཞི་ག་ཤེད་རྗེ་བརྟན་མ། ཡོ་ཉ་མ། མཆེ་བ་མ། འཇོམས་མ་རྣམས་དང་། སྤྱི་བོ་ལ་སོགས་པའི་གནས་ཉི་ཤུ་རྩ་བཞིར། པུ། ཛཱ། ཨོ། ཨ། གོ། ར། དེ། མ། ཀ། ཨོ། ཏྲི། ཀོ། ཀ། ལ། ཀ། ཧི། པྲེ། གྲི། སཽ། སུ། ན། སི། མ། ཀུ། ཁམས་དང་བཅས་པ་རྣམས་དཔའ་བོ་དང་དཔའ་མོ་རྣམས་སུ་གྱུར་པ་ནི་སྤྱི་བོ་པུ་ལི་ར་མ་ལ་ཡར་ཁཎྜ་ཀ་པ་ལི་དང་། རབ་ཏུ་གཏུམ་མོ།། སྤྱི་གཙུག་ཛཱ་ལན་དྷ་རར་མ་ཧཱ་ཀམ་ཀ་ལ་དང་། གཏུམ་པའི་མིག་ཅན་མ། ན་བ་གཡས་པ་ཨུ་རྒྱན་ཏུ་ཀམ་ཀ་ལ་དང་། འོད་ལྡན་མ། ལྷག་པ་ཨར་བུ་ཏར་མཆེ་བ་རྣམ་པར་གཙིགས་པ་དང་། སྣ་ཆེན་མ་སྟེ་གནས།། ན་བ་གཡོན་པ་གོ་ད་ཝ་རིར་སུ་ར་བཻ་རི་དང་། བརྟན་པའི་བློ་ཅན་མ། སྨིན་མའི་དབུས་ར་མེ་ཤྭ་རིར། འོད་དཔག་མེད་དང་། མིའུ་ཐུང་མ།། མིག་གཉིས་དེ་ཝཱི་ཀོ་ཊར་

༄ རྡོ་རྗེའི་འོད་དང་། ཡང་ག་རེ་དབང་ཕྱུག་མ། ཕྲག་པ་གཉིས་མ་ལ་བཟར་རྡོ་རྗེའི་སྒྲུ་དང་། ཤིང་གྲིབ་མ་སྐྱེ་ཉེ་བའི་གནས་རྣམས་ཕྱུགས་ཀྱི་འཁོར་ལོ་ཁ་མདོག་ལྗང་པོ་ནམ་མཁའ་ལ་སྤྱོད་པའོ།། མཆན་ཁྲུང་གཉིས་ཀ་མ་རུ་པར་ཨཾ་ཀུ་ཧྲི་དང་ཨེ་ཧྲུ་པ་ཏི། ཀུ་མ་གཉིས་ཨོ་ཏྲེར་རྡོ་རྗེ་རལ་པ་ཅན་དང་། འཇིགས་བྱེད་ཆེན་མོ་སྐྱེ་ཞིང་། ཀྱེ་བ་ཏྲི་ཤ་ཀུ་ནེར་དཔའ་བོ་ཆེན་པོ་དང་། རླུང་གི་ཤུགས་ཅན་མ། ཀླ་རྩེ་ཀོ་ས་ལར་རྡོ་རྗེ་ཧཱུྃ་མཛད་དང་། ཆང་འཐུང་མ་སྐྱེ་ཉེ་བའི་ཞིང་།། ཁ་ག་ཡིང་ཀར་རབ་ཏུ་བཟང་པོ་དང་ཤུ་མ་དེ་ཝི། མགྲིན་པ་ལམ་པ་ཀར་རྡོ་རྗེ་བཟང་པོ་དང་། ཤིན་ཏུ་བཟང་མོ་སྐྱེ་ཚན་དོ། སྙིང་ཀུན་ཙོར་འཇིགས་བྱེད་ཆེན་པོ་དང་ཏ་ན་མ། འདོམས་བར་ཏེ་མ་ལ་ཡར་མིག་མི་བཟང་དང་། ཁ་ག་ན་སྐྱེ་ཉེ་བའི་ཚན་དོ། རྣམས་གསུང་གི་འཁོར་ལོ་ཁ་དོག་དམར་པོ་ས་ལ་སྤྱོད་པའོ།། མཚན་མ་པྲེ་ཏ་པུ་རིར་སྟོབས་པོ་ཆེ་དང་འཁོར་ལོའི་ཤུགས་ཅན་མ། བཤང་ལམ་གྲི་ཧ་དེ་བར་རིན་ཆེན་རྡོ་རྗེ་དང་། །ཁཎྜ་རོ་ཧ་སྐྱེ་འདུ་བ། བརླ་གཉིས་སཽ་རཥྚྲར་ཧ་གྲིན་དང་། ཤོན་ཊི་ནི། བྱིན་པ་གཉིས་སུ་ཝརྣ་དྭཱི་པར་ནམ་མཁའི་སྙིང་པོ་དང་། འཁོར་ལོའི་གོ་ཆ་མ་སྐྱེ་ཉེ་བའི་འདུ་བ། སོར་མོ་བཅུ་དྲུག་ན་ག་རར་དཔལ་ཧེ་རུ་ཀ་དང་། ཤིན་ཏུ་དཔའ་མོ།། ཐོལ་གོང་སིན་དྷུ་རར་པདྨ་གར་གྱི་དབང་ཕྱུག་དང་། སྟོབས་ཆེན་མ་སྐྱེ་དུར་ཁྲོད། མཐེ་བོང་བཞི་མ་རོར་རྣམ་པར་སྣང་མཛད་དང་འཁོར་ལོ་སྦྲུར་མ། པུས་མོ་གཉིས་ཀུ་ལུ་ཏར་རྡོ་རྗེ་སེམས་དཔའ་དང་། བཙོན་འགྲུས་ཆེན་མོ་སྐྱེ་ཉེ་བའི་དུར་ཁྲོད་རྣམས་སྐུའི་འཁོར་ལོ་ཁ་དོག་དཀར་པོ་ས་འོག་ན་སྤྱོད་པའོ།། ལྷ་དེ་རྣམས་ཀྱི་ཚུལ་གོང་དུ་བཤད་པ་བཞིན་གསལ་བཏབ་ལ། ཨོཾ་ཨཱཿ ཧཱུྃ་སཏྭ་ཏྭེ་ར་ཡོ་གི་ནི་སྲུ་ལ་ལྷག་ཙིཏྟ་བཛྲ་སྭ་བྷཱ་ཝ་ཨཏྨ་ཀོ་ཧཾ༔ ཞེས་བརྗོད་ཅིང་། བདག་གིས་བསྒོམས་པའི་ཕྱི་ནང་གི་དཀྱིལ་འཁོར་འཇམ་བུའི་གླིང་ན་

༄༅ བཀུགས་པའི་སྤྲུལ་སྐུ། འོག་མིན་ན་བཞུགས་པའི་ལོངས་སྐུ་རྣམས་དབྱེར་མེད་པར་གྱུར་ནས་གཉིས་སུ་མེད་པ་རྡོ་རྗེའི་རང་བཞིན་བདག་ཡིན་སྙམ་དུ་དྲན་པ་ལན་གསུམ་བྱས་ལ། ༀ་བཛྲ་ཤུད་དྷ་སརྦ་དྷརྨ་བཛྲ་ཤུད་དྷོ་ཧཾ་ ཞེས་བརྗོད་པས་སྐུ་གསུང་ཐུགས་རྡོ་རྗེའི་རང་བཞིན་རྣམ་པར་དག་པ་བདག་ཡིན་སྙམ་དུ་བསམ་མོ༎ དེ་ནས་གནས་རྣམས་སུ་བྲི་བའི་གདན་ལ། སྙིང་ཁར། ༀ་ཧ། རྡོ་རྗེ་སེམས་དཔའ་དཀར་པོ། མགོ་བོར་ ན་མ་ཧི། རྣམ་པར་སྣང་མཛད་སེར་པོ། སྤྱི་གཙུག་ཏུ་སྭཱ་ཧཱ་ཧུ་པད་མ་གར་གྱི་དབང་ཕྱུག་དམར་པོ༎ ཕྲག་པ་གཉིས་སུ། བཽ་ཥཊ་ཧེ། དཔལ་ཧེ་རུ་ཀ་ནག་པོ། མིག་གཉིས་སུ། ཧཱུྃ་ཧཱུྃ་ཧོ། རྡོ་རྗེ་ཉི་མ་དམར་སེར༎ ཡན་ལག་ཐམས་ཅད་ལ། ཕཊ་ཧཾ། རྟ་མཆོག་ལྗང་ཁུ་སྟེ་དཔའ་བོའི་གོ་ཆ་དང་། ལྟེ་བར་ༀ་བཾ་རྡོ་རྗེ་ཕག་མོ་དམར་མོ༎ སྙིང་ཁར་ ཧཾ་ཡོཾ་ གཤིན་རྗེ་མ་སྔོན་མོ། ཁར་ ཧྲིཾ་མོཾ་ རྨོངས་བྱེད་མ་དཀར་མོ། མགོ་ལ་ ཧྲིཾ་ཧྲིཾ་ བསྐྱོད་བྱེད་མ་སེར་མོ། སྤྱི་གཙུག་ཏུ། ཧཱུྃ་ཧཱུྃ། སྐྲག་བྱེད་མ་ལྗང་ཁུ། ཡན་ལག་རྣམས་ལ ཕཊ་ཕཊ། ཙཎ་ཊི་ཀ་དུད་ཁ་སྟེ་དཔའ་མོའི་གོ་ཆ་བཀོད་ལ། ཡབ་ཀྱི་གནས་སུ་ཡུམ་དང་། ཡུམ་གྱི་གནས་སུ་ཡབ་གཉིས་སུ་མེད་པར་བསམས་ཏེ། ཡི་གེའི་རྣམ་པ་ཉིད་ལྷའི་ངོ་བོར་བསྒོམ་པ་ནི་གོ་ཆ་དགོད་པའོ༎ དེ་ནས་འབར་བའི་ཕྱག་རྒྱ་དཔྲལ་བའི་དབྱིས་སུ་བསྐོར་ཞིང་། ཛཿ ཞེས་བརྗོད་ནས་སྙིང་ཁའི་ཧཱུྃ། ལས་འོད་འཕྲོས་པས་རང་བཞིན་གྱིས་གྲུབ་པའི་དཀྱིལ་འཁོར་སངས་རྒྱས་དང་བྱང་ཆུབ་སེམས་དཔའ་ཐམས་ཅད་ཀྱིས་བསྐོར་བ་མདུན་དུ་སྤྱན་དྲངས་པ་ལ་ཕྱི་མ་ལྟར་མཆོད་ནས། ཛཿ་ཧཱུྃ་བཾ་ཧོཿ། ཞེས་བརྗོད་པས་རང་ལ་བསྟིམས་ནས། ༀ་ཡོ་ག་ཤུད་དྷ་སརྦ་དྷརྨ་ཡོ་ག་ཤུད་དྷོ་ཧཾ། ཞེས་བརྗོད་པས་གཉིས་སུ་མེད་པར་གྱུར་པར་བསམ་པ་ནི་ཡེ་ཤེས་པ་གཞུག་པའོ༎ ཡང་དབང་གི་ལྷ་ཌཱ་ཀ་ཌཱ་ཀི་གཉིས་ཀྱི་དཀྱིལ་འཁོར་ལ་སངས་རྒྱས་དང་

༄༅ བྱང་ཆུབ་སེམས་དཔའ་དང་། ཁྲོ་བོ་དང་། ཁྲོ་མོ་དང་། མཆོད་པའི་ལྷ་མོའི་ཚོགས་དཔག་ཏུ་མེད་པས་བསྐོར་བ་སྤྱན་དྲངས་པ་ལ་ཕྱི་མ་བཞིན་མཆོད་ནས། དེ་བཞིན་གཤེགས་པ་ཐམས་ཅད་ཀྱིས་བདག་ལ་མངོན་པར་དབང་བསྐུར་དུ་གསོལ་ཞེས་གསོལ་བ་བཏབ་པས། ལྷ་རྣམས་ཀྱིས། ཇི་ལྟར་བལྟམས་པ་ཙམ་གྱིས་ནི། ལྷ་རྣམས་ཀྱིས་ནི་ཁྲུས་གསོལ་ལྟར། ལྷའི་ཆུ་ནི་དག་པ་ཡིས། དེ་བཞིན་བདག་གིས་དབང་བསྐུར་རོ།། ཨོཾ་སརྦ་ཏ་ཐཱ་ག་ཏ་ཨ་བྷི་ཥེ་ཀ་ཏ་ས་མ་ཡ་ཤྲཱི་ཡེ་ཧཱུཾ། ཞེས་གསུང་ཞིང་དབང་བསྐུར་ནས། བཀྲ་ཤིས་ཀྱི་གླུ་དང་། བགེགས་སྐྲོད་པ་དང་། མཆོད་པ་མཛད་པས་ཡེ་ཤེས་ཀྱི་ཆུས་ལུས་ཐམས་ཅད་གང་། དྲི་མ་ཐམས་ཅད་དག། ཆུའི་ལྷག་མ་སྤྱི་བོར་ལུད་པས། བདེ་བ་ཆེན་པོའི་ལྷ་ལྔ་དང་། དམ་ཚིག་གི་ལྷ་རྣམས་ལ་རྡོ་རྗེ་སེམས་དཔའ། ཐུགས་ཀྱི་འཁོར་ལོ་ལ་མི་བསྐྱོད་པ། གསུང་གི་འཁོར་ལོ་ལ་འོད་དཔག་མེད། སྐུའི་འཁོར་ལོ་ལ་རྣམ་པར་སྣང་མཛད་དུ་གྱུར་པར་བསམ་པ་ནི་རིགས་བདག་གིས་རྒྱས་གདབ་པ་སྟེ། རྒྱས་པར་བསྒོམ་པའི་ཚུལ་ལོ།། སྐྱབས་སུ་འགྲོ་བ་དང་། སེམས་བསྐྱེད་པ་དང་། དགའ་བ་གསུམ་སྔོན་དུ་སོང་ནས་བསྲུང་པའི་འཁོར་ལོ་རྫོགས་པར་བསྒོམས་ལ། སྤྱི་བོར་བླ་མའི་ཞུག་གཉིས་སམ། བླ་མ་དངོས་དཀོན་མཆོག་གསུམ་གྱི་རང་བཞིན་དུ་བསྒོམ་པ་ལ། མོས་པ་དྲག་པོ་བྱས་པས། ལུས་ལ་ཐིམ་པའི་ཚུལ་གྱིས། ནང་གི་སླ་ཚུལ་འདྲིས་པས། ལུས་ཀྱི་དཀྱིལ་འཁོར་གསལ་བར་བྱས་པ་མན་ཆད་སྔ་མ་ལྟར་བསྒོམ་པ་ནི་འབྲིང་གི་ཚུལ་ལོ།། སྔོན་དུ་བསྲུང་བའི་འཁོར་ལོ་ཡང་མི་བསྒོམ་ཞིང་ནང་གི་དཀྱིལ་འཁོར་བསྒོམ་པ་འབའ་ཞིག་ལམ་དུ་བྱེད་པའི་ཕྱིར། སོ་ཚ་བཅིང་བ་མན་ཆད་ཀྱང་མི་བྱེད་པར་ལུས་ཀྱི་དཀྱིལ་འཁོར་གསལ་བཏབ་ནས། སྔགས་ཀྱིས་བྱིན་གྱིས་བརླབས་ལ། དེ་ཉིད་ལ་ཡིད་མཉམ་པར་འཇོག་པ་ནི་བསྡུས་པའི་ཚུལ་ཏེ། བདག་

༄༅ ཉིད་སངས་རྒྱས་སུ་བསྐྱེད་པའོ། དེ་ནས་ལྷ་རྣམས་ཀྱི་ཐུགས་ཁའི་ས་བོན་ལས། ལས་ཀྱི་ཁ་ཊྭཱཾ་ག་དང་མཐུན་པའི་སྔགས་ཀྱི་ཕྲེང་བ་འཕྲོས་པས་ཡབ་ཀྱི་ཞལ་དང་། ཡུམ་གྱི་ཞལ་དང་། ཐྲ་ག་དང་། རྡོ་རྗེའི་ཕྱམ་ནས་འཁོར་བ་དང་། རྣལ་འབྱོར་མ་བཅུ་གཉིས་ཀྱི་ནི་ཐུགས་ཁའི་ས་བོན་ལ་གཡོན་དུ་འཁོར་བ། དེ་དག་ལས་ཀྱང་། ཕྱི་རོལ་དུ་འོད་ཟེར་འཕྲོས་པས། །སངས་རྒྱས་དང་བྱང་ཆུབ་སེམས་དཔའ་ཐམས་ཅད་ཀྱི་རྒྱུད་བསྐུལ་བར་བསམ་ཞིང་། ༀ་ཤྲཱི་བཛྲ་ཧེ་ཧེ་རུ་རུ་ཀཾ་ཧཱུཾ་ཧཱུཾ་ཕཊ། ཌཱ་ཀི་ནི་ཛྭ་ལ་སམ་བྷ་ར་སྭཱ་ཧཱ། ཨ་བཛྲ་བཻ་རོ་ཙ་ནཱི་ཡེ་ཧཱུཾ་ཧཱུཾ་ཕཊ་སྭཱ་ཧཱ། ༀ་ཧྲཱི་ཧ་ཧ། ཧཱུཾ་ཧཱུཾ་ཕཊ། ༀ་སརྦ་བུདྡྷ་ཌཱ་ཀི་ནཱི་ཡེ། བཛྲ་ཝརྞ་ནཱི་ཡེ་ཧཱུཾ་ཧཱུཾ་ཕཊ་སྭཱ་ཧཱ། ཅེས་པ་ལ་སོགས་པ་གང་མོས་པ་བཟླ་བ་ནི་བཟླས་པའི་རྣལ་འབྱོར་ཏེ་བསྐྱེད་པའི་རིམ་པའོ།། །རྫོགས་རིམ་བསྒོམ་པར་འདོད་པས་རང་གི་ལྟེ་བར་པད་མ་འདབ་མ་བརྒྱད་པའི་སྙིང་པོར་ཟླ་བའི་སྟེང་དུ་རྡོ་རྗེ་སེམས་དཔའ་རྡོ་རྗེ་སྙེམས་མ་དང་གཉིས་སུ་མེད་པའི་ཐུགས་ཁར་ཧཱུཾ་བསམ་པ་ལས་འོད་འཕྲོས་པས་གཙོ་བོ་ནས་རིམ་པས་དཀྱིལ་འཁོར་དང་། སྣོད་བཅུད་གསལ་བཏབ་པ་ལ་དམིགས་པ་གཏད་པས། ཐམས་ཅད་འདར་ཞིང་། གཡོ་བར་བསྒོམས་ནས། འོད་ཟེར་ཚུར་བསྡུས་པས་ཐམས་ཅད་རིམ་གྱིས་ཁྲིའི་ཧེ་རུ་ཀའི་བར་དུ་ཐིམ་ཞིང་། དེའི་ཡང་ཡུམ་ཡབ་དང་། ཡབ་ཀྱང་ཞལ་གཅིག་ཕྱག་གཉིས་པར་བསྡུས་ནས། དེའང་ལྟེ་བའི་རྡོ་རྗེ་སེམས་དཔའ་དང་། དེ་ཡང་ཡུམ་ཡབ་དང་ཡབ་ཀྱང་ཐུགས་ཁའི་ཧཱུཾ་དང་། དེའང་རིམ་གྱིས་ཐིག་ལེ་ལ་ཐིམ་ཞིང་། ཐིག་ལེའང་མཐའ་ཡལ་བར་བསྒོམས་ནས། མི་དམིགས་པའི་ངང་ལ་བློ་གཞག་པ་ནི་རྡོ་རྗེ་སེམས་དཔའ་བསྒོམ་པའོ།། ཡང་རང་གི་ལྟེ་བར་པད་མ་འདབ་མ་བཞི་པར་ཤར་ནས་གཡོན་སྐོར་གྱིས། ས་ཧྲུང་། ཆུ་ཧྲུང་། མེ་ཧྲུང་། ཧྲུང་ཧྲུང་གི་རང་བཞིན་ལ་སེར་པོ།།

༄༅ ཞ་དཀར་པོ། །ར་དམར་པོ། །ཡ་ལྗང་ཁུ་དང་། །དབུས་སུ་ནམ་མཁའི་རྒྱང་གི་རང་བཞིན་ ཐིག་ལེ་སྔོན་པོ་རྣམས་དམིགས་ནས། དབུགས་ཕྱིར་རྒྱུ་བའི་ཚེ། ལ་ལས་འོད་ཟེར སྐུད་པ་འབྲིང་པོ་འི་ཚད་ཙམ་སྣ་བུག་གཡོན་ནས་མདུན་དུ་ཐད་ཀར་སོར་བཅུ་དྲུག་གི་བར་དུ་ཐུང་ཞིང་། ནང་དུ་འཇུག་པའི་ཚེ་ལ་ཉིད་ལ་སྡུར་ ཐིམ་པར་བསམས་ནས། རྒྱང་ཁ་སྦྱོར་བྱའོ༎ དེ་ལྟར་རྟག་ཏུ་བསྒོམས་པས། དུ་བ་ལྟ་བུའི་རྟགས་མཐོང་བའི་ཚེ ལ་ཞ་ལ་བསྒྲིམས་ནས། ཞ་ལས་འོད་དཀར་པོ་འི་ལྡང་འཇུག་ལ་སོགས་པ་སྔ་མ་ལྟར་བསྒོམ་པས། སྨིག་རྒྱུ་ལྟ་བུའི་རྟགས་འབྱུང་ངོ་། དེའི་ཚེ་ཞ་ར་ལ་བསྒྲིམས་ནས། འོད་དམར་པོ་འི་ལྡང་འཇུག་ལ་སོགས་པ་བསྒོམས་པས་མེ་ཁྱེར་ལྟ་བུའི་རྟགས་འབྱུང་ངོ་། །དེའི་ཚེ་ར་ཡ་ལ་བསྒྲིམས་ནས། འོད་ལྗང་ཁུ་འི་ལྡང་འཇུག་ལ་སོགས་པ་བསྒོམས་པས་མར་མེ་ལྟ་བུའི་རྟགས་འབྱུང་ངོ༎ དེ་ནས་ཡ་དབུས་ཀྱི་ཐིག་ལེ་ལ་བསྒྲིམས་ནས། འོད་དང་རྒྱང་ལྡང་འཇུག་མི་བསྒོམ་པར། ཐིག་ལེ་ཉིད་ལ་ཡིད་གཏད་དེ། རྒྱང་ཁ་སྦྱོར་བསྒོམས་པས་ནམ་མཁའ་སྤྲིན་མེད་པ་ལྟ་བུའི་རྟགས་འབྱུང་ངོ་། དེའི་མཐར་མཐོང་བའི་ལམ་གྱི་ཡེ་ཤེས་སྐྱེ་བར་འགྱུར་རོ། ཡི་གེ་བཟླ་བའོ༎ ཡི་གེ་དེ་དག་གི་རྗོད་དུ། །ཐིག་ལེ་དམིགས་ནས་སྔ་མ་ལྟར་བསྒོམ་པ་ནི་ཐིག་ལེ་བཟླ་བ་རྫོགས་པའི་རིམ་པའོ༎ མཉམ་པར་བཞག་པའོ༎ ༄༅ །དེ་ནས་སྟོང་པའི་ངང་ལས། སྐད་ཅིག་གིས་རང་ ཧེ་རུ་ཀ་ཡབ་ཡུམ་གྱི་སྐུར་དམིགས་པའི་ཐུགས་ཁའི་ཧཱུྃ་ལས་འོད་འཕྲོས་པས་ནང་དང་ཕྱིའི་དཀྱིལ་འཁོར་དང་། སྣོད་བཅུད་ཐམས་ཅད་གསལ་བར་དམིགས་ནས་བདག་གི་སོ་དང་སེན་མོ་ལ་སོགས་པའི་ཁམས་ ཉི་ཤུ་རྩ་བཞི་ནི་ ཁཎྜ་ཀ་པ་ལི་ལ་སོགས་པའི་དཔའ་བོ། །ཉི་ཤུ་རྩ་བཞིའི་ངོ་བོར་རྣམ་པར་དག་ཅིང་། དེ་དག་གི་རྟེན་མི་ཕྱེད་མ་ལ་སོགས་པའི་རྩ་རྣམས་ནི་རྣལ་འབྱོར་མ་ཉི་ཤུ་རྩ་བཞིའི་ངོ་བོར་རྣམ་པར་དག་གོ་

༄ ཞེས་བསམ་ཞིང་། དཔའ་བོ་ཧེ་རུ་ཀ་བཞིའི་ཐུགས་བརྗོད་པས་ཀྱང་བརྟན་པར་བྱ་བ་ནི། ཁམས་དང་རྩའི། དག་པ་དང་། ཡབ་ཀྱི་རྩ་སྔགས་ཀྱིས་རུས་པའི་རྒྱན་དྲུག་རིགས་དྲུག་གི་ངོ་བོར་དཔལ་ཧེ་རུ་ཀ་དང་། ཨ་ཀ། ལ་སོགས་པས་འཁོར་ལོ་ལ་སོགས་པའི་རྒྱན་དྲུག་དང་། དཔའ་བོ་དྲུག་དང་། ཡུམ་གྱི་རྩ་སྔགས་ཀྱིས་མགྲིན་པའི་ཕྲེང་བ་རྡོ་རྗེ་ཕག་མོ།། ཡབ་ཀྱི་སྙིང་པོས་མི་མགོའི་དོ་ཤལ་དང་། ཉེ་སྙིང་གིས་རྣ་རྒྱན་དང་། ཡུམ་གྱི་སྙིང་པོས་གླང་པོ་དང་སྟག་གི་ལྤགས་པ་དང་། ཨ་བཾ་ལ་སོགས་པས་སྐ་རགས། དཔའ་མོ་དྲུག་དང་གཙོ་མོའི་སྙིང་པོ་ལ་སོགས་པ་དཔའ་མོ་སུམ་བཅུ་སོ་བདུན་གྱི་སྔགས་ཀྱིས་ཕྱག་མཚན་དང་། མཚམས་བཞིའི་ཐོད་པ་དང་། ཡུམ་གྱི་ཉེ་སྙིང་གིས་མི་མགོའི་དབུ་རྒྱན་རྣམས་ཐོགས་དང་། ལྷ་དེ་དག་གི་ངོ་བོར་དྲན་པར་བྱ་ཞིང་། ཁ་ཊྭཱཾ་ག་ནི་ལྷའི་སྐུ། ཤེས་རབ་ཌཱ་མ་རུ་འི་སྒྲ། ཉིན་མོ་བཅོམ་ལྡན་རྡོ་རྗེ་ཅན། རྣལ་འབྱོར་མ་ནི་མཚན་མོར་བཤད།། ཅེས་དག་པ་དྲན་པར་བྱས་ནས་དཔའ་མོ་དང་། གོ་ཆ་ཆེན་པོས་བསྲུངས་ལ། སུམ་བྷའི་སྔགས་ལན་གཉིས་ཀྱིས་ཕྱོགས་མཚམས་བཅིངས་ཏེ། བདག་དང་སྣང་བ་ཐམས་ཅད་ལྷའི་དཀྱིལ་འཁོར་བརྗོད་པ་དང་། གྲགས་པ་ཐམས་ཅད་སྔགས་སེམས་ཀྱི་རྟོག་པ་ཐམས་ཅད་ཡེ་ཤེས་ཀྱི་ཆོ་འཕྲུལ་དུ་བསྒོམས་ནས། ཡབ་ཀྱི་ཁང་པ་བརྒྱད་པ་བརྗོད་པས་བྱིན་གྱིས་བརླབས་ལ། ཡུལ་རྣམས་ལ་ཞེན་མེད་པར་ལོངས་སྤྱོད་པ་ནི། སྤྱོད་ལམ་གྱི་རྣལ་འབྱོར་རོ།། །དེ་ནས་མངོན་པར་བཤམས་པའི་གཏོར་མ་སུམ་བྷ་བས་བསང་། སྭ་བྷཱ་ཝས་སྟོང་པར་སྦྱངས་པའི་ངང་ལས། ཡམ་ལས་རླུང་དང་། རམ་ལས་མེའི་སྟེང་དུ། ཨ་ལས་ཐོད་པ་ཡངས་པར། ཨ་ལས་ཟླ་བའི་སྟེང་དུ། ཤར་ནས་གཡས་སྐོར་དང་།། དབུས་སུ། གོ། ཀུ། ད། ཧ། ན་ལས་བ་ལང་། ཁྱི། རྟ། གླང་པོ་ཆེ། མིའི་ཤ་དང་།། དེའི་སྟེང་དུ། བི། མུ། ཤུ། མ། ར། ལས་དྲི་ཆེན། དྲི་

༄༅ ཆུ་བྱང་ཆུབ་ཀྱི་སེམས། ཤ་ཆེན་གྱི་དངས་མ། ར་ཀྟ། དེའི་སྟེང་དུ། ཧཱུྃ། བྷྲཱུྃ། ཨ། ཛྲཱི། ཁཾ། ལས་ཆོས་ཀྱི་དབྱིངས་ཀྱི་ཡེ་ཤེས། མེ་ལོང་ལྟ་བུ། མཉམ་པ་ཉིད། སོ་སོར་རྟོག་པ། བྱ་བ་གྲུབ་པའི་ཡེ་ཤེས་སུ་བསམས་པའི་སྟེང་དུ། ཨོཾ་དཀར་པོ་མགོ་ཐུར་དུ་ལྟ་བ། དེའི་སྟེང་དུ། ཨ་ལས་ཟླ་བའི་སྟེང་དུ། ཧཱུྃ་ལས་སྣ་ཚོགས་ཧཱུྃ་གིས་མཚན་པ་ལས། འོད་ཟེར་འོག་ཏུ་འཕྲོས་པས་རླུང་གཡོས་ཤིང་། མེ་སྦར་བས་རྫས་རྣམས་བཙོ་ཞིང་བཀོལ་བའི་རླངས་པ་གྱེན་དུ་སོང་བས་བསྐུལ་ནས། ཨ་དང་། ཟླ་བ་དང་། སྣ་ཚོགས་རྡོ་རྗེ་ལས་བདུད་རྩི་བབས་ཤིང་། འོད་ཟེར་རླངས་པ་དང་བཅས་པ་ཕྱོགས་བཅུར་འཕྲོས་པས་དེ་བཞིན་གཤེགས་པ་ཐམས་ཅད་ཀྱི་ཐུགས་ཁ་ནས་ཡེ་ཤེས་ཀྱི་བདུད་རྩི་ས་གང་བའི་ཐོད་པ་དཔག་ཏུ་མེད་པ་སྤྱན་དྲངས་པ། སྣ་ཚོགས་རྡོ་རྗེ་དང་། ཟླ་བ་དང་། ཨོཾ་དང་བཅས་པ་རྣམས་གཏོར་མ་ལ་ཐིམ་པས་ཁ་དོག། ཧྲི། ཧོ། ནུས་པ་ཕུན་སུམ་ཚོགས་པའི་བདུད་རྩིའི་རྒྱ་མཚོ་ཆེན་པོར་བསམས་ལ། ཨོཾ་ཨཱཿ ཧཱུྃ་དང་། ཧཿ ཧོཿ ཧྲཱིས། བྱིན་གྱིས་སབརླབ་བོ།། དེ་ནས་མདུན་གྱི་ནམ་མཁར་སྐད་ཅིག་གིས་ལྷ་དྲུག་བཅུ་རྩ་གཉིས་ཀྱི་དཀྱིལ་འཁོར་དམིགས་ལ་གཙོ་བོའི་ཐུགས་ཁའི་ཧཱུྃ་ལས་འོད་འཕྲོས་པས་དུར་ཁྲོད་བརྒྱད་ཀྱང་ཡོངས་སུ་རྫོགས་པའི་དཀྱིལ་འཁོར་བརྒྱད་དུ་གྱུར་པ་ཡེ་ཤེས་པ་དང་རོ་གཅིག་པར་གྱུར་པའི་ལྷ་རྣམས་ཀྱི་ཞལ་ནས་འོད་ཀྱི་སྦུ་གུ་བྱུང་བའི་ལམ་ནས་གསོལ་བར་བསམ་ཞིང་། རྡོ་རྗེ་ཐལ་མོ་ཁ་སྦྱོ་ལ། ཨོཾ་བཛྲ་ཨ་ར་ལི་ཧོ་ཛཿ ཧཱུྃ་བཾ་ཧོཿ བཛྲ་ཌཱ་ཀི་ནི་ས་མ་ཡ་སྟྭཾ་དྲི་ཤྱ་ཧོ།། ཨ་ཨཱཿ ཧཱུྃ་ཞེས། ལྷ་རམ་འཁོར་ལོའི་གྲངས་དང་མཉམ་པ་དང་། དཔའ་བོ་ཉི་ཤུ་རྩ་བཞིའི་ཕྲེང་ཐུགས་ཀྱིས་ཀྱང་དུལ་ནས། ཕྱི་ནང་ཡིད་ལས་བྱུང་བས་མཆོད་ལ།

༄༅། ཆང་པ་བརྒྱད་པ་གཉིས་ཀྱིས་བསྟོད་དེ། འདོད་པའི་དོན་གསོལ་བ་བཏབ་ལ། ཡི་གེ་བརྒྱ་པ་བཟློད་ཅིང་། ནོངས་པ་བཟོད་པར་གསོལ་ནས་བཟླ་ལྷུས་ཡེ་ཤེས་པ་གཤེགས་སུ་གསོལ་ལ།། དམ་ཚིག་པ་བདག་ལ་བསྡུའོ།། འཇིག་རྟེན་པ་ལ་ནི་མཁའ་འགྲོ་སྤྱིའི་གཏོར་མས་རང་དབུལ་ལོ།། གཏོར་མའི་རྣལ་འབྱོར་རོ།། ཁ་ཟས་གཏོར་མ་ལྟར་བྱིན་གྱིས་རླབས་ནས། རང་ཧེ་རུ་ཀར་དམིགས་པའི་ལྟེ་བར་གཏུམ་མོའི་མེ་འབར་བའི་ལུས་ཡོངས་སུ་གང་བའི་ཁྲོད་ན་སྙིང་ཁར་དཀྱིལ་འཁོར་གྱི་ལྷ་ཚོགས་དང་། ནང་གི་གཙོ་བོའི་རིགས་བདག་ཏུ་སྣ་མ་བཀྲུགས་ཤིང་། ཕྱོ་བར་དུར་ཁྲོད་པ་རྣམས་དང་། ཁམས་གསུམ་གྱི་སེམས་ཅན་ཐམས་ཅད་གནས་པར་བསམས་ལ། ལག་པའི་མཆོད་པས། ལག་པའི་ལྷ་མཆོད་ཅས། ལག་པ་གཉིས་དགང་བླུགས། ཁ་ཧོམ་བྱུང་། ཁ་ཟས་བསྲེག་རྫས་སུ་དམིགས་ཏེ། ཞིམ་དུ་ཞེན་པར་མི་བྱ་ཞིང་། རོ་མྱོང་པར་ཟོས་ནས། ལྷག་མ། ཨོཾ་ཨུཙྪིཥྚ་བ་ལིན་ཏ་བྷཀྵ་སི་སྭཱ་ཧཱ། ལྷག་མ་ལ་དབང་པའི་འབྱུང་པོ་ལ་སྦྱིན་ནོ། ཁ་ཟས་ཀྱི་རྣལ་འབྱོར་རོ།།

༄༅། དེ་ལྟར་རྣལ་འབྱོར་བཞི་ཡན་ལག་དང་བཅས་པ་གོམས་པ་ལས་བྱུང་བའི་ཏིང་ངེ་འཛིན། སྤྲོས་བཅས་དང་། སྤྲོས་མེད་དང་། ཤིན་དུ་སྤྲོས་མེད་ཀྱིས་བརྟན་པར་བྱས་པས། འཇིག་རྟེན་ལས་འདས་པའི་ཡེ་ཤེས་སྐྱེས་པ་དང་། གཞན་གྱི་དོན་དུ། ཀུན་དུ་བཟང་པོའི་སྤྱོད་པ་སྤྱད་པས། བྱང་ཆུབ་སེམས་དཔའི་ས་བཅུ་ཉིས་བགྲོད་དེ། ཉེ་བའི་རྒྱུས་མཚམས་སྦྱར་ནས། རང་དང་གཞན་གྱི་དོན་ལྷུན་གྱིས་གྲུབ་པའི་རྡོ་རྗེ་འཆང་ཆེན་པོའི་གོ་འཕང་ཐོབ་པར་འགྱུར་རོ།། གནས་སྐབས་ཀྱི་འབྲས་བུ་ནི་ཞར་ལ་འབྱུང་། བ་ཉིད་དོ། འདི་ཡང་རང་གི་སློབ་མ་མཆོག ཛི་ཤྲིག་དེ་ལྟར་ཀྱིས་སྐུལ་ནས། འཕགས་པས་སྦྱར་པའི་དགེ་བ་

༄༅། ཞེས། འགྲོ་ཀུན་ཏེ་དུ་ཀར་སྒུར་ཅིག། སློབ་དཔོན་ལུ་ཨི་པའི་རྗེས་སུ་འབྲང་བའི། དཔལ་འཁོར་ལོ་བདེ་མཆོག་གི་དཀྱིལ་འཁོར་གྱི་སྒྲུབ་པའི་ཐབས་འདི་ནི། འཕགས་པས་ཕྱུགས་མོ་ལུག་གི་ལོ་སྨིན་དྲུག་གི་ཟླ་བའི་ཚེས་ཉི་ཤུ་ལྔའི་ཉིན་པར། ཤིང་ཀུན་གྱི་མཁར་དུ། རྩང་ཞིང་གསལ་བའི་ཚིག་གི་རྣམ་པར་སྦྱར་བའི་ཡི་གེ་པ་ནི་ཨ་ཙ་ར་འོ།། དགེའོ།།

ཡིདྲ་གཉིས་པ་རྫོགས་སོ།།

DEM-CHOG TANTRA.

Fascicule III.

༄༅། །དཔལ་འཁོར་ལོ་བདེ་མཆོག། རྡོ་རྗེ་རྣལ་འབྱོར་མ།

དཔལ་སྒྲུ་མ་ཆེན་མོ། སྒྲོལ་མ་རྣམས་བཞུགས་སོ།།

གསུམ་པ།།

༄༅། །དཔལ་འཁོར་བདེ་མཆོག །རྡོ་རྗེ་རྣལ་འབྱོར་མ། ནཱ་རོ་པ་ལ་བརྒྱུད་པའི་ལུ་ཡི་པའི་ཡན་ལག་གལ་བདུན་པ།

༄༅། ན་མོ་གུ་རུ་ཝཛྲ་ཌ་ར་ཀཱ་ཡ་ ན་མ། ཤྲཱི་ཙ་ཀྲ་སཾ་བ་ར་མ་ཎྜ་ལ་ཧཱུྃ༔ དུས་གསུམ་བདེ་བར་གཤེགས་པའི་ཡེ་ཤེས་སྐུ། ཐུགས་རྗེ་ཆེན་པོས་ཐབས་ཚུལ་སྣ་ཚོགས་ཀྱིས། གདུལ་བྱ་ཀུན་མཁྱེན་སར་ལ་འགོད་མཛད་པ། བླ་མེད་བླ་མའི་ཞབས་ལ་ཕྱག་འཚལ་ལོ།། ཆོས་དབྱིངས་རང་བཞིན་ཡེས་ཤེ་ཆེན་པོ་འི་སྐུ། སྤྲུལ་པའི་འོད་འཕྲོ་ཤེས་རབ་ཕག་མོས་འཁྱུད། བྱང་ཆུབ་ཕྱོགས་ཆོས་དཔའ་བོ་དཔའ་མོ་འི་ཚོགས། སྲིད་ཞིའི་དབང་ཕྱུག་ཀུན་ལ་ཕྱག་འཚལ་ལོ། ཉེ་བར་བཀོད་དང་བདག་པོས་མ་བཟུང་དང་། གསང་བའི་རྫས་དང་ཟག་མེད་བདེ་ཆེན་དང་། ཀུན་དུ་བཟང་པོ་འི་མཆོད་སྤྲིན་ཆེན་པོ་ནི། ནམ་མཁའ་དག་དང་མཉམ་པས་རྟག་ཏུ་མཆོད། ཐོག་མེད་དུས་ནས་ཉོན་མོངས་དབང་གྱུར་བས། ལུས་ངག་ཡིད་ཀྱིས་སྡིག་པ་ཅི་བགྱིས་དང་། བགྱིད་དུ་ཙལ་དང་དེ་ལ་ཡིད་རང་བའི། ཉེས་པའི་ཚོགས་རྣམས་མགོན་པོ་འི་སྤྱན་སྔར་བཤགས། དེང་ནས་བྱང་ཆུབ་སྙིང་པོར་མཆིས་ཀྱི་བ། ཐུགས་རྗེ་འི་བདག་ཉིད་བླ་མ་དམ་པ་དང་། ཡོན་ཏན་ཐར་ལས་རྒྱལ་དང་དམ་པའི་ཆོས།། གནས་གསུམ་མཁའ་འགྲོའི་ཚོགས་ལ་བདག་སྐྱབས་མཆི། གསང་བ་བླ་མེད་འཁོར་ལོ་སྡོམ་པ་ཡི། ཐུན་མོང་བ་དང་ཁྱད་པར་མད་ཚིག་ཀུན། བདག་གིས་ཡོངས་སུ་གཟུང་ཞིང་བྱང་ཆུབ་བར། ལུས་ངག་ཡིད་ཀྱིས་འབད་དེ་བསྲུང་བར་བགྱི། དུས་གསུམ་ཕྱོགས་བཅུའི་འཇིག་རྟེན་ཐམས་ཅད་ན། རྒྱལ་དང་རྒྱལ་སྲས་རང་རྒྱལ་དགྲ་བཅོམ་དང་། སོ་སོའི་སྐྱེ་བོའི་དགེ་བ་ཅི་མཆིས་པ། མ་ལུས་པ་ལ་རྗེས་སུ་ཡིད་རང་ངོ་།། ཕྱོགས་བཅུའི་བདེ་གཤེགས་སྲས་དང་བཅས་རྣམས་ཀྱི། འགྲོ་

༄༅། བཞི་དོན་དུ་བྱང་ཆུབ་ཐུགས་བསྐྱེད་ལྟར། བདག་གིས་ཀྱང་ནི་བྱང་ཆུབ་སེམས་བསྐྱེད་ཅིང་།། བྱང་ཆུབ་སྤྱོད་པ་བླ་མེད་སྤྱོད་པར་བགྱི། མ་ལུས་ཕྱོགས་བཅུའི་ཞིང་ན་བཞུགས་གྱུར་པའི། རྒྱལ་བ་ཀུན་གྱི་དྲུང་དུ་བདག་མཆིས་ཏེ། མཐའ་ཡས་སེམས་ཅན་ཚོགས་རྣམས་བསྒྲལ་བའི་ཕྱིར། བླ་མེད་ཆོས་ཀྱི་འཁོར་ལོ་བསྐོར་བར་བསྐུལ། འགྲོ་ཀུན་ཀུན་མཁྱེན་གོ་འཕང་ལ་གནས་བར། ནམ་མཁའི་མཐར་ཐུག་གྱུར་པའི་སངས་རྒྱས་རྣམས། སྐུ་ངན་མི་འདའ་བཞུགས་ནས་གདུལ་བྱ་ཡི། དོན་ཀུན་མཛད་པར་བདག་གི་གསོལ་བ་འདེབས། བདག་གིས་སེམས་ཅན་ཀུན་གྱི་དོན་སླད་དུ། ཧེ་རུ་ཀ་དཔལ་གོ་འཕང་བསྒྲུབ་པའི་ཕྱིར། ཟབ་མོ་འཁོར་ལོ་སྡོམ་པའི་ལམ་གྱི་མཆོག། རིམ་པ་གཉིས་ལ་ཡང་དག་གནས་པར་བགྱི།། དེ་ལས་བྱུང་བའི་དགེ་བའི་རྩ་བ་མཆོག། དྲི་མེད་རབ་ཏུ་དཀར་བ་གང་ཡོད་དེས། སྐུ་གསུམ་བདག་ཉིད་ཧེ་རུ་ཀར་གྱུར་ནས། འཁོར་འདས་མ་ལུས་ཡོངས་སུ་འདྲེན་པར་ཤོག། རྡོ་རྗེ་འཛིན་པ་ཁྱོད་ཀྱིས་ལེགས་བསྒྲུབས་པའི། གནས་པ་འདི་ནི་ལེགས་པར་གནས་པ་སྟེ། ལམ་མཆོག་འདི་ཡིས་རིང་པོར་མི་ཐོགས་པར། རང་གཞན་དོན་རྫོགས་ཧེ་རུ་ཀར་འགྱུར་རོ།། བླ་མ་མཆོག་དང་ཀུན་བཟང་ཧེ་རུ་ཀའི། བཀའ་དྲིན་ཆེན་པོས་བདག་ཀྱང་ལེགས་བསྒྲུབས་ནས། དངོས་གྲུབ་ཆེན་པོས་བདག་ཡིད་ཚིམ་མཛོད་ལ། སངས་རྒྱས་ཡུལ་དུ་གཤེགས་ནས་སླར་ཡང་བྱོན། ཚུལ་འདི་ནི་མའི་མ་གསང་བ་བླ་ན་མེད་པ་འཁོར་ལོ་སྡོམ་པའི་རྒྱུད་ཀྱི་རྗེས་སུ་འབྲངས་ནས། རྣལ་འབྱོར་གྱི་དབང་ཕྱུག་ཆེན་པོ་ལཱུ་ཡི་པའི་དགོངས་པ། དཔལ་ན་རོ་ཏ་པ་ལས་བརྒྱུད་དེ་འོངས་པའོ།། ༎ ༄༅། ཚིགས་སུ་བཅད་པར་གང་གིས་བརྩེབས་ཞེ་ན། དཔལ་ལྡན་བླ་མ་ཆོས་ཀྱི་རྗེ་མཁྱེན་རབ་ཀྱི་དབང་ཕྱུག་སྐྱ་པ་པཎྜི་ཏ་ཆེན་པོའི་ཞབས་རྡུལ་སྤྱི་བོས་ལེན་ཅིང་། དེ་ཉིད་ཀྱིས་རྗེས་སུ་བཟུང་བའི་དགེ་ཚུལ་རྡོ་རྗེ་རིན་པ། བློ་གྲོས་རྒྱལ་

༄ མཚན་དཔའ་བཟང་པོ་ཞེས་བྱ་བས། ཆུ་ཕོ་བྱི་བའི་ལོ། རྟ་པའི་ཟླ་བའི་ཚེས་བརྒྱད་ལ་བྱང་ངོས་ཡི°ཧྲུ་ཙོར་ཁབ་ཏུ་སྒྱུར་བའོ།། ।།དགེའོ།།

༄༅། དཔལ་འཁོར་ལོ་བདེ་མཆོག་གི་དཀྱིལ་འཁོར་གྱི་སྟོད་པའི་རབ་ཏུ་བྱེད་པ་ཞེས་བྱ་བ། བླ་མ་དམ་པའི་ཞབས་ལ་ཕྱག་འཚལ་ལོ།། ཚོགས་གཉིས་དཔལ་ལས་བྱུང་གྱུར་ཞིང་། སྟོང་ཉིད་སྙིང་རྗེ་དབྱེར་མེད་བདག། བདེ་ཆེན་གསང་བ་མི་ཟད་པ། ཧེ་རུ་ཀ་ལ་ཕྱག་འཚལ་ལོ། དཔའ་བོ་རྣལ་འབྱོར་མ་རྣམས་ཀྱིས། །འཁོར་ལོ་སྐོར་མཛད་སྤྲིན་ཞིའི་དཔལ། བདེ་མཆོག་རྡོ་རྗེ་ཕག་མོ་ཡིས། ཀུན་ནས་འཁྱུད་ལ་ཕྱག་འཚལ་ལོ། ཆོས་ཀྱི་དབྱིངས་ལས་བྱུང་གྱུར་ཞིང་བུད་མེད་རྒྱུ་མའི་ཚོ་འཕྲུལ་གྱིས། ཡེ་ཤེས་སྒྱུ་མ་ཀུན་སྐྱེད་པ། རྡོ་རྗེ་ཕག་མོར་ཕྱག་འཚལ་ལོ། བདེ་ཆེན་འཁོར་ལོ་འི་ཤར་གནས་ཤིང་། བྱམས་པ་ཆེན་པོ་འི་ངོ་བོ་ཉིད། བྱིན་གྱིས་རློབ་པའི་ལས་མཛད་པ། མཁའ་འགྲོ་མ་ལ་ཕྱག་འཚལ་ལོ། མགོན་པོའི་གཡོན་ཞལ་མདུན་གནས་ཤིང་། བཏང་སྙོམས་ཆེན་པོ་འི་ངོ་བོ་ཉིད། འཕྲིན་ལས་རྫས་སུ་སྒྲུབ་མཛད་པ། ལྷ་མ་ལའང་ཕྱག་འཚལ་ལོ། །དཔལ་གྱི་རྒྱབ་ཞལ་མདུན་གནས་ཤིང་། དགའ་བ་ཆེན་པོ་འི་ངོ་བོ་ཉིད། ཆོས་ཀྱི་འཁོར་ལོ་བསྐོར་མཛད་པ། དུམ་སྐྱེས་མ་ལ་ཕྱག་འཚལ་ལོ། རྗེ་བོ་འི་གཡས་ཞལ་མདུན་གནས་ཤིང་། སྙིང་རྗེ་ཆེན་པོ་ ངོ་བོ་ཉིད། དབང་བསྒྱུར་བའི་ལས་མཛད་པ། གཟུགས་ཅན་མ་ལ་ཕྱག་འཚལ་ལོ། ཀུན་ཀྱང་ཡོན་ཏན་ངོ་བོ་སྟེ། སེར་སྣ་ལ་སོགས་སྐྱོན་སྤོང་ཞིང་། དཀྱིལ་འཁོར་སྙིང་པོར་རྣམ་རོལ་བ། བདེ་ཆེན་འཁོར་ལོར་ཕྱག་འཚལ་ལོ། །ཤར་རྩི་བས་ཕྱུ་ཡིར་མི་ཕྱེད་དང་། སོ་དང་སེན་མོ་འི་ཁམས་སྤོང་བ། ཕོད་པའི་དུམ་བུ་རབ་གཏུམ་མོ།། མཉམ་པར་སྦྱར་ལ་ཕྱག་འཚལ་ལོ།། བྱང་ཕྱོགས་ཛ་ལན་དྷ་ར་རུ། ཕྲ་གཟུགས་སྣ་དང་སྒྲ་སྤོང་བ། གིང་དུས་ཆེན་པོ་གཏུམ་མིག་མ། རྣམས་འཇུག་མཆོག་ལ་ཕྱག་འཚལ་ལོ། ནུབ་ཕྱོགས་ཨུ་རྒྱན་

ཧཱུྃ བཛྲ་མ་དང་། ཕྲགས་པ་དྲི་མའི་ཁམས་སྦྱོང་བ། ཀཾ་ཀ་ལ་དང་འོད་ལྡན་ན་མ། ཀུན་ཏུ་སྦྱོར་ལ་ཕྱག་འཚལ་ལོ། ཧཱུྃ་ཕྱོགས་ཨར་བུར་གཡོན་མ་དང་། ཤའི་ཁམས་ནི་ཡོངས་སྦྱོང་བ། མཆེ་བ་རྣམ་རྩིགས་སྣ་ཆེན་མ། ཡང་དག་སྦྱོར་ལ་ཕྱག་འཚལ་ལོ། །ཤར་ཧཱུྃ་གོ་ད་ཝ་རི་རུ། ཕུང་ཆུ་རྩ་རྒྱུས་ཁམས་སྦྱོང་བ། སྤུ་ར་མླི་རི་བརྟན་གྲོ་མ། གཉིས་མེད་བཞུགས་ལ་ཕྱག་འཚལ་ལོ། ཧཱུྃ་རྒྱབ་ར་མེར་དུ་སྲབ་སྐྲེས། རྡུས་པ་དྲི་མའི་ཁམས་སྦྱོང་བ། འོད་དཔག་མེད་དང་ཁའི་རི། ཀུན་ནས་སྦྱོར་ལ་ཕྱག་འཚལ་ལོ། ནུབ་བྱང་དེ་ཝཱི་ཀོ་ཊར་ནི། སྨོམ་དང་མཆིན་པའི་ཁམས་སྦྱོང་བ། རྡོ་རྗེ་འོད་དང་ལང་ཀའི་དབང་། སྐམས་པར་ཆགས་ལ་ཕྱག་འཚལ་ལོ། བྱང་ཤར་མ་ལར་དབང་མ་དང་། སྙིང་གི་ཁམས་ནི་ཡོངས་སྦྱོང་བ། རྡོ་རྗེ་སྐུ་དང་ཤིང་གྲིབ་མ། ཁ་སྦྱོར་མཆོག་ལ་ཕྱག་འཚལ་ལོ། ཀུན་ཀུང་ཐུགས་ཀྱི་ཧེ་བོ་སྟེ། སེམས་དང་ཞེ་སྡང་རྣམ་པར་སྦྱོང་། མཁའ་ལ་སྤྱོད་པའི་རྩལ་འཛིན་མ། ཐུགས་ཀྱི་འཁོར་ལོར་ཕྱག་འཚལ་ལོ། །ཤར་རྩིབས་ཀུམ་དུར་སྐྱོན་མ་དང་། མིག་གི་ཁམས་ནི་ཡོངས་སྦྱང་བ། སྨྲ་གུ་ཅན་དད་ས་སྤྱངས་མ། རྣམ་པར་རོལ་ལ་ཕྱག་འཚལ་ལོ། །བྱང་ཕྱོགས་ཨོ་ཏྲར་འཛུག་མ་དང་། མཁྲིས་པའི་ཁམས་ནི་རྣམ་སྦྱོང་བ། རྡོ་རྗེ་རལ་པ་འཛིགས་བྱེད་མ། དགའ་མཀྲུར་སྤྱོད་ལ་ཕྱག་འཚལ་ལོ། ནུབ་ཕྱོགས་ཏྲ་ཤ་ཀུ་ནེ་རུ། མ་མོ་གློ་བའི་ཁམས་སྦྱང་བ། དཔལ་བོ་ཆེན་པོ་རླུང་ཤུགས་མས། ཉེ་བར་འཁྲིལ་ལ་ཕྱག་འཚལ་ལོ། ཧཱུྃ་ཕྱོགས་རྩིབས་ཀྱི་ཀོ་ས་ལར། མཆན་མོ་རྒྱུ་མའི་ཁམས་སྦྱོང་བ། རྡོ་རྗེ་ཧཱུ། མཛོད་ཆང་འཕུང་མ། བདེ་བས་མྱོས་ལ་ཕྱག་འཚལ་ལོ། །ཤར་ཧཱུྃ་འཛམས་ཀྱི་ཀ་ལིང་ཀར། བསིལ་སྦྱིན་རྒྱས་པའི་ཁམས་སྦྱོང་། རབ་ཏུ་བཟང་དང་ལྡང་ལྷ་མོ། རྩེ་ཞིང་རོལ་ལ་ཕྱག་འཚལ་ལོ། །ཧཱུྃ་རྒྱབ་ལམ་པར་ཚ་བ་དང་། ཧྥུ་བའི་ཁམས་ནི་ཡོངས་སྦྱོང་བ། རྡོ་རྗེ་བཟང་པོ་བཟང་མོ་ཡིས། རྣམ་པར་མཆོད་ལ་ཕྱག་འཚལ་ལོ། ནུབ་བྱང་ཀན་རྩིར་

༄༅ གསོལ་མ་དང་། བཤང་པའི་ཁམས་ནི་སྤྱོང་མཛད་པ། འཇིགས་བྱེད་ཆེ་དང་ཏ་ན་མ། བདེ་བས་དགྱེས་ལ་ཕྱག་འཚལ་ལོ། བྱང་ཤར་ཧི་མ་ལ་ཡ་རུ། རངས་མ་རྒྱུས་པའི་དངས་མ་སྤྱོང་། མིག་མི་བཟང་དང་ཁ་ག་ན། རྣམ་པར་རྩེན་ལ་ཕྱག་འཚལ་ལོ། །ཀུན་ཀྱང་གསུང་གི་ངོ་བོ་སྟེ། ངག་དང་འདོད་ཆགས་རྣམ་པར་སྤྱོང་། ས་ལ་སྤྱོད་པའི་ཚུལ་འཛིན་པ། གསུང་གི་འཁོར་ལོར་ལ་ཕྱག་འཚལ་ལོ།། ཤར་རྩེ་བས་བྲི་ཏར་གཟུགས་ཅན་དང་། བད་ཀན་ཁམས་ནི་རྣམ་སྤྱོང་བ། སྟོབས་ཆེན་འཁོར་ལོའི་ཤུགས་ཅན་མ། གཉིས་མེད་རོལ་ལ་ཕྱག་འཚལ་ལོ། བྱང་རྩེ་བས་གྲི་ཏར་སྐྱི་མ་དང་། ནག་གི་ཁམས་ནི་ཡོངས་སྤྱོང་བ། རིན་ཆེན་རྡོ་རྗེ་དུམ་སྐྱེས་མས། ཀུན་ནས་མཆོད་ལ་ཕྱག་འཚལ་ལོ། ནུབ་ཀྱི་རྩེ་བས་ཀྱི་སུ་ར་ཊ་ཊྲར། རྒྱུ་སྦྱིན་མ་དང་བྲག་སྤྱོང་མ། ཏ་མགྲིན་དང་ནི་ཤེན་ཊེ་ནི། ཀུན་དུ་རོལ་ལ་ཕྱག་འཚལ་ལོ། ལྷོ་ཕྱོགས་སུ་ཕར་ཧ་དེ་པར། སྦྱོར་བྲལ་རྡུལ་གྱི་ཁམས་སྤྱོང་བ། མཁའ་སྙིང་འཁོར་ལོའི་གོ་ཆ་མས། ནི་བར་བསྟེན་ལ་ཕྱག་འཚལ་ལོ། ཤར་ལྷོ་མཚམས་ཀྱི་ནག་རར། སྟུ་གུ་མ་དང་ཆེར་སྤྱོང་མ། ཧེ་དུ་ཀ་དཔལ་དཔའ་མོ་དང་། ཟུང་དུ་འཇུག་ལ་ཕྱག་འཚལ་ལོ། །ལྷོ་ནུབ་སིན་དྷུར་གུབ་མ་དང་མཆི་མའི་ཁམས་ནི་ཡོངས་སྤྱོང་བ། པདྨ་པ་གར་དབང་སྟོབས་ཆེན་མས། ཡོངས་སུ་མཆོད་ལ་ཕྱག་འཚལ་ལོ། །ནུབ་བྱང་མ་རོར་འཆོད་མ་དང་། མཆིལ་མའི་ཁམས་ནི་རབ་སྤྱོང་བ་རྣམ་སྣང་འཁོར་ལོ་སྒྱུར་མ་ཡི། བདེ་བས་དགྱེས་ལ་འཚལ་ལོ། བྱང་ཤར་རྩེ་བས་ཀྱི་ཀུ་ལུ་ཏར། ཡིད་བཟངས་མ་དང་སྣབས་སྤྱོང་བ། རྡོ་རྗེ་སེམས་དཔའ་བཙོན་ཆེན་མས། རྣམ་པར་མཆོད་ལ་ཕྱག་འཚལ་ལོ ཀུན་ཀྱང་སྐུའི་ངོ་བོ་སྟེ། ལུས་དང་ཧེ་སྨུག་རྣམ་པར་སྤྱོང་། ས་འོག་སྤྱོད་པའི་ཚུལ་འཛིན་པ། སྐུའི་འཁོར་ལོར་ལ་ཕྱག་འཚལ་ལོ། དཀྱིལ་འཁོར་ཤར་གྱི་སྒོར་གནས་ཤིང་། ཞེ་དང་དཀུག་པའི་ལས་མཛད་པ། བྱ་རོག་གདོང་ཅན་བྱ་རོག་ལྷར། བསྐམ་གཟུགས་

༄༅ མ་ལ་ཕྱག་འཚལ་ལོ། །དཀྱིལ་འཁོར་བྱང་གི་སྒོར་གནས་ཤིང་། །འབེབས་དང་དྲག་པོ་ཡི་ལས་མཛད་པ། འུག་པའི་གདོང་ཅན་འུག་པ་ལྟར། རྣམ་བཀྲིངས་མ་ལ་ཕྱག་འཚལ་ལོ། དཀྱིལ་འཁོར་ནུབ་ཀྱི་སྒོར་གནས་ཤིང་། བཅིང་དང་དབང་གི་ལས་མཛད་པ། ཁྱིའི་གདོང་ཅན་ནོར་སྲུངས་ལྟར། གཡེལ་མེད་མ་ལ་ཕྱག་འཚལ་ལོ། །དཀྱིལ་འཁོར་ལྷོ་ཡི་སྒོར་གནས་ཤིང་། གཉུག་དང་རྒྱས་པའི་ལས་མཛད་པ། ཕག་གི་གདོང་ཅན་ཕག་བཞིན་དུ། རྟག་མེད་མ་ལ་ཕྱག་འཚལ་ལོ། །ཤར་ལྷོ་ཡི་གྲྭར་ནི་ལེགས་བཞུགས་ནས། བརྟན་པའི་དུག་དང་དབུལ་སེལ་ཞིང་། རྒྱལ་བ་ལ་མ་ལུས་མཉེས་བྱེད་པ། གཤིན་རྗེ་བརྟན་མར་ལ་ཕྱག་འཚལ་ལོ། ལྷོ་ནུབ་གྲྭར་ནི་ལེགས་བཞུགས་ནས། འཆི་བདག་ཉེས་སྤྱོད་ཀུན་སེལ་ཞིང་། དཀྱིལ་འཁོར་པ་ཀུན་མཛེས་བྱེད་མ། གཤིན་རྗེའི་པོ་ཉར་ཕྱག་འཚལ་ལོ། ནུབ་བྱང་གྲྭར་ནི་ལེགས་བཞུགས་ནས། གཡོ་བའི་དུག་དང་ཁྲོ་འཇོམས་ཤིང་། དབྱངས་མཆོག་ཀུན་གྱི་དབྱངས་ལྡན་མ། གཤིན་རྗེ་མཆེ་བ་མར་ཕྱག་འཚལ། བྱང་ཤར་གྲྭར་ནི་ལེགས་བཞུགས་ནས། བགེགས་དང་གཡེལ་བ་རྣམས་སེལ་ཅིང་། ཞལ་དང་ཕྱག་ཞབས་ཀུན་བསྐྱོད་མ། གཤིན་རྗེ་འཇོམས་མར་ལ་ཕྱག་འཚལ་ལོ། ཀུན་ཀུང་འཕྲིན་ལས་ངོ་བོ་སྟེ། ལས་ངན་ཕྲ་རྡོག་རྣམ་པར་སྦྱོང་། ཀུན་དུ་སྤྱོད་པའི་ཚུལ་འཛིན་པ། དམ་ཚིག་འཁོར་ཡོར་ཕྱག་འཚལ་ལོ། ཡེ་ཤེས་རིན་ཆེན་ལས་གྲུབ་ཅིང་། རྒྱན་རྣམས་ཀུན་གྱིས་རྣམ་པར་མཛེས། ལུས་དང་ཞིང་ཀུན་ཡོངས་སྐྱོང་བ། གཞལ་ཡས་ཁང་ལ་ཕྱག་འཚལ་ལོ། ཕྱི་རོལ་ཁོར་ཡུག་ལེགས་གནས་ནས། དཀྱིལ་འཁོར་པ་ཀུན་མཆོད་བྱེད་ཅིང་། སྒྲུབ་པ་པོ་ལ་མཆོག་སྩོལ་བ། དུར་ཁྲོད་གནས་པ་རྣམས་ལ་འདུད། སྟོང་ཉིད་ཡེ་ཤེས་རྡོ་རྗེའི་དངོས་བདུད་དཔུང་ངེས་པར་འཇོམས་བྱེད་ཅིང་། མི་ཕྱེད་རྣལ་འབྱོར་པའི་དཔལ་བསྲུང་བའི་འཁོར་ཡོར་ཕྱག་འཚལ་ལོ། ཐུགས་དང་ཏིང་ངེ་འཛིན་བརྟེན་ཞིང་། ཕྱི་ནང་གསང་བ་དེ་ཁོ་ནའི། མཆོད་པ

༄༅ ཀྱུ་ཧ་ཛོས་མཆོད་བགྱིད་ཀྱིས། དངོས་གྲུབ་མ་ལུས་བདག་ལ་བསྩོལ། བདེ་མཆོག་འཁོར་ལོ་བསྟོད་བགྱིས་པའི། དགེ་བའི་བདག་གཞན་བདེ་ཀུན་ལ། འཆི་མེད་སྤྱོད་ནས་བདེ་བའི་མཆོག། བདེ་ཆེན་ཧེ་རུ་ཀར་གྱུར་ཅིག། དཔལ་བདེ་མཆོག་འཁོར་ལོ་འི་དཀྱིལ་འཁོར་གྱི་ལྷ་ཚོགས་ལ་བསྟོད་པའི་རབ་ཏུ་བྱེད་པ་འདི་ནི། སྟོན་པ་ཤེས་རབ་ཅེས་བྱ་བས་བསྐུལ་ནས། དགེ་སློང་སྔགས་འཆང་པ་འཕགས་པ་ཞེས་བྱ་བས་ལྕགས་མོ་ལུག་གི་ལོ། ནག་པའི་ཟླ་བའི་ཚེས་ཉི་ཤུ་བཞིའི་ཉི་མ་གྲུང་གི་ཆ་ལ། ཙོང་ཁ་འི་ཕྲེང་ཆེན་པོར་ཤིན་ཏུ་སྨར་དུ་སྦྱོར་བའི་ཡི་གེ་བ་ནི་ཨ་ཙ་ར་ལགས་སོ། དགེའོ།།

༄༅། ཨོཾ་སྭ་སྟི་ཧཱུྃ། སྐུ་གསུམ་ཡེ་ཤེས་ལྷའི་དངོས། མཁའ་འགྲོ་འི་དབང་ཕྱུག་བཅོམ་ལྡན་འདས། འཁོར་ལོ་སྡོམ་པ་ལ་བཏུད་དེ། དབང་གིས་བྱ་བ་མདོར་བསྡུས་བཤད། འཁོར་ལོ་གསུམ་རིམ་རྣལ་འབྱོར་ཉིད། གང་གིས་ཁམས་གསུམ་སེམས་ཅན་གནས། རྡོ་རྗེ་འཆང་གི་གནས་ཐོབ་པའི། དབང་བསྐུར་ཆོ་གའི་རིམ་བཤད། དབང་བསྐུར་དཀྱིལ་འཁོར་སྟོན་འགྲོ་བར། རྡོ་རྗེ་འཆང་གིས་གསུངས་པ་སྟེ། འོན་ཀྱང་དཀྱིལ་འཁོར་དེ་རང་བཞིན། ཅི་ཡིན་དེ་ནི་འདི་ལྟར་བཤད། རི་མོར་གནས་པའི་ལས་དང་ནི། ཐིག་ལས་ཚོན་དཀྱུའི་རིམ་པ་བསྟན། འགྲོ་བ་འདི་དག་རང་བཞིན་གྱིས། གྲུབ་པའི་དཀྱིལ་འཁོར་གཉིས་མེད་པའོ།། བཅོས་མ་གཉིས་ཀྱི་ངོ་བོ་གང་། དེ་ནི་གདུལ་བྱའི་དབང་ལས་འདོད། མཁས་པའི་བསྒྲུབ་བྱ་དེ་མིན་ཏེ། ཡང་དག་དོན་མཐོང་གྲོལ་ཕྱིར་རོ།། འཁོར་ལོ་གསུམ་གྱི་དཀྱིལ་འཁོར་གྲུབ། དཀྱིལ་འཁོར་ལྷ་རྣམས་གྲུབ་པའོ།། དེའི་དབང་བསྐུར་ལ་སོགས་རིམ། ཅི་ནས་མ་གྲུབ་ཡང་གྲུབ་བྱེད། དེ་ཡི་རང་བཞིན་མི་ཤེས་རྣམས། རྟོགས་དུ་བྱ་བར་བཞེད་པ་སྟེ། དབང་བསྐུར་ཚོགས་རིམས་ཀུན་རྫོབ་ཏུ། ཐ་སྙད་དུ་ནི་གྲུབ་པའོ།། སློབ་དཔོན་ལ་སོགས་དབྱེ་བ་ཡིས། དབང་བསྐུར་

༄༅ རྣམས་པ་བཞི་བཤད་དེ། རྒྱུའི་དབང་སོགས་དབྱེ་བ་ཡིས། བཞི་པོ་དེ་ནི་བཅུ་བཞི་འོ༎ དེ་འང་ལྟ་སྟེ། དབང་བསྐུར་གྱི་སྔོན་དུ་དཀྱིལ་འཁོར་འགྲོ་བའི་འཐད་པ། གང་དུ་འཇུག་པའི་ཡུལ་དཀྱིལ་འཁོར་གྱི་རབ་ཏུ་དབྱེ་བ། བཅོས་མ་གཉིས་སྤངས་ཏེ་རང་བཞིན་གྱིས་གྲུབ་པའི་དཀྱིལ་འཁོར་ལ་བརྟེན་པའི་ཚུལ། དོན་དམ་པར་སྒོམ་པ་ལས་གྲོལ་ཡང་། ཀུན་རྫོབ་ཏུ་དབང་བསྐུར་བ་དགོས་པའི་འཐད་པ། དབང་གི་རྣམ་གཞག་སྤྱིར་བསྟན་པའོ༎ བསྙེན་པ་སྔོན་དུ་སོང་བ་ཡིས། དང་པོ་བདག་གི་རྣལ་འབྱོར་བསྒོམ། སྔགས་ཚོགས་ཀྱིས་མཆོད་གཏོར་མ་སྦྱིན། བུམ་པའི་ཆོ་ག་ལེགས་བྱས་ལ། དཔའ་བོ་རྣལ་འབྱོར་མ་རྣམས་མཆོད། སློ་ཡི་རྣམས་གཞག་སྔོན་འགྲོ་བས། མཎྜལ་ཕུལ་ལ་བདེན་པ་བརྗོད། གདོང་གཡོག་བཅིངས་ལ་མེ་ཏོག་གཏད། བསྐྱུང་ཞིང་བྱིན་བརླབས་འཇོད་པ་ནི། བྱང་སེམས་བསྐྱེད་དེ་གསང་བར་གདམས། ནང་དུ་བཅུག་ལ་གསོལ་བ་གདབ། དམ་ཚིག་བསྒྲགས་ལ་ཐུན་མོང་དང་། ཁྱད་པར་གྱི་ནི་སྡོམ་པ་སྦྱིན། ལེགས་སྦྱངས་དངོས་གཞིའི་ཆོ་ག་བྱད། དམ་ལ་གཞག་ཅིང་ཡེ་ཤེས་དབབ། མེ་ཏོག་དོར་ལ་དཀྱིལ་འཁོར་བསྟན། འཇུག་པ་ཡི་ནི་ཆོ་ག་འོ༎ དབང་གི་དོན་དུ་གསོལ་བ་གདབ། དབང་བསྐུར་རྣམ་པ་བཅུ་བཞི་ཡིས། དེ་ནས་དབང་ནི་བསྐུར་བར་བྱ། སྔགས་དང་ཆུ་དང་ཅོད་པན་དང་། རྡོ་རྗེ་དྲིལ་བུ་མིང་གི་དབང་། བརྟུལ་ཞུགས་གཉིས་དང་ལུང་བསྟན་དང་། སློབ་དཔོན་དབང་དང་རྗེས་གནང་དང་། གསང་བ་ཤེས་རབ་ཡེ་ཤེས་དང་། བཞི་པ་ཡང་ནི་དེ་བཞིན་ནོ། སློབ་དཔོན་ལ་སོགས་བཞི་པོ་ཡང་། སྔོན་འགྲོ་དས་གཞི་མཇུག་དེ་ངས། གསུམ་གསུམ་གྱིས་ནི་ཡང་དག་བསྡུས། གཞན་དོན་བྱ་བའི་རིམ་པའོ༎ རང་གི་དམ་ཚིག་གསོ་འདོད་ན། མདུན་དུ་དཀྱིལ་འཁོར་བསྒྲུབས་མཆོད་ནས། སློབ་དཔོན་གྱི་ནི་ཆོ་ག་རྣམས། དཀྱིལ་འཁོར་གཙོ་བོས་མཛད་པར་བསམ། ཆོ་གའི་གོ་རིམས་སྤར་དང་མཚུངས། རྗེས་

1

ཀྱི་བྱ་བ་གཞན་དང་འདྲ། དོན་ཀྱང་གཏོར་འགྲོན་མ་གཏོགས་པ། གཞན་ནི་གཤེགས་སུ་གསོལ་བ་མེད། ལུས་ཀྱི་དཀྱིལ་འཁོར་ལ་བརྟེན་ཕྱིར། དབང་གི་བྱ་བ་མདོར་བསྡུས་པའོ།། ཟབ་མོ་འི་རྒྱུད་ལ་བརྟེན་ནས་ནི། རྣལ་འབྱོར་དབང་ཕྱུག་དྲིལ་བུ་པས། དབང་བསྐུར་ཆོ་གའི་རིམ་པ་མཛད། དེ་ཡི་མདོར་བསྡུས་བདག་གིས་སྦྱར། དེ་ལས་བྱུང་བའི་དགེ་བ་དེས། འགྲོ་ཀུན་ལམ་མཆོག་འདིར་ཞུགས་ནས། སྒྲིབས་པའི་དྲི་མ་ཀུན་སྤངས་ཏེ། རྫོགས་པའི་བྱང་ཆུབ་ཐོབ་པར་ཤོག། ལུས་ཀྱི་དཀྱིལ་འཁོར་ལ་བརྟེན་ཏེ་དབང་བསྐུར་བའི་ཆོ་གའི་མདོར་བསྡུས་འཕགས་པའི་མིང་དང་ལྡན་པས་སྦྱར་བ་རྫོགས་སོ།། དགེའོ།།

DEM-CHOG TANTRA.

༄༅། དཔལ་འཁོར་ལོ་བདེ་མཆོག། རྡོ་རྗེ་རྣལ་འབྱོར་མ།

དཔལ་སྒྲུ་མ་ཆེན་མོ། སློབ་མ་རྣམས་བཞུག་སྭོ།།

ཧཱུྃ བདེ་མཆོག་ལུས་དཀྱིལ།།

ༀ བདེ་མཆོག་ལུས་དཀྱིལ།།

༄༅། །དཔལ་འཁོར་ལོ་བདེ་མཆོག་གི་ལུས་ཀྱི་དཀྱིལ་འཁོར་དུ་བདག་ཉིད་འཇུག་ཅིང་དབང་བླང་བའི་ཆོ་ག་ཞེས་བྱ་བ། བླ་མ་དང་དཔལ་ཧེ་རུ་ཀ་ལ་ཕྱག་འཚལ་ལོ།། དབང་གི་དབང་གིས་དབང་བྱའི་འབྲས། བསྒྲུབ་ཕྱིར་དབང་རབ་སྐུར་མཛད་པའི། བླ་མ་མཆོག་ལ་ཕྱག་འཚལ་ནས། དབང་ཉིད་ལམ་དུ་བྱ་བ་བཤད།། དེ་ལ་འཁོར་ལོ་བདེ་མཆོག་གི་ལུས་ཀྱི་དཀྱིལ་འཁོར་དུ་དབང་བསྐུར་བ་ཐོབ་ཅིང་། འདིའི་རྣལ་འབྱོར་ལ་ཡིད་བརྟན་པས། རང་གིས་ཉིང་ངེ་འཛིན་གྱི་དཀྱིལ་འཁོར་ལ་དབང་བླངས་པས་བྱང་ཆུབ་བསྒྲུབ་པའི་ཕྱིར། དབེན་པའི་གནས་སུ་ཏེན་དང་། ཕྱི་ནང་གི་མཆོད་པ་དང་། གཏོར་མ་གསུམ་དང་། བུམ་པ་གཉིས་དང་། རྡོ་རྗེ་དྲིལ་བུ་ལ་སོགས་པ་འདིར་དགོས་པའི་རྫས་དང་། མཆོད་པའི་ཡོ་བྱད་རྣམས་སྔ་གོན་དུ་བྱས་ལ། རྣལ་འབྱོར་ལ་མཉམ་པར་འཇོག་ནུས་པའི་གྲོགས་དང་བཅས་ཏེ་འཁོད་ནས། མཁའ་འགྲོ་སྤྱི་གཏོར་ལྷར་སྡོན་འགྲོའི་གཏོར་མས་དེར་འདུས་པའི་འབྱུང་པོའི་ཚོགས་ཚིམ་པར་བྱས་ལ། གསང་སྔགས་ལྷ་བར་མི་དབང་བ་བསྐྲད་ནས། དཔང་བ་རྣམས་ལ་ཕྲོགས་བཅོལ་ཏེ། གཏོར་མ་དེར་ལ། རྣལ་འབྱོར་ལ་གནས་

༄༅། །ཡར་གསོལ་བ་བཏབ་ནས། ཡི་གེ་བརྒྱ་པས་རྒྱུད་སྦྱངས་ཏེ། ནལ་འབྱོར་བསྒོམ་པ་དང་། བཟླས་པ་དང་། བདག་བསྐྱེད་ལ་མཆོད་པའི་བར་བྱའོ།། དེ་ནས་མཆོད་རྫས་རྣམས་སྦྱང་བསང་། སྭ་བྷ་ཝས་སྦྱངས་པའི་ངང་ལས་ཨ་ལས་ཐོད་པ་རྣམས་ཀྱི་ནང་དུ། མཆོད་ཡོན། ཞབས་བསིལ། མེ་ཏོག། སྤོས། མར་མེ། དྲི། ཞལ་ཟས། གཞན་ཡང་འདོད་པའི་ཡོན་ཏན་ལྔ་ལ་སོགས་པ་མཆོད་པའི་ཡོ་བྱད་དཔག་ཏུ་མེད་པས། ས་དང་། ནམ་མཁའ་དང་། བར་སྣང་གང་བར་བསྐྱེད་ནས་སོ་སོའི་རྟགས་ཀྱིས་བྱིན་གྱིས་བརླབ་པར་བྱའོ།། དེ་ནས་མདུན་དུ་དམིགས་པའི་རྟེན་ཡོད་དམ། མེད་ཀྱང་རུང་སྟེ། སྐད་ཅིག་གིས་རི་རབ་ཀྱི་སྟེང་། བསྲུང་འཁོར་གྱི་ནང་དུར་ཁྲོད་བརྒྱད་ཀྱིས་བསྐོར་བའི་དབུས་སུ། གཞལ་ཡས་ཁང་གྲུ་བཞི། སྒོ་བཞི། རྒྱན་ཐམས་ཅད་ཀྱིས་བརྒྱན་པའི་ནང་འཁོར་ལོ་རིམ་པ་ལྔའི་ལྟེ་བར་རང་གི་བླ་མ་འཁོར་ལོ་བདེ་མཆོག་རྣམ་པ་སྐུ་ལ་ལྷ་དྲུག་བཅུ་རྩ་གཉིས་དང་ལྡན་པ་ཡུམ་རྡོ་རྗེ་ཕག་མོ་དང་གཉིས་སུ་མེད་པ་དང་། ཕྱོགས་བཞིར་སྙིང་པོའི་རྣལ་འབྱོར་མ་བཞི། མཚམས་བཞིར་ཐོད་པ་བདུད་རྩིས་གང་བ་བཞི་སྟེ། བདེ་ཆེན་གྱི་འཁོར་ལོ་དང་དེའི་ཕྱི་རོལ་དུ་ཐུགས་དང་། གསུང་དང་། སྐུའི་འཁོར་ལོ་དང་། དེའི་ཕྱི་རོལ་འོག་གི་གཞི་ལ་ཞབས་པར་སྒོ་མཚམས་མ་རྣམས་རང་གིས་བསྒོམས་པ་ལྟ་བུའི་རྣམ་པ་ཅན་དམིགས་ནས། རིགས་བདག་གིས་རྒྱས་གདབ་པའི་བར་བདག་བསྐྱེད་ལྟར་བསྒོམས་པ་ལ། ཕྱི་དང་། ནང་དང་། མཉེས་པ་དང་། ཡིད་ལས་བྱུང་བ་དང་། བསྟོད་པའི་བར་གྱིས་མཆོད་ནས། གཏོར་མ་ག།སྤྱིཾ་ཀྱི་དང་པོ་འཁོར་ལོ་བདེ་མཆོག། གཉིས། །ཆོས་སྐྱོང་། གསུམ་པ་མཁའ་འགྲོ་སྤྱི་རེ་གཏོར་མའི་ཚོགས་དཔལ་ལོ།། དེ་ནས་མཚན་ཉིད་དང་ལྡན་པའི་བུམ་པ་གཉིས་བཤམས་པ་བསངས་ཤིང་སྦྱངས་པའི་ངང་ལས་པད་མ་དང་ཟླ་བའི་སྟེང་དུ་ཧཱུྃ་ལས་

༄ རིན་པོ་ཆེའི་བུམ་པ་ལྔའི་གོས་དང་། དཔག་བསམ་གྱི་ཤིང་རིས་བརྒྱན་པ་བསྐྱེད་ལ། རྣམ་རྒྱལ་གྱི་བུམ་པར་དཀྱིལ་འཁོར་ཡོངས་སུ་རྫོགས་པའི་གདན་དང་། ལས་ཐམས་ཅད་པའི་བུམ་པར་བདེ་ཆེན་གྱི་དཀྱིལ་འཁོར་འབར་ཞིག་གི་གདན་དམིགས་ལ་གཉིས་ཀའི་ནང་དུ་ཨཱ་ལཱི་གཉིས་ལས་ཟླ་བ། དེའི་སྟེང་དུ། ཡ་ར་ལ་ཝ་ཀྵ་དང་བཅས་པའི་ཀཱ་ལི་གཉིས་ལས་ཉི་མ། རྣམ་རྒྱལ་གྱི་ཉི་ཟླ་ཁ་སྦྱོར་གྱི་བར་དུ། ལྷ་རྣམས་ཀྱི་ས་བོན་རྣམས་དང་། ལས་ཐམས་ཅད་པར་བདེ་ཆེན་ལྷ་ལྔའི་ས་བོན་བཀོད་ནས། དེ་དག་འདྲེས་པ་ལས་རྣམ་རྒྱལ་དུ་ལྷ་དྲུག་བཅུ་རྩ་གཉིས་དང་། ལས་ཐམས་ཅད་པར་ལྷ་ལྔ་བསྐྱེད་ནས། རིགས་བདག་གིས་རྒྱས་གདབ་པའི་བར་བདག་བསྐྱེད་ལྟར་བྱས་པ་ལ། བསྟོད་པའི་བར་གྱིས་མཆོད་ནས། རང་གི་སྙིང་ཁ་ནས་སྔགས་ཀྱི་འོད་ཟེར་གཟུངས་ཐག་ལ་བརྟེན་ཏེ་སོང་བས་ལྷ་རྣམས་ཀྱི་ཐུགས་བསྐུལ་ནས་སྐུ་ཐམས་ཅད་ལས་བདུད་རྩིའི་རྒྱུན་བབས་པས་བུམ་པ་གང་བར་བསམ་ཞིང་། རྣམ་རྒྱལ་ལ། ཨོཾ་སརྦ་བུད་དྷ་ཌཱ་ཀི་ནཱི་ཡེ་བཛྲ་ཝརྞ་ནཱི་ཡེ་ཧཱུྃ་ཧཱུྃ་ཕཊ་སྭཱ་ཧཱ། ཞེས་པ་དང་། ཨོཾ་ཀ་ཀཱ་སྱེ། ཨུ་ལཱུ་ཀ་སྱེ། ཤྭ་ན་སྱེ། སུ་ཀ་ར་སྱེ། ཡ་མ་ད་ཏི། ཡ་མ་དཱུ་ཏི། ཡ་མ་དཾ་ཥྚྲི་ཎི། ཡ་མ་མ་ཐ་ནི་ཧཱུྃ་ཧཱུྃ་ཕཊ། ཨོཾ་ཨ་ན་ཡ་ཧོ་བྷ་ག་ཝན་བིདྱ་ར་ཛ་ཧཱུྃ།། ཞེས་ཅི་རིགས་པ་བཟླ་ཞིང་། ལས་ཐམས་ཅད་པ་ལ། ཨོཾ་སུམྦྷ་ནི་སུམ་བྷ་ཧཱུྃ་ཧཱུྃ་ཕཊ། ཨོཾ་གྲྀཧྞ་གྲྀཧྞ་ཧཱུྃ་ཧཱུྃ་ཕཊ། ཨོཾ་གྲྀཧྞ་པ་ཡ་གྲྀཧྞ་པ་ཡ་ཧཱུྃ་ཧཱུྃ་ཕཊ། ཨོཾ་ཨ་ན་ཡ་ཧོ་བྷ་ག་ཝན་བིདྱ་ར་ཛཱ་ཡ་ཧཱུྃ་ཧཱུྃ་ཕཊ་ཞེས་པ་དང་། ཨོཾ་སརྦ་ཏ་ཐཱ་ག་ཏ་ཨ་བྷི་ཥེ་ཀ་ཏ་ས་མ་ཡ་ཤྲཱི་ཡེ་ཧཱུྃ། ཞེས་ཅི་རིགས་པ་བཟླས་ནས་སླར་ཡང་མཆོད་ཅིང་བསྟོད་ལ། དུང་ཆོས་ཀྱི་ཆུ་བླུགས་པས་ཐམས་ཅད་འོད་དུ་ཞུ་བ་ལས་བྱུང་བའི་ཆུར་བསྒྱུར།། བུམ་པའི་ཆོ་ག།། །དེ་ནས་རང་ཉིད་ཀྱིའི་ཏེ་དུ་ཀ་ཐུག་གཉིས་པར་བརྩམས་ལ། བླ་མ་དང་གཙོ་བོ་ཐ་མི་དད་པའི་མདུན་དུ་དབང་

༄ ཐྲང་སྐྱེ། ཐྲ་མས་མཛོད་ཀྱུ་རྣམས་དེས་མཛོད་ལ། ལས་ཀྱི་བྱ་བ་རྣམས་དེའི་ཕྱུགས་ཁ་ནས་གྲུལ་པའི་ཧེ་རུ་ཀ་ཕྱུག་གཉིས་པས་མཛོད་ཅིང་། སློབ་མའི་བྱ་བ་རྣམས་རང་གིས་དངོས་སུ་བྱའོ།། དེའང་མཉལ་ཕྱུལ་ནས་མི་ཏོག་དང་བཅས་པས་ཐལ་མོ་སྦྱར་བ་ལ་བླ་མས། ཆོས་རྣམས་གཟུགས་བརྙན་ལྟ་བུ་སྟེ། གསལ་ཞིང་དག་ལ་རྟོག་པ་མེད། གཟུང་དུ་མེད་ཅིང་བརྗོད་དུ་མེད། རྒྱུ་དང་ལས་ལས་ཡང་དག་བྱུང་། དེ་བཞིན་དེ་ཉིད་ངེས་པར་བྱུང་། བདེན་པ་དེ་ཡིས་དཀྱིལ་འཁོར་ནི། གཟུགས་བརྙན་གསལ་བར་སློབ་མ་རྣམས། ཀུན་གྱིས་དྲི་མེད་མཐོང་པར་ཤོག། ཅེས་ལན་གསུམ་གྱིས་བདེན་པའི་སྟོབས་བརྗོད་ནས། ཨ་ཁཾ་ཧྲི་ར་ཧཱུྃ་གིས་གདོང་གཡོགས་འཆིངས་ཤིང་། མི་ཏོག་གི་ཕྲེང་བ་གཏད། ལས་ཐམས་ཅད་པའི་ཆུ་དང་སུམྦྷ་བསང་། བདུད་རྩི་ལྟེ་ལ་གཞག་ཅིང་། ཨོཾ་ཨཱཿཧཱུྃ་ཡིས་བྱིན་གྱིས་བརླབ། བུ་ཁྱོད་སུ་ཅི་ལ་དགའ། ཞེས་དྲིས་པའི་ལན་དུ། སྐལ་བཟང་བདག་བདེ་བ་ཆེན་པོ་ལའོ།། ཞེས་པ་དང་། དེས་བྱ་ལ་ཅི་ཞིག་བྱ་ཞེས་པའི་ལན་དུ། སངས་རྒྱས་མཆོག་གི་དམ་ཚིག་གོ། ཞེས་ལན་བཏབ་ནས། རང་གི་སྙིང་གི་ནང་དུ་ཀུན་རྫོབ་བྱང་ཆུབ་ཀྱི་སེམས་ཀྱི་ངོ་བོ་ཟླ་བའི་སྙིང་དུ། དོན་དམ་བྱང་ཆུབ་སེམས་ཀྱི་ངོ་བོ། རྡོ་རྗེ་དཀར་པོ་རྩེ་མོ་ལྔ་པ་བསམས་ནས། དངོས་སུ་རྡོ་རྗེས་གཏུག་ཅིང་། ཨོཾ་བཛྲ་ཡོ་ག་ཙིཏྟ་ཨུཏ་པ་ད་ཡ་མི། སུ་ར་ཏ་ས་ཏྭ་ཡ་ཧཱུྃ་ཧོ། ཨཱ་རཏྣ་བཛྲ་ཡ་ཐ་སུ་ཁཾ། ཞེས་པས་བྱང་ཆུབ་ཀྱི་སེམས་བསྐྱེད་ནས། ཕྱི་བོར་རྡོ་རྗེས་གཏུགས་ལ། དེང་ཁྱོད་ལ་དེ་བཞིན་གཤེགས་པ་ཐམས་ཅད་ཀྱིས་བྱིན་གྱིས་རློབ་པར་འགྱུར་གྱིས། དེ་བཞིན་གཤེགས་པ་ཐམས་ཅད་ཀྱི་གསང་བ་དམ་པ་འདི། དེ་བཞིན་གཤེགས་པ་ཐམས་ཅད་ཀྱི་དཀྱིལ་འཁོར་དུ་མ་ཞུགས་པ་རྣམས་ལ་སྨྲ་བར་མི་བྱ་ཞིང་། མ་དད་པ་རྣམས་ལ་སང་མ་ཡིན་ནོ།། །ཞེས་གསང་བར་གདམས། སློ་མས་ལུས་ཀྱི་དཀྱིལ་

ༀ་ འཁོར་གྱི་སྙིང་དུ་ཁྲིད་པར་བསམ་ཞིང་། ཛཿཧཱུྃ་བཾ་ཧོཿ ཞེས་བརྗོད་དོ། ། ཕྱིའི་འདུག་པའོ། །དེ་ནས་ རྨི་ལམ་ང་མི་རྟོག་དང་བཅས་པས། གང་ གི་དྲིན་ གྱིས་བདེ་ཆེན་ཉིད། སྐད་ ཅིག་ ཉིད་ལ་འཆར་བ་གང་། བླ་ མ་ རིན་ ཆེན་ ལྟ་ བུའི་ སྐུ། རྡོ་ རྗེ་ཅན་ཞབས་ པད་ལ་འདུད། སངས་རྒྱས་ཀུན་གྱི་རང་བཞིན་སྐུ། སློབ་དཔོན་ལ་ནི་བདག་སྐྱབས་མཆི། ཅེས་པས་བླ་མ་དང་། དཔའ་བོ་རྣལ་འབྱོར་མ་འཁོར་ལོ། རྣལ་འབྱོར་གནས་ལ་བདག་སྐྱབས་མཆི། ཞེས་པས་དཀྱིལ་ འཁོར་གྱི་ལྷ་རྣམས་ལ་སྐྱབས་སུ་སོང་ནས། དོན་ དམ་ སྒོ་བའི་སེང་གེ་རྣལ་འབྱོར་ཞེས་བྱ་བ། ཉོན་མོངས་གཅོད་པའི་དོན་ལ་ངེས་དུ་མཁས་གྱུར་པ། སྲིད་པའི་ཉེས་བརྒྱ་སྐྱིད་ ཙ་ཉོན་ མོངས་ཆོད་མཛད་ལ། རྣལ་འབྱོར་ དོན་དམ་རྒྱལ་པོ་དེ་ཉིད་བདག་ལ་གྲུབ་པར་མཛོད། ཞེས་ལན་གསུམ་དུ་གསོལ་བ་གདབ་པོ།། །དེ་ནས་བླ་མས། །དེ་བཞིན་གཤེགས་པ་ཀུན་གྱི་གནས། ཧེ་རུ་ཀ་དཔལ་གྲོང་ཁྱེར་མཆོག། སྙིང་པོ་འི་དཀྱིལ་འཁོར་འདི་རུ་ནི། བདག་གིས་སློབ་མ་གཞུག་པར་བགྱི།། ཞེས་ལན་གསུམ་གྱིས་རང་གི་སྐུའི་ དཀྱིལ་ འཁོར་ ལ་ གསོལ་བ་བཏབ་ པར་བསམ་མོ། དེ་ ནས་ བླ་ མས། རྨོ་པ་ཡེན་ དུ་གཞུག་པའི་ཕྱིར། གང་ནས་གང་མའི་ རྨི་ལ་ ནི། །བུ་ ཁྱོད་ ཀྱིས་ ནི་ སྲུང་བ་སྟེ། གྲོལ་བའི་རྒྱུ་ནི་དེ་ལས་གཞན། ཐབས་ ནི་ ཅི་ཡང་ཡོད་མ་ཡིན། ཞེས་གསུང་བ་ཁས་བླངས་པའི་ཕྱིར། གཙོ་བོས་ཇི་ལྟར་བཀའ་སྩལ་པ། དེ་དག་ཐམས་ཅད་བདག་གིས་བགྱི།། ཞེས་ལན་གསུམ་བརྗོད་ནས། ཐུན་མོང་གི་སྨོན་པ་ཁས་བླངས་པའི་ཕྱིར། བླ་མའི་ གསུང་ གི་རྗེས་སུ་ཟློ་བར་ བསམ་ཞིང་། སྲས་བཅས་ སངས་རྒྱས་ཐམས་ ཅད་དང་། དཔའ་བོ་རྣལ་འབྱོར་མ་རྣམས་ཀུན། བདག་ལ་དགོངས་པར་མཛད་དུ་གསོལ། །བདག་གི་མིང་འདི་ཞེས་བགྱི་བ་ཡིས། དུས་འདི་ནས་ནི་བཟུང་ནས་སུ། ཇི་སྲིད་བྱང་ཆུབ་

༄ སྙིང་པོ་རི་བར། ཇི་ལྟར་དུས་གསུམ་མགོན་པོ་རྣམས། བྱང་ཆུབ་ཏུ་ནི་ངེས་མཛད་
པའི། བྱང་ཆུབ་སེམས་ནི་བླ་ན་མེད། དམ་པ་བདག་གིས་བསྐྱེད་པར་བགྱི། ཚུལ་ཁྲིམས་
ཀྱི་ནི་བསྡམ་པ་དང་། དགེ་བའི་ཆོས་ནི་སྡུད་པ་དང་། སེམས་ཅན་དོན་བྱེད་ཚུལ་
ཁྲིམས་གསུམ། སོ་སོར་བརྟན་པོར་གཟུང་བར་བགྱི། སངས་རྒྱས་ཆོས་དང་དགེ་འདུན་སྟེ།
བླ་ན་མེད་པའི་དཀོན་མཆོག་གསུམ། སངས་རྒྱས་རྣལ་འབྱོར་ལས་སྐྱེས་པའི། སྡོམ་
པ་དེང་ནས་བརྟན་པོར་གཟུང་། རྡོ་རྗེ་རིགས་མཆོག་ཆེན་པོ་ལ། རྡོ་རྗེ་དྲིལ་བུ་ཕྱག་
རྒྱ་ཡང་། །ཡང་དག་ཉིད་དུ་གཟུང་བར་བགྱི། སློབ་དཔོན་དག་ཀྱང་གཟུང་བར་བགྱི།
རིན་ཆེན་རིགས་མཆོག་ཆེན་པོ་ཡི། །དམ་ཚིག་ཡིད་དུ་འོང་བ་ལ། ཉིན་རེ་ཞིང་ནི་
དུས་དྲུག་ཏུ། སྦྱིན་པ་རྣམ་བཞི་རྟག་ཏུ་སྦྱིན། །བྱང་ཆུབ་ཆེན་པོ་ལས་བྱུང་བའི། པད་
མའི་རིགས་ཆེན་དག་པ་ལ། ཕྱི་ནང་གསང་བ་ཐེག་པ་གསུམ། དམ་པའི་ཆོས་ནི་མ་
ལུས་གཟུང་།། ལས་ཀྱི་རིགས་མཆོག་ཆེན་པོ་ལ། སྡོམ་པ་ཐམས་ཅད་ལྡན་པར་ནི། ཡང་
དག་ཉིད་དུ་གཟུང་བར་བགྱི། མཆོད་པའི་ལས་ཀྱང་ཅི་ནུས་བགྱི། བྱང་ཆུབ་སེམས་ནི་
བླ་མེད་མཆོག། །དམ་པ་བདག་གིས་བསྐྱེད་བགྱིས་ནས། སེམས་ཅན་ཀུན་གྱི་དོན་གྱི་ཕྱིར།
བདག་གིས་སྡོམ་པ་མ་ལུས་གཟུང་། མ་བསྒྲལ་བ་རྣམས་བདག་གིས་བསྒྲལ། མ་གྲོལ་བ་བདག་
རྣམས་བདག་གིས་དགྲོལ། དབུགས་མ་ཕྱིན་པ་དབུགས་དབྱུང་ཞིང་། སེམས་ཅན་མྱ་ངན་
འདས་ལ་དགོད།། །ཞེས་ལན་གསུམ་བརྗོད་ནས། ཁྱད་པར་གྱི་སྡོམ་པ་གཟུང་བའི་ཕྱིར།
སངས་རྒྱས་ཆོས་དང་དགེ་འདུན་ལ། །རྟག་ཏུ་བདག་ནི་སྐྱབས་སུ་མཆི། རྣལ་འབྱོར་
གསང་སྔགས་མཁའ་འགྲོ་མ། འཁོར་ལོ་གསུམ་གྱི་བདག་ཉིད་ཅན། ཀུན་ལ་རྟག་ཏུ་
སྐྱབས་སུ་མཆི། དཔའ་བོ་དཔའ་མོ་དབང་ཕྱུ་མོ། བྱང་ཆུབ་སེམས་དཔའི་བདག

༄ ཉིད་ཆེ། ཁྱད་པར་དུ་ཡང་སློབ་དཔོན་ལ། རྟག་པར་བདག་ནི་སྐྱབས་སུ་མཆི། ཧེ་རུ་ཀ་དཔལ་ཇོག༔ དཔའ་བོ། །ཉལ་འབྱོར་མ་དང་སྣང་མཛོད་ཇོགས། བྱང་ཆུབ་སེམས་དཔའ་དཔག་མེད་པ། ཐམས་ཅད་བདག་ལ་དགོངས་སུ་གསོལ། བདག་ནི་དུས་འདི་ནས་བཟུང་སྟེ། ཐེ་སྲིད་གཉིས་མེད་ལ་གནས་པར། དེ་དེ་ཚངས་སྤྱོད་གཉིས་མེད་པ། །ཉི་ཤུ་རྩ་གཉིས་ལེགས་པར་བསྲུང་།། ཞེས་ལན་གསུམ་བརྗོད་པས་དམ་ཚིག་བླང་ངོ་། དེ་ནས་བླ་མས།། ཨོཾ་སརྦ་ཤྲིག་ནན། ན་མཿ སརྦ་ཏ་ཐཱ་ག་ཏེ་བྷྱོཿ བི་ཤྭ་མུ་ཁེ་བྷྱཿ སརྦ་ཐཱ་ཁཾ་ཨུད་ག་ཏེ། སྥ་ར་ཎ་ཨི་མཾ་ག་ག་ན་ཁཾ་སྭཱ་ཧཱ་དཾ་བ་ཡིན་ཏེ་སྭཱ་ཧཱ།། ཞེས་པས་བགེགས་རྣམས་ལ་གཏོར་མ་གསུམ་བྱིན་ནས། སྲུམ་ཧཱུའི་ཕྱགས་དང་བཅས་པའི་ཏིང་ཡོ་དང་། ཚང་བུ་ལན་གསུམ་བྱིན་པས་ཀྱང་བསྐྲད་ལ། གྲུ་གྲུལ་གྱི་དུད་པས་བདུག་ཅིང་། ཡུངས་དཀར་གྱིས་བྲབ། སུམྦྷའི་ཕྱགས་ཀྱི་མཐར་བགེགས་གང་དག་མི་འགྲོ་བ་དེ་དག་གི་མགོ་ཚལ་པ་བརྒྱར་འགས་པར་འགྱུར་རོ། ཞེས་གསུང་བས་བགེགས་སྤྱངས་ནས། རང་གི་སྡིག་པ་ཀཾ་གི་རྣམ་པར་སྣ་བུག་ནས་འཐོན་ཏེ་རིལ་ལ་ཐིམ་པ་གཡས་སུ་ཡེ་ཤེས་ཀྱི་མེ་དང་། གཡོན་དུ་ཆུ་མཆོར་དོར་བར་བསམ་ཞིང་། ཨོཾ་བཛྲ་ཌ་ཀ་ཁ་ཁ་ཁཱ་ཧི་ཏེ་ཁཱ་ཧི་ཏེ་སརྦ་པཱ་པཾ་ད་ཧ་ན་བྷསྨིཾ་ཀུ་རུ་ཡེ་སྭཱ་ཧཱ། ཞེས་ཡང་ཡང་བརྗོད་པས་སྡིག་པ་སྦྱངས་ནས། ལས་ཐམས་ཅད་པའི་བུམ་པས་བཀྲུ་ཞིང་། ཐེ་ཀྱུར་བཟླས་པ་ལ་སོགས་པའི་ཕྱགས་དང་། ཚོགས་སུ་བཅད་པ་བརྗོད་པས་དྲི་མ་སྦྱང་ངོ་། དེ་ནས་སྭ་བྷཱ་བའི་སྔགས་ཀྱིས་རང་ཉིད་སྟོང་པར་སྦྱངས་པའི་ངང་ལས་སྐད་ཅིག་གིས་སྤྱི་ཡི་ཧེ་རུ་ཀ་ཕྱག་བཅུ་གཉིས་པ་ཡུམ་དང་བཅས་རྫིང་ལུས་ཀྱི་དཀྱིལ་འཁོར་གྱི་ལྷ་ཚང་བ་གོ་ཆ་གཉིས་དང་བཅས་པ་དམིགས་སུ་

༄༅ པ་ཡ། སངས་རྒྱས་དང་བྱང་ཆུབ་སེམས་དཔའ་ཐམས་ཅད་ཧཱུ་ཡི་དང་། ཀཱུ་ཡིའི་རྣམ་པར་ཐིམ་ཞིང་། བླ་མས་ཧཱུ་ཡི་ཀཱུ་ཡི་བརྗོད་པས་བྱིན་གྱིས་རློབ་པར་བསྒོམ་པ་ནི། ནང་དུ་འཇུག་པའི་དངོས་གཞིའོ།། དེ་ལྟར་ཐོབ་པའི་དམ་ཚིག་མི་ཉམས་པར་སྲུང་དུ་གཞུག་པའི་ཕྱིར། བླ་མས་ཡེ་ཤེས་གང་གིས་ཁྱོད་དེ་བཞིན་གཤེགས་པ་ཐམས་ཅད་དང་། །དཔའ་བོ་དང་། །རྣལ་འབྱོར་མ་ཐམས་ཅད་ཀྱི་དངོས་གྲུབ་ཀྱང་ཐོབ་པར་འགྱུར་ན་དངོས་གྲུབ་གཞན་ལྟ་ཅི་སྨོས། ཁྱོད་ཀྱིས་དཀྱིལ་འཁོར་ཆེན་པོ་མ་མཐོང་བ་རྣམས་ཀྱི་མདུན་དུ་སྨྲ་བར་མི་བྱ་སྟེ། བུ་ཁྱོད་དམ་ཚིག་ཉམས་པར་གྱུར་ཏ་རེ། ཞེས་བསྒྲུངས་པའི་ཕན་ཡོན་དང་། ཧེ་རུ་ཀ་དཔལ་དེང་ཁྱོད་ཀྱི། སྙིང་ལ་ཡང་དག་ཞུགས་པར་གྱུར། གལ་ཏེ་ཚུལ་འདི་སྨྲས་ན་ནི། དེ་མ་ཐག་ཏུ་དྲལ་ཏེ་པ་ཤིགས། ཞེས་མ་བསྒྲུངས་པའི་ཉེས་དམིགས་དང་། །འདི་ནི་ཁྱོད་ཀྱི་དམྱལ་བའི་ཆུ། དམ་ཚིག་འདས་ན་སྲེག་པར་བྱེད། དམ་ཚིག་བསྲུངས་ན་དངོས་གྲུབ་ནི། རྡོ་རྗེ་བདུད་རྩི་ཡི་ཆུ་འདིས་འགྲུབ། ཨོཾ་པཉྩ་ཨ་མྲྀ་ཏ་ཨུད་ཀ་ཋ་ཋ་ཋ ཿཧཱུཾ།། ཞེས་པས་བདུད་རྩི་བླུད་པས་ཕན་ཡོན་དང་། ཉེས་དམིགས་གཉིས་ཀ་དང་། ཁྱོད་ཀྱིས་སྨད་པར་མི་བྱ་ཞིང་། དམ་ཚིག་དང་འགལ་མི་བྱ་སྟེ། །དམྱལ་ལ་སོགས་པར་འགྲོ་འགྱུར་རོ།། ཞེས་བླ་མའི་བཀའ་ཉན་པར་བསྒོ་བས། དམ་ལ་བཞག་ནས་དེ་བཞིན་གཤེགས་པ་ཐམས་ཅད་དང་། དཔའ་བོ་དང་། རྣལ་འབྱོར་མ་ཐམས་ཅད་ཀྱིས་བདག་ལ་བྱིན་གྱིས་རློབས་ཤིག། དཔལ་ཧེ་རུ་ཀ་བདག་ལ་དབབ་པར་མཛོད་ཅིག། །ཞེས་ལན་གསུམ་གསོལ་བ་བཏབ་སྟེ། དངོས་པོ་དང་མཚན་མ་ལ་མ་ཞེན་པའི་ངང་ལས། རང་ཧེ་རུ་ཀར་དམིགས་པའི་རྐང་པའི་འཁྱིལ་གྱི་ཧཱུྃ་ལས། ཡེ་ཤེས་ཀྱི་མེ་འབར་བས་སྡིག་པ་དང་རྟོག་པ་ཐམས་ཅད་བསྲེགས།

༄ ལུས་ཀྱི་ལྷ་ཐམས་ཅད་གསལ་བཏབ། སངས་རྒྱས་དང་བྱང་ཆུབ་སེམས་དཔའ་ཐམས་ཅད་དང་། དཔའ་བོ་དང་། རྣལ་འབྱོར་མ་ཐམས་ཅད་བདེ་མཆོག་གི་ལྷའི་རྣམ་པས་བདག་ལ་ཐིམ་པར་བསམ་ཞིང་། གུ་གུལ། གྱི་ལའི་བྲུན། ཟླ་མཚན་དང་ལྡན་པའི་འདམས་དཀྲིས་ཀྱི་རས་བསྒྲིགས་པས་བདུག་ནས། ཟླ་མས་ཡབ་ཡུམ་གྱི་སྙིང་པོ་དང་། ཨོཾ་ཧྲཱིཿ་མ་ཧཱ་སུ་ཁཾ་ཧྲཱ་ཨ་ཧཱ་ཤ་ཡ་ཧཱུྃ། ཨ་ཤྲཱི་ཧེ་རུ་ཀ་བཛྲ་མ་ཧེ་བཛྲ་ཧ་ཧཱ་ཧེ་མ་ཧེ་སྭཱ་ཧཱ། ཞེས་གསུང་བར་བསམ་ཞིང་ཡིད་གཟུང་ངོ་། དེ་ནས་སྤྱི་བོར་རྡོ་རྗེ་བཞག་ནས། ཧྲཱིཿ་བརྗོད་བརྟན་པར་བསམ་མོ། ཡེ་ཤེས་དབབ་པའོ།། དེ་ནས་ཨོཾ་བྲ་ཧི་ཚ་བཛྲ་ཧོས་མི་ཧོག་གི་ཕྲེང་བ། ཟླ་མའི་ཐུགས་ཁའི་གཙོ་བོ་ལ་ཕྱུལ་ནས། ཟླ་མས། ཨོཾ་བྲ་ཧི་གྲི་ཧྣ་སྭ་མི་མཾ་ས་ཧྲ་མ་ཧཱ་བ་ལ་ཨོཾ་ཞེས་གསུང་ཞིང་མི་ཧོག་མགོར་བཞག་ནས། རང་གི་མིག་འབྲས་གཉིས་སུ། ཨ་བསྐྱེད་ལ།། ཧེ་རུ་ཀ་དཔལ་དེང་ཁྱོད་ཀྱི། མིག་འབྱེད་པར་ནི་བརྩོན་པར་མཛོད། ཀྱེ་བས་ཐམས་ཅད་མཐོང་འགྱུར་བ། རྡོ་རྗེ་དེ་མིག་ནི་བླ་ན་མེད། ཨོཾ་བཛྲ་ནེ་ཏྲ། ཨ་པ་ཧ་ར་པ་ཊ་ལ་ཧྲི༔ ཅེས་པས་གདོང་གཡོགས་ཕྱེ་ལ། རང་བཞིན་གྱིས་ནི་དག་པའི་བདག། ལུས་ནི་རང་བཞིན་དྲིམ་མེད། དཔའ་བོ་དཔའ་མོ་དབང་མོ་འི་གནས། དཀྱིལ་འཁོར་ལ་ནི་དེ་ཁྱོད་ལྟོས། དེ་ནས་གནས་དང་དེ་གནས་ཚོགས། བདག་ཉིད་དཀྱིལ་འཁོར་ལུས་དཀྱིལ་འཁོར། །ཡང་ནས་བྱང་ཆུབ་ཕྱོགས་ཀྱི་ཆོས། སུམ་བཅུ་རྩ་བདུན་རང་བཞིན་ཏེ། རྩ་ནི་སུམ་བཅུ་རྩ་བདུན་པའོ།། །ལྷའི་དཀྱིལ་འཁོར་དཀྱིལ་འཁོར་པ། དཔལ་ནི་ཧེ་རུ་ཀའི་ནི། ཡན་ལག་ཡན་ལག་ཉེར་བསྟན་ཏོ། ཞེས་གསུང་པས་སྐུའི་དཀྱིལ་འཁོར་བསྟན་ནས། བདག་གི་ཡིད་ཀྱིས་ཀྱང་མངོན་སུམ་ལྟར་བལྟའོ།། དེ་ནས་མཎྜལ་ཕུལ་ལ། ཆོས་བདེན་བདག་ཉིད་བསམ་མི་ཁྱབ། བདག་ལ་དབང་ནི་བསྐུར་དུ་གསོལ། ཞེས་ལན་གསུམ་གསོལ་

༄ བ་བཏབ་ནས། བདག་བླ་མའི་མཉྫུ་དྲྀ་རིན་པོ་ཆེའི་ཁྲི། པད་མ་དང་། ཉི་མའི་གདན་ལ་བཞུགས་པའི་དཔལ་ཧེ་རུ་ཀར་དམིགས་པའི་སྟེང་དུ། གདུགས་དཀར་པོ་དང་། ཕྱོགས་ཐམས་ཅད་ནས་མཆོད་པ་སྣ་ཚོགས་ཀྱིས་མཆོད་པར་བསམ་ཞིང་། གཙོ་བོའི་ཐུགས་ཁ་ནས་འཁྲོས་པའི་ཁྲོ་མཚམས་མ་བརྒྱད་ཀྱིས་བགེགས་ཐམས་ཅད་བསྐྲད། མཆོད་པ་ཐམས་ཅད་ཀྱིས་མཆོད། བཀྲ་ཤིས་བརྗོད། ཁྲུས་གསོལ་ཏེ། མེ་ཏོག་གི་ཆར་ཕབ་པས། ཤིས་པ་མཇོད་པར་བསམ་མོ། དེ་ནས་བླ་མའི་ནང་གི་ཧེ་རུ་ཀ་ཡབ་ཡུམ་གྱི་ཐུགས་ཁ་ནས་སྔགས་ཀྱི་ཕྲེང་བ་འཁྲོས་པས་རང་གི་སྙིང་ཁར་ཞུགས་ནས། སྙིང་ཁའི་ཧཱུྃ་གི་མཐའ་མར་གཡོན་སྐོར་དུ་འཁོར་བས། སྔགས་ཀྱི་དབང་ཐོབ་པར་བསམ་ཞིང་། ཨོཾ་ཤྲཱི་བཛྲ་ཧེ་ཧེ་རུ་རུ་ཀཾ་ཧཱུྃ་ཧཱུྃ་ཕཊ། ཌཱ་ཀི་ནི་ཛྭ་ལ་སམྦྷཱ་ར་སྭཱ་ཧཱ། ཨོཾ་ཝཛྲ་བཻ་རོ་ཙ་ནི་ཡེ་ཧཱུྃ་ཧཱུྃ་ཕཊ་སྭཱ་ཧཱ།། ཞེས་ལན་གསུམ་བརྗོད་ནས། བཅོམ་ལྡན་བདག་ལ་སྐུ་ལ་ལགས་ཀྱིས། བཅོམ་ལྡན་བདག་ལ་བྱིན་གྱིས་རློབས། ཞེས་ལན་གསུམ་བརྗོད་དེ་མེ་ཏོག་སྣར་དབུལ། །བླ་མས་ཕྲེང་བ་དེ་ཉིད་སྔགས་སུ་བྱིན་གྱིས་བརླབས་ནས། བཅོམ་ལྡན་འདི་ལ་སྐུ་ལ་ལགས་ཀྱིས། བཅོམ་ལྡན་འདི་ལ་བྱིན་གྱིས་རློབས། ཞེས་གསུང་ཞིང་མེ་ཏོག་ཕྱི་བོར་བཞག་པར་བསམ་པ་ནི་སྔགས་ཀྱི་དབང་ངོ་། ༄ །དེ་ནས་རིག་པའི་དབང་ལྔ་བླང་བའི་ཕྱིར། བདག་དང་། རྣམ་རྒྱལ་གྱི་བུམ་པ་སྭ་ཧཱ་ཡས་སྦྱངས་པའི་ངང་ལས། པད་མ་དང་། ཟླ་བའི་སྟེང་དུ་ཧཱུྃ་ལས་རྡོ་རྗེ་ཧཱུྃ་གིས་མཚན་པ་ལས་འོད་འཕྲོས་སེམས་ཅན་ཐམས་ཅད་ཀྱི་དོན་བྱས། སླར་འདུས་པ་ལས་མི་བསྐྱོད་པ་སྔོན་པོ། ཞལ་གཅིག་ཕྱག་གཉིས་པ། རྡོ་རྗེ་དྲིལ་བུ་འཛིན་པས་ཡུམ་ལ་འཁྱུད་པ། ཡུམ་མ་མ་ཀཱི་སྔོན་མོ། གྲི་གུག་དང་ཐོད་པ་འཛིན་པ་དང་མཉམ་པར་སྦྱར། གཉིས་ཀ་འང་རུས་པ་དང་། རིན་པོ་ཆེས་བརྒྱན་པའི་དཔྲལ་བར་ཨཾ། མགྲིན་པར་ཨཱཿ སྙིང་

༄༅ ཁར་ཧཱུྃ་བཀོད་ནས། དབང་རྫས་ཀྱི་མི་བསྐྱོད་པ་ཡབ་ཡུམ་སྙོམས་པར་ཞུགས་ནས་ཞུ་བ་ལས་བྱུང་བའི་རྒྱུར་བཟླས་ནས། དཀྱིལ་འཁོར་གྱི་ལྷ་རྣམས་ལ། ཁྱེད་ཀྱིས་བདག་ལ་དབང་བསྐུར་དུ་གསོལ་ཞེས་གསོལ་བ་བཏབ་པས། གཙོ་བོ་དེ་ཐུགས་ཁ་ནས་སྤྲུལ་པའི་དབང་གི་ལྷ་དྲུག་བཅུ་རྩ་གཉིས་ནམ་མཁར་བྱོན་ནས། གཙོ་བོས། ཇི་ལྟར་བཟླམ་པ་ལ་སོགས་པ་དང་། ཨོཾ་སརྦ་ཏ་ཐཱ་ག་ཏ་ཨ་བྷི་ཥེ་ཀ་ཏ་ས་མ་ཡེ་ཤྲཱི་ཡེ་ཧཱུྃ། ཙཀྲ་བཱི་ར་ཧཱུྃ་ཨ་བྷི་ཥིཉྩ་མི། ཀ་ཀྵ་སྭཱ།། ལ་སོགས་པའི་སྔགས་ཀྱི་མཐར། ཨོཾ་བཛྲ་ཧྲ་ཡ་ཨ་བྷི་ཥིཉྩ་ཧཱུྃ། ཞེས་གསུང་ཞིང་བུམ་པའི་ཆུས་དབང་བསྐུར། སྙིང་པོའི་རྣལ་འབྱོར་མ་བཞིས་རྡོ་རྗེའི་གླུ་ལེན། དཔའ་བོ་དང་རྣལ་འབྱོར་མ་རྣམས་ཀྱིས་བཀྲ་ཤིས་བརྗོད། སྒོ་མཚམས་མ་རྣམས་ཀྱིས་བགེགས་བསྲུང་ཅིང་མཆོད། དབང་གི་ཆུ་རྒྱུན་དེས། ང་མཐིལ་ཡན་ཆད་གང་། དྲི་མ་ཐམས་ཅད་དག། མི་བསྐྱོད་པས་དབུ་བརྒྱན་པ་ནི་ཕྱིའི་དབང་ངོ་། སྙིང་ཁའི་ཧཱུྃ་ལས་འོད་འཕྲོས་པས། སངས་རྒྱས་ཐམས་ཅད་མི་བསྐྱོད་པའི་རྣམ་པས་སྤྱན་དྲངས་པ། །སྙིང་ཁའི་སྒོ་ནས་ལུས་ལ་ཐིམ་པས་བདག་མི་བསྐྱོད་པར་གྱུར་པ་ནི་ནང་གི་དབང་ངོ་། །དེ་ནས་དངོས་སུ་མཆོད་ནས། ཆུའི་དབང་ཐོབ། ཞེ་སྡང་དག། རྣམ་ཤེས་གནས་གྱུར། མེ་ལོང་ལྟ་བུའི་ཡེ་ཤེས་དང་། མི་བསྐྱོད་པའི་དངོས་གྲུབ་ཐོབ་པར་བསམ་མོ། ༄༅ །ཡང་སྣང་བའི་ངང་ལས། རང་གི་སེམས་དང་དབུ་བརྒྱན། ཨཾ་ལས་རིན་པོ་ཆེ་ཨཾ་གིས་མཚན་པ་ལས་རིན་ཆེན་འབྱུང་ལྡན་སེར་པོ་རིན་པོ་ཆེ་དང་དྲིལ་བུ་འཛིན་པ། ཡུམ་རིན་ཆེན་སྒྲོལ་མ་དང་སྦྱོར་བར་དམིགས་ནས། །གནས་གསུམ་བྱིན་གྱིས་བརླབས་ལ། དབང་གི་ལྷ་རྣམས་ལ་གསོལ་བ་བཏབ་པས། ལྷ་རྣམས་ཀྱིས། སངས་རྒྱས་རྣམས་ཀྱིས་རབ་བརྟགས་པའི། དབུ་རྒྱན་དབང་བསྐུར་ཕྱིན་པར་བྱ། ཅེས་པ་དང་། ཡུམ་གྱི་ནི་སྙིང་གི་མཐར། །ཨ་བྷྲ་ཏི་ཥྛ་མ་ཧཱ་སུ་ཀུ་ཊ་ཧཾ་ཞེས་པས། དབང་རྫས་ཀྱི་རིན་ཆེན་

༄ དཔལ་འཁོར་ལོ་བདེ་མཆོག།

༄ འབྱུང་ལྡན་ཆུ་བ་ལས་བྱུང་བའི་དབུ་རྒྱན་སྤྱི་བོར་བཞག་ནས། ཐོ་མ་ལྟར་བྲུམ་པའི་ཚུས་དབང་བསྐུར་ལུས་ཐམས་ཅད་གང་། དྲི་མ་ཐམས་ཅད་དག། རིན་ཆེན་འབྱུང་ལྡན་གྱིས་དབུ་བརྒྱན་པ་ནི་ཕྱིའི་དབང་ངོ་། །དབྲལ་བའི་ཨོཾ་ལས་འོད་འཕྲོས་པས། སངས་རྒྱས་རྣམས་རིན་ཆེན་འབྱུང་ལྡན་གྱི་རྣམ་པས་སྤྱན་དྲངས་པ། དབྲལ་བ་ནས་ལུས་ལ་ཐིམ་པས། རང་ཉིད་རིན་ཆེན་འབྱུང་ལྡན་གྱི་ངོ་བོར་གྱུར་པ་ལ་མཆོད་ནས། ཅོད་པན་གྱི་དབང་ཐོབ། ང་རྒྱལ་དང་སེར་སྣ་དག། ཚོར་བ་གནས་གྱུར། མཉམ་པ་ཉིད་དང་། རིན་ཆེན་འབྱུང་ལྡན་གྱི་དངོས་གྲུབ་ཐོབ་པར་བསམ་མོ།། ༄ །།ཡང་སྙིང་པའི་ངང་ལས། རང་གི་སེམས་དང་། རྡོ་རྗེ་ཧྲཱིཿ་ལས་པད་མ་ཧྲཱིཿ་གིས་མཚན་པ་ལས་འོད་དཔག་མེད་དམར་པོ། པད་མ་དང་དྲིལ་བུ་འཛིན་པ། ཕྱམ་གོས་དཀར་མོ་དང་སྦྱོར་བར་དམིགས་ནས། གནས་གསུམ་བྱིན་གྱིས་བརླབས་ལ། དབང་གི་ལྷ་རྣམས་ལ་གསོལ་བ་བཏབ་པས། ལྷ་དེ་རྣམས་ཀྱིས། འདི་ནི་སངས་རྒྱས་ཐམས་ཅད་དེ། ཧེ་རུ་ཀ་དཔལ་དབང་བསྐུར་བས།། དེ་རིང་ཁྱོད་ནི་དབང་བསྐུར་རོ། རབ་ཏུ་གྲུབ་ཕྱིར་རྡོ་རྗེ་བཟུང་། ཨོཾ་ཤྲཱི་ཧེ་རུ་ཀ་ཨ་ ཧྲྀ་ད་ཡ་ཧཱུཾ། ཨ་བྷི་ཥིཉྩ་མི། ཧྲཱིཿ་བྲི་ར་ས་མ་ཡ་ཧཱུཾ། ཞེས་པས་དབང་རྫས་ཀྱི་འོད་དཔག་མེད་ཆུ་བ་ལས་བྱུང་བའི་རྡོ་རྗེ་ལག་པ་གཡས་པར་གནང་བ། སྙིང་ཁར་བཟུང་བ་ཚུལ་སོགས་པ་དབང་བསྐུར་བས། ལུས་ཐམས་ཅད་གང་། དྲི་མ་ཐམས་ཅད་དག། འོད་དཔག་ཏུ་མེད་པས་དབུ་བརྒྱན་པ་ཕྱིའི་དབང་ངོ་། །མགྲིན་པའི་ཧྲཱིཿ་ལས་འོད་འཕྲོས་པས་སངས་རྒྱས་ཐམས་ཅད་འོད་དཔག་མེད་ཀྱི་རྣམ་པས་སྤྱན་དྲངས་པས། མགྲིན་པ་ནས་ལུས་ལ་ཐིམ་པས། རང་ཉིད་འོད་དཔག་མེད་ཀྱི་ངོ་བོར་གྱུར་པ་ལ་མཆོད་ནས། རྡོ་རྗེའི་དབང་ཐོབ། འདོད་ཆགས་དག། འདུ་ཤེས་གནས་གྱུར། སོ་སོར་རྟོག་པ་དང་། འོད་དཔག་ཏུ་མེད་པའི་དངོས་གྲུབ་ཐོབ་

༄༅ པར་བཙམ་མོ། ༄༅ །ཡང་སྟོང་པའི་ངང་ལས་རང་གི་སེམས་དང་། དྲིལ་བུ། ཁཾ་ལས་རལ་གྲི་ཁཾ་གིས་མཚན་པ་ལས། དོན་ཡོད་གྲུབ་པ་ལྗང་ཁུ། རལ་གྲི་དང་། དྲིལ་བུ་འཛིན་པས་ཡུམ་དམ་ཚིག་སྒྲོལ་མ་དང་སྦྱོར་བར་དམིགས་ནས་གནས་གསུམ་བྱིན་གྱིས་བརླབས་ལ། དབང་གི་ལྷ་རྣམས་ལ་གསོལ་བ་བཏབ་པས་ལྷ་དེ་རྣམས་ཀྱིས། འདི་ནི་རྣལ་འབྱོར་མ་ཀུན་གྱི། ཤེས་རབ་དབྱིངས་ཀྱི་རྗེས་འགྲོར་བཤད། ཁྱོད་ཀྱིས་ཀྱང་ནི་རྟག་ཏུ་ཟུང་། བྱང་ཆུབ་མཆོག་ཏུ་རྒྱལ་བས་བཞེད། བཛྲ་གྷཎྚ་ཨ་ཞེས་པས། དབང་རྫས་ཀྱི་དོན་ཡོད་གྲུབ་པ་ཕྲུ་བ་ལས་བྱུང་བའི་དྲིལ་བུ་ལག་པ་གཡོན་པར་གཏད་པ་དགྱིལ་བ་ལ། ཆུ་ལ་སོགས་པས་དབང་བསྐུར། ལུས་ཐམས་ཅད་གང་། དྲི་མ་ཐམས་ཅད་དག། དོན་ཡོད་ཕྲུ་བ་པས་དབུ་བརྒྱན་པ་ཕྱིའི་དབང་ངོ།། །འཚོགས་མའི་ཁཾ་ལས་འོད་འཕྲོས་པས་སངས་རྒྱས་ཐམས་ཅད་དོན་ཡོད་གྲུབ་པའི་རྣམ་པས་སྤྱན་དྲངས་པ། འཚོགས་མ་ནས་ལུས་ལ་ཐིམ་པས། རང་ཉིད་དོན་ཡོད་གྲུབ་པའི་ངོ་བོར་གྱུར་པ་ལ་མཆོད་ནས། དྲིལ་བུའི་དབང་ཐོབ། ཕྱག་རྟགས་དག། འདུ་བྱེད་གནས་གྱུར། བྱ་བ་གྲུབ་པ་དང་། དོན་ཡོད་གྲུབ་པའི་དངོས་གྲུབ་ཐོབ་པར་བསམ་མོ།། ༄ །ཡང་སྟོང་པའི་ངང་ལས། རང་གི་སེམས་ཧཱུྃ་ལས་འཁོར་ལོ་ཧཱུྃ་གིས་མཚན་པ་ལས་རྣམ་པར་སྣང་མཛད་དཀར་པོ་འཁོར་ལོ་དང་དྲིལ་བུ་འཛིན་པ། ཡུམ་སངས་རྒྱས་སྤྱན་མ་དང་སྦྱོར་བར་དམིགས་ནས་གནས་གསུམ་བྱིན་གྱིས་བརླབས་ལ། དབང་གི་ལྷ་རྣམས་ལ་གསོལ་བ་བཏབ་པས། ལྷ་དེ་རྣམས་ཀྱིས། ཨོཾ་བུདྡྷ་ཏེ་ཛུ་ཀ་ཨ་དྷི་པ་ཏི་ཧཱུྃ། ཨ་བྷི་ཥིཉྩ་མི། བུདྡྷ་ཏེ་ཛུ་ཀ་ཐུ་མ། ཨ་དྷི་ཊི་ཀ་ཏཿ ཀྱེ་དཔལ་ཆེ་གེ་མོ་རྡོ་རྗེ་ཞེས་བྱ་བའི་དེ་བཞིན་གཤེགས་པའོ་ཞེས་དབང་བསྐུར་ཏེ། འདི་ལ་དབང་རྫས་མེད་དོ།། ཡང་ཆུ་ལ་སོགས་པས་དབང་བསྐུར། ལུས་ཐམས་ཅད་གང་། དྲི་མ་ཐམས་ཅད་དག། རྣམ་པར་སྣང་མཛད་

༄༅ ཀྱི་དབུ་བརྒྱན་པར་བཟམ་པ་ནི་ཕྱིའི་དབང་ངོ་། །སྤྱི་བོའི་ཧཱུྃ་ལས་འོད་འཕྲོས་པས་སངས་རྒྱས་ཐམས་ཅད་རྣམ་པར་སྣང་མཛད་ཀྱི་རྣམ་པས་སྤྱན་དྲངས་པ། སྤྱི་བོ་ནས་ཞུས་ལ་ཐིམ་པས། རང་ཉིད་རྣམ་པར་སྣང་མཛད་ཀྱི་རང་བཞིན་དུ་གྱུར་པ་ལ་མཆོད་ནས། མིང་གི་དབང་ཐོབ། གཏི་མུག་དག། གཟུགས་ཀྱི་ཕུང་པོ་གནས་གྱུར། ཆོས་ཀྱི་དབྱིངས་དང་། རྣམ་པར་སྣང་མཛད་ཀྱི་དངོས་གྲུབ་ཐོབ་པར་བཟམ་མོ། རིག་པའི་དབང་ལྔ་འོ།། ༄༅ །།དེ་ནས་པད་དང་ཟླ་བའི་སྟེང་དུ་རང་གི་སེམས་ཧཱུྃ་ལས་ རྡོ་རྗེ་དཀར་པོ་ཧཱུྃ་གིས་མཚན་པ་ལས། རྡོ་རྗེ་སེམས་དཔའ་དཀར་པོ་རྡོ་རྗེ་དང་དྲིལ་བུ་འཛིན་པ། ཡུམ་རྡོ་རྗེ་སྙེམས་མ་དང་སྦྱོར་བར་དམིགས་ནས། གནས་གསུམ་བྱིན་གྱིས་བརླབས་ནས། དབང་གི་ལྷ་རྣམས་ལ་གསོལ་བ་བཏབ་པས། ལྷ་དེ་རྣམས་ཀྱིས། འདི་དེ་སངས་རྒྱས་ཐམས་ཅད་དེ། ཧེ་རུ་ཀ་དཔལ་ཕྱག་ན་གནས། ཁྱོད་ཀྱིས་ཀྱང་ནི་རྟག་ཏུ་ཟུང་། ཧེ་རུ་ཀ་དཔལ་བརྟུལ་ཞུགས་བརྟན། ཨོཾ་སརྦ་ཏ་ཐཱ་ག་ཏ་སིདྡྷི་བཛྲ་ས་མ་ཡ་ཏིཥྛ་བཛྲ་ཨེ་ཥ་ཏྭཾ་དྷ་ར་ཡ་མི་ཧཱུྃ་ཧ་ཧ་ཧོ་ཧ།། ཞེས་པས་སངས་རྒྱས་ཐམས་ཅད་ཀྱི་ཐུགས་གཉིས་སུ་མེད་པའི་ཡེ་ཤེས་ཀྱི་ངོ་བོ། རྡོ་རྗེ་བྱིན་པ་བླངས་ནས། སྙིང་གི་ནང་ཡང་དེ་ལྟ་བུའི་རྡོ་རྗེ་སེམས་དཔའ་བསྒོམ་པ་ནི་རྡོ་རྗེའི་བརྟུལ་ཞུགས་སོ།། ༄༅ །།ཡང་པད་མ་དང་ཉི་མའི་སྟེང་དུ་རང་གི་སེམས་ཧཱུྃ་ལས་རྡོ་རྗེ་ཧཱུྃ་གིས་མཚན་པ་ལས་འཁོར་ལོ་བདེ་མཆོག་ཞལ་བཅུ་གཉིས་པ། ཡུམ་རྡོ་རྗེ་ཕག་མོ་དང་གཉིས་སུ་མེད་པར་དམིགས་ནས། གནས་གསུམ་བྱིན་གྱིས་བརླབས་ལ། དབང་གི་ལྷ་རྣམས་ལ་གསོལ་བ་བཏབ་པས། དབང་གི་ལྷ་དེ་རྣམས་ཀྱིས། ཁ་ཊྭཾ་ག་དང་ཌཱ་མ་རུ། ཧེ་རུ་ཀ་དཔལ་ཁ་ཊྭཾ་ག། རྣལ་འབྱོར་མ་ནི་ཌཱ་མ་རུ། རྡོ་རྗེར་ཁ་ཊྭཾ་རྡོ་རྗེར་བཅས། དྲིལ་བུ་སིལ་སིལ་སྒྲ་སྒྲོགས་ཤིང་། ཚངས་པའི་སྐུད་ཐོགས་རྣལ་འབྱོར་བདག། ཁ་ཊྭཾ་ག་དང་རྣལ་འབྱོར་སྟོད།

༄༅ དཔའ་བོ་ཆེན་པོས་བླང་བར་བྱིས།། ཞེས་པས་ལག་པ་གཡས་པར་གསུང་གི་རྡོ་རྗེ་ཌ་མ་རུ་དང་། གཡོན་པར་ཐུགས་ཀྱི་རྡོ་རྗེ་ཐོད་པ་བདུད་རྩིས་གང་བ་དང་། ཁྲུ་མོར་སྐུའི་རྡོ་རྗེ་ཁ་ཊྭཾ་ག། སེ་རལ་ཁར་གཉིས་སུ་མེད་པའི་རྡོ་རྗེ་ཚངས་པའི་སྐུད་པས་བཅིངས་ནས། སྙིང་གི་ནང་དུ་ཡང་དེ་ལྟ་བུའི་ཧེ་རུ་ཀ་བསྒོམ་པ་ནི། ཐུན་མོང་མ་ཡིན་པའི་བརྟུལ་ཞུགས་ཏེ་སློབ་མའི་དབང་ངོ་།། ༄། །དེ་ནས་མཎྜལ་ཕུལ་ལ། དཔའ་བོ་ཆེན་པོ་མི་རྟོག་པའི་····དབང་བསྐུར་བ་ནི་བདག་ལ་སྩོལ། སེམས་ཅན་ཀུན་གྱི་དོན་གྱི་ཕྱིར། རྡོ་རྗེ་སློབ་དཔོན་བདག་གྱུར་མཛོད། ཞེས་ལན་གསུམ་གྱིས་རྡོ་རྗེ་སློབ་དཔོན་གྱི་དབང་གི་དོན་དུ་གསོལ་བ་བཏབ་ནས། དབང་རྟགས་རིན་པོ་ཆེའི་ཁྲི་སེང་གེས་བཏེག་པ་པད་མ་དང་ཉི་མར་ལོས་པའི་སྟེང་དུ། རང་གི་སེམས་པ་ཧཱུྃ་ལས་རྡོ་རྗེ་སྔོན་པོ་ཧཱུྃ་གིས་མཚན་པ་ལས་འོད་འཕྲོས་སེམས་ཅན་ཐམས་ཅད་ཀྱི་དོན་བྱས། སླར་འདུས་ནས་གཅིག་ཏུ་འདྲེས་པ་ལས་རང་ཉིད་རྡོ་རྗེ་འཆང་ཆེན་པོ། སྐུ་མདོག་སྔོན་པོ་རྡོ་རྗེ་དང་དྲིལ་བུ་འཛིན་པ། ཡུམ་ལ་འཁྱུད་པ། མཚན་དང་དཔེ་བྱད་འབར་བ། ཡུམ་རྡོ་རྗེ་སྙེམས་མ་སྐུ་མདོག་སྔོན་མོ། གྲི་གུག་དང་ཐོད་པ་འཛིན་པ། གཉིས་ཀའང་རུས་པ་དང་རིན་པོ་ཆེས་བརྒྱན་པར་གྱུར་པ་ལ་གོ་ཆ་གཉིས་བཅིངས་ཏེ། དབང་གི་ལྷ་ཐམས་ཅད་ཀྱིས་འདི་ནི་སངས་རྒྱས་ཐམས་ཅད་ལ་སོགས་པ་སྔགས་དང་བཅས་པས་ལག་པ་གཡས་པར་རྡོ་རྗེ་བྱིན་ནས་ཐོག་མཐའ་མེད་པའི་སེམས་དཔའ་ནི། རྡོ་རྗེ་སེམས་དཔའ་དགའ་བ་ཆེ། ཀུན་ཏུ་བཟང་པོ་ཀུན་བདག་ཉིད། རྡོ་རྗེ་སྙེམས་ཚུལ་བདག་པོའི་མཆོག། ཞེས་དེ་ཁོ་ན་ཉིད་གསུངས་ཤིང་དྲན་པས་རང་གི་སེམས་ཐུགས་རྡོ་རྗེ་དང་། འདི་ནི་རྣལ་འབྱོར་མ་ལ་སོགས་པས། དྲིལ་བུ་གཡོན་དུ་བྱིན་ནས། སྟོང་པ་ངོ་བོ་ཉིད་ཀྱིས་དག། ངོ་བོ་ཉིད་ཀྱིས་སྟོང་གྲོལ་བྱས། རང་བཞིན་དག་པའི་སེམས་ལྡན་པ། སྟོང་པ་དམ་པ་བྱེད་པར་འགྱུར། ཞེས་གསུང་ཞིང་དེ་ཁོ་

༄༅ ན་ཉིད་དྲན་པས། ངག་གསུང་རྡོ་རྗེ་དང་། རྡོ་རྗེ་ཆེ་དང་དྲིལ་བུ་ཆེ། ཧཱུྃ་ཤིག་རྡོ་རྗེར་བྱིན་གྱིས་བརླབས། དེ་རིང་རྡོ་རྗེ་སློབ་དཔོན་གྱུར། སློབ་མའི་ཚོགས་རྣམས་བསྡུ་བར་བྱིས། དེ་བཞིན་གཤེགས་པ་ཐམས་ཅད་ཀྱི། འདའ་བ་དུ་ནི་མི་མཛད་པ། དམ་ཚིག་ཕྱག་རྒྱ་ཞེས་སུ་བཤད། ཡིད་ཀྱི་ལུས་ནི་བརྟན་ཕྱིར་རོ། །ཞེས་ཕྱག་རྒྱའི་དེ་ཁོ་ན་ཉིད་གསུངས་ཤིང་། དེའི་དོན་རང་གིས་དྲན་པར་བྱས་པས། ལུས་སྐུ་རྡོ་རྗེར་གྱུར་པ་ལ་སྒྱུ་མ་བཞིན་དུ་ཐྲམ་པའི་ཚུལ་སོགས་པས་དབང་བསྐུར་བས། དྲི་མ་ཐམས་ཅད་དག། སློབ་དཔོན་གྱི་བྱ་བ་མཐའ་དག་ལ་དབང་བར་བྱས་ནས་མི་བསྐྱོད་པས་དབུ་བརྒྱན་པ་ལ། དབང་གི་ལྷ་ཐམས་ཅད་ཀྱིས། ཨོཾ་སུ་བྲ་ཏིཥྛ་བཛྲ་ཡེ་སྭཱ་ཧཱ། ཞེས་བརྗོད་ཅིང་མེ་ཏོག་གི་ཆར་ཕབ་པས་ཁམས་གསུམ་གྱི་ཆོས་ཀྱི་རྒྱལ་པོར་མངའ་གསོལ་བར་བསམ་པ་ནི། རྡོ་རྗེ་སློབ་དཔོན་གྱི་དབང་ངོ༎ ༎

༄༅ དེ་ནས་བླ་མས་རྡོ་རྗེ་སློབ་དཔོན་གྱི་བྱ་བ་མཐར་ཕྱིན་པར་བྱ་བའི་ཕྱིར། དེ་ཉིད་རིག་པའི་རྟུལ་འབྱོར་པས། མི་བྱ་བ་ནི་ཟུང་ཟད་མེད། དེ་ཉིད་ཤེས་ནས་དེ་ནས་ནི། དཔའ་བོས་འདོད་པ་ལྷ་སྤྱོད་དོ༎ ཞེས་ཀུན་དུ་སྤྱོད་པ་དང་། བདག་ཉིད་དཔའ་བོ་ཀུན་གྱི་དངོས། བདག་ཉིད་ལྷ་མོ་ཀུན་གྱི་གནས། དེ་ཕྱིར་བདག་གིས་ཐམས་ཅད་བྱ། བདག་ཉིད་ཧེ་རུ་ཀ་མཆོད་དོ༎ ཞེས་ལྷ་མཆོད་པ་དང་། རྟེན་ཅིང་འབྲེལ་པར་འབྱུང་ཆོས་ཅན། །སེམས་ཅན་སྒྱུ་མའི་རང་བཞིན་ནོ། །ཁམས་གསུམ་དེ་ལྟར་ཤེས་ནས་ནི། སེམས་ཅན་དོན་ནི་མཉམ་མེད་བྱས། ཞེས་སེམས་ཅན་གྱི་དོན་གྱི་རྗེས་སུ་གནང་བ་རྣམས་གནང་བར་བསམ་མོ༎ ༄༅ །དེ་ནས་བླ་མ་ཤཱཀྱ་ཐུབ་པའི་རྣམ་པ་འཛིན་པས། བདག་གི་སྤྱི་བོར་མི་འཛིགས་པ་སྦྱིན་པའི་ཕྱག་རྒྱ་གཏུགས་ཏེ། འདི་སྐད་ང་ཡིས་ལུང་བསྟན་ཏེ། འཁོར་ལོ་གསུམ་[illegible]་བདག་[illegible]ད་ཅན། ཁྱང་ཉིད་སངས་རྒྱས་ཀུན་རང་བཞིན། ཧེ་རུ་ཀ་དཔལ་

༄ ཞེས་བྱ་བའི། དེ་བཞིན་དུ་ཤེགས་པ་ཉིད་ཡིན་ནོ། ཨོཾ་བྲཱུཾ་ཧི་ཧུ་ཀི་ཧྲ་ཀི་ཧྲི་ཎ་ཧཱུཾཿ ཕཊ་ཏ་ཐཱ་ག་ཏ་སིད་དྷ་ས་མ་ཡེ་སྭཱཧཱ། ཧཱུར་ཧཱུ་ཕཊ་སྭཱ། ཁམས་གསུམ་གྱི་ནི་རྒྱལ་སྲིད་ཆེ། དཔལ་ལྡན་ཡོན་ཏན་འབྱུང་བའི་གནས། བདུད་ཚོགས་ཀུན་ལས་རྣམ་རྒྱལ་ཞིང་། ཕྱོང་ཕྱིར་མཆོག་ཏུ་རྟོགས་པ་ཡིན། ཞེས་གསུང་ཞིང་ལུང་བསྟན་ནས། དབུགས་ཕྱུང་བར་བསམ་མོ། །དེ་ལྟར་བླ་མའི་ལུས་ཀྱི་དཀྱིལ་འཁོར་དུ་བུམ་པའི་དབང་ཐོབ། ལུས་ཀྱི་དྲི་མ་དག། བསྐྱེད་པའི་རིམ་པ་བསྒོམ་པ་ལ་དབང་། སྤྲུལ་པའི་སྐུ་ཡི་རྟེན་འབྲེལ་མཛོད་དུ་བྱས་ཞེས་བརྟན་པར་བྱའོ། བུམ་པའི་དབང་ངོ།། ༄ །དེ་ནས་གསང་དབང་གི་དོན་དུ་མཎྜལ་ཕུལ་ནས། སྐྱོབ་མེད་སྐྱོབ་པ་སྐྱབས་མེད་སྐྱབས། དཔལ་ནི་འཁོར་ལོ་བདེ་བའི་མཆོག། རྒྱུ་མེད་པར་ནི་ཐུགས་རྗེ་ཆེ། མགོན་མེད་བདག་གི་མགོན་མཛོད་ཅིག། བདག་ཉིད་ཆེ་ཁྱོད་ཟེ་ལྟ་བར། གཙོ་བོས་བདག་ཀྱང་དེ་འདྲར་མཛོད། འཁོར་བ་འདམ་གྱི་ཚོགས་ཤང་དུ། བྱིང་བ་སྐྱབས་མེད་བདག་ལ་སྐྱོབས།། ཞེས་ལན་གསུམ་གསོལ་བ་བཏབ་ནས། གདོང་གཡོགས་ལ་འབྲུ་གསུམ་བཀོད་ཅིང་། བདུད་རྩི་ཕྱིན་གྱིས་བརླབས་ཏེ། བླ་མ་དཀྱིལ་འཁོར་གྱི་གཙོ་བོ་དང་གཉིས་སུ་མེད་པ། ཡབ་ཡུམ་སྙོམས་པར་ཞུགས་པའི་བདེ་བའི་ཐུགས་དེ་བཞིན་གཤེགས་པ་ཐམས་ཅད་བཀུག་པ་ཞལ་དུ་ཞུགས་ཐུགས་ཁར་འོད་དུ་ཞུ། གསང་བའི་གནས་ནས་ཐིག་ལེའི་རྣམ་པས་བབས་པས་བདག་གི་ལྕེ་ཐོག་ཏུ་གནང་བར་བསམ་ཞིང་། བླ་མས། འདི་ནི་དཔའ་བོ་ལྷ་མོ་རྣམས། དམ་ཚིག་སྨད་བྱུང་ཆེན་པོ་སྟེ། ཁམས་ལྔ་ལྡན་པ་རོས་རྟོགས་བྱེད། བདེ་བ་གང་དེ་ལྷུང་བར་གྱིས། ཇི་ལྟར་རྡོ་རྗེ་འཆང་ཚོགས་ཀྱིས། སྟོན་ཆད་སྲས་ནི་དབང་བསྐུར་བ། དེ་བཞིན་དུ་ནི་བྱང་ཆུབ་སེམས། བཟང་པོས་བུ་ཁྱོད་དབང་བསྐུར་རོ། །ཞེས་གསུངས་ནས་བཅང་བ་མྱངས་པས་ལུས་ཐམས་ཅད་གང་ཞིང་། རང་

༄༅། བཞིན་བརྒྱུད་ཟུའི་རྣམ་པར་རྟོག་པ་འགགས་ནས་གསུང་རྣམ་པར་དག་པ་འོད་དཔག་མེད་དུ་བསྒོམས་ལ། ཨ་ཧོ་མ་ཧཱ་སུ་ཁཾ༔ ཞེས་ལན་གསུམ་བརྗོད། དེ་ནས་ཨོཾ་ཨཱཿ ཧཱུྃ་གིས་གཏོང་གཡོགས་ཕྱེ་ལ། བྱང་ཆུབ་ཀྱི་སེམས་ཀྱི་དཀྱིལ་འཁོར་དུ་གསང་བའི་དབང་ཐོབ། ངག་གི་དྲི་མ་དག། ཙཎྜ་ལི་བསྒོམ་པ་ལ་དབང་། ཡོངས་སྒྲུབ་རྫོགས་པའི་སྐུའི་རྟེན་འབྲེལ་མཛོད་དུ་བྱུས་པར་བསམ་མོ། །གསང་བའི་དབང་ངོ་།། ༄༅ །།དེ་ནས་ཤེས་རབ་ཡེ་ཤེས་ཀྱི་དབང་གི་དོན་དུ་མཎྜལ་ཕུལ་ནས། སྔ་མ་བཞིན་གསོལ་བ་བཏབ་ལ། གཏོང་གཡོགས་ཏེ་འབྲུ་གསུམ་བརྗོད་ཅིང་ཕྱིན་གྱིས་བརླབས་ནས། རང་སྐད་ཅིག་གིས་བདེ་མཆོག་ཕྱག་བཅུ་གཉིས་པར་དམིགས་པ་ལ། བླ་མས་རིག་མ་ཡོངས་སུ་དག་པ་རྡོ་རྗེ་ཕག་མོར་བྱིན་གྱིས་བརླབས་པ་བཟུང་སྟེ། །ལྷ་མོ་འདི་ནི་ཕྱག་རྒྱ་ཆེ། །མཐའ་ཡས་བདེ་བ་སྦྱིན་པ་མོ། རྣམ་པ་ཀུན་དུ་ཕྱག་རྒྱ་ཡོངས། བུ་ཡིས་བླ་མེད་མཆོད་པར་གྱིས། ཅེས་གསུང་ནས་གནང་བ་དང་། དེ་ནས་རིག་མ་དེས། དཔའ་བོ་བྱང་ཆུབ་སེམས་ཟ་བར། ཁྱོད་ནི་སྤྱོ་བ་ཡིན་ནམ་ཅི། །དྲི་ཆེན་དྲི་ཆུ་སྣབས་དང་ཁྲག། རྩོགས་ཟ་ད་ལྷ་ཡིད་ཆེས་སམ། རྗེས་སུ་མཐུན་སྦྱོར་དམ་ཚིག་བཟང་། ཇི་ལྟར་དགའ་བ་སྦྱོར་ཅིག་བྱ། ཅེས་གསུངས་པའི་ལན་དུ། ཇི་ལྟར་གསུངས་པའི་དམ་ཚིག་རྫོགས། །ལྷ་མོ་བདག་ནི་ཅིས་མི་སྤྱོ། །བུད་མེད་རྟག་གུས་ཅིས་མི་བྱ། པད་མ་མཆོད་པར་ཅིས་མི་བགྱིད།། །ཞེས་ལན་བཏབ་པས། ལྷ་མོ་དེ་དགྱེས་ནས། པད་མ་ཁྲ་ཛ་ཧོ་ཅེས་གསུང་ཞིང་། རྩ་མཆོག་ཏུ་གྱུར་པའི་ཧཱུྃ་བསྐྱེད་ནས། དེ་པང་དུ་ཕྱིན་པ་རྡོ་རྗེ་ཕག་མོར་གསལ་བར་དམིགས་ཏེ། སྐུ་གསུང་ཐུགས་དང་། གནས་ལྔ་དང་། མཁའ་དང་གསང་བ་བྱིན་གྱིས་བརླབས་ནས། ལྷན་ཅིག་སྐྱེས་པའི་ཡེ་ཤེས་མངོན་དུ་བྱ་སྙམས་པས་སྙོམས་པར་ཞུགས་པས། དགའ་བ། མཆོག་དགའ དགའ་བྲལ་གྱི་དགའ་བ། ལྷན་ཅིག་སྐྱེས་

༄ པའི་དགའ་བ་རྣམས་སྐྱེས་ཏེ། བདེ་སྟོང་ཟུང་འཇུག་གི་ཏིང་ངེ་འཛིན་ལ་མཉམ་པར་བཞག་གོ།། །ཨ་མོ་དེས། དང་ནས་བཟུང་སྟེ་བུ་ཁྱོད་ཀྱིས། ཇི་སྲིད་བྱང་ཆུབ་སྙིང་པོ་འི་བར། མི་འདྲར་སེམས་ཅན་ཐམས་ཅད་ཀྱི། དོན་ནི་བདག་ཉིད་ཀུན་གྱིས་གྱིས། ཞེས་ཐེས་སུ་གནང་ནས། གཏོར་གཡོགས་ཕྱི་ལ། ཧྲ་གའི་དཀྱིལ་འཁོར་དུ། ཤེས་རབ་ཡེ་ཤེས་ཀྱི་དབང་ཐོབ། ཡིད་ཀྱི་དྲི་མ་དག། པོ་ཉའི་ལམ་བསྒོམ་པ་ལ་དབང་། ཆོས་ཀྱི་སྐུའི་རྟེན་འབྲེལ་མངོན་དུ་བྱས་པར་བསམ་མོ། ཤེས་རབ་ཡེ་ཤེས་ཀྱི་དབང་ཐོབ།། ༄ །དེ་ནས་དབང་བཞི་པའི་དོན་དུ་མཚོན་ཚུལ་ནས། ཁྱོད་ཞབས་པདྨ་བའི་བཀའ་དྲིན་གྱིས། གཙོ་བོ་དབང་བསྐུར་རྣམ་གསུམ་ཐོབ། །དེ་རིང་རིན་ཆེན་བཞི་པ་ཡང་། བདག་ལ་བཀའ་དྲིན་བསྐྱབ་ཏུ་གསོལ།། ཞེས་ལན་གསུམ་གསོལ་བ་བཏབ་ནས། གཏོར་གཡོགས་ལ་འབྲུ་གསུམ་བཪྫོད་ཅིང་བྱིན་གྱིས་བརླབས་ཏེ། ལུས་དཀྱིལ་ཀུང་ལག་པ་མཉམ་བཞག་གི་ཕྱག་རྒྱ་དངས་པ་ལ་བླ་མས། འདི་ནི་རང་ཉིད་མཐོང་པ་སྟེ། །ཕྱི་རོལ་ཡུལ་ནི་སྣང་བ་པའོ། རིགས་འདི་བོར་ནས་དེ་ལས་ནི། གཞན་པའི་ཐབས་ཀྱི་སངས་རྒྱས་མེད། རིག་མའི་བརྟུལ་ཞུགས་སྤྱོད་ཅིག་བྱ། བརྟུལ་ཞུགས་རྣམས་ཀྱི་བླ་མའི་བླ། ཞེས་གསུངས་པའི་དོན་མཐར་ཐུག་དེ་ཁོ་ན་ཉིད་ཀྱི་རྡོ་རྗེ་ཕག་མོ་ནི་རང་གི་སེམས་ཉིད་སྤྲོས་པ་ཐམས་ཅད་དང་བྲལ་བ་ཡིན་ལ། དེ་ཉིད་ཤེས་རབ་ཀྱི་ཕ་རོལ་ཏུ་ཕྱིན་མ་འང་ཡིན་ནོ་སྙམ་དུ་བསམས་ནས་མི་རྟོག་པའི་ངང་ལ་ཡིད་གཞག་གོ། །དེ་ནས་གཏོར་གཡོགས་ཕྱི་ལ། དོན་དམ་པ་བྱང་ཆུབ་སེམས་ཀྱི་དཀྱིལ་འཁོར་དུ་དབང་བཞི་པ་ཐོབ། བག་ཆགས་དང་བཅས་པའི་སྒྲིབ་པ་ཐམས་ཅད་སྦྱངས། བསམ་གྱིས་མི་ཁྱབ་པའི་ལམ་བསྒོམ་པ་ལ་དབང་། ངོ་བོ་ཉིད་ཀྱི་སྐུའི་རྟེན་འབྲེལ་མངོན་དུ་བྱས་པར་བསམ་མོ། དབང་བཞི་པའོ།། ༄ དེ་ནས་ལུས་དང་ལོངས་སྤྱོད་ཐམས་

༄༅། ཅད་ཡོན་དུ་ཕུལ་ནས། དེང་ནས་བཙམས་ཏེ་བདག་བྲན་དུ། ཁྱེད་ལ་བདག་ནི་འབུལ་ལགས་ན། ཁྱོད་ཀྱིས་སློབ་མར་གཟུང་བ་དང་། ཆ་ཡིས་ཀྱང་ནི་སྤུད་དུ་གསོལ། ཞེས་པས་གཏང་རག་དབུལ་ལོ།། །དེ་ནས་ཕྱི་ནང་གི་ལྷ་རྣམས་མཆོད་པའི་ཕྱིར། ཚོགས་ཀྱི་འཁོར་ལོ། ལྷག་གཏོར། བཀྲ་ཤིས་དང་བཅས་པའི་བར་ཚོ་ག་ལས་འབྱུང་བ་ལྟར་བྱ་སྟེ། མདུན་བསྐྱེད་ལ་མཆོད་ཅིང་བསྟོད་ནས། མ་འབྱོར་བ་དང་ཉམས་པ་དང་། གང་ཡང་བདག་རྨོངས་བློ་ཡིས་ནི། བགྱིས་པ་དང་ནི་བགྱིད་རྩལ་བ། །དེ་ཀུན་མགོན་པོས་བཟོད་པར་གསོལ། ཞེས་ཉེས་པ་བཟོད་པར་གསོལ་ནས། འཇིག་རྟེན་དང་འཇིག་རྟེན་ལས་འདས་པའི་དངོས་གྲུབ་མ་༄ ལུས་པ་རྩལ་དུ་གསོལ་ཞེས་གསོལ་བ་བཏབ་པས། སེམས་ཅན་ཐམས་ཅད་བདེར་གྱུར་ཅིག། སེམས་ཅན་ཐམས་ཅད་སྒྲིབ་མེད་པར། གང་གི་ལམ་གྱིས་གྲོལ་འགྱུར་བ། དེས་ནི་སངས་རྒྱས་ཉིད་ཐོབ་ཤོག། ཅེས་དགེ་བའི་རྩ་བ་བསྔོས་ནས། དཀྱིལ་འཁོར་ལ་མ་བསྙེམས་པའི་ལྷ་དང་། གཏོར་མའི་འགྲོན་རྣམས། ཨོཾ་ཁྱེད་ཀྱིས་སེམས་ཅན་དོན་ཀུན་མཛད། རྗེས་སུ་མཐུན་པའི་དངོས་གྲུབ་གསོལ། སངས་རྒྱས་ཡུལ་དུ་གཤེགས་ནས་ཀྱང་། སླར་ཡང་བྱོན་པར་མཛད་དུ་གསོལ། །ཨོཾ་བཛྲ་མུཿ་གཤེགས་སུ་གསོལ་ནས། རས་བྲིས་ཀྱི་དཀྱིལ་འཁོར་ལ་བསྙེམ་པ་ནི། རབ་ཏུ་གནས་པའི་མཆོག་ཏུ་འགྱུར་བའི་ཕྱིར་བརྟན་པར་བཞུགས་སུ་གསོལ་ལོ།། རྟེན་མེད་ན་ཡེ་ཤེས་པ་གཤེགས་སུ་གསོལ་ལ། དམ་ཚིག་པ་བདག་ལ་བསྡུའོ།། དེ་ནས་བདག་ཉིད་གོ་ཆ་གསུམ་གྱིས་བསྲུངས་ལ། ལས་ཀྱི་རྗེས་བསྡུས་ནས། གནས་སྐབས་དང་རྗེས་སུ་འབྲེལ་པའི་རྣལ་འབྱོར་གྱིས་གནས་པར་བྱའོ། །དབང་བསྐུར་བླ་མ་ལས་ཐོབ་བཞིན། རང་གིས་བླངས་ཤིང་གོམས་བྱས་པས། མ་ལུས་རྒྱལ་བས་གཅིག་ཅར་དུ། ཉིད་ཇི་བཞིན་དུ་དབང་བསྐུར་འགྱུར། འདིའི་ཚུལ་གྱིས་གཞན་དག་ཀྱང་། རྗེས་སུ་གཟུང་བར་

༄ ཧུང་ཨོད་ཀྱི། དོན་ཀྱང་མ་སྨིན་པ་ལ་མིན། གང་ཕྱིར་མཆོག་གི་ལས་ཡིན་ཕྱིར། སྒྲུབ་པའི་གཙོ་བོས་སྦྱར་བའི་གཞུང་། རིམ་པ་ཉིན་ལས་བརྒྱད་པ། ཚུལ་འདི་དཔལ་ལྡན་ས་སྐྱའི། །ཁྱད་པར་འཕགས་པའི་དཔལ་འབྱོར་ཡིན། །དུ་ཁལ་དུ་ར་མིས་ཀྱིས་བསྐྱལ་ཞིང་། དེའི་ཞབས་ཀྱང་འདུན་པའི་ཏོར། །འཕགས་པས་བཀོད་པའི་དགེ་བ་ཡིས། །བདག་པ་ཞེན་ཏེ་དུ་ཀར་གྱུར་ཅིག།། ༄ །།སློབ་དཔོན་རྡོ་རྗེ་དྲིལ་བུ་པའི་གཞུང་གི་རྗེས་སུ་འབྲང་བ། །འཁོར་ལོ་བདེ་མཆོག་ལུས་ཀྱི་དཀྱིལ་འཁོར་དུ་བདག་ཉིད་འཇུག་ཅིང་དབང་བླང་བའི་ཆོ་ག་འདི་ནི། འཕགས་པས་རྩ་མོ་བྱའི་ལོ། ས་གའི་ཟླ་བའི་ཚེས་ཉི་ཤུ་བདུན་ལ་ཤིང་ཀུན་དུ་སྦྱར་བའི་ཡི་གེ་པ་ནི་ཨ་ཙར་དོ།། དགེའོ།།

༄༅། །དཔལ་འཁོར་ལོ་སྡོམ་པའི་རིམ་པ་ལྔའི་མན་ངག་ཅེས་བྱ་བ།།

༈ དཔལ་རྡོ་རྗེ་མཁའ་འགྲོ་ལ་ཕྱག་འཚལ་ལོ། །གང་གི་དྲིན་གྱིས་སྐད་ཅིག་ལ། གཉིས་མེད་ཡེ་ཤེས་ཉེར་འཆར་བ། །བླ་མའི་ཞབས་ལ་ཕྱག་འཚལ་ནས། བསྒོམ་པའི་རིམ་པ་འདིར་བཤད་བྱ།། །དེ་ལ་ཡང་དག་པའི་བླ་མས་ཁྲི་དང་ནང་གི་བདག་ཉིད་ཀྱི་འཁོར་ལོ་སྡོམ་པའི་དཀྱིལ་འཁོར་དུ་དབང་བསྐུར་བ་དང་། འདི་ཉིད་ཀྱི་བྱིན་གྱིས་བརླབས་ཀྱིས་ཡོང་སུ་སྨིན་པར་བྱས་ཤིང་། གདམས་པ་དང་། རྗེས་སུ་བསྟན་པ་ཉེ་བར་ཐོད་པ་བསྐྱེད་པའི་རིམ་པ་ལ་དམིགས་པ་ཙུང་ཟད་བརྟན་པ་རྫོགས་པའི་རིམ་པ་བསྒོམ་པར་འདོད་པའི་གང་ཟག་གིས་ཐོ་རངས་ལ་སོགས་པའི་དུས་སུ་སྟན་བདེ་བ་ལ་དཀྱིལ་མོ་ཀྲུམས་ཀྱིས་འདུག་ལ། འདི་ཉིད་ཀྱི་བསྐྱེད་པའི་རིམ་པ་བསྒོམ་པ་སྔོན་དུ་སོང་ནས། རང་གི་སྙིང་ཁའི་ཧཱུྃ་ལས་འོད་འཕྲོས་པས་ཕྱིའི་སྣོད་བཅུད་ཐམས་ཅད་རང་གི་ལུས་ལ་བསྡུ། ལུས་ཡང་སྔའི་སྒོ་ནས་རང་གི་ཐུགས་ཁར་བསྡུ། རང་ཉིད་ཕྱག་གཉིས་པར་བསྡུས་པའི་སྤྱི་བོར་བླ་མ་བསྒོམས་ལ། མོས་གུས་དྲག་ཏུ་བསྒོམ་ཞིང་བདག་གི་རྒྱུད་ལ་ཡང་དག་པའི་ཏིང་ངེ་འཛིན་བསྐྱེད་དུ་གསོལ་ཞེས་གསོལ་བ་གདབ། དེ་ནས་སྙིང་གི་ནང་དུ་ཨ་ཟླ་བའི་དཀྱིལ་འཁོར་སྲན་མ་ཕྱེད་ཚལ་ཙམ་གྱིས་སྟེང་དུ་རང་གི་ཤེས་པ་ཐིག་ལེ་དཀར་དམར་ཡུངས་དཀར་ཙམ་གཅིག་ཏུ་བསམས་ལ། །དེ་ལ་སེམས་གཟུང་རིམ་གྱིས་རླུང་ཡང་ཁ་སྦྱར་འཇམ་པོ་བྱ། །གོམས་ནས་སེམས་ཟིན་པ་དང་ཡིད་གཞན་དུ་མི་འགྲོ་ཞིང་རྩེ་གཅིག་ཏུ་གནས་པ་དང་། བདེ་གསལ་གྱི་ཏིང་ངེ་འཛིན་སྐྱེའོ། དེ་ལ་བསྟན་པ་དང་དབང་པོ་གཞན་ལ་ཡང་སྒྲོ་སྐྱེ། རྟེན་འགྲོ་ཕྱི་མ་ལྟར་བྱས་ལ། དངོས་བཞིའི་ཚེ་མིག་གི་འབྲས་བུ་གཉིས་ཀྱི་ནང་དུ། །ཟླ་བ་ལ་གནས་པའི་ཐིག་ལེ་དཀར་པོ་ཤིན་ཏུ་ཕྲ་བ་རེ་བསྒོམས་ལ། མིག་གཙུམས་ལ་ཡིད་གཟུང་། ཙུང་ཟད་ཐེན་པ་དང་གཟུགས་སྣ་ཚོགས་ལ་བལྟ་

༄ ཞིང་། ཐིག་ལེ་ལ་ཡིད་གཏད་དེ་གཞན་ལ་སེམས་འཕྲོ་མི་གཞུག། དེ་གོམས་པས་ཐིག་ལེའི་རྣམས་པ་གསལ་ཞིང་། གཟུགས་གང་མཐོང་བའི་སྟེང་དུ་ཏིང་ངེ་འཛིན་སྐྱེའོ།། དེ་ལ་བརྟན་པ་ཙུང་ཟད་ཐོབ་པ་དང་། ཐིག་ལེ་དེ་སྙིང་ཁར་བསྡུས་ལ། སྙིང་ཁའི་ཐིག་ལེ་དེ་སྔར་བས་ཀྱང་གསལ་ཞིང་འབར་བར་བསྒོམས་ནས་མཉམ་པར་བཞག་པའི་ཏིང་ངེ་འཛིན་མཆོག་སྐྱེའོ།། དེའི་རྗེས་ལ་རྣ་བར་སྒྲོ་སྟེ། སྔོན་འགྲོ་སྔར་ལྟར་བསྒོམས་ལ། དངོས་གཞི་ལ་རྣ་བ་གཉིས་ཀྱི་ནང་དུ་ཟླ་བ་ལ་གནས་པའི་ཐིག་ལེ་སྔོན་པོ་གཉིས་བསྒོམས་པ་སྒྲ་མེད་པའི་ས་ཕྱོགས་སུ་ཡིད་གཟུང་། ཙུང་ཟད་བྲིན་པ་དང་། སྒྲ་སྐད་ཚོགས་མཉེན་ཞིང་ཐིག་ལེ་ལ་ཡིད་གཏད་དེ། གཞན་དུ་སེམས་འཕྲོ་མི་གཞུག། དེ་གོམས་པས་ཐིག་ལེ་དམིགས་པ་གསལ་ཞིང་། སྒྲ་གང་དུ་ཐོས་པའི་སྟེང་དུ་ཏིང་ངེ་འཛིན་སྐྱེའོ།། །དེ་ལ་བརྟན་པ་ཙུང་ཟད་ཐོབ་པ་དང་། ཐིག་ལེ་དེ་སྙིང་ཁའི་ཐིག་ལེ་ལ་བསྡུས་པས་ཐིག་ལེ་དེ་སྔར་བས་ཀྱང་གསལ་ཞིང་འབར་བར་བསྒོམས་ལ། མཉམ་པར་བཞག་པའི་ཏིང་ངེ་འཛིན་མཆོག་སྐྱེའོ།། །དེའི་རྗེས་ལ་སྣར་སྒྲོ་སྟེ་སྔོན་འགྲོ་སྔར་ལྟར་བསྒོམས་ལ། དངོས་གཞི་ལ་སྣ་བུག་སོ་སོ་འམ། བུ་གའི་འཛོམ་སོ་འི་ནང་དུ་ཟླ་བའི་སྟེང་དུ་ཐིག་ལེ་སེར་པོ་བསྒོམ་ལ། དྲི་མི་བྲོ་བའི་སར་ཡིད་གཟུང་། །ཙུང་ཟད་བྲིན་པ་དང་། དྲི་སྣ་ཚོགས་བསྣམས་ཞིང་ཐིག་ལེ་ལ་ཡིད་གཏད་དེ། གཞན་དུ་སེམས་འཕྲོ་མི་གཞུག། དེ་ལ་གོམས་པས་ཐིག་ལེའི་དམིགས་པ་གསལ་ཞིང་། དྲི་གང་ཚོར་བའི་སྟེང་དུ་ཏིང་ངེ་འཛིན་སྐྱེའོ། དེ་ལ་བརྟན་པ་ཙུང་ཟད་ཐོབ་པ་དང་། ཐིག་ལེ་དེ་སྙིང་ཁའི་ཐིག་ལེ་ལ་བསྡུས་པས་ཐིག་ལེ་དེ་སྔར་བས་ཀྱང་གསལ་ཞིང་། འབར་བར་བསྒོམས་ལ་མཉམ་པར་བཞག་པའི་ཏིང་ངེ་འཛིན་མཆོག་སྐྱེའོ། དེའི་རྗེས་ལ། ལྕེར་སྒྲོ་སྟེ། སྔོན་འགྲོ་སྔར་ལྟར་བསྒོམས་ལ་དངོས་གཞི་ལ་ལྕེའི་རྩ་བར་ཟླ་བའི་སྟེང་དུ་ཐིག་ལེ་

༄༅ དམར་པོ་བསྒོམས་ལ། རོ་མི་ཀྱང་བར་ཡིད་གཏུང་། །ཚུར་ཟད་བྱིན་པ་དང་། རོ་སྣ་ཚོགས་ཀྱང་ཞིང་། ཐིག་ལེ་ལ་ཡིད་གཏད་དེ། གཞན་དུ་སེམས་འཕྲོར་མི་གཞུག། དེ་ལ་གོམས་པས་ཐིག་ལེའི་དམིགས་པ་གསལ་ཞིང་། རོ་གང་མྱོང་བའི་སྟེང་དུ་ཏིང་ངེ་འཛིན་སྐྱེ་རོ། དེ་ལ་བརྟན་པ་ཚུར་ཟད་ཐོབ་པ་དང་། ཐིག་ལེ་དེ་སྙིང་ཁའི་ཐིག་ལེ་ལ་བསྡུས་ལ། ཐིག་ལེ་དེ་སྔར་བས་ཀྱང་གསལ་ཞིང་འབར་བར་ བསྒོམས་ནས་མཉམ་པར་བཞག་པས་ཏིང་ངེ་འཛིན་མཆོག་སྐྱེ་རོ།། །དེའི་རྗེས་ལ་ལུས་ལ་སྦྱོ་སྦྱོ། སྔོན་འགྲོ་སྔར་ལྟར་བསྒོམས་ལ། དངོས་གཞི་ལ་གསང་གནས་ཀྱི་རྩ་བའི་ནང་ངམ། དཔྲལ་བར་ཟླ་བའི་སྟེང་དུ་ཐིག་ལེ་ཐུང་ཁྲུ་བསྒོམས་ལ། གང་ལ་འཇང་མི་རེག་པར་ཡིད་གཏུང་། ཚུར་ཟད་བྱིན་པ་དང་། རེག་བྱ་སྣ་ཚོགས་ལ་རེག་ གཅིང་ཀྱང་ས་ལ། ཐིག་ལེ་ལ་ཡིད་གཏད་དེ། གཞན་དུ་སེམས་འཕྲོར་མི་གཞུག། དེ་ལ་གོམས་པས་ཐི་ལེའི་དམིགས་པ་གསལ་ཞིང་། རེག་བྱ་གང་ལ་རེག་པའི་སྟེང་དུ་ཏིང་ངེ་འཛིན་མཆོག་སྐྱེ་རོ།། དེ་ལ་བརྟན་པ་ཚུར་ཟད་ཐོབ་པ་དང་། ཐིག་ལེ་དེ་སྙིང་ཁའི་ཐིག་ལེ་ལ་བསྡུས་པས་ཐིག་ལེ་དེ་སྔར་བས་ཀྱང་གསལ་ཞིང་འབར་བར་བསྒོམས་ནས། མཉམ་པར་བཞག་པས་ཏིང་ངེ་འཛིན་མཆོག་སྐྱེ་རོ། །དེའི་རྗེས་ལ་ཀུན་དུ་གཡོ་བའི་ཡིད་ལ་དམིགས་ ཞིང་བསྒོམ་ཏེ། སྔོན་འགྲོ་སྔར་ལྟར་བསྒོམས་ལ། དངོས་གཞི་ལ་སྙིང་ཁའི་ཐིག་ལེ་དཀར་དམར་གྱི་སྟེང་དུ་དེ་བས་ཕྲ་བའི་ཐིག་ལེ་དམར་སྐྱ་གཅིག་བསྒོམས་ལ། །རིན་དུ་དབེན་པའི་གནས་སུ་ཡིད་གཏུང་ངོ་། ཚུར་ཟད་བྱིན་པ་དང་ཉོན་མོངས་པ་སྣ་ཚོགས་སྐྱེ་བའི་ཡུལ་དང་བཅས་པའི་གནས་སུ་བསྒོམ་ཞིང་། འདོད་ཆགས་ལ་སོགས་པའི་ཉོན་མོངས་པ་གང་སྐྱེས་པའི་ཡུལ་དང་། །ཉོན་མོངས་པ་ཀུན་དུ་རྒྱུ་བ་ཉིད་ཐིག་ལེ་སྔོན་པོ་ལ་བསྒོམ་ཞིང་ཡིད་གཏུང་ངོ་། དེ་གོམས་པས་ཐིག་ལེའི་དམིགས་པ་གསལ་ཞིང་། ཉོན་མོངས་

༄ པ་མི་སྤྲོ་བ་འམ་ཙུད་ཟད་སྤྲོས་ཀྱང་རང་ཡུལ་དུ་འགྱུར་རོ།། །དེ་ལ་ཙུང་ཟད་བརྟན་པ་ཐོབ་པ་དང་། ཐིག་ལེ་དེ་འོག་གི་ཐིག་ལེ་དམར་རྒྱ་ལ་ཐིམ། དེའང་འོག་གི་ཐིག་ལེ་དཀར་དམར་ལ་ཐིམ། །དེའང་ཟླ་བ་ལ་ཐིམ་ཟླ་བའང་ནམ་མཁའ་ལ་སྤྲིན་ཡལ་བ་ལྟར་ཡལ་ནས་སྟོང་པ་ལ་མཉམ་པར་བཞག་པས་ནི་གནས་མཆོག་སྐྱེ་རོ།། །མཐར་མཉམ་གཞག་ལས་ལྡང་བའི་ཚེ་སྐད་ཅིག་གིས་ཟླ་བ་དང་། ཐིག་ལེ་རྣམས་རིམ་གྱིས་སྒྲུབ་པར་བལྟ་ཞིང་། རང་ཉིད་ཧེ་རུ་ཀ་དང་། ཕྱིའི་ཆོས་རྣམས་ཀྱང་སྣང་བཞིན་དུ་རང་བཞིན་མེད་པར་བལྟས་ལ་ལྡང་ངོ་། དེ་ལྟར་སོ་སོའི་རྟགས་མ་བྱུང་གི་བར་དུ་བསྒོམས་ཤིང་། མཐར་ཕྱིན་པ་ན་སྟོང་པ་ཞི་གནས་དང་། བདེ་གསལ་ལྷག་མཐོང་གི་ཏིང་ངེ་འཛིན་སྐྱེས་ནས། ཏིང་ངེ་འཛིན་གྱི་རྒྱུན་དེས་མཐོང་ལམ་གྱི་ཡེ་ཤེས་སྐྱེས་ནས། སངས་རྒྱས་ཉིད་འབྱུང་བར་འགྱུར་རོ་ཞེས་གསུངས་སོ། ས་བོན་དང་བཅས་པའི་བདག་བྱིན་གྱིས་བརླབ་པའི་རིམ་པའོ།། ༄ །གཞན་ཡང་འདི་ཉིད་ཀྱི་བསྒོམ་པའི་ཚུལ་གཉིས་པ་ནི་བསྐྱེད་པའི་རིམ་པ་ནས། བླ་མ་ལ་གསོལ་བ་གདབ་པའི་བར་ཟླ་མ་ལྟར་བསྒོམས་ལ། རྩོལ་བ་མེད་པར་སྣའི་སྒོ་ནས་རླུང་ཞི་བའི་ཚུལ་གྱིས་དྲུར་གཞུག་གོ། དེ་ནས་རླུང་ཕྱིར་རྒྱུ་བའི་ཚེ་རྟོག་བཅས་ཀྱི་ཡིད་འོང་ཁ་དོག་དམར་སྨུག་གི་ཚུལ་དུ་སྙིང་ཁ་ནས་འགྲོགས་ཏེ། རླུང་གང་ནས་རྒྱུ་བའི་སྣ་བུག་གི་སྒོ་ནས་ཕྱིར་མི་འབུད་པར། ཕྱིལ་དེ་འཕྱིལ་བར་བསམ། ནང་དུ་འཇུག་པའི་ཚེ་རླུང་དང་འགྲོགས་ནས་སྙིང་གི་བར་དུ་སྟིག གནས་པའི་ཚེ། སྙིང་གི་ནང་དུ་ཐིམ་ནས་མི་གཡོ་བར་བསམ། དེ་ལྟར་གྲངས་མི་གཟུང་ཞིང་སེམས་རྣམ་པར་མི་གཡེང་བར་རྒྱུན་དུ་བསྒོམས་པས། རླུང་ནང་དུ་འཇུག་པ་དང་གནས་པའི་ཤས་ཆེ་བར་འགྱུར་ཞིང་། དེའི་ཚེ་མི་རྟོག་པའི་ཏིང་ངེ་འཛིན་ཡང་སྐྱེ་བར་འགྱུར་རོ། དེ་ལ་བརྟེན་ནས་དབང་པོ་རྣམས་ལ་སྦྱོ་བར་བྱ་སྟེ། རྩལ་དེ་ཉིད་ཀྱིས་སྣ་སྒོ་ནས་རླུང་ཕྱིའི་

༈ འགྲོ་ནང་འདུག་གནས་པ་དང་བསྡུན་ནས་མིག་ནས་འོད་དཀར་པོ་དང་། ན་བ་ནས་ནག་པོ་དང་། སྣ་ནས་སེར་པོ་དང་། ལྕེ་ནས་དམར་པོ་དང་། གསང་གནས་ནས་ལྗང་ཁུ་འབྱུང་བ་དང་། འདུག་པ་དང་དེ་ཉིད་དུ་གནས་པར་རིང་དུ་བསྒོམས་པས། ནང་དུ་འདུག་པ་དང་། གནས་པ་ཤས་ཆེ་བར་འགྱུར་ཞིང་། དེའི་ཚེ་ཡུལ་སོ་སོའི་སྟེང་དུ་མི་རྟོག་པ་སྐྱེས་པ་དང་། གོང་གི་ཚུལ་བཞིན་དབང་པོ་ལྔའི་འོད་རྣམས་རིམ་པས་སྙིང་ཁར་བསྡིམས་ནས་མཉམ་པར་བཞག་པས་མི་རྟོག་པའི་ཏིང་ངེ་འཛིན་མཆོག་སྐྱེ་བར་འགྱུར་རོ།། མཉམ་བཞག་ལས་ལྡང་བའི་ཚུལ་ཡང་སྔ་མ་དང་མཚུངས་པ་ཉིད་དོ། །དེ་ལྟར་རྣལ་འབྱོར་གཉིས་ཀ་ལ་གོམས་པས་གནས་སྐབས་སུ་བསྐལ་པའི་ཡུལ་རྣམས་མཐོང་བ་ལ་སོགས་པའི་མངོན་པར་ཤེས་པ་རྣམས་འབྱུང་ཞིང་། མཆོག་གི་དངོས་གྲུབ་ཀྱང་ཐོབ་པར་འགྱུར་རོ། ས་བོན་མེད་པའི་བདག་བྱིན་གྱིས་བརླབ་པ་སྟེ། བདག་བྱིན་གྱིས་བརླབ་པའི་རིམ་པའོ།།

དེ་ནས་འདིའི་རིམ་པ་གཉིས་པ་བསྒོམས་པའི་ཚུལ་ནི། སྔོན་འགྲོ་སྔ་མ་ལྟར་བསྒོམས་ལ། ལུས་ཀྱི་འཁྲུལ་འཁོར་དང་ལྡན་པས་སྣ་བུག་གང་ནས་རྒྱུ་བ་ནས། རླུང་ལྡང་འདུག་གནས་པ་ཅི་བདེར་ལེན་འགག་རྒྱུར་བཙུག་ནས། །མཐར་འདུག་པའི་ཚེ་རླུང་འོད་ཀྱི་ཚུལ་དུ་རྡུབས་ནས་སྟེང་འོག་གི་རླུང་ཁ་སྦྱར་བས། ལུས་ཐམས་ཅད་འོད་ཀྱིས་གསལ་བར་བྱས་པའི་མཐུས་སྤྱི་བོ འི་མཐོ་གང་ཙམ་གྱི་སྟེང་དུ་ཧཱུྃ་ཧྲོ་སྐུ་ལས་བྱུང་བའི་སྣ་ཚོ གས་རྡོ་རྗེ་ཤར་དཀར། ལྷོ་སེར། ནུབ་དམར། །བྱང་ལྗང་། །ཕྱི་བ་སྔོན་པོར་བསྐྱེད་པའི་ནང་དུ་ཆོས་འབྱུང་དམར་སྐྱ་སྟེང་དུ་ཟུར་གསུམ་དང་། འོག་ཏུ་ཟུར་ཅིག་པའི་ནང་དུ། རྡོ་རྗེ་དམར་པོ་རྩེ་ལྔ་པའི་སྟེང་གི་རྩེ་མོར་ཟླ་བ་ལ་གནས་པའི་ཧཱུྃ་དཀར་དམར་བསམས་པའི་སྟེང་གི་ཐིག་ལེ་ཤིན་དུ་ཕྲ་བ་ལ་ཡིད་གཏད་དོ།། རླུང་མ་ཐུབ་ན་རིམ་གྱིས་བཏང་ལ། །ཡང་

༄༅ སྟར་བཞིན་རླུང་ཁ་སྦྱར་ལ་བསྒོམ་མོ། །གལ་ཏེ་སེམས་གཡེངས་ན་ཐིག་ལེ་ལས་འོད་ཟེར་དཀར་དམར་འོག་ཏུ་འཕྲོས་པས། །སྤྱི་གཙུག་ཚངས་པའི་བུ་ག་ནས་མར་ཞུགས་ཤིང་། རིམ་གྱིས་ལུས་ཐམས་ཅད་འོད་ཟེར་དཀར་དམར་གྱིས་གང་བའི་ལུས་བདེ་བ་དང་། སེམས་མི་རྟོག་པར་གྱུར་བར་བསམ་ཞིང་། རླུང་ཁ་སྦྱར་ཡང་ཡང་བསྒོམས་པས་སེམས་མི་གཡེང་བར་འགྱུར་རོ།། བརྟན་ཞིང་གོམས་པས་བདེ་བ་དང་། མི་རྟོག་པའི་ཏིང་ངེ་འཛིན་རྒྱུན་མི་ཆད་པ་དང་། མཉམ་པར་འཇོག་པ་དང་། ལྡང་བའང་འདོད་པ་ཙམ་ལ་རག་ལས་པར་འགྱུར་རོ།། དེ་ནས་གཞན་ལ་སྦྱོ་བ་ནི། སྔོན་འགྲོ་སྟར་བཞིན་བསྒོམས་ལ། སྤྱི་བོའི་སྣ་ཚོགས་རྡོ་རྗེ། ཆོས་འབྱུང་རྡོ་རྗེ་དང་བཅས་པ་མིག་གི་འབྲས་བུ་གཉིས་ཀྱི་ནང་དུ་བསྒོམ་ཞིང་། རླུང་གི་རྣལ་འབྱོར་དང་། སེམས་གཡེངས་ན་ལུས་ཀྱི་ནང་ན་མར་སྦྱོ་བ་སྔ་མ་ལྟར་བསྒོམས་པས། གཟུགས་ཀྱིས་མི་གཡེང་ཞིང་གཟུགས་ཀྱི་སྟེང་དུ་ཏིང་ངེ་འཛིན་སྐྱེ་བ་དང་། ལྷའི་མིག་གི་མངོན་པར་ཤེས་པ་འཆར་བར་འགྱུར་རོ།། དེ་ལ་བརྟན་པ་དང་། རྣ་བ་གཉིས་ཀྱིས་ནང་དུ་དམིགས་ནས། སྒྲས་མི་གཡེང་ཞིང་། སྒྲ་ཡི་སྟེང་དུ་ཏིང་ངེ་འཛིན་སྐྱེ་བ་དང་། ལྷའི་རྣ་བའི་མངོན་པར་ཤེས་པ་སྐྱེས་ཀྱི་པར་དུ་བསྒོམ་མོ། དེ་ལ་བརྟན་པ་དང་། སྣའི་བུ་ག་གཉིས་སུ་དམིགས་ནས། དྲིས་མི་གཡེངས་ཞིང་། དྲིའི་སྟེང་དུ་ཏིང་ངེ་འཛིན་སྐྱེ་བ་དང་། སྣའི་མངོན་པར་ཤེས་པ་སྐྱེས་ཀྱི་བར་དུ་བསྒོམ་མོ། དེ་ལ་བརྟན་པ་དང་། ལྕེའི་དཀྱིལ་དུ་དམིགས་ནས། རོས་མི་གཡེང་ཞིང་། རོ་འི་སྟེང་དུ་ཏིང་ངེ་འཛིན་སྐྱེ་བ་དང་། ལྕེའི་མངོན་པར་ཤེས་པ་སྐྱེས་པའི་བར་དུ་བསྒོམ་མོ། དེ་ལ་བརྟན་པ་དང་རྡོ་རྗེ་རྩེ་མོ་དང་། སྨིན་མཚམས་གཉིས་ཀྱི་བར་དུ་རེག་འཇོག་དུ་དམིགས་ནས། རེག་བྱས་མི་གཡེང་ཞིང་རེག་བྱའི་སྟེང་དུ་ཏིང་ངེ་འཛིན་སྐྱེ་བ་དང་། ལུས་ཀྱི་མངོན་

ཧཱུྃ པར་ཤེས་པ་སྐྱེས་པའི་བར་དུ་བསྒོམ་མོ། དེ་ལ་བརྟན་པ་དང་སྙིང་གི་ནང་དུ་དམིགས་ནས། ཕྱི་ནང་གི་ཆོས་ཀྱི་རྣམ་པ་ཡིད་ལ་བྱེད་པས་མི་གཡེང་ཞིང་། ཆོས་ཀྱི་དབྱིངས་ཀྱི་སྟེང་དུ་ཏིང་ངེ་འཛིན་སྐྱེ་བ་དང་། ཕ་རོལ་གྱི་སེམས་ཤེས་པའི་མངོན་པར་ཤེས་པ་སྐྱེས་ཀྱི་བར་དུ་བསྒོམ་མོ།། དེ་ནས་སྙིང་ཁ་ཆོས་ཀྱི་འཁོར་ལོ་འི་ལྟེ་བའི་ཧཱུྃ་དང་བཅས་པ་རྣམས་ལ་གནས་པའི་ཡི་གེ་རེ་ཐིག་ལེ་རྣམས་ལ་རིམ་པ་བཞིན་སེམས་གཟུང་ཞིང་འོད་སྤྲོ་བ་དང་། རླུང་ཁ་སྦྱར་གྱི་བསྒོམས་པ་གོམས་པའི་རྣལ་འབྱོར་གྱིས་ཟག་པ་ཟད་པའི་མངོན་པར་ཤེས་པ་འཆར་བར་འགྱུར་རོ། དེ་ནས་སྤྱི་བོ་བདེ་བ་ཆེན་པོ་འི་འཁོར་ལོ་འི་ལྟེ་བའི་ཧཾ་དང་། ཙ་འདབ་ཀྱི་ཡི་གེ་རྣམས་ལ་ཐིག་ལེ་བཀོད་པ་ལ་རིམ་པ་བཞིན་སེམས་གཟུང་ཞིང་འོད་སྤྲོ་བ་དང་། རླུང་ཁ་སྦྱར་གྱི་བསྒོམ་པ་གོམས་པའི་རྣལ་འབྱོར་གྱིས། གནས་རིས་གོང་མའི་ལྷའི་ཚོགས་མཐོང་བ་དང་། བདེ་བ་ཆེན་པོ་འི་ཏིང་ངེ་འཛིན་སྐྱེ་བར་འགྱུར་རོ།། ཧཱུྃ །དེ་ནས་མགྲིན་པ་ལོངས་སྤྱོད་ཀྱི་འཁོར་ལོ་འི་ལྟེ་བའི་ཨོཾ་དང་འདབ་མའི་ཡི་གེ་རྣམས་ལ་ཐིག་ལེ་བཀོད་པ་ལ་རིམ་པ་བཞིན་སེམས་གཟུང་ཞིང་འོད་སྤྲོ་བ་དང་། རླུང་ཁ་སྦྱར་གྱི་བསྒོམ་པ་གོམས་པའི་རྣལ་འབྱོར་གྱིས་བསྟན་བཅོས་ཐམས་ཅད་ཤེས་པ་དང་། ཚིག་གི་མཆོག་འགྲུབ་པར་འགྱུར་རོ།། དེ་ནས་ལྟེ་བ་སྤྲུལ་པའི་འཁོར་ལོ་འི་ལྟེ་བའི་ཨཾ་དང་། ཙ་འདབ་ཀྱི་ཡི་གེ་རྣམས་ལ་ཐིག་ལེ་བཀོད་པ་ལ་རིམ་པ་བཞིན་སེམས་བཟུང་ཞིང་། འོད་སྤྲོ་བ་དང་། རླུང་ཁ་སྦྱར་གྱི་བསྒོམ་པ་གོམས་པའི་རྣལ་འབྱོར་གྱིས་ལྷའི་མཆོག་ལས་སྐྱེས་པའི་བུ་མོ་རྣམས་ལ་ལོངས་སྤྱོད་པ་དང་། སྤྲུལ་པ་དང་། ལོངས་སུ་སྤྱོད་པའི་རྫུ་འཕྲུལ་ཡང་ཐོབ་པར་འགྱུར་རོ།། རྣམ་པ་སྣ་ཚོགས་པའི་རྡོ་རྗེའི་རིམ་པའོ།། །གཞན་ཡང་འདི་ཉིད་ཀྱི་བསྒོམ་པའི་ཚུལ་གཉིས་པ་ནི་སྔོན་དུ་འགྲོ་བ་སྦྱོར་མ་དང་མཚུངས་ཤིང་། དངོས་གཞི་ལ་སྣའི་སྒོ་ནས་རླུང་རྒྱུ་བ་བརྟགས་པས། ཕཡས་

༄ ནས་རྒྱ་ན་ཕྱིར་འགྲོ་བའི་ཚེ་མཛོད་སྤུར་ཉི་མའི་དཀྱིལ་འཁོར་སེན་མོ་ བཀྲིཾས་པ་ཙམ་གཅིག་བསྒོམས་པ་ལ་རླུང་རྣམས་ཐིམ་པར་བསམ།། ཡང་ཕྱིར་རྒྱུ་བའི་ཚེ་ཉི་མའི་སྟེང་དུ་ཟླ་བའི་དཀྱིལ་འཁོར་ཉི་མའི་ཚད་དང་མཉམ་པ་གཅིག་བསམས་པ་ལ་རླུང་བསྟེམ། ཡང་གསུཾ་པ་རྒྱུ་བའི་ཚེ་ཟླ་བའི་སྟེང་དུ་སྐར་མ་ལྷ་བུའི་ཐིག་ལེ་ལྔ་བསམ་པར་བྱ་སྟེ། དབུས་སུ་སྔོན་པོ། ཤར་དཀར་པོ། ལྷོ་སེར། ནུབ་དམར། བྱང་ལྗང་པར་དམིགས་པ་ལ་རླུང་བསྟེམ། གལ་ཏེ་སྣ་བུག་གཡོན་ནས་རྒྱུ་ན། ཐོག་མར་ཟླ་བ་བསྒོམ་ཞིང་། དེའི་སྟེང་དུ་ཉི་མ་བསྒོམ་ལ། གཞན་ཐ་མ་དང་འདྲ། དེ་ལྟར་རླུང་ཕྱིར་རྒྱུ་བའི་ཚེ་ཉི་ཟླ་ཐིག་ལེ་དང་བཅས་པ་ལ་རླུང་བསྟེམ། འཇུག་པ་དང་གནས་པའི་ཚེ་གང་ཡང་ཡིད་ལ་མི་བྱ། ཚུལ་དེ་ལྟར་ཡུན་རིང་དུ་བསྒོམས་པས་ཉི་ཟླ་ཐིག་ལེ་དང་བཅས་པ་མངོན་གསུམ་དུ་མཐོང་བ་ལྟར་གསལ་བར་གྱུར་བའི་ཚེ། མཐའ་མའི་ཐིག་ལེ་བཞི་དབུས་ཀྱི་ཐིག་ལེ་སྔོན་པོ་ལ་ཐིམ། དབུས་ཀྱི་ཐིག་ལེ་དེའང་ཉི་ཟླ་སྟེང་མ་ལ་ཐིམ། དེའང་འོག་མ་ལ་ཐིམ། དེའང་ནམ་མཁའ་ལ་ཕྱིན་ཡལ་བ་ལྟར་མི་དམིགས་པར་གྱུར་བར་བསྒོམ་ཞིང་། དེའི་ཚེ་ཕྱི་ནང་གི་ཆོས་ཐམས་ཅད་ཀུང་མི་དམིགས་པའི་ངང་ལ་མཉམ་པར་བཞག་པས། མི་རྟོག་པའི་ཡེ་ཤེས་སྐྱེ་བར་འགྱུར་རོ།། དེ་ཉིད་ཐབས་ཀྱི་ཆ་དང་བྲལ་བར་བསྒོམས་པས། མཐོང་བའི་ལམ་གྱི་ཡེ་ཤེས་སྐྱེ་བར་འགྱུར་རོ།། ས་བོན་མེད་པའི་སྣ་ཚོགས་རྡོ་རྗེ་རིམ་པ་སྟེ། སྣ་ཚོགས་རྡོ་རྗེ འི་རིམ་པ་གཉིས་པའོ།།

༄ དེ་ནས་འདིའི་རིམ་པ་གསུམ་པ་འབྒོམ་པའི་ཚུལ་ནི། །བསྐྱེད་པའི་རིམ་པ་བསྒོམས་པ་ནས། བླ་མ་ལ་གསོལ་བ་འདེབས་པའི་བར་སྔར་བཞིན་བྱས་ནས། །དངོས་གཞི་ལ་དངོས་དང་། ཡེ་ཤེས་ཀྱི་རིག་མ་ལ་རྟེན་པ་གཉིས་ཡོད་པ་ལས། །འདིར་ཡེ་ཤེས་ཀྱི་རིག་མ་ལ་རྟེན་པའི་ཚུལ་བརྗོད་པར་བྱའོ། །དེའང་རང་ཉིད་ཧེ་རུ་ཀ་ཡུག་གཉིས་པར་བསྒྱུས་པའི་མདུན་དུ་བདག་

༄༅ གིས་ཡོངས་སུ་སྨིན་པའི་མིའི་བུ་མོ་མཚན་ཉིད་དང་ལྡན་པ་གཅིག་དམིགས་ལ། །དེ་སྐད་ཅིག་གིས་རྡོ་རྗེ་ཕག་མོར་བསྐྱེད་ནས་གསལ་བར་བཟླ་བ་ནི་བདག་དང་ཕྱག་རྒྱ་ལྷར་བསྐྱེད་པའོ། །དེ་ནས་རང་གི་གསང་གནས་མི་དམིགས་ཏེ་སྟོང་པའི་ངང་ལས་ཧཱུཾ་ལས་རྡོ་རྗེ་སྔོན་པོ་རྩེ་མོ་ལྔ་པ་ལྟེ་བར་ཧཱུཾ་གིས་མཚན་པ། །བྷང་ལས་རྡོ་རྗེ་ནོར་བུ་དམར་པོ་བུ་གར་ཧཱུཾ་གྱིས་མཚན་པར་བསྐྱེད། །ཡབ་ཀྱི་ལྟེ་བར་ཡུམ་གྱི་སྙིང་པོ། །སྙིང་ཁར་ཡུམ་གྱི་ཉེ་སྙིང་། མགྲིན་པར་ཡབ་ཀྱི་སྙིང་པོ། །དཔྲལ་བར་ཡབ་ཀྱི་ཉེ་སྙིང་དགོད། ཡུམ་གྱི་བྷ་ག་མི་དམིགས་ཏེ། །སྟོང་པའི་ངང་ལས་ཨ་ལས་པདྨ་དམར་པོ། །འདབ་མ་གསུམ་པ་ཨས་མཚན་པ། ཀྲཾ་ལས་ཟེའུ་འབྲུ་སེར་པོ་བུ་གའི་ནང་དུ་ཀྲཾ་གིས་མཚན་པར་བསྐྱེད། །ཡུམ་གྱི་ལྟེ་བར་ཡབ་ཀྱིས་སྙིང་པོ། །སྙིང་ཁར་ཡབ་ཀྱི་ཉེ་སྙིང་། །མགྲིན་པར་ཡུམ་གྱི་སྙིང་པོ་དང་། དཔྲལ་བར་ཡུཾ་གྱི་ཉེ་སྙིང་དགོད་པ་ནི། །གསང་སྔགས་ཀྱིས་དག་པར་བྱ་བའོ། །དེ་ནས་ལྷན་ཅིག་སྐྱེད་པའི་ཡེ་ཤེས་མངོན་དུ་བྱ་སྙམ་པའི་ཆོས་ཀྱི་འདུ་ཤེས་དང་ལྡན་པས་ཐོག་མར་ཡུམ་གྱི་གཟུགས་ལ་བལྟ་བ་དང་། །དེ་ནས་གླུ་དབྱངས་ལ་སོགས་པའི་སྒྲ་ལ་མཉན་པ་དང་། དྲི་བསྣམ་པ་དང་། །རེག་པ་དང་། །འཁྱུད་པ་དང་ཙུམ་བྷ་ལ་སོགས་པ་བྱས་པས་དགའ་བའི་བདེ་བ་སྐྱེ་ལ། །དེ་དག་ཀྱང་རང་གི་ངོ་བོས་སྟོང་པའི་རྒྱས་བཏབ་ནས་ཟུང་འཇུག་བསྒོམ་པ་ལ་བསླབ་བོ། །དེ་ནས་དབང་པོ་གཉིས་སྦྱར་བས་མཆོག་ཏུ་དགའ་བ་དང་། །བསྐུབས་པ་དང་། །བསྐུབ་པའི་སྦྱོར་བས་དགའ་བྲལ་གྱི་དགའ་བ་དང་། །ཁམས་གཉིས་རང་གི་དབང་གི་གནས་སུ་འདུས་པ་ལྷན་ཅིག་སྐྱེས་པའི་ཡེ་ཤེས་སྐྱེས་པར་བསྒོམ་ཞིང་བདེ་སྟོང་ཟུང་འཇུག་གི་ཉམས་བསྐྱང་ངོ་།། གལ་ཏེ་ཏིང་ངེ་འཛིན་གསལ་ཞིང་བདེ་བ་ཆེར་འཕེལ་བས་ཁམས་ཉམས་ཀྱིས་རྫོགས་ནས། རྡོ་རྗེ་ཁྲུ་ཚུར་སྙིང་ཁར་བསྣོལ་ཞིང་། །བཟློགས་ནས།

༄༅ མིག་སྟེང་དུ་དཀྲུད་པ་དང་། སྨིན་པོ་འི་ཞལ་བྲང་ཅིང་། །ཧཱུཾ་དྲག་ལ་རིང་བ་ཉི་ཤུ་རྩ་ཅིག་ཙམ་བརྗོད་པས་བཟློག་གོ། དེ་ལྟར་ཡུན་རིང་དུ་གོམས་པས་ལྷན་ཅིག་སྐྱེས་པའི་ཡེ་ཤེས་སྐྱེ་ཞིང་། །རྗེས་ཐོབ་ལ་འང་དྲན་པའི་རྣལ་འབྱོར་རྒྱུན་མ་ཆད་པར་བྱའོ།། །ལག་པས་མཆོད་པའི་ཕྱག་རྒྱའི་སྐོར་ནས་བསྟན་པ་དང་། །དངོས་ཀྱི་ཕྱག་རྒྱ་ཆེན་པའི་དབང་གསུམ་པས་ཡེ་ཤེས་རྗེས་སུ་དྲན་པའི་སྒོ་ནས་ཏིང་ངེ་འཛིན་བསྐྱེད་པར་གསུངས་པའི་བསྒོམ་པའི་ཚུལ་གཞན་ཡིན་ཏེ། །འདིར་སྔ་མ་ཉིད་ཀྱིས་ཆོག་པར་བསམས་སོ། །དེ་ལས་དོན་གྱི་ཡེ་ཤེས་སྐྱེས་པ་སྐྱོང་བ་ནི་ནོར་བུ་འགེངས་པའི་རིམ་པ་བཞི་པ་ཡིན་ཏེ། །བསྒོམ་པའི་ཚུལ་འབྱོར་གཞན་མེད་པ་ཉིད་དོ། །ནོར་བུ་འགེངས་པའི་རིམ་པ་གསུམ་པའོ།། ༄ །།དེ་ནས་འདིའི་རིམ་པ་བཞི་བསྒོམ་པའི་ཚུལ་ནི་བསྐྱེད་པའི་རིམ་པ་བསྒོམ་ནས་ལུས་ཀྱི་ལྷ་རྣམས་རང་རང་གི་གནས་སུ་ཐིམ། ཡུམ་ཡང་འོད་ཀྱི་ཚུལ་གྱིས་སྣ་བུག་གཡོན་གྱི་ལམ་ནས་སྙིང་ཁར་ཐིམ། ཐུ་བ་མཐའ་ཆད་ཀྱི་འཇོམས་གྲུ་གསུམ་གྱི་ནང་དུ། ཆོས་འབྱུང་དམར་སྐྱ་གདེངས་ཀ་ཅན་དུ་ཕྱོགས་པའི་དཀྱིལ་དུ་ཡི་གེ་ཧཱུའི་རྩེ་མོ། དབུས་སུ་ཐིག་ལེ་དཀར་པོ། ཤར་དུ་སྔོན་པོ། ལྷོར་སེར་པོ། ནུབ་ཏུ་དམར་པོ། བྱང་དུ་ལྗང་ཁུ་བསྒོམས་ལ་སྟེང་འོག་གི་རླུང་ནང་དུ་དྲངས་ནས། །དབུས་ཀྱི་ཐིག་ལེ་ལ་ཐིམ་པས་ཐིག་ལེ་རྣམས་ཤིན་དུ་གསལ་བར་གྱུར་བ་ལ་དམིགས་ཤིང་རླུང་ཁ་སྦྱར་བསྒོམ་པར་བྱའོ། ཡུན་རིང་དུ་གོམས་པས་ལྟེ་བའི་གནས་སུ་ཉིད་འབར་བར་འགྱུར་བའི་ཚེ་ཐིག་ལེ་ཞུ་ལས་མེ་ཁ་ཏོག་ཐུ་ཀྲིན་དུ་འབར་བ། རོ་མའི་ནང་ནས་སོང་བ་སྣ་བུག་གཡས་ནས་འཐོན་ཏེ། ཕྱོགས་བཅུའི་དེ་བཞིན་གཤེགས་པ་ཐམས་ཅད་ཀྱིས་ཤངས་བུག་གཡས་ནས་ཞུགས་ནས། གཏུམ་མོའི་མེ་དང་འདྲེས་ཏེ་ཀྱིན་དུ་སོང་བས་ དེ་བཞིན་གཤེགས་པ་རྣམས་ཀྱི་སྤྱི་བོ་ནས་བྱང་ཆུབ་ཀྱི་སེམས་ཀྱི་རྒྱུན་བབས་པ་ཤངས་བུག་གཡོན་ནས་དྲངས་བ། བདག་གི་སྤྱི་

༄༅ གཙུག་ཛ་ལན་དྷ་རའི་བུ་ག་ནས་ཞུགས་ན། ས་ཙྪ་དབུ་མ་ནས་ཕྱི་བར་བབས་ཤིང་
འཕྲོ་བ། ཐིག་ལེ་ལྷའི་འོད་ཀྱིས་གསལ་བར་བྱས་པས་བདེ་བ་དང་། སྣོད་འཐིལ་བར་བསམ་
ཞིང་། རྡུང་ཁ་སྦྱར་ཡང་ནས་ཡང་དུ་བསྒོམས་པས་ཕྱི་བའི་དཀྱིལ་འཁོར་དབུལ་གྱི་མི་
ཡོང་ལྟར་དཀར་ཞིང་སྲ་ལ། འཇམ་པ་དང་། སྣོད་དང་། བདེ་བ་རྒྱས་པར་འགྱུར་
པ་དང་། བྱང་ཆུབ་ཀྱི་སེམས་སྙིང་ཁར་འཕྲོ་བ་ལ་ཐུ་མ་ལྟར་བསྒོམས་པས། བརྟན་
པ་དང་། མཐོན་པར་ཤེས་པ་ལྔ་འཆར་བར་འགྱུར་རོ།། །དེ་ནས་མཁྲིན་པར་འཕྲོ་བ་
ལ་དམིགས་ཏེ་བསྒོམས་པས། འཇིག་རྟེན་གྱི་ཁམས་ཀྱི་ནོར་ཐམས་ཅད་ལ་ལོངས་སྤྱོད་པ་
དང་། ཚངས་པའི་དབྱངས་དང་རྫུས་བཞིན་གྱི་དཀྱིལ་འཁོར་ཁེབས་པར་འགྱུར་ལ། མཁྲིན་
པ་ནས་འཕྲོས་ནས་དབྱུང་པ་ལ་སོགས་པའི་ཚིགས་དང་། ཡན་ལག་རྣམས་སུ་འཕྲོ་བ་
ལ་དམིགས་པ་གཏད་པས་སྲིད་མེད་ཀྱི་བུའི་སྟོབས་དང་མཉམ་པ་དང་། ཛུ་འཕྲུལ་དུ་མ་
སྟོན་ནུས་པར་འགྱུར་རོ། དེ་ནས་སྤྱི་བོ་བདེ་ཆེན་དུ་འཕྲོ་བ་ལ་དམིགས་པ་བརྟན་པས་
མི་རྟོག་པའི་ཏིང་ངེ་འཛིན་དང་། གཙུག་ཏོར་གྱི་གཞི་འདང་འགྲུབ་པར་འགྱུར་རོ།། ཛ་
ལན་དྷ་རའི་རིམ་པ་བཞི་པའོ།། ༄༅ །།དེ་ནས་རིམ་པ་ལྔ་པ་བསྒོམ་པའི་ཚུལ་ནི།
བསྐྱེད་པའི་རིམ་པ་བསྒོམས་པའི་མཐར་སྙིང་གི་ནང་དུ་ཟླ་བའི་དཀྱིལ་འཁོར་གྱི་སྟེང་དུ་ཧཱུྃ་
དམར་སྐྱ་བསྒོམས་པ་ལས་འོད་འཕྲོས་པས་ཁམས་གསུམ་སྣོད་བཅུད་ཐམས་ཅད་ལ་ཕོག་
ཅིང་། དེ་ཐམས་ཅད་རང་གི་ལུས་ལ་བསྡུ། ལུས་ཡང་ཡབ་ལ་ཐིམ། ཡབ་ཐུགས་
ཁའི་ཧཱུྃ་ལ་ཐིམ། ཧཱུྃ་གི་ཞབས་ཀྱུ་ཁོག་པ། ཁོག་པ་མགོ། མགོ་ཟླ་ཚེས། ཟླ་ཚེས་
ཐིག་ལེ། ཐིག་ལེ་ནཱ་ད། ནཱ་ད་ཡལ་ནས་སྟོང་པར་གྱུར་ཏེ། མི་དམིགས་པའི་ངང་
ལ་མཉམ་པར་བཞག་གོ།། གོམས་ན་མི་དམིགས་པའི་ཏིང་ངེ་འཛིན་ཐེ་ཙམ་འཇོད་
པ་འབྱུང་བར་འགྱུར་རོ། །དེ་ལས་ལྡང་བའི་ཚེ་སྐད་ཅིག་གིས་རང་ཧེ་རུ་ཀར་བཞེངས་

༄༅ ལ་ཧཱུྃ་ཞེས་བརྗོད་པས་ཡུམ་དང༌། ལུས་ཀྱི་དཀྱིལ་འཁོར་ལྷ་དང་བཅས་པ་དང༌། སྣང་བཅུད་ཐམས་ཅད་གསལ་བར་དམིགས་ལ། ཐམས་ཅད་ཀྱང་རང་གི་སེམས་ཀྱི་རྣམ་པར་འཕྲུལ་པ་རྨི་ལམ་ལྟ་བུ་རི་སྣམ་དུ་བསམས་ནས་རྣལ་འབྱོར་གཞན་ལ་འཇུག་པར་བྱའོ།། དེ་ལྟར་རྒྱུན་དུ་རྣལ་འབྱོར་དུ་བྱས་པས་འཇིག་རྟེན་གྱི་ཆོས་བརྒྱད་ལ་བསོགས་པར་འགྲོ་བའི་རྟོག་པ་དང༌། ངེས་ཀུན་ནས་བསླང་བའི་སྤྱོད་པ་འཇིག་པར་འགྱུར་རོ། བསམ་གྱིས་མི་ཁྱབ་པའི་རིམ་པ་ལྔ་པའོ།། །དེ་ལྟར་བསྐྱེད་པའི་རིམ་པ་དང༌། རྫོགས་པའི་རིམ་པ་རིམ་པ་ལྔ་པ་སྟེ། རིམ་པ་གཉིས་ཟུང་འཇུག་ཏུ་བསྒོམས་པས་ཏིང་ངེ་འཛིན་བརྟན་ཞིང༌། དུ་བ་ལ་སོགས་པའི་རྟགས་རྣམས་ངེས་པར་མཐོང་བའི་ཚེ། ཇི་སྐད་བཤད་པའི་སྤྱོད་པ་རྣམས་སྤྱད་པས་འཇིག་རྟེན་ལས་འདས་པའི་ཡེ་ཤེས་སྐྱེས་ནས། ས་དང་ལམ་ཐམས་ཅད་བགྲོད་དེ། རིང་པོ་མི་ཐོགས་པར་དཔལ་རྡོ་རྗེ་འཆང་ཆེན་པོར་འགྱུར་བ་ཉིད་དོ། །རིམ་པ་ལྔའི་བསྒོམ་ཚུལ་རབ་གསལ་བ། །རྗེ་བཙུན་བླ་མས་མཛད་ཀྱང་ཙང་བ་དང༌། །གསལ་བའི་ཚུལ་ལ་སློ་བས་བསྐུལ་བའི་ངོར། །བདག་གིས་བརྩེབས་པའི་ཉོངས་པ་བཟོད་པར་གསོལ། དགེ་བས་བདག་དང་སེམས་ཅན་མ་ལུས་པ། །ལམ་ཚུལ་འདི་ལ་ཞུགས་ནས་སྲིད་ཞིའི་མཐའ། །རྣམ་པར་སྤངས་ནས་དོན་གཉིས་འབྱོར་གྱུར་པའི། །ཏེ་རུ་ཀ་དཔལ་ཉིད་དུ་འགྱུར་པར་ཤོག།། རྒྱལ་བུ་འདི་ཡིག་དེ་ལྟར་ཞེས་བྱ་བས་དགོངས་ཤིང༌།། དུ་གལ་དུར་མིས་ཀྱིས་ཆེད་ཆེར་དོན་དུ་གཉེར་ཏེ། རྒྱང་རིང་པོ་ནས་བསྐུལ་བའི་དོན་དུ། དགེ་སློང་ཐུགས་འཆང་པ་འཕགས་པ་ཞེས་བྱ་བས། ས་ཕོ་སྟག་གི་ལོ། དབྱར་ཟླ་ར་བའི་ཚེས་ཉི་ཤུ་ལྔ་ལ་དཔལ་ས་སྐྱའི་ཆོས་གྲྭ་ཆེན་པོར་སྦྱར་བའོ། །ཡི་གེ་པ་ནི་གནས་རྙིང་གི་བཙུན་པ་ཡེ་ཤེས་སེང་གེ་ཞེས་བྱ་བའོ།། རྫོང་སྦྲེང་གཞུང་གི་པར་ཁང་དུ་པར་དུ་བསྒྲུན་པའོ།། མ་མོ། སློབ་ལོ་ཁམས་ལེའུ་ཞེས་པ་རྫོགས་སོ།། སརྦ་མངྒ་ལམ།། བཀྲ་ཤིས་དགེའོ།།

D. B. Press—217—500—4-1-1918.